THE
PERFECT
TEAM

THE PERFECT TEAM

THE BEST PLAYERS, COACH,
AND GM—LET THE DEBATE
BEGIN!

DOUBLEDAY
New York London Toronto Sydney Auckland

PUBLISHED BY DOUBLEDAY
a division of Random House, Inc.

DOUBLEDAY and the portrayal of an anchor with a dolphin are registered
trademarks of Random House, Inc.

Book design by Michael Collica

Library of Congress Cataloging-in-Publication Data

The perfect team / NBA.
   p. cm.
   1. Basketball players—United States—Biography. 2. Basketball players—
Rating of—United States. I. National Basketball Association.
   GV884.A1P45 2006
   796.323'092'2—dc22

2005049387

ISBN 0-385-50146-3

PRINTED IN THE UNITED STATES OF AMERICA

10 9 8 7 6 5 4 3 2 1

First Edition

Contents

Foreword by Chuck Daly. vii

Chapter One:
  Larry Bird (Forward)—Confidence
  by Jackie MacMullan 1
Chapter Two:
  John Havlicek (Forward/Guard)—Perpetual Motion
  and Hustle *by Bob Ryan* 27
Chapter Three:
  Allen Iverson (Guard)—Courage
  by John Smallwood 49

Chapter Four:

Magic Johnson (Guard)—Leadership
by Mark Heisler 71

Chapter Five:

Michael Jordan (Guard)—The Will to Win and Competitive
Spirit *by Paul Ladewski* 91

Chapter Six:

Jason Kidd (Guard)—Selflessness and Sacrifice
by Steve Popper 117

Chapter Seven:

Bill Laimbeer (Center)—Intensity
by Bryan Burwell 147

Chapter Eight:

Shaquille O'Neal (Center)—The Will to Dominate
by Tom Friend 171

Chapter Nine:

Oscar Robertson (Guard)—Versatility
by Lyle Spencer 191

Chapter Ten:

Bill Russell (Center)—Pride
by Frank Deford 217

Chapter Eleven:

Bill Walton (Center)—Precision
by Sam Smith 237

Chapter Twelve:

Jerry West (Guard)—Dealing with Pressure
by Scott Ostler 263

Chapter Thirteen:

Phil Jackson (Head Coach)—Flexibility and the Power
to Motivate *by Charley Rosen* 289

Chapter Fourteen:

Red Auerbach (General Manager)—Basketball IQ
by Dan Shaughnessy 311

Foreword

The NBA's Perfect Team?
Let the Debate Begin

by Chuck Daly

Assembling the perfect NBA team is a daunting if not impossible task. So many great players have left an indelible imprint on the game during the league's six decades. How can one narrow the list to a mere twelve? It is a formidable assignment, yet one that is also fun and sure to invite debate.

Whether someone prefers Bill Russell to Wilt Chamberlain or Oscar Robertson to Magic Johnson, the necessary attributes of assembling such a team remain the same—rebounding, shooting, passing, ball-handling, defensive skills, and so on. Yet those aren't sufficient in and of themselves. Individual brilliance may electrify crowds, but in the end, people come to see teams play as teams and win.

When we think of building a basketball team, we usually do it by the numbers: one (point guard), two (shooting guard), three (small forward), four (power forward), and five (center). Debates usually center on who was the greatest point guard of all time, who was the greatest power forward, etc. Combine the best ever at each position and you would have the perfect team, or so the theory goes.

That will give you a team of great players, but will it be a great team? Many think that the Dream Team, which I coached at the 1992 Olympics in Barcelona, was the perfect team. Maybe so, but when I was named coach, I had many nights of trial and tribulation. How would I find enough court time for all those great players? Worse, the international game is forty minutes, eight fewer minutes than NBA games. All I thought about was, How am I going to play all these great players in only forty minutes? I wondered if some of the big-name scorers would be able to take a backseat and play power forward. Could this team play together?

I needn't have worried. I tried to mix things up. I opened every game and every half with a different starting lineup. I never put a clock on them, but they all played seventeen to eighteen minutes, except for Michael Jordan, who usually played twenty-three to twenty-four minutes because of injuries to other players. Each player accepted his role. It was amazing. That team was so majestic and handled itself so well, never once did I call a time-out.

As the Dream Team demonstrated, the essential attribute is unselfishness, which ties together all of the other attributes. Players have to buy into your system, and be willing to accept the role you, as the coach, have assigned to them.

My Pistons were just such a team, one that did all the little things that win championships. It started with defense and with rebounding, so the other team got only one crack to score. At the other end, we moved the ball around, players set screens, and we crashed the boards. It's a solid formula that works.

To execute this plan, we had players up front who did not care about stats but instead were willing to challenge every shot and fight for every rebound. Players such as Bill Laimbeer, Rick Mahorn, Dennis Rodman, and John Salley.

We had a terrific backcourt with Joe Dumars, Vinnie Johnson, and Isiah Thomas. Thomas played point guard and Dumars played two-guard, but each could play the other position, while Johnson provided instant scoring off the bench. Swingman Mark Aguirre also put up points for us. We had a better offense than people gave us credit for, but again, it all started with defense, and with our playing as a team.

Best of all, each player could step into a variety of roles. Ideally, a perfect team would have replaceable parts. That's why we won two championships in Detroit. And the members of the NBA's Perfect Team are players who could excel in many different roles.

So who makes up the NBA's Perfect Team, and how and why were they chosen? The individuals profiled on these pages—guards Jerry West, Oscar Robertson, Magic Johnson, Jason Kidd, and Allen Iverson; forwards Michael Jordan, John Havlicek, Larry Bird, and Bill Laimbeer; centers Bill Russell, Bill Walton, and Shaquille O'Neal; head coach Phil Jackson; and general manager Red Auerbach—embody qualities that all winning teams must possess. Such qualities include ability to deal with pressure, versatility, leadership, competitive drive, selflessness, courage, perpetual motion, confidence, intensity, pride, precision, will to dominate, flexibility/ability to motivate, and basketball IQ.

These players, along with the coach and general manager, were chosen because a large part of their individual success, and ultimately team success, depended on one particular characteristic. Together these players form not only a dream team of sorts but also a cohesive one. Should other attributes be brought into the mix, there isn't any doubt other players would qualify. Yet selecting such a team is an inexact science.

When presented with the NBA's Perfect Team list, as selected by a group of NBA experts, two glaring omissions in my mind were Kareem Abdul-Jabbar, the NBA's all-time leading scorer, and Wilt Chamberlain, who dominates the NBA record book. One can argue that the omissions don't end there. What about Bob Pettit and Elgin Baylor?

It is quite evident that given the vast number of great players who have played in the NBA, one can actually come up with several versions of the Perfect NBA team and technically be right. The team selected and featured on these pages simply wouldn't have any opposition. Putting together a team across generations is a little bit like highlight films: you never miss a shot and you never lose.

So with this in mind, the list is not meant to end the debate; its goal is only to further the conversation and highlight twelve of not only the most remarkable players of all time but twelve who would constitute the most cohesive team based on the attributes selected.

The players chosen for the NBA's Perfect Team also offered their Perfect Teams. Whom did Magic Johnson select as his starting center? Did Bill Russell select himself or his friend and on-court rival Wilt Chamberlain? Find out in the pages to come.

First, though, here are my observations and thoughts on the twelve players who compose the NBA's Perfect Team. I coached some of them, in Detroit and in Barcelona as part of the Dream Team, and I coached against most of them, so I know firsthand what they brought to the game. The other players I have slightly removed impressions of. But I watched them closely enough to realize they are some of the all-time greats.

GUARDS

Leadership: Magic Johnson

The point guard is the leader of the offense, the coach on the floor. The offense begins and often ends with the point guard, who likely handles the ball on every possession.

The point guard should be a player who, number one, has the ability to move the ball where it needs to go. The point guard sees the whole floor, understands the flow of the game, and finds a way to get the ball to the right player. He should have knowledge similar to the coach in terms of what the team is trying to do on offense.

But the point guard also needs to be able to score. Sometimes delivering the ball to the right player means taking it to the hoop himself. Moreover, because of the shot clock, the point guard often ends up with the ball in his hands with four to five seconds on the clock, and he has to create a shot or take one from long range.

There is no question that Magic Johnson was one of the outstanding leaders of the game. He proved that beyond basketball. Not many people have his ability, his size, and his heart. More important, he is one of only a handful of people—on and off the basketball court—who can get others to follow. That is a rare ability. Isiah Thomas, whom I coached in Detroit, was like that.

Magic saw the game differently than other players. He saw two or three steps ahead. He knew where his teammates were going to be before they did, and because of that, they would find the ball waiting for them instead of the other way around.

His offensive game developed over time, as he took over more of the scoring load from Abdul-Jabbar. He could be a point guard, shooting guard, small forward, power forward, and, of course, center, the position he played against the 76ers in Game 6 of the 1980 NBA Finals. Who will ever forget that performance? I know I won't. I had a front-row seat as an assistant coach on Philadelphia's bench.

Dealing with Pressure: Jerry West

Jerry West defined the shooting guard position. There were shooting guards before West, but the Lakers great made the two-guard position what it is. Two-guards after West are still searching to become him. Most of the great two-guards of today learned how to play the position; Jerry West was born with the ability.

West could score from anywhere, with or without help. His shot off the dribble was second to none, and his instincts were remarkable. Coaches put so much pressure on that position to score, but no more pressure than West put on himself. He simply refused to quit, refused to accept failure. That is what made him so good at crunch time. That is why he was Mr. Clutch.

Versatility: Oscar Robertson

The Big O was the greatest ever at controlling a team and controlling a game. Though he did not penetrate much, he was a gifted scorer and passer. Like Magic, Robertson was one of those rare players who made his teammates better. Average players became good ones when they took the floor with him.

Robertson displayed great patience and court sense. If he was open for a fifteen-footer and saw a teammate who had a ten-footer, he would pass the ball. He always wanted the best shot, and he patiently waited until it came open.

Scoring, rebounding, distributing the basketball—Robertson invented the triple-double that Magic later popularized. Was he more versatile than Magic? I don't know, but versatility is the word that defines the Big O.

Selflessness/Sacrifice: Jason Kidd

Kidd's true ability is pushing the ball up the floor. Out in the open court, he is one of the best ever. He is always looking to pass, and every team he has played on has been successful because of Kidd.

Celtics great Bob Cousy was like that, too, setting up teammates. But the big difference in the latter-day era is going end to end, getting deep, and breaking down defenses, and nobody does that better than Kidd.

Courage: Allen Iverson

Allen Iverson is not only one of the great all-time scorers, he is the ultimate rubber ball. He has probably been knocked down more than anyone I've ever seen, but he gets up and plays as if nothing happened. He may be one of the smallest players on the floor, but he is not intimidated. He plays the game in the air.

There are not many like him. Isiah Thomas was somewhat like that, a very tough-minded guard who played through a lot of injuries. Both Thomas and Iverson have a lot of heart. You wonder what they would have been like with a little more height. I said once that Thomas might have been the best player in history if he were five inches taller, and that could apply to Iverson, too.

FORWARDS

Competitive Drive: Michael Jordan

You don't know anything about a player until you coach him. For me, as great as Jordan seemed to be while watching him from the opposing bench or from the broadcast booth, I didn't understand how good he was until I coached him in the 1992 Olympics.

Jordan combined the best traits of many players into one remarkable package. He was as mentally tough as anyone, and played with great intensity from the first minute to the last. Like West, he wanted the ball at the end, and like West, he usually came through.

Ultimately, Jordan combined unbelievable talent with unbelievable competitiveness. I learned that firsthand when I beat him at a round of golf in Barcelona during the 1992 Olympics. The next season, I coached the Nets. We hosted the Bulls, and we simply could not stop Jordan. And every time he ran by me after making a bucket, he reminded me about that round of golf.

Confidence/Intuition/Instinct: Larry Bird

Larry Bird probably beat us more with big plays than anyone. Yes, everyone remembers his steal against us in the 1987 Eastern Conference Finals, when we were about to win Game 5 at the Boston Garden and seemed headed to the NBA Finals.

But I also remember a game in Hartford, Connecticut, when we set up our defense to prevent Bird from getting open in the corner for his patented three-pointer. With the defense we had, Bird shouldn't have been able to get the ball there, much less get a shot off, but he found a way.

That was Bird. He had an incredible ability to score, to rebound, to anticipate, to pass—to do everything. It was like the Celtics had a point guard at forward, one who could see the floor and distribute the ball or score at will. He was impossible to defend.

Perpetual Motion/Hustle: John Havlicek

Motion is the word to define John Havlicek. Others may have had more ability, but his hustle made him the guy who could always get open. He drove defenders nuts as they chased him all over the floor. Maybe the only player of this era who is comparable is Reggie Miller, and even he did not move as much as Hondo.

Havlicek was the ultimate Sixth Man, a player who came off the bench to spark his team. He would run up and down the floor, crash the boards, and hit shots. By the fourth quarter, weary defenders could no longer keep up, and Havlicek took over.

CENTERS

Mental Toughness/Pride: Bill Russell

No argument about Bill Russell, who won more championships (eleven) than any player in any team sport. But, critics say, he averaged only 15.1 points per game. So what? Russell could score, but the Celtics did not need points from him.

They needed rebounding, defense, and leadership, and he delivered. Like I said earlier, the Perfect Team is made up of players who know and accept their roles, and Russell's role was to cover the lane with his timing, athletic skills, reach, and superb positioning. He stood up to any challenge, and he treated any missed shot or loose ball as his personal property.

This Perfect Team is an offensive team, and Russell would play the same role for them that he did for the Celtics: swatting shots, collecting rebounds, and firing outlet passes to start the break.

Will to Dominate: Shaquille O'Neal

Shaq combines incredible physicality with a soft touch around the basket. Don't let that soft touch deceive you—the Big Diesel is the most physical player in the history of the game.

Indeed, if Shaq gets the ball down low, it is over. Just get out of the way. But Shaq does more than just overpower opponents. He has great agility, has developed into an excellent passer, and has a variety of shots. His power, however, is what defenders fear most, and with good reason.

Precision: Bill Walton

Bill Walton played during the 1970s on the Blazers teams, which were the most beautiful executing teams I have seen in this league. And it all started with Walton, the most precise center at both ends of the court. He even looked the part of precise.

Walton played a game like Bill Russell, only with more offense. Like Russell, he used his intelligence and understanding to dominate within the Blazers' team concept. His skill as a passer allowed the Blazers to run their offense through Walton, while his defensive abilities made the lane a no-man's-land for opponents. He set screens, crashed the boards, and did the little things. If not for the injuries, Walton would have enjoyed a career that would have made him an all-time great.

Intensity: Bill Laimbeer

Bill Laimbeer was not the most physically gifted player, but he worked hard to overcome that. He had an incredible mind for the game. He studied extensively, examined the angle of opponents' shots so he could position himself for rebounds, and had a deft touch from three-point range. He and Isiah perfected that pick-and-pop play, a variation on the pick-and-roll that had Laimbeer popping outside for a three-pointer.

Laimbeer also had an unusual toughness and fire. During the 1990 NBA Finals, we split two games at home against the Blazers. We then traveled to Portland, where we had not won in seventeen years. I was distraught. Our team was beat up.

The day before Game 3, I taped a TV show with Laimbeer as my guest, and he looked into the camera and guaranteed that we would win two games in Portland. The next day, in Game 3, we did not play well at the start. But Laimbeer's fire got our guys going and ticked off the Blazers. He got into their heads, and had them so upset that it took them out of their game. We went on to win Game 3 and the next two games, and to take the series as well.

GENERAL MANAGER

Basketball IQ: Red Auerbach

I would imagine that there was never an NBA All-Star Game during the 1950s and 1960s without at least three players from Red Auerbach's Celtics. He was way ahead of the curve when it came to building a team.

Auerbach had a formula, and then he went out and found players to match his design. All you have to do is look at the number of rings to see how successful he was, and how there could be no other choice for general manager.

HEAD COACH

Flexibility/Ability to Motivate: Phil Jackson

It takes leadership and intelligence to succeed as a coach. Phil Jackson would rank in the top 1 to 2 percent in terms of intelligence, and he has always been a leader. He also brings a tremendous understanding of the game.

Jackson's teams played a different style of offense—one built around ball and people movement—that proved highly successful. But he also is a great defensive coach, and all champions play great defense. That is where coaching comes in—a coach has to convince his team to play defense, to trust one another so they will rotate on defense, and to rebound. Jackson did that in Chicago, and he did that in Los Angeles, to great effect.

To be on my perfect team, a player has to have won a championship, and almost every member of this team has one or more rings. Winning a championship is the ingredient that defines a player.

As for my perfect team, it is pretty hard to argue with the Dream Team. They had a mystique about them that will never be matched. The 1992 Olympics were an out-of-this-world experience. That group, which came to Barcelona already tabbed as the Dream Team, had a lot to live up to. If anything, they exceeded expectations.

What about your perfect team? Maybe your team has Kareem Abdul-Jabbar and Wilt Chamberlain. I certainly wouldn't argue with that. You want Bob Cousy in the backcourt? Okay by me. It's your team. The NBA's Perfect Team is not the end, but rather just the start.

Let the debate begin. . . .

THE PERFECT TEAM

Chapter One

LARRY BIRD—Forward

Confidence

by Jackie MacMullan

I n 1986 the NBA concocted a novel way to spice up its weekend of All-Star festivities—a three-point contest for the top marksmen in the league to show off their shooting prowess.

On the day of the competition, Boston Celtics forward Larry Bird sauntered into the locker room where his fellow participants were dressing.

"Hey, guys," Bird chortled. "Which one of you is going to finish second?"

It's one thing to say it. It's another thing to back it up. Bird validated his bravado by easily outdistancing

Craig Hodges 22–12 in the finals—even though he had finished fourth in the preliminary round and just barely advanced. But as the field narrowed, Bird's shooting improved. The higher the stakes, the more confident he became.

"I'm the three-point king!" he gleefully announced within seconds of winning the competition.

He was also a three-time NBA champion, the leader of an irreverent Celtics team whose swagger served notice that losing was out of the question. No deficit was too large to overcome, and no one player was too dominating for them to contain. Boston derived much of its personality from Bird, who was as adept at making grand pronouncements as he was at fulfilling them.

Consider Game 4 of the 1984 Finals against the Los Angeles Lakers. The Celtics had already lost one home game and been trampled in Game 3, 137–104, at the Forum to fall behind 2–1 in the best-of-seven series. Before the critics could level the Celtics for their miserable performance, Bird landed the first blow. He called his team "a bunch of sissies" and recommended they report to the nearest emergency room for twelve heart transplants. The stinging words quickly produced the desired results in his own locker room. Boston returned home angry and edgy. Yet their captain wasn't done talking. The final salvo Bird delivered was directed toward the Lakers.

"We will win the world championship," he declared.

To do so, Bird knew he had to shake free from Michael Cooper, L.A.'s superb wiry forward, who lay in bed at night with his wife and watched game films of his celebrated Celtics opponent. Boston also needed to be more physical with the Lakers to prevent them from running the Celtics ragged with their transition game.

With goading from both Bird and teammate M. L. Carr, forward Kevin McHale permanently changed the tenor of the series in Game 4 when he clotheslined Lakers forward Kurt Rambis as he drove to the basket on the break. A rejuvenated Boston team, which had fallen behind by ten (68–58) at halftime and was down five with a minute left in regulation, forced overtime on a Robert Parish three-point play and a pair of Bird free throws. Larry almost won it in regulation with an off-balance leaner that rolled off the rim. As the Celtics huddled up Bird assured his teammates, "Get me a good look, and I'll win it for us."

That look came with sixteen seconds to play in OT, shortly after Lakers star Magic Johnson missed two free throws.

"I was coming across the lane," Bird recalled, "and faked one way, then went the other. Cooper fell down, and that meant Magic had to pick me up. I was actually glad Magic was on me. He was a great defender, but I knew I could post him up."

Bird systematically backed Johnson in, then swished a turn-around jumper over his outstretched hand. The Celtics won the game, 129–125, and they went on to win the championship—just as Bird had predicted they would. Bird went home with the league MVP trophy and the grudging admiration of his NBA rivals, who knew better than to question whether number 33 would honor his words with actions.

"At that point of my career, I had all the confidence in the world," Bird said. "When I took a shot, I believed it was going in, every time. I had taken so many shots, I couldn't imagine missing. I only thought in positive terms.

"People talk about being in a 'zone.' I've been there. It's when you just know you've got control of the whole game. It's hard to explain, but your reactions are quicker, and the rim looks bigger, and your eyes have better focus.

"I've always done a lot of shooting on my own in the summer. I got to the point where I could hit eighty to a hundred in a row without missing. That leads to a feeling of 'Give me the ball. I know I can make it.'"

Even later in his career, ravaged by injuries to his heels, elbow, and back that limited his practice time, Bird didn't abandon his strut. In 1990 he ventured to New York City to play the Knicks amid whispers that his game was in decline. Late in the first quarter he received the ball in the right corner of the court. Parish set a pick to free him, leaving Knicks center Patrick Ewing, a full three inches taller than Bird, to sprint out and cover him on the switch.

"Here's what I'm going to do," Bird growled. "I'm going to fake once, drive past you, then put in an underhand scoop layup."

Ewing, crouching lower into his defensive stance, shot back, "Like hell you are."

Bird rose up as if to shoot the jumper, then put the ball on the floor. He scooted past Ewing underneath, then upfaked once more.

As Ewing scurried to recover, the most confident player in the NBA proceeded to do exactly what he said he'd do: he rolled in an underhand scoop shot against the irritated center for two points.

"Face!" Bird said softly as he ran back down the court. His body may have been on borrowed time, but his mind was still itching to spar with anyone who would take him on, particularly a friend like Ewing, who committed the egregious error of doubting him.

"If someone said I couldn't do something," Bird said, "I wasn't going to stop until I did it."

In fact, it was an offhand comment by Parish before the inaugural three-point contest at the 1986 All-Star Game that supplied Bird with all the motivation he needed.

"Robert said there was no way I was going to win it," Bird said. "He said all the little guards out on the perimeter who make their living hitting shots like that would. He just couldn't see a six-foot-nine-inch forward going out and doing it.

"I was ticked. I went in there saying, 'I'm going to show him.' "

Bird spent hours after practice preparing for the competition with Celtics teammates Danny Ainge and Scott Wedman, two excellent long-ball shooters. He left nothing to chance, importing red, white, and blue balls into his workout, knowing they would be used in the competition and would be worth a point more than the regular balls. He positioned the five racks around the three-point arc in deliberate fashion, always placing them in the same spot, with the seams lined up uniformly. He simulated timed rounds and tallied his results in his head. By the time he arrived in Dallas, Bird wasn't just the most confident contestant, he was also the most prepared.

He also enjoyed another advantage that prompted him to issue his now-famous declaration of superiority: an uncommon level of concentration that enabled him to block out any distractions. That, Bird believed, helped develop a reservoir of confidence that was not easily drained.

"For some guys, going out and being part of a big event like that with all sorts of people cheering and talking to you and making noise is difficult," Bird said. "To me, it was nothing. I got out there and focused on the rim and blocked everything else out. When I did that, the basket looked big enough to fit *two*."

Bird agreed to defend his three-point title in 1987 in Seattle, but soon developed severe problems with his shooting elbow and refrained from issuing any bold predictions. On the morning of the three-point competition he woke up and tried to straighten his elbow, but it remained locked up. He quickly dialed up Dan Dyrek, his physical therapist, who spent the hours leading up to the competition manipulating the elbow to regain some of its flexibility. As Bird pulled on his uniform and walked onto the court, he turned to his girlfriend (now wife), Dinah Mattingly, and said, "If I win this year, I'll never lose again."

He defended his title by edging Detlef Schrempf and Cooper and took particular pleasure in beating fourth-place finisher Ainge, who had helped him prepare in 1986 but had vowed to beat him in 1987.

The All-Star venue switched to Chicago in 1988, and again Bird strolled into the locker room asking who would finish behind him. The muted response from the players led him to believe that he had already eliminated half the field with his pregame histrionics.

Bird's primary challenger that day was Dale Ellis, one of the top snipers in the league. But Bird was healthy and had eased himself into the kind of rhythm that made shooting threes as easy as tossing rolled-up shirts into a laundry basket. Ellis had put up a score of 15 when Bird took the court as the final contestant. He revealed a hint of a smile when he got to the last rack, then buried the first three balls. He had already ensured at least a tie with Ellis when he lofted the final red, white, and blue ball, extending his index finger to signify number one as it took flight. The ball dropped through, and his reputation as a clutch performer was further cemented.

Asked how long he planned to enter the three-point competition, Bird answered, "Until I lose." Laughter accompanied his answer. Would anyone else ever win it?

They would. Bird missed all but six games the following season after undergoing heel surgery. Ellis took the three-point crown in his absence. Bird returned in 1990 in Miami, but by then chronic back problems had joined his balky heels as a persistent—and often debilitating—distraction. He sat out twenty-two games in 1989–90 and missed countless more workouts.

"I lose confidence when I'm not practicing," Bird said. "When I was out there and I hadn't practiced, I didn't have the same feeling. It was like going in to take a test and you didn't study, and you don't know what's on the test. When you study and you know what's on there, it's a breeze to go through it."

His back woes, which would later require fusion surgery, made every aggressive movement a chore. He was simply no longer himself in 1990, and it showed in the three-point shootout.

"I didn't even finish the final rack [of balls]," Bird said. "When the horn went off, I couldn't believe it. Somehow my timing was off. I must have been too slow moving around. I was shocked. In my mind, I was going to win it. I never—ever—went there thinking about finishing second."

Bird finished sixth and never participated again.

Two years later, in 1992, Bird announced his retirement. He was in constant pain and could no longer play with the passion and fervor that had set him apart. When he finally gave up the game that had made him wealthy beyond his dreams, he announced that it was the happiest day of his life. His body simply could not absorb any more pounding.

"People think confidence comes from your physical abilities," Bird said. "That's partly true. But basketball is a mental game. I always prided myself on being able to convince myself to do whatever it took. After all the injuries, I couldn't do that anymore."

It was a humbling experience to have the confidence stripped away. It had been his most valuable weapon for most of his athletic life, beginning when he was a teenager growing up in rural Indiana. Back then, Bird devoted most of his time to baseball until he went to visit relatives and accepted an invitation to play some pickup basketball.

Wearing jeans, a T-shirt, and tennis sneakers, an outfit that became his signature "uniform," Bird caught the ball and instinctively fired it up. He loved the sound it made when it swished through the strings. When he shot it again, the ball bounced around the rim and fell in. He took three more shots, and they too were good. He reveled in the attention it generated among his cousins and brothers. He was good at this game. He never forgot the surge of adrenaline that accompanied that summer afternoon.

"Basketball always made me feel good," Bird said. "I was a lot more comfortable on the court than I was off it."

Anxious to reproduce that feeling, he practiced incessantly, shooting as many as 800 shots a day. Being good was one thing; being great required the kind of dedication and single-mindedness that was second nature to Bird. He had spent most of his young life trying to match the efforts of his two older brothers, Mark and Mike, who showed little mercy when tormenting their younger sibling. His brothers were bigger and stronger, which meant Bird had to work harder and longer. He had to develop a thick exterior and learn to experience his share of failure. He consistently played against guys two and three years older than him, so by the time he played alongside his peers, the game seemed easy.

In his sophomore year of high school, Bird was chosen for the varsity team but broke his ankle and missed most of the season. He showed up at the gymnasium every day after school anyway and soon discovered that if he balanced his crutches in the right fashion, he could invent some dribbling drills, practice his passing, and shoot free throws.

"I got to the point where I shot so many free throws, I thought my arm was going to fall off," Bird said. "I had no other choice. I couldn't play with the guys. It became part of my routine."

That routine led to an average of 500 free throws a day, and an NBA career free-throw shooting percentage of 88.6 percent.

Even though Bird had seen little action because of his ankle injury in his sophomore season, coach Jim Jones still put him on the postseason roster. He practiced with the team leading up to the state tournament, but had no idea if there was a spot for him in the rotation.

"When I first came back, I had trouble running," Bird said. "My calf was real small. I focused on passing to everyone else, because I didn't have the lift in my legs. Guys couldn't believe the passes I was making."

During his rehabilitation from his injury, everything was more difficult to execute. When he finally got healthy and shed the cast, Bird had learned to shoot under the most cumbersome conditions. Thus, when Jones tapped him on the shoulder and told him to go into a key playoff game against Paoli, Bird was ready. He buried a couple of key jumpers, then found himself at the line with two free throws to win it. He sank them both and was mobbed by his teammates. Asked how he was able to hit such pressure shots after missing most of the season, Bird explained that he merely closed his eyes and visualized all the free throws he had taken—with and without the crutches.

"It never occurred to me that I'd miss," he said. "I hardly ever missed when I practiced."

Up until his junior season of high school, Bird preferred to be a setup man and rebounder, but his obvious shooting skills became too critical to ignore. During one game his coach issued a proclamation that changed Bird's game forever.

"We were playing a game against Jasper [High School]," Bird said. "At halftime coach Jones came up to me and said, 'Larry, if you don't start shooting, you're not playing.'

"I knew I had open looks that I was passing up, but I just loved getting the ball to the other guys. But after Coach Jones said that, I said, 'Okay, you want me to score. How many do you want?' "

He finished with a game-high twenty-eight points. That performance only reinforced what Bird already knew: he could score at will. He had spent so much time practicing his offensive arsenal that he was able to dribble—and shoot—deftly with both hands. His coach played a significant role in developing Bird's work ethic. In the summer Jones would stop by to watch his players shoot, then tell them he'd be back to check on them. Sometimes he'd come back in an hour. Other times he'd play eighteen holes, shower, and come back—four hours or more later. Many times Bird would yearn to quit practicing and go for a swim or have lunch, but he lived in fear of Coach Jones returning and not finding him working on his game.

As Bird grew older he realized that his work ethic instilled confidence not only in himself but also in his teammates. During his pro career, Bird established himself as a pregame fixture at Boston Garden, taking hundreds of shots in preparation for that night's opponent.

"People asked me why I took so many shots before our Celtics games," Bird said. "It wasn't so much for me. I figured if it came down to one shot at the end of the game, I wanted my teammates to know I could hit it."

He proved it time and time again, but never more spectacularly than in back-to-back games during the 1984–85 season. The Celtics were hosting the Portland Trail Blazers at the Garden, and Bird scored forty-eight points in a game that featured four lead changes in the final seventeen seconds. Yet it was Boston that had the last word. The Celtics called time, down one, and were looking for Parish in the post, but Jerome Kersey deflected the inbounds pass. Dennis Johnson grabbed the ball and relayed it to Bird in the corner.

"There were two seconds on the clock," Bird recalled. "I had two guys on me—Clyde Drexler and Cliff Robinson. I got the ball, threw 'em a head fake, and dropped it in from deep in the corner as I was losing my balance."

As Bird fell out of bounds, his twenty-footer sailed up and in, clinching the 128–127 victory.

Two nights later, in the Hartford Civic Center, Bird and the Celtics became embroiled in another tight game. This time Boston was trading hoops with the Detroit Pistons. Bird, who was guarded by Kent Benson because of an injury to Pistons forward Dan Roundfield, had already racked up thirty points and ten boards. He had thoroughly enjoyed each basket. It was Benson who had snubbed Bird when he was a college freshman at Indiana, making snide comments and refusing to allow him to participate in their preseason pickup games. Bird, who was a shy, awkward kid, never forgot how Benson belittled him and the other freshmen, making an uncomfortable situation even worse.

"I don't know why Detroit put him on me that night—maybe because he had some size—but I was glad," Bird said.

Just as they had been two nights before, Boston was down one with the ball and four seconds to play when Bird took the inbounds pass and drove past Benson.

"I got the ball about ten feet from the basket," Bird said. "It was a real good look. Benson wasn't going to stop me. He didn't have the quickness. That was it."

For the second time in as many games, Bird had hit the game-winner at the buzzer.

"I never said anything to [Benson]," he said. "Watching his face was enough. I remember the night when Kevin McHale got fifty-six points. At the time, it was a Celtics record. In the last quarter he had

Benson on him, and he was just embarrassing him. Benson got so pissed he got himself thrown out of the game. I was so happy watching him walk off the court."

Even though Bird's confidence was tested each time he attempted to play at the next level, going from high school to college to the NBA, his issues rarely revolved around what was happening on the court. When he chose to play for Indiana, he had no doubt he was talented enough, even though skeptics questioned his quickness.

"When I first got there, the guys would scrimmage every day, but because we were freshmen, none of us ever got a chance to get in," Bird said. "Me, Wayne Radford, and Jim Wisman just sat there, waiting for a chance. There was this kid that came off the bench for Indiana named [John] Laskowski. I watched him play, and I remember turning to Jim Wisman and saying, 'I'll have his job.' I wasn't expecting to start or anything. I knew Bobby Knight wouldn't want to start a freshman. But I knew if I got a chance to play, I was taking someone's job. I used to say to Jim all the time, 'He'll have to play me.'

"I just knew it."

It was one pronouncement Bird never had a chance to prove. He never stole Laskowski's job because he left Indiana before the basketball season began. He possessed all the skills he needed on the floor, but he lacked the same ease off the court. He found the schoolwork too difficult, the classes too big, and the students too sophisticated. Bird was too shy and self-conscious to ask questions or get the extra help he needed. He was a small-town kid from a poor family that couldn't provide him with the fashionable clothes that everyone else on campus seemed to be wearing.

One afternoon he packed up his belongings, hitchhiked from Bloomington back home to French Lick, and never returned. He transferred to Indiana State, was forced to sit out a season, and, by undergoing the agonizing exercise of watching and not playing, added a new dimension to his burgeoning résumé: court awareness. He saw plays develop before his teammates did. He studied how the better players moved without the ball, and how patience rewarded teams with success. This added knowledge left him impatient to take the floor and refine his game.

"When I was finally eligible, the first game I played in was so easy I couldn't believe it," Bird said. "We had played about eight or nine minutes of the first half when I said to myself, 'I have complete control of this whole game.' I remember walking off thinking, 'Geez, if this is the way it is, then I'm going to beat this league up.' "

He did. In 1976–77, Bird's first year of eligibility at Indiana State, he averaged 32.8 points a game, the highest average of his career in either college or the pros. He routinely put up gaudy numbers like the forty-two points, eleven rebounds, and seven assists he submitted on January 10 of that season against Butler. To him, Butler was just another in a line of opponents—until one of their forwards began chirping about how he would shut Bird down when they met again in three weeks.

"I can't remember his name," Bird said, "but I remember what he said. He was going to take care of Bird. I went out and dropped forty-seven on him at his place. He didn't have a whole lot to say after that."

Bird went undefeated in his senior season before losing to Magic Johnson and Michigan State in the NCAA championship game, which remains, more than twenty-five years later, the most highly rated college basketball game in history. The Spartans flummoxed Bird with a trapping zone that left him double- or triple-teamed at every turn. His frustration was evident in all facets of the game, including his 5-for-8 shooting from the free-throw line.

The results of that game rankled Bird, and while he acknowledged Michigan State was the better team, he knew he would now prepare for his transition to the pros with a new set of doubters nipping at him. His mantra was familiar: *I'll show them.*

"Everyone was saying all the same things," Bird recalled. "They all said, 'He came from a small town and a small college. He's never been tested.'

"So I go down to Celtics training camp in Marshfield [Massachusetts]. I'm playing against guys like Dave Cowens, Rick Robey, and M. L. Carr. Normally veterans don't go to summer camp. They were down there to see me. I knew.

"I remember going back and saying, 'Maybe the games are different, but this isn't that hard.' "

Bird expected to be tested. Carr was the designated veteran who took it upon himself to gauge the mettle of the rookie, whom forward Cedric Maxwell had already jokingly tagged as "The Great White Hope."

"M.L. was right up on me," Bird said. "He was bumping me and pushing me. I knew what he was doing, but I was ready. I knew I was good enough. Even so, when we scrimmaged at night, I held back a little bit. I didn't want to overdo it. I wanted to be accepted by those guys."

It happened soon enough. The Celtics won a championship in 1981, Bird's second season in the league, in dramatic fashion. They had fallen behind 3–1 in the Eastern Conference Finals to the Philadelphia 76ers, who were led by Julius Erving, the graceful, explosive forward whose early dominance had the Sixers confidently predicting the series was over.

Bird was acutely aware of Erving's standing. He had met Dr. J in an exhibition game in Houston and was grateful for the genuine greeting the future Hall of Famer gave him. Although he was as impressed as anyone with Erving's game, Bird was not intimidated. He dissected Erving as if he were any other player, in search of a weakness he could exploit.

"He was tough for us to guard, especially in the beginning," Bird said. "We knew he wanted to go baseline, so we'd try to send help there. We'd edge our big guy over. But Julius was so quick that sometimes our guys couldn't get over there in time, and then you knew that meant he was going to dunk on you.

"We got smarter about him as we went along. We made him go to the middle, and that took away some of his comfort level."

Bird's strategy included making Erving work harder than he wanted to when the Celtics had the ball. Although Bird did not have to contend solely with Erving on the defensive end (that job often fell to Maxwell or McHale), it was Dr. J's exclusive job to stop Bird.

"My size was my big advantage," he said. "I knew if I could get him in the post, he'd be in trouble. The other key thing was to run [the Sixers] off our picks. I was set up better than most. Robert

[Parish] used to set great picks. Those picks would buy me just enough time to get a good look at the basket."

Although he did not publicly guarantee a victory against Philadelphia in Game 5, Bird and his teammates talked confidently in the locker room about their chances before the game. Late in the fourth quarter Bird took a pass from Nate Archibald and saw Erving glide over to defend him.

"We were down two points," Bird recalled. "We had to win that game, or we were out. I hit a leaner underneath him. I'll never forget it. The ball hit the rim, bounced straight up in the air, and fell in."

Boston beat the Sixers 111–109 that day and went on to stun the basketball world by toppling Philadelphia to advance to the Finals. Bird followed the lead of veterans Tiny Archibald, Maxwell, and Chris Ford and stayed focused on one game at a time rather than the more daunting task of winning three in a row.

"No one had given us a chance [to come back]," he said. "But we won one, and then the next, and then all of a sudden it was 3–3. I always like the Celtics' chances when it's 3–3."

Over the next six years, Bird, Parish, and McHale evolved into one of the most dominating front lines in NBA history. The trio formed an alliance predicated on the trust and confidence they had in each other.

"I knew with Robert and Kevin that I didn't have to always take the shot," Bird said. "I could pass the ball. If I had an off shooting night, I could rebound. It didn't matter to me if I got the last look. It was more rewarding sometimes to make the last pass."

The Big Three carried themselves with an aura that proved to be both intimidating and entertaining. In 1985, when the team was finishing up its annual West Coast swing, Utah veteran Pace Mannion chatted with Bird before the game and predicted a victory for the Jazz, pointing out that Boston was shorthanded (Dennis Johnson, Parish, and Quinn Buckner were all sidelined with injuries) and probably fatigued from their long road trip.

"We've got you tonight," Mannion said.

"We'll see," Bird answered.

He turned, walked into the locker room, and relayed Mannion's words to his team.

"We were so beat up M.L. had to start," Bird said. "But we still went up something like 34–6 in the first quarter. Kevin was just torturing their big center, Mark Eaton. He killed that poor kid. Thurl Bailey was on me, and I was hitting everything."

McHale and Bird fed off each other's success. They were so hot they took turns yelling to Utah coach Frank Layden on the bench, "C'mon, Frank. Is this the best you've got? Don't you have anyone over there who can guard us?"

Bird submitted a triple-double and was one steal shy of a quadruple-double. When coach K. C. Jones realized his prize forward was close to the milestone, he offered to send him back in, but Bird declined.

"That was a great win," Bird said. "It would have been easy for us to just pack it in on the last game of a long road trip. As it was, Kevin and I were coming off the All-Star Game, and we had been on the road something like seventeen or eighteen days. But you challenge us, and we're going to respond."

The most epic challenges of his career came from the Lakers. Although the showdowns were often billed as Larry versus Magic, the two rarely guarded each other. Yet Bird knew Earvin Johnson had prepared just as hard and just as long as he had. He also knew Magic's most valuable weapon was his unselfishness.

"Magic was a passer who, when he needed to score, had the confidence to score," Bird said. "That made him very, very dangerous. If his team wasn't going the way it was supposed to go, you knew he was going to step up and put the ball in the basket. Magic Johnson could have averaged twenty-eight points a game in this league if he wanted to. I could have averaged thirty points if I wanted to. But both of us had other things we'd rather do.

"I remember one year leading the league in scoring for a short time. Someone pointed it out to me, and I said, 'No way. It's not going to happen.' I wanted no part of that. I still wanted to be a rebounder and a passer. There had never been a Celtics player that led the league in scoring and won a championship. I looked it up. I wasn't going to be the first."

Although playing against Magic was always the story line, Bird's true nemesis in the series was the defensive-minded Cooper, who will be forever known as the one player who could slow Bird down.

"He was the toughest I ever had to face," Bird said. "He limited my shots. Cooper was smaller than me, and he always played me so close. When I got the ball and tried to make a move against him, I was always afraid they'd call a charge on me.

"When Cooper was out there, I knew that meant if I got shots, I better be in position to make them, because when he was playing me, I wasn't going to get as many good looks."

Cooper was a master at denying the entry pass and pushing his opponents out of shooting range. He was a fundamentally sound player who almost always boxed out, thus limiting second-chance shots.

"I knew I could score on him," Bird said, "but it was never going to be easy."

Although Bird felt Cooper had earned his moniker as a legitimate irritant to his game, he was incredulous when people suggested that Milwaukee's Paul Pressey or Houston's Rodney McCray and Robert Reid fell into a similar category.

He took care of both those false assumptions in 1986, beginning with the Bucks. In 1982 Milwaukee was responsible for Bird's most demoralizing moment as a pro when they swept the Celtics in four games in the playoffs. Four years later Boston had long since avenged those defeats, but Bird still enjoyed a certain satisfaction in drubbing the Bucks.

His team had already taken a commanding 3–0 lead in the 1986 Eastern Conference Finals when Bird thrust the dagger through the entire team with his Game 4 performance.

Milwaukee had pulled within three, 95–92, in the fourth quarter when D.J. fouled out and K. C. Jones was forced to put Parish, McHale, and Bill Walton in the frontcourt and Bird in the backcourt. Bird threw the ball in to Parish, who, being doubled, kicked it back out to Bird. He launched a three. It was so dead on, the strings didn't even move. The Bucks called time, then coughed up the ball, and this time Bird threw it inside to Walton. Walton was immediately doubled, so he kicked it back out to Bird again, who launched another three-pointer. 101–92. The stunned Milwaukee players shuffled back to their bench. Bird had broken their spirit.

The final possession of the night also landed in Bird's hands. He stood in the corner, watching the game clock dwindle down to nothing. With Boston holding a 103–94 lead, no one even bothered to sprint out to guard Bird on the wing. He barked, "Isn't anyone coming to get me?" No one moved. He stood, fiddled with the ball until the shot clock ticked down to 0:01, then sank another three-pointer, exaggerating his follow-through as he walked off the court.

"I was halfway to the locker room by the time the buzzer sounded," he said. "I never even saw that last one go in. I just heard the boos from the Milwaukee fans."

After the game, beleaguered Bucks coach Don Nelson saluted Bird, then offered, "I'm not sure the Celtics aren't on a different planet compared to us mortal teams."

Next on Boston's docket was a surprising Houston team, which had eliminated the Lakers in the West. The Rockets sported twin towers Akeem (later Hakeem) Olajuwon and Ralph Sampson and were managed by former Boston coach Bill Fitch. The Celtics had built up a 3–1 series lead when a fight broke out between Sampson and Celtics guard Jerry Sichting in Game 5. The fisticuffs ignited a raucous Houston crowd, and Boston limped home, 111–96 losers.

Bird made it clear to his teammates that Houston was too dangerous to take to seven games. "We need to win this one now," he told McHale in practice. "I'm going to get every rebound tomorrow." McHale responded, "I'll get every one you don't get."

True to their word, both Bird and McHale dominated the glass in a Game 6 win. Bird was everywhere, accomplishing a triple-double of twenty-nine points, eleven rebounds, and twelve assists. He stole the ball three times and even won a jump ball against the seven-footer Olajuwon. Boston was cruising, up by twenty-four points, when Bird fielded a behind-the-back pass by Walton late in the third quarter. Instead of driving to the hole and drawing the foul, Bird weaved in and out of three Houston defenders toward the sideline, then let a flailing, falling three-pointer go. Bird wasn't going for the basket—he was going for the kill.

"The plan was to break their backs," Bird said. "I wanted that series over. I just had one of those great days. I remember saying after the game, 'If I feel this way all the time, I should quit playing.' I just felt as though I was controlling what happened out there. I was stealing the ball, moving well, getting pretty much anything I wanted."

There have been some occasions when Bird's most impressive performances have started out with mediocre results. In the first quarter of Game 7 of the Eastern Conference Semifinals against the Atlanta Hawks on May 2, 1988, Bird shot just two of seven from the floor and appeared uncharacteristically lethargic. Although the Celtics stayed close with the Hawks, there was an uneasy feeling among the Boston Garden faithful. When was Larry going to turn it up?

He waited until the final quarter, after Atlanta star Dominique Wilkins had already put thirty-one points on the board. Although Bird's shooting performance had been forgettable up to that point, it had no bearing on the decisions he would make going forward. "I never let a bad shooting night stop me from taking them," he said.

With his team's playoff livelihood hanging in the balance, Bird's competitive juices stirred. He scored twenty of his thirty-four points in the final quarter on nine-of-ten shooting. Wilkins, meanwhile, answered with sixteen points of his own in those last twelve minutes. Together, they embarked on a thrilling shootout that has become part of NBA lore.

For nearly two minutes, the two players traded baskets. First it was a Bird lefty three-point bank shot. 93–90, Celtics. Wilkins answered with a three-pointer, then added a deep corner jumper. Bird offset that with a lefty shot in the lane. Wilkins countered with a pull-up fourteen-footer. Bird, in turn, buried a twenty-footer. Wilkins coaxed in a tough banker.

And so it went, down to the final minutes, as both forwards took turns making improbable pressure shots.

"I had it going in that fourth quarter," Bird recalled, "but so did he. I knew how *I* felt. I was just hoping he didn't feel as good as I did. I remember thinking, *Please, miss a shot. Just one.* Every time he put one up, I'd be watching and hoping . . . but he was on fire."

In the end, the experienced Celtics team held fast, and the young Hawks team blinked. Bird drained a long three for a 112–105 cushion, and while 'Nique countered with an impossible jump hook and a follow of his own missed dunk in the final minutes, the Celtics held on to win, 118–116. Afterwards Wilkins conceded, "When Larry is in a rhythm like that, he's hard to stop."

Bird saluted Wilkins, then pointed to his team's experience as the difference down the stretch.

"The Hawks were young and up and coming," Bird said. "Even so, you just knew they'd never beat us in a seven-game series. We wouldn't let it happen. We could steal one at their place, but they could never do that at Boston Garden."

In fact, after Atlanta had gone up 3–2 in the series but then lost Game 6 on their own floor, Bird said simply, "They had their chance. Now it's our turn, and we won't blow it."

They didn't.

As the Big Three aged and began breaking down because of injury, the series win over Atlanta became, in retrospect, one of their final glorious stands. They lost that same spring to Detroit in the Eastern Conference Finals, and Bird began facing his future, which would include spending most of his final season in a full body brace when he wasn't playing.

After his retirement, he stayed close to the game, both as a coach and as general manager for the Indiana Pacers. Some of today's superstars walk with the same kind of swagger that marked his Celtics years. Others merely talk the game, without the preparation or the resolve to translate that into championship play.

Bird looks back and marvels at his own unwavering confidence. Sometimes it was as subtle as betting former Knicks trainer Mike Saunders five dollars he could bank in a three-pointer against his team—then going out and doing it. Other times it was as demonstrative as the sixty points he dropped on Atlanta in a game in New Orleans on March 12, 1985, just days after McHale had set a new team record with fifty-six points.

"It is the greatest feeling in the world to go out there and know you can do almost anything you want," he said. "When I was on top of my game, I felt that way almost every night."

His career totals include 21,791 points, 8,974 rebounds, 5,695 assists, and 1,556 steals, yet there is no official way to document Bird's true worth.

Too bad they don't keep stats on the number of confident predictions fulfilled.

LARRY BIRD'S PERFECT TEAM

Point Guard—Leadership

You've got to be able to lead by example. We had plenty of guys who talked about how great they were going to be, but they didn't always go out and do it. Magic Johnson was the kind of leader who practiced hard, played hard, and led with authority. The Lakers always fed off whatever Magic was doing or feeling.

Shooting Guard—Dealing with Pressure

I'll take Reggie Miller. I have never seen one guy hit more shots to tie or win a game, especially in hostile places like New York and Boston. The pressure never seemed to get to him. I can remember one time when I was coaching him in Indiana. We had a situation where we needed a shot in the final seconds. We designed a play where Travis Best was going to come off a pick and shoot it, with Reggie as an option on the play. Well, Travis came off the pick, hit the rim, and missed the shot. Reggie came up to me afterwards and said, "Coach, no disrespect, but you need to give me the ball at the end of the game." He was right.

Forward—Competitive Drive

That's Michael Jordan. He is the most competitive guy I ever played against. He was all about getting the job done. He proved that when he got his team to win seventy-two games. And from what I understand, he was competitive as hell in practice too.

Forward—Confidence

I think if you ask Magic, me, or Michael, we all felt we were the most confident player on the floor. When you believe you are the most confident, then you play that way.

Center—Mental Toughness

Obviously I never played with Bill Russell, but I've been around him, and I can see that he is a good choice. Nobody wins that many championships on just physical ability alone. You have to have the head for it too.

Sixth Man—Versatility

Kevin McHale. No question about it. I tell these guys who complain about coming off the bench now, "You guys are idiots. Kevin McHale used to come off the bench, and you couldn't carry his jock." Kevin could be anything he wanted. He came into the league as a defensive player, but then all of a sudden he was a scorer. He had a slew of devastating low post moves. By the end, he was shooting three-pointers. He could have averaged twenty-five points and ten rebounds a night. I asked him why he didn't, and he said, "You start putting up numbers like that, and they'll expect it every night." He was happy just being great. He didn't want to be the MVP or the best. He just wasn't interested in that.

Forward—Perpetual Hustle and Motion

This answer might surprise you. There was a guy named Ronnie Lee who was all over the floor. He didn't have a lot of skills. He was an all right, not a good shooter. He was an all right, not a great defensive player. But if there was a loose ball, he'd knock down three guys to get it. I remember once we were playing against Detroit in the Pontiac Silverdome, and he saved a ball from going out of bounds. He slid off the court into the seats, and by the time I looked around, he was already back on the court. He just never stopped moving.

Guard—Selflessness

I think you could make a case for either Jason Kidd or John Stockton, because neither one of those guys looked to shoot unless he had to. But my choice for most selfless player would be Robert Parish. Talk about a guy who gave up a lot for the team. He sacrificed everything and never said a word. We never would have won those championships without him, but he didn't want to hear about that. He didn't like the attention.

Guard—Courage

I'll take Micheal Ray Richardson. That guy would get his shot blocked three times in a row, and I guarantee you he was coming back at you. You could never relax when you played against him. He was a helluva player, and he was fearless. He'd take it to the hole against guys twice his size and think nothing of it.

Center—Will to Dominate

Certainly Michael Jordan was like that, and Shaquille O'Neal is like that among the current players. But I'll take Wilt Chamberlain. You can talk about Shaq all you want, but Wilt *averaged* fifty points a game. He scored a hundred points in a game. He led the league in assists one year. He blocked shots. Now that's a guy who dominates.

Center—Precision

Bill Walton. He played the game the way it should be played. He didn't commit a lot of turnovers. He always hit the open man. He could pass the ball, he always boxed out, and he was great at starting the fast break. Offensively, he used a lot of back-cuts. He was a pleasure to watch.

Center—Intensity

Hell, we were all intense. Me, Magic, and Michael. But you know who else was pretty intense—Patrick Ewing. I couldn't believe the change that overcame him after he went to Georgetown. When he played high school ball in [Massachusetts], he was giving the fans the finger, going at people in the stands. People were always on him, that was part of the problem, because he was so big. But then you see him a couple of years later, and he was a different kid. He's still incredibly intense, but it's channeled in the right direction. I think you've got to give [Georgetown coach] John Thompson some credit for that.

General Manager—Basketball IQ

Red Auerbach. There's absolutely no question about it. He made some of the greatest deals in the history of the game. It's not even close. He not only got all these great guys for the Celtics, he got them to give their all. The one interesting thing about Red was once they put in the salary cap, he didn't want any part of it anymore. He liked trading players for players, not players for cap space.

Head Coach—Ability to Motivate

Pat Riley is my all-time favorite coach, but you've got to give it to Phil Jackson. I mean, nine championships is pretty good.

LARRY BIRD—FORWARD

PERSONAL: Born December 7, 1956, in West Baden, IN . . . 6–9/220 (2.06 m/100 kg) . . . full name: Larry Joe Bird.

HIGH SCHOOL: Springs Valley (French Lick, IN).

COLLEGE: Indiana, then Northwood Institute (IN), then Indiana State.

TRANSACTIONS/CAREER NOTES: Selected after junior season by Boston Celtics in first round (sixth pick overall) of 1978 NBA draft. . . . Adviser, Celtics (1992–93 through 1996–97). . . . President of basketball operations, Indiana Pacers (July 11, 2003–present).

CAREER HONORS: Elected to Naismith Basketball Hall of Fame (1998). . . . Member of gold-medal-winning U.S. Olympic team (1992). . . . Boston Celtics all-time steals leader with 1,556 (1979–80 through 1991–92).

COLLEGIATE RECORD

NOTES: *The Sporting News* College Player of the Year (1979). . . . Naismith Award winner (1979). . . . Wooden Award winner (1979). . . . *The Sporting News* All-America first team (1978, 1979).

Season	Team	G	Min	FGM	FGA	Pct	FTM	FTA	Pct	Reb	Ast	Pts	Averages		
													RPG	APG	PPG
74–75	IU					Did not play									
75–76	ISU				Did not play—transfer student										
76–77	ISU	28	1,033	375	689	.544	168	200	.840	373	122	918	13.3	4.4	32.8
77–78	ISU	32	—	403	769	.524	153	193	.793	369	125	959	11.5	3.9	30.0
78–79	ISU	34	—	376	707	.532	221	266	.831	505	187	973	14.9	5.5	28.6
Total		94	—	1,154	2,165	.533	542	659	.822	1,247	434	2,850	13.3	4.6	30.3

NBA REGULAR-SEASON RECORD

HONORS: NBA Most Valuable Player (1984, 1985, 1986). . . . NBA Rookie of the Year (1980). . . . All-NBA first team (1980, 1981, 1982, 1983, 1984, 1985, 1986, 1987, 1988). . . . All-NBA second team (1990). . . . NBA All-Defensive second team (1982, 1983, 1984). . . . NBA All-Rookie team (1980). . . . Long Distance Shootout winner (1986, 1987, 1988).

| | | | | | | | | | | Rebounds | | | | | | | | Averages | | |
Season	Team	G	Min	FGM	FGA	Pct	FTM	FTA	Pct	Off	Def	Tot	Ast	St	Blk	TO	Pts	RPG	APG	PPG
79–80	Bos	82	2,955	693	1,463	.474	301	360	.836	216	636	852	370	143	53	263	1,745	10.4	4.5	21.3
80–81	Bos	82	3,239	719	1,503	.478	283	328	.863	191	704	895	451	161	63	289	1,741	10.9	5.5	21.2
81–82	Bos	77	2,923	711	1,414	.503	328	380	.863	200	637	837	447	143	66	254	1,761	10.9	5.8	22.9
82–83	Bos	79	2,982	747	1,481	.504	351	418	.840	193	677	870	458	148	71	240	1,867	11.0	5.8	23.6
83–84	Bos	79	3,028	758	1,542	.492	374	421	.888	181	615	796	520	144	69	237	1,908	10.1	6.6	24.2
84–85	Bos	80	3,161	918	1,760	.522	403	457	.882	164	678	842	531	129	98	248	2,295	10.5	6.6	28.7
85–86	Bos	82	3,113	796	1,606	.496	441	492	.896	190	615	805	557	166	51	266	2,115	9.8	6.8	25.8
86–87	Bos	74	3,005	786	1,497	.525	414	455	.910	124	558	682	566	135	70	240	2,076	9.2	7.6	28.1
87–88	Bos	76	2,965	881	1,672	.527	415	453	.916	108	595	703	467	125	57	213	2,275	9.3	6.1	29.9
88–89	Bos	6	189	49	104	.471	18	19	.947	1	36	37	29	6	5	11	116	6.2	4.8	19.3
89–90	Bos	75	2,944	718	1,517	.473	319	343	.930	90	622	712	562	106	61	243	1,820	9.5	7.5	24.3
90–91	Bos	60	2,277	462	1,017	.454	163	183	.891	53	456	509	431	108	58	187	1,164	8.5	7.2	19.4
91–92	Bos	45	1,662	353	758	.466	150	162	.926	46	388	434	306	42	33	125	908	9.6	6.8	20.2
Total		897	34,443	8,591	17,334	.496	3,960	4,471	.886	1,757	7,217	8,974	5,695	1,556	755	2,816	21,791	10.0	6.3	24.3

THREE-POINT FIELD GOALS: 1979–80, 58-for-143 (.406); 1980–81, 20-for-74 (.270); 1981–82, 11-for-52 (.212); 1982–83, 22-for-77 (.286); 1983–84, 18-for-73 (.247); 1984–85, 56-for-131 (.427); 1985–86, 82-for-194 (.423); 1986–87, 90-for-225 (.400); 1987–88, 98-for-237 (.414); 1989–90, 65-for-195 (.333); 1990–91, 77-for-198 (.389); 1991–92, 52-for-128 (.406). Total: 649-for-1727 (.376).

PERSONAL FOULS/DISQUALIFICATIONS: 1979–80, 279/4; 1980–81, 239/2; 1981–82, 244/0; 1982–83, 197/0; 1983–84, 197/0; 1984–85, 208/0; 1985–86, 182/0; 1986–87, 185/3; 1987–88, 157/0; 1989–90, 173/2; 1990–91, 118/0; 1991–92, 82/0. Total: 2279/11.

NBA PLAYOFF RECORD

NOTES: NBA Finals Most Valuable Player (1984, 1986). . . . Holds career playoff record for most defensive rebounds—1,323.

Season	Team	G	Min	FGM	FGA	Pct	FTM	FTA	Pct	Off	Def	Tot	Ast	St	Blk	TO	Pts	RPG	APG	PPG
79–80	Bos	9	372	83	177	.469	22	25	.880	22	79	101	42	14	8	33	192	11.2	4.7	21.3
80–81	Bos	17	750	147	313	.470	76	85	.894	49	189	238	103	39	17	62	373	14.0	6.1	21.9
81–82	Bos	12	490	88	206	.427	37	45	.822	33	117	150	67	23	17	38	214	12.5	5.6	17.8
82–83	Bos	6	240	49	116	.422	24	29	.822	20	55	75	41	13	3	19	123	12.5	6.8	20.5
83–84	Bos	23	961	229	437	.524	167	190	.879	62	190	252	136	54	27	87	632	11.0	5.9	27.5
84–85	Bos	20	815	196	425	.461	121	136	.890	53	129	182	115	34	19	57	520	9.1	5.8	26.0
85–86	Bos	18	770	171	331	.517	101	109	.927	34	134	168	148	37	11	47	466	9.3	8.2	25.9
86–87	Bos	23	1,015	216	454	.476	176	193	.912	41	190	231	165	27	19	71	622	10.0	7.2	27.0
87–88	Bos	17	763	152	338	.450	101	113	.894	29	121	150	115	36	14	49	417	8.8	6.8	24.5
89–90	Bos	5	207	44	99	.444	29	32	.906	7	39	46	44	5	5	18	122	9.2	8.8	24.4
90–91	Bos	10	396	62	152	.408	44	51	.863	8	64	72	65	13	3	19	171	7.2	6.5	17.1
91–92	Bos	4	107	21	42	.500	3	4	.750	2	16	18	21	1	2	6	45	4.5	5.3	11.3
Total		164	6,886	1,458	3,090	.472	901	1,012	.890	360	1,323	1,683	1,062	296	145	506	3,897	10.3	6.5	23.8

THREE-POINT FIELD GOALS: 1979–80, 4-for-15 (.267); 1980–81, 3-for-8 (.375); 1981–82, 1-for-6 (.167); 1982–83, 1-for-4 (.250); 1983–84, 7-for-17 (.412); 1984–85, 7-for-25 (.280); 1985–86, 23-for-56 (.411); 1986–87, 14-for-41 (.341); 1987–88, 12-for-32 (.375); 1989–90, 5-for-19 (.263); 1990–91, 3-for-21 (.143); 1991–92, 0-for-5. Total: 80-for-249 (.321).

PERSONAL FOULS/DISQUALIFICATIONS: 1979–80, 30/0; 1980–81, 53/0; 1981–82, 43/0; 1982–83, 15/0; 1983–84, 71/0; 1984–85, 54/0; 1985–86, 55/0; 1986–87, 55/1; 1987–88, 45/0; 1989–90, 10/0; 1990–91, 28/0; 1991–92, 7/0. Total: 466/1.

NBA ALL-STAR GAME RECORD

NOTES: NBA All-Star Game Most Valuable Player (1982).

Season	Team	Min	FGM	FGA	Pct	FTM	FTA	Pct	Rebounds Off	Def	Tot	Ast	PF	DQ	St	Blk	TO	Pts
1980	Bos	23	3	6	.500	0	0	—	3	3	6	7	1	0	1	0	3	7
1981	Bos	18	1	5	.200	0	0	—	1	3	4	3	1	0	1	0	2	2
1982	Bos	28	7	12	.583	5	8	.625	0	12	12	5	3	0	1	1	4	19
1983	Bos	29	7	14	.500	0	0	—	3	10	13	7	4	0	2	0	5	14
1984	Bos	33	6	18	.333	4	4	1.000	1	6	7	3	1	0	2	0	2	16
1985	Bos	31	8	16	.500	5	6	.833	5	3	8	2	3	0	0	1	4	21
1986	Bos	35	8	18	.444	5	6	.833	2	6	8	5	5	0	7	0	4	23
1987	Bos	35	7	18	.389	4	4	1.000	2	4	6	5	5	0	2	0	2	18
1988	Bos	32	2	8	.250	2	2	1.000	0	7	7	1	4	0	4	1	2	6
1990	Bos	23	3	8	.375	2	2	1.000	2	6	8	3	1	0	3	0	3	8
1991	Bos							Selected but did not play—injured										
1992	Bos							Selected but did not play—injured										
Total		287	52	123	.423	27	32	.844	19	60	79	41	28	0	23	3	31	134

THREE-POINT FIELD GOALS: 1980, 1-for-2; 1983, 0-for-1; 1985, 0-for-1; 1986, 2-for-4; 1987, 0-for-3; 1988, 0-for-1; 1990, 0-for-1. Total: 3-for-13 (.231).

HEAD COACHING RECORD

BACKGROUND: Special assistant, Boston Celtics (1992–93 through 1996–97).
HONORS: NBA Coach of the Year (1998).

Season	Team	Regular Season W	L	Pct	Finish	Playoffs W	L	Pct
97–98	Ind	58	24	.707	2nd/Central Division	10	6	.625
98–99	Ind	33	17	.660	1st/Central Division	9	4	.692
99–00	Ind	56	26	.683	1st/Central Division	13	10	.565
Total (3 years)		147	67	.687	Total (3 years)	32	20	.615

NOTES: 1998—Defeated Cleveland, 3–1, in Eastern Conference First Round; defeated New York, 4–1, in Eastern Conference Semifinals; lost to Chicago, 4–3, in Eastern Conference Finals. 1999—Defeated Milwaukee, 3–0, in Eastern Conference First Round; defeated Philadelphia, 4–0, in Eastern Conference Semifinals; lost to New York, 4–2, in Eastern Conference Finals. 2000—Defeated Milwaukee, 3–2, in Eastern Conference First Round; defeated Philadelphia, 4–2, in Eastern Conference Semifinals; defeated New York, 4–2, in Eastern Conference Finals; lost to Los Angeles, 4–2, in NBA Finals.

Chapter Two

JOHN HAVLICEK—
Forward/Guard

Perpetual Motion and Hustle

by Bob Ryan

C edric Maxwell was twenty-one years old, a fit
and eager first-round draft choice of the hallowed Boston Celtics, when he first encountered
the phenomenon known as John Havlicek.

"John came into camp late," Maxwell recalled.
"The rest of us were already there for a week or so.
Well, John came in and he *never* stopped running. He
hit the floor and he was running. The rest of us were
trying to get into shape. He was ready to run."

John Havlicek was then thirty-seven, and this
would be his sixteenth, and final, NBA season.

"I thought it would be a good indoctrination for him to find out what this new game was all about," Havlicek explained.

The only flaw in that reasoning was that the rest of the NBA really wasn't like that, either before or since. Havlicek's game was his and his alone. Since professional basketball began to assume its present shape in 1946, there has been one combination of stamina and versatility like John Havlicek, and that was John Havlicek.

The following premise really is non-negotiable: John Havlicek was the greatest forward-guard swingman in NBA history. There was no one between six feet and six-eight who could effectively guard him, and there were very few in that size range he couldn't take care of at the other end of the floor. He represented the greatest king on the chessboard for his coaches that has ever been available to anyone.

He scored the first of his 26,395 regular-season points on a dunk in the old Madison Square Garden in 1962, and he scored the last on a free throw with twenty-nine seconds remaining in a dramatic farewell against the Buffalo Braves in which he scored twenty-nine points before a capacity Boston Garden crowd of 15,276, very few of whom could see clearly through the tears that were flooding the ancient building.

In those sixteen seasons, he played on eight championship teams. He was first-team All-NBA four times and second-team All-NBA six times, the first of those as a premier Sixth Man in 1964 and the last of those as a venerated *éminence grise* twelve years later. He was either first- or second-team All-Defensive eight times, and the only reason there aren't more of these selections on his résumé is that the award wasn't instituted until 1968, when he had already been in the league for five seasons. He played in thirteen consecutive All-Star Games, breaking into double figures eleven times, including a twenty-six-point output in 1968 when, in an uncharacteristic burst of immodesty, he declared he thought he deserved to be the MVP (it was given to Hal Greer, who shot 8-for-8).

But he is not remembered for those numbers as much as he is for his unique style of play. There have been a lot of players properly cited for their unrelenting hustle. No one, for example, ever played harder than Jerry Sloan. Hustle, however, is one thing, and unceasing movement is another. The one man in NBA history who went the longest with the mostest, if you will, was John Havlicek.

"John Havlicek?" pondered Walt "Clyde" Frazier, who played against Havlicek for eleven seasons. "Perpetual motion. Tireless. Relentless. You just never knew where he would be. He was a dangerous man."

Chris Ford, who would later play for and coach the Celtics, played against Havlicek for six seasons. "Perpetual motion," he smiled. "He always kept on moving."

Added Kathy (Mrs. Chris) Ford, "I can remember Chris saying, 'I've got to go chase John Havlicek tonight.' "

"He was constantly in motion," said Ernie DeGregorio, the 1973–74 NBA Rookie of the Year. "And he was probably the smartest player I've ever played against."

"Most people would say to me, 'Slow down, will you?' said Bill Bradley, the Princeton and New York Knicks' Hall of Famer who would serve three terms in the U.S. Senate after retiring from basketball. "My game was running. But John Havlicek ran *me.*"

Simple location helped produce that John Havlicek. Growing up in Lansing, Ohio, he yearned for a bicycle. But his parents said no.

"It wasn't so much that my parents couldn't afford it," he explained in his 1976 autobiography *Hondo: Celtics Man in Motion,* "or didn't want to spend the money. We lived right on Route 40. And when I say we lived right on it, I mean just that. The house was smack on a curve, and our front door was no more than ten or twelve feet from the highway. When a big truck would go by at night, the house would vibrate. Consequently, they never wanted me to have a bicycle, because they thought it was too dangerous."

So while his friends were pedaling around the neighborhood, young Johnny Havlicek was picking 'em up and laying 'em down. "It was a tortoise-and-hare situation," he wrote. "They'd still get there first, but I'd be pulling in right after."

There was more.

"Maybe that's where I began to develop my stamina," he continued. "I do have a theory about my ability to change direction. I used to play a game with myself. I used to go up into the woods—they were only about a hundred yards from my house—just looking for animals, or just to be alone. I'd take a path to get to the top of the hill, but on the way down I'd run without taking the path. In doing so, I would dodge trees, using all kinds of different fakes and maneuvers. I fell down many times. But maybe I developed some of the instincts for the shuffle step doing all those various things I did running down that hill."

What he did not know at the time was that he was also something of a genetic freak. A bit later in life he went for a chest X-ray.

"My lungs were so big," Havlicek explained, "they needed two plates."

An old-fashioned Chip Hilton-esque three-sport star in high school, he just naturally gravitated to the ol' State U as part of a marquee basketball recruiting class that included Jerry Lucas and Larry Siegfried. His Ohio State team would win a national title in his sophomore season and finish as a frustrated runner-up to Cincinnati the following two seasons. Through it all, Havlicek was essentially the Robin to the Batman that was Jerry Lucas, who remains one of the greatest high school and college players ever. Lucas was both an unstoppable basketball force and a fascinating human being. Whereas Havlicek was the classic hardworking B-student who drank his milk to the bottom of the glass and looked both ways before crossing, Lucas was an eccentric genius who could skip class all semester and still post As by pulling off the classic all-nighter prior to the exam.

Lucas may have been a breed apart off the court, but it was John Havlicek who was a breed apart on it. The other players were pretty fit, but they were like fifty-year-old fat guys compared to John Havlicek.

"We were supposed to run a mile in under six minutes before October 15," Havlicek said. "We'd go out to have the cross-country team pace us. I did my miles in 4:50 and 4:52 my junior and senior years. There wasn't anyone close to me. I was basically keeping up with the cross-country team. It was always easy for me to run. It was something I took pride in. I wanted to do it to impress the coach too."

Lucas had been one of the stars on the acclaimed 1960 Olympic basketball team. Havlicek felt that he too should have been picking up one of those precious gold medals, and it remains one of his great career frustrations.

"Not making the 1960 Olympic basketball team is probably my most bitter disappointment in sports," he wrote in *Hondo,* "and I will never get over it. You only get one chance. I knew I should have been there, and I wasn't."

By the end of his senior year, John Havlicek was six-five and 195 pounds of sinewy muscle and energy. He participated easily in coach Fred Taylor's up-tempo offense, and he was as good a mid-sized defensive player as there was in the country. He was dedicated, determined, and diligent. The Boston Celtics, meanwhile, were coming off a fifth championship in six years and were, next to the Harlem Globetrotters, the most famous basketball team in the world. They would be picking ninth and last in the first round, and it was known that coach and general manager Red Auerbach liked both Havlicek and Bradley forward Chet Walker, a clever, six-foot-six scoring machine. But Syracuse selected Walker, thus making John Havlicek a Celtic.

Before going to Boston, however, Havlicek made an interesting detour. He had been an All-State quarterback in high school, and the home-state Browns had drafted him even though he hadn't played any football for Woody Hayes at Ohio State. Havlicek was intrigued enough to attend a mini-camp, where it was determined that four years away from the game had been too long for him to regain his quarterback skills. But the Browns thought he had a decent chance to become a wide receiver, and he played well enough during the exhibition season to last until the last cut. It came down to John Havlicek versus a rookie out of Maryland named Gary Collins, and the Browns chose Collins.

Gary Collins played ten productive seasons for the Browns, catching 331 passes, good for 5,299 yards. He was also a good enough punter to lead the league with a 46.7 average in 1965. The Browns made a good choice, all right.

The Celtics made a better one.

In the annals of the NBA, there has never been a better inherent match of team and draft choice than the marriage vows that were taken in 1962 between the Boston Celtics and twenty-two-year-old John Havlicek. For Havlicek was a runner, and the Boston Celtics were the consummate running team.

The kid was a spotty jump shooter, but that didn't matter. He was smart, he could run, and he could play defense. There was a place for him. With the incomparable Bill Russell at the absolute peak of his physical powers (twenty-eight years old at the start of the season, he would average 16.8 points and 23.6 rebounds a game), the Celtics were the class of the league. Tom Heinsohn and Satch Sanders were a classic offense-defense forward duo. Frank Ramsey was the league's reigning Sixth Man. Sam and K. C. Jones were starters-in-waiting in the backcourt.

And then there was Bob Cousy.

The Cooz, aka "Mr. Basketball," was thirty-four, and on many nights he was really feeling his age. He was on the verge of retirement. But in the autumn of his career, into his life dropped a kid who would help make professional life so much easier. The partnership of Bob Cousy and John Havlicek lasted only one year, but what an intriguing year it was.

Cousy's game was passing, and Havlicek's game was running and cutting. John Havlicek's rookie season basically consisted of his taking full advantage of the old master's passing expertise. "All I did that year," Havlicek said, "was run around and catch passes from Cousy."

He caught enough of them to score 14.3 points per game. It didn't take long for opponents to see that the Celtics, already the best team in the league, had just added not only a very good young player to the cast but a very good young player whose peripatetic style meshed perfectly with that of his team.

"When I first saw him," recalled Jerry West, "I said, 'Why can't *we* get players like that?' "

As both Cousy and Russell, just to name two, had discovered before him, Red Auerbach was the perfect coach for a player who had specific skills. Auerbach knew what to do with a passer like Cousy. Auerbach knew what to do with a defensive and rebound-oriented center like Russell. And now Auerbach knew what to do with a young sprinter such as John Havlicek.

"Just run people," said Havlicek. "That's what he told me."

"I didn't want to handle the ball," Havlicek explained, "and I didn't have to, not with Cousy out there. My game in college was running, but now it was even easier, because if you ran and got open, Cousy would find you."

"Our style was perfect for him," said Tom Heinsohn, who started off as the young man's roommate and wound up as his coach on two championship teams. "Cousy was the master of the long, downcourt pass, and Havlicek could catch them. That first year, 90 percent of his baskets must have been layups."

"John Havlicek was, by far, the best finisher I played with in my thirteen years," confirmed Cousy. "In terms of having someone to finish other than my old roomie Bill Sharman, who was a perimeter player, John was the best. He could catch the ball, put it to the floor, and finish with anyone.

"One complements the other," Cousy continued. "The point guard doesn't want to give it to a guy who's going to screw it up. And the receiver loves to play with someone who will give him the ball where all he has to do is take a dribble or two and lay it in. He had great hands. I can't remember him turning it over. He was just so solid."

Havlicek was a forward, and he thought of himself as nothing else, but before too long Auerbach had other ideas. Ramsey, the consummate Sixth Man, was nearing retirement, and Auerbach wanted to groom Havlicek as a replacement. Defense as a guard was not going to be a problem, of course.

Ramsey willingly tutored the kid in the art of being a proper Sixth Man: always sit close to Red. Always have your warm-up suit unbuttoned or unzipped so that it can be shed instantly when your name is called. Ramsey also was willing to share the many tricks of the trade. In later years Havlicek would earn a reputation as one of the great sneaky (but always clean) players in the league.

The Celtics were 59–22 in the regular season, cruising home in the Eastern Division with a ten-game bulge over Syracuse. They needed seven games to get past a good Cincinnati team in the first round, and then they defeated the Lakers in six for their fifth title in succession and sixth in seven years. John Havlicek was no adjunct. He may not have started any games, but he played enough to finish third on the team in minutes played during the regular season. In just one year he had become an integral part of the world's greatest basketball team.

One year later he was practically indispensable. He had increased his per-game minutes to 32 and his scoring average to 19.9. He had gone home and worked on his jump shot, making himself much more of a viable threat in the half-court game than he had been as a rookie. There was no Bob Cousy to make life cushy, but John Havlicek had no trouble adjusting to the K. C. Jones style. He was essentially the same player he had always been, except that he was better. Year after year, he would get better.

"His work ethic was always so good," said West. "Because of that, he got a little better every year. That's the sign of a great player—someone who makes subtle improvements every year."

"We came away that first season thinking that John would be a nice NBA player," agreed Cousy. "But none of us saw a potential Hall of Famer or that he would have the career he's had, because he just didn't shoot that well. So it's a credit to him that he worked the way he did to make himself into a shooter."

"I went back to Columbus in the summer of 1963 and got a job with the Division of Parks," he wrote in *Hondo*. "I was able to play a lot of basketball."

In the company of Ohio State buddies Lucas, Siegfried, Mel Nowell, and Joe Roberts (in other words, the four other starters on the 1960 NCAA championship team), he played lots and lots of basketball that summer. "I worked on my basic ball-handling, on how to use a pick properly, and how to dribble with my head up when I was in the middle of a fast break," he noted. "I came back to Boston in the proper frame of mind, much more confident of my ability to play guard in the NBA."

His game had broadened, and his circumstance had changed a bit too. It didn't take him very long to discover that he had been a bit sheltered during his rookie year.

"Auerbach never yelled at rookies," Heinsohn pointed out. "And you know how sincere and dedicated John was. Well, we're in St. Louis early that second year, and at halftime Red starts in on him. I mean, John just about started crying. He was beside himself. I went over to him, put my arm around him and said, 'John, all this means is that Red is saying you're no longer a rookie.' "

In year three he became a true Celtic legend because of one play. Game 7, Eastern Conference Finals between the Celtics and the 76ers. Protecting a 110–107 lead in the waning seconds, the Celtics had a twenty-four-second violation. Wilt Chamberlain dunked one at the other end with five seconds left to cut the lead to one. Eschewing a time-out, Russell quickly grabbed the ball and threw it in. But his in-bounds pass hit the guy wire that ran from the balcony to the basket. That was a turnover.

Hal Greer put the ball in play. Havlicek was guarding Walker. The assumption was that he would take a jump shot as the seven-one Chamberlain, the six-ten Johnny Kerr, and the six-nine Luke Jackson crashed the boards. But Havlicek foiled the plan by deflecting the in-bounds pass over to Sam Jones to save the game and the series.

The play was plenty timely and dramatic as it was, but the incident had legs that keep it going to this day in greater Boston because Celtics announcer Johnny Most's call was played and replayed and still stands as one of the great emotional descriptions of an athletic feat ever recorded. "Havlicek Stole the Ball!" became a phrase and concept that elevated him from mere great player to official icon.

His stature continued to grow. The Celtics won championships in 1965 and 1966, and in '66 his reputation went up a little more when Auerbach inserted him into the starting lineup after the Celtics had dropped behind the Cincinnati Royals, two games to one. That turned out to be the spark the team needed to come back and win the series. As Auerbach had before him, player-coach Russell continued to employ Havlicek as a Sixth Man for the next two seasons.

That was A-OK with John Havlicek. "I really liked the role of Sixth Man," he declared in *Hondo.* "Every team has five starters, but only on the Celtics was there the mystique of being the Sixth Man. You stood alone and you had your own little thing to be proud of. Since I was averaging more minutes than some of the starters, I had a sense of accomplishment. I never clamored to be a starter. I was receiving publicity and recognition as a Sixth Man, and I was perfectly happy with things the way they were. On occasion I would be inserted into the starting lineup during the playoffs, which served as an ego-massager."

In a replay of the '66 scenario, Havlicek had such an ego massage: Russell called upon him as a savior when the Celtics got behind Detroit, two games to one, in a 1968 series. He had eighteen points, twelve rebounds, and thirteen assists as the Celtics evened the series and had a 31–10–12 game when they clinched it in Game 6. He followed that with games of thirty-five, twenty-nine, twenty-nine, nine (oops), twenty-nine, twenty-nine, and twenty-one points as the Celtics came back from a 3–1 deficit to defeat Philadelphia.

Russell wasn't going to fool around with any Sixth Man stuff in the Finals against L.A. Havlicek played all but two minutes of a possible 291 as the Celtics took out the Lakers in six.

That's right: he played 289 out of 291 minutes, all of them at top speed. The following year he played all but two minutes in a five-game conquest of Philadelphia and all but four minutes in a six-game triumph over New York.

With the exception of a very brief period at the start of the 1969–70 season, he was now a starter for life. The Sixth Man days were behind him. He was simply too good not to be out there every second he was available, and since he was always available, he had to start. The man did not get into foul trouble, and he did not get tired. So why shouldn't he play?

At the start of the 1969–70 season, John Havlicek was twenty-eight years old and in possession of six championship rings. He had been the perfect fit with a superbly crafted Celtics team that had been built around the unique athletic and personal genius of Bill Russell. But Russell retired in the summer of '69. The Celtics were going to be a very different team.

In the first part of his career, a period lasting from 1962 through 1969, John Havlicek had been part of sport's greatest team. He had gradually expanded his role, and he had become the team's best all-around player, but as long as Bill Russell was around, it was Bill Russell's team, and rightly so. As brilliant as Havlicek was, he had still been merely the best of all the pilot fish who had been making a living off the Big Fella.

Now he was himself the Main Man.

The biggest names in the game, apart from centers, were Oscar Robertson and Jerry West; they were the All-League backcourt every year from 1961–62 through 1966–67, before West was nudged out by Dave Bing in 1967–68. It was heresy in some quarters to suggest that someone in their size range was better. But by 1969 the truth was that John Havlicek was the best all-around player in the league.

He would submit conclusive proof in the next two seasons, when he simply carried the Boston Celtics as they attempted to make their way in the NBA without Bill Russell, the greatest winner of them all. In the 1969–70 season, Havlicek led the team in scoring (24.2), rebounds (7.8), and assists (6.8). The following season he increased those totals to 28.9, 9.0, and 7.5. He didn't lead the team in rebounds because young Dave Cowens, a certified backboard-eater, had joined the team.

But the numbers that separated Havlicek from the pack were these: 45.4 and 45.1. Those were his *average* minutes per game. Yes, they were league-leading totals.

Tom Heinsohn was the coach. He was, and is, a devotee of the running game. He believes that a good running game is not a sometime thing, that it requires a commitment that begins on the first day of training camp, and that this dedication, even more than speed, is what really matters. How fortunate for him, therefore, that John Havlicek was on his team. The John Havlicek who had come into the NBA running in 1962 was still running in 1971 and 1972 and would still be running in his final year of 1978. Final year? How about final possession?

In the NBA there is running, and there is running. In the history of the league, there have been some great running teams, most notably the '80s "Showtime" teams in L.A. Those teams, quarterbacked by Magic Johnson, featured greyhounds such as James Worthy, Michael Cooper, and Byron Scott. They had more sheer speed and more sheer athleticism than the Celtics ever had. They ran well, but they didn't run as much as John Havlicek did when he played for the Boston Celtics.

"The way we ran," Heinsohn explained, "was to run the court and then run a circle route under the basket. Guards essentially run from foul line to foul line. Centers, if they run at all, run from dotted line to dotted line. But our forwards went baseline to baseline and then, if we didn't have a shot, exchanged along the baseline. And we did that all game. Our forwards took the long route."

But that's just talking about fast breaks. John Havlicek took no time off when it became a half-court game. That's when he went into plan B, running without the ball and running without the ball and running without the ball.

"He kept running you into picks," said DeGregorio. "And he was just so smart. He had more knowledge of the game than anyone else. He knew how to take you inside. He could shoot over you. He could go back-door."

As time went on, he developed a complete offensive game. He was a very strong driver. His deceptive strength enabled him to withstand blows and thus convert countless old-fashioned three-point plays. He had extraordinary body control, which enabled him to avoid many a rival hoping to take a charge.

He became an excellent shooter. He was not a great one-on creator, but he was an exceptional catch-and-shoot marksman. He knew how to use a good pick. He had excellent range and would have flourished in the age of the three-point shot. He was, of course, an excellent foul shooter.

One thing everyone remembers was his signature bank shot. But unlike other celebrated bank shooters—Sam Jones, Rudy Tomjanovich, and Tim Duncan come to mind—his specialty was unique. He liked to bank on straightaway shots, especially on the move.

"That's something that evolved gradually," he said. "I always figured the square was there to help you. After a while, you learn to put it up there with the right touch. If it goes in clean, fine. If it doesn't, you might get the rebound. One thing I was always good at was following my own shots."

All this came into play in Game 6 of the 1974 Finals against Milwaukee. Trailing by two late in the first overtime, Don Chaney took the ball from Bob Dandridge. Havlicek came out of the pack, leading the fast break. He rushed at Kareem Abdul-Jabbar at full speed and attempted about a twelve-foot banker—straight on.

"I had Abdul-Jabbar moving backwards," Havlicek explained in *Hondo,* "and if I stopped suddenly, there was no way he could recover quickly enough to come forward and block my shot."

The ball was a bit long, but Havlicek beat a startled Abdul-Jabbar to the ball ("I was always good at following my own shots") and banked in his own follow-up to create a second overtime.

By far the greatest area of personal improvement came in his passing. The reluctant ball-handler of his youth became one of the great passers in the game. He eventually mastered all the standard passes. He was a truly excellent passer off the drive. He learned how to make good entry passes to pivotmen. He ran a great fast break.

And he became almost Cousy-like with his ability to throw the long baseball pass, often to a streaking Dave Cowens, the runningest center ever seen. Among his other physical attributes, Havlicek was blessed with large, strong hands. This, of course, was what had intrigued the Cleveland Browns.

The early '70s were not easy years for John Havlicek. He had once been part of as smart and basketball-savvy a group as the sport has ever known. One reason Russell had been a successful player-coach (two titles in three years) was the identity of the core group. Havlicek, Don Nelson, Satch Sanders, Sam Jones, Larry Siegfried, Bailey Howell, and Wayne Embry hardly needed coaching. The Celtics actually operated in a town meeting style, with Embry keeping track of minutes in his head for substitution purposes, Siegfried serving as the de facto offensive coordinator, and Russell masterminding the defense and making all final decisions.

Two years later a prime-of-life Havlicek found himself playing with talented kids such as Cowens, Jo Jo White, and Steve Kuberski, and it was a shock. Things that seemed logical to him were not so logical to them, and he had many exasperating moments on the floor. One night when things had not gone very well he allowed himself to be quoted to the effect that he was now a part of "the dumbest team I've ever played on."

But the old Celtics were a once-in-a-lifetime experience, and Havlicek had to move on. Things took a significant turn for the better when Auerbach brought in Paul Silas prior to the 1972–73 season. The six-foot-seven forward was the league's premier offensive rebounder, a superb defensive player, and a man with a very forceful personality. This was a man who would have fit in with the old Celtics, and both Havlicek and Cowens, who now had help on the boards, embraced him. The Celtics won sixty-eight games and might very well have won championship number twelve if Havlicek, who had convened the '73 playoffs by dumping fifty-four points on the Atlanta Hawks (eighteen of twenty-four shooting), had not been injured in Game 3 of the second-round series with the Knicks.

What transpired certainly enhanced the Havlicek legend. Playing without him, the Celtics lost Game 4 of that series in double overtime, losing a sixteen-point fourth-quarter lead to fall behind in the series, 3–1. Playing almost exclusively with his left arm (four of his six baskets were southpaw efforts), Havlicek scored eighteen points in Game 5 as the Celtics kept the series alive. They won again in Game 6, forcing a seventh game in Boston. But this time the Knicks were not quite as deferential toward Havlicek as they had been in the two previous games, in which they appeared to be treating him more like visiting royalty than a feared opponent. Truth be told, he was bluffing his way through with one arm, and in Game 7 they exploited his vulnerability, forcing him into turnovers. New York won, 94–78.

But playing as well as he did with one arm added to the growing legend that was John Havlicek. A year later the Celtics made it all the way, running through Buffalo and New York in Game 6, when it appeared that he had led the team to victory by scoring nine of the team's eleven points, only to see the amazing Abdul-Jabbar pull the game out with a seventeen-foot corner hook. Game 7 belonged to the Celtics, however, as Cowens got off to a great start and the Celtics triumphed in Milwaukee, 102–87.

He had won his first six titles as part of Russell's team. This was his first as captain of Havlicek's team.

"I can't ever remember being any happier than after winning that game," he declared in *Hondo*. "I never had so much fun before, because the new group of Celtics had a feeling for celebration that far exceeded that of the old generation. It was a matter-of-fact thing when we won—at least until 1969. I'm sure, though, that back in 1957, when they won their first one, things were different."

The Celtics were a nice blend of veterans and young Turks, but there was no doubt who had done the most to create this first post-Russell championship. The 1974 Finals will always serve as Exhibit A when the subject of John Havlicek's superhuman stamina, endurance, and indomitable will come up for discussion. He was then thirty-four years of age and had been playing at his unmatched non-stop pace for twelve years. But he played 94 percent of the available minutes in that series.

That's correct. He played forty-five, forty-one, forty-five, forty-eight, forty-seven, fifty-eight, and forty-six minutes in those seven games. Game 6 was a chore, even for him. He played all fifty-eight minutes in that double-overtime classic, during which he had thirty-six points, nine rebounds, and four assists. "People said that after that game I didn't look like my normal self," he recalled. In *Hondo* he wrote, "I was really depressed after the game. I had never come out of the game during the entire fifty-eight minutes and I was exhausted. People kept telling me I didn't look like myself, and the next day I discovered what they were talking about. I saw a picture of myself in the paper, and I wouldn't have known it was me if it weren't for the caption underneath the picture and the number 17 on the guy's jersey. My eyes were sunken and I looked horrible."

The game had ended around midnight, Boston time, and on Sunday afternoon at 1:00 P.M. Eastern Standard Time he was back out there for forty-six minutes in Game 7.

Move the clock ahead two years and you'll find that not much had changed. The opponent in the Finals was Phoenix, and the twist in the plot was that John Havlicek, in the first game of the first series against Buffalo, had sustained a torn plantar fascia in the arch of his left foot. He was trying to fight his way through the pain. Told that he needed to soak his foot in ice for three hours daily, he reasoned that if three were good, then six or seven must be twice as good, and so that's what he did. He carried a little turquoise dish pan around for the remainder of the playoffs, and now he was in the Finals for the eighth time. He might not have been as productive as he usually was, but he was still John Havlicek, and the team sure wasn't going to win without him.

He was practically a sloth by his standards, playing forty, thirty-four, thirty-one, and forty-one minutes in the first four games, which left the team tied at two games apiece entering Game 5. He was now an injured thirty-six-year-old playing as much on sheer determination as anything else. How much more could he possibly have to give?

Try fifty-eight minutes.

The big Celtic hero in that epic Game 5 was Jo Jo White, who hit big shot after big shot in the fourth quarter and throughout the three overtimes as the Celtics staggered home as 128–126 victors. But John Havlicek wasn't bad either, with twenty-two points, nine rebounds, and eight assists, to go along with his defense and his brainpower. The Celtics went out to Phoenix thirty-six hours later to win a thirteenth championship.

He would never win another championship, but he would go on

being John Havlicek. The Celtics had one last stand in 1977, taking a favored 76er team to seven games before losing. A thirty-seven-year-old John Havlicek did his part by defending Julius Erving doggedly, never allowing the younger Dr. J to go off on any of his fearsome tangents. It just seemed that wherever Dr. J wanted to go, Havlicek was already there.

His sixteenth, and final, season was not a very pleasant one. The Celtics were in disarray, but the one area of stability was in the backcourt, where Dave Bing and Havlicek performed with class and dignity. The team won only thirty-two games, but there was one worth remembering, and that was the last.

April 9, 1978, was his last day in a Celtics uniform. The opponents were the Buffalo Braves, a team that liked to get up and down the floor. This was good. John Havlicek was going to go out running.

Entering the fourth quarter, Havlicek had twelve points. That would have been an acceptable farewell for the typical thirty-eight-year-old (his thirty-eighth birthday having taken place the day before). But the fates had something more in store.

Four minutes and three seconds into the final period, John Havlicek swished one from the left corner. On the next possession he came off a pick. As Johnny Most would have said, "Bang!"

Now the crowd was into it. A minute and a half later, he was fouled on the fast break. He made both free throws. With 3:04 left, he made a reverse layup off the fast break, and now we are talking pandemonium in Boston Garden. John Havlicek is suddenly thirty-eight going on twenty-eight going on eternal.

With 2:16 remaining, coach Satch Sanders sent in Ernie DeGregorio. Oh, if only he had done so earlier. For Ernie was nothing less than Bob Cousy's spiritual son. Havlicek came into the game running the floor and catching passes from the best passer of one era, and now he was going to spend the last two minutes and sixteen seconds of his career running the floor and catching passes from the best passer of another era.

What happened was positively chilling. At 1:24, Havlicek ran the floor, took a pass from DeGregorio, got fouled, and sank two free throws. At 1:09, DeGregorio found him for a fast-break layup. Eleven seconds later, Ernie D hit Havlicek for a reverse layup. There was no way to describe the crowd's reaction to what was going on. What they were witnessing wasn't history so much as fantasy. It was the most symbolically meaningful action ever to take place in an otherwise meaningless NBA game. Ernie D was sending John Havlicek, the ultimate running man, out of the game on a running extravaganza.

Ernie and John weren't done. With forty-one seconds left, Havlicek converted his own rebound. Twelve seconds later, DeGregorio found him one more time. Havlicek was fouled. He made the first and missed the second, and that was it. Dave Bing replaced him with fifteen seconds left.

In his final game, thirty-eight-year-old John Havlicek had scored seventeen points in the fourth quarter. He finished with twenty-nine points, nine rebounds, and four assists. He had played forty-one minutes.

"That wasn't the way I had been taught to play," said DeGregorio. "I had been taught to look for whoever was open. But that day I was only looking for one man. I had never played like that before, but this was something special. Larry Fleisher [head of the Players' Association, as well as Havlicek's agent] told me he had never seen anything like that game. I know I was practically bawling myself. John Havlicek just meant so much to the game."

"I remember it well," said Cedric Maxwell. "It was like watching Secretariat run. And the way Ernie kept finding him. Ernie kept flipping him passes, and it was like the opposing team was in slow motion. You knew John was going to get it, and you knew John was going to score."

Nearly three decades have passed, and many interesting things have happened in the NBA. Magic, Larry, and Michael have come and gone. The Buffalo team in question has moved to San Diego and on to Los Angeles, where they are known as the Clippers. The game is universal in a way that was unimaginable in 1978. Yes, many things have happened, but the NBA has not produced another John Havlicek. There have been great passers, great scorers, great everythings, but no person who has brought the peculiar package of endurance and versatility to the sport that was John Havlicek.

No one averages forty-five minutes a game. No one runs and runs and runs the way John Havlicek did. Tom Heinsohn once said that when John Havlicek retires, they'll cut him open and coils and sprockets and springs will pop out. Everyone nodded and everyone laughed. Everyone half-expected it to be true.

Don't even try to compare any other swingman to John Havlicek. Scottie Pippen? Please. Dan Majerle? Sorry. Chris Ford says that Rip Hamilton has some of the move-without-the-ball ideas in his game, but it stops there. In keeping with the universal appeal of the modern NBA, Havlicek himself says that he sees a little of himself in Manu Ginobili, an Argentine who probably has never heard of John Havlicek.

That's nice of John Havlicek to say, but he's being too charitable. The next John Havlicek has yet to materialize. John Havlicek played two positions at an All-Star level. His unparalleled stamina enabled his coach to keep him in games while every rival coach had to rest his own star. In his time, John Havlicek positively affected more games than any other noncenter, and that includes Oscar Robertson, Jerry West, Elgin Baylor, and Julius Erving.

There was no start-to-finish career like it. Try this one. In his final season the Celtics, like many other teams, ran into problems with winter storms that forced game postponements. A number of games had to be rescheduled. So it was that, at age thirty-seven, John Havlicek played back-to-back-to-back games in which he averaged forty minutes a game and scored twenty, thirty-two, twenty-seven, and twenty-five points.

In sixty-six hours.

By the way, in his sixteenth, and final, season, he played all eighty-two games.

"He was the epitome of what the Celtics stood for in those days," suggested Bill Bradley.

As far as basketball players are concerned, he was in fact the epitome of epitome.

JOHN HAVLICEK'S PERFECT TEAM

First Team

Forward—Larry Bird: Won't be denied. Utterly persistent.

Forward—Michael Jordan: No weaknesses. Undeniably persistent.

Center—Bill Russell: Greatest winner of all time.

Guard—Magic Johnson: Second-greatest winner of all time. Made everyone better. Great will to win.

Guard—Oscar Robertson: The best player I've ever played against.

Sixth Man

Forward—Kevin McHale: An anomaly in the post.

Second Team

Forward—Elgin Baylor: Great rebounder and scorer. Undeterred going to the basket.

Forward—Karl Malone: Strong, aggressive, and a great combination inside-outside player.

Center—Kareem Abdul-Jabbar: Impossible sky-hook. Great scorer and clutch foul shooter too.

Guard—Jerry West: Quickest release and quickest player to guard. Very long arms.

Guard—Kobe Bryant: As talented as anyone.

Center—Wilt Chamberlain: Most dominant player with regard to strength in my era.

Coach and General Manager

Red Auerbach: Architect of winning, master of managing players as a coach. Knew all the rules and loopholes. Daring as a general manager. A gambler: Russell, Bird, etc. If I can't have him as my GM, I'll take Jerry West.

JOHN HAVLICEK—FORWARD/GUARD

PERSONAL: Born April 8, 1940, in Martins Ferry, OH . . . 6–5/205 (2.03 m/97.6 kg) . . . full
name: John J. Havlicek . . . nickname: Hondo.
HIGH SCHOOL: Bridgeport (OH).

COLLEGE: Ohio State.

TRANSACTIONS/CAREER NOTES: Selected by Boston Celtics in first round of 1962 NBA draft.

CAREER HONORS: Elected to Naismith Memorial Basketball Hall of Fame (1983). . . . NBA 35th Anniversary All-Time Team (1980) and One of the 50 Greatest Players in NBA History (1996).

MISCELLANEOUS: Member of NBA championship team (1963, 1964, 1965, 1966, 1968, 1969, 1974, 1976). . . . Selected as wide receiver by Cleveland Browns in seventh round of 1962 National Football League draft. . . . Boston Celtics all-time leading scorer with 26,395 points (1962–63 through 1977–78).

COLLEGIATE RECORD

NOTES: *The Sporting News* All-America second team (1962). . . . Member of NCAA championship team (1960).

													Averages		
Season	Team	G	Min	FGM	FGA	Pct	FTM	FTA	Pct	Reb	Ast	Pts	RPG	APG	PPG
58–59	Ohio State					Freshman team did not play intercollegiate schedule									
59–60	Ohio State	28	—	144	312	.462	53	74	.716	205	—	341	7.3	—	12.2
60–61	Ohio State	28	—	173	321	.539	61	87	.701	244	—	407	8.7	—	14.5
61–62	Ohio State	28	—	196	377	.520	83	109	.761	271	—	475	9.7	—	17.0
Total		84	—	513	1,010	.508	197	270	.730	720	—	1,223	8.6	—	14.6

NBA REGULAR-SEASON RECORD

HONORS: All-NBA first team (1971, 1972, 1973, 1974). . . . All-NBA second team (1964, 1966, 1968, 1969, 1970, 1975, 1976). . . . NBA All-Defensive first team (1972, 1973, 1974, 1975, 1976). . . . NBA All-Defensive second team (1969, 1970, 1971).

															Averages		
Season	Team	G	Min	FGM	FGA	Pct	FTM	FTA	Pct	Reb	Ast	PF	DQ	Pts	RPG	APG	PPG
62–63	Bos	80	2,200	483	1,085	.445	174	239	.728	534	179	189	2	1,140	6.7	2.2	14.3
63–64	Bos	80	2,587	640	1,535	.417	315	422	.746	428	238	227	1	1,595	5.4	3.0	19.9
64–65	Bos	75	2,169	570	1,420	.401	235	316	.744	371	199	200	2	1,375	4.9	2.7	18.3
65–66	Bos	71	2,175	530	1,328	.399	274	349	.785	423	210	158	1	1,334	6.0	3.0	18.8
66–67	Bos	81	2,602	684	1,540	.444	365	441	.828	532	278	210	0	1,733	6.6	3.4	21.4
67–68	Bos	82	2,921	666	1,551	.429	368	453	.812	546	384	237	2	1,700	6.7	4.7	20.7
68–69	Bos	82	3,174	692	1,709	.405	387	496	.780	570	441	247	0	1,771	7.0	5.4	21.6
69–70	Bos	81	3,369	736	1,585	.464	488	578	.844	635	550	211	1	1,960	7.8	6.8	24.2
70–71	Bos	81	3,678	892	1,982	.450	554	677	.818	730	607	200	0	2,338	9.0	7.5	28.9
71–72	Bos	82	3,698	897	1,957	.458	458	549	.834	672	614	183	1	2,252	8.2	7.5	27.5
72–73	Bos	80	3,367	766	1,704	.450	370	431	.858	572	529	195	1	1,902	7.1	6.6	23.8

		G	Min	FGM	FGA	Pct	FTM	FTA	Pct	Rebounds Off	Def	Tot	Ast	St	Blk	TO	Pts	Averages RPG	APG	PPG
73–74	Bos	76	3,091	685	1,502	.456	346	416	.832	138	349	487	447	95	32	—	1,716	6.4	5.9	22.6
74–75	Bos	82	3,132	642	1,411	.455	289	332	.870	154	330	484	432	110	16	—	1,573	5.9	5.3	19.2
75–76	Bos	76	2,598	504	1,121	.450	281	333	.844	116	198	314	278	97	29	—	1,289	4.1	3.7	17.0
76–77	Bos	79	2,913	580	1,283	.452	235	288	.816	109	273	382	400	84	18	—	1,395	4.8	5.1	17.7
77–78	Bos	82	2,797	546	1,217	.449	230	269	.855	93	239	332	328	90	22	204	1,322	4.0	4.0	16.1
Total		1,270	46,471	10,513	23,930	.439	5,369	6,589	.815	—	—	8,007	6,114	476	117	204	26,395	6.3	4.8	20.8

PERSONAL FOULS/DISQUALIFICATIONS: 1973–74, 196/1; 1974–75, 231/12; 1975–76, 204/1; 1976–77, 208/4; 1977–78, 185/2. Total: 3281/21.

NBA PLAYOFF RECORD

NOTES: NBA Finals Most Valuable Player (1974). . . . Shares NBA Finals single-game record for most points in an overtime period—9 (May 10, 1974, vs. Milwaukee). . . . Shares single-game playoff record for most field goals made—24 (April 1, 1973, vs. Atlanta).

Season	Team	G	Min	FGM	FGA	Pct	FTM	FTA	Pct	Reb	Ast	PF	DQ	Pts	Averages RPG	APG	PPG
62–63	Bos	11	254	56	125	.448	18	27	.667	—	17	28	1	130	0.0	1.5	11.8
63–64	Bos	10	289	61	159	.384	35	44	.795	—	32	26	0	157	0.0	3.2	15.7
64–65	Bos	12	405	88	250	.352	46	55	.836	—	29	44	1	222	0.0	2.4	18.5
65–66	Bos	17	719	153	374	.409	95	113	.841	—	70	69	2	401	0.0	4.1	23.6
66–67	Bos	9	330	95	212	.448	57	71	.803	—	28	30	0	247	0.0	3.1	27.4
67–68	Bos	19	862	184	407	.452	125	151	.828	—	142	67	1	493	0.0	7.5	25.9
68–69	Bos	18	850	170	382	.445	118	138	.855	—	100	58	2	458	0.0	5.6	25.4
71–72	Bos	11	517	108	235	.460	85	99	.859	—	70	35	1	301	0.0	6.4	27.4
72–73	Bos	12	479	112	235	.477	61	74	.824	—	65	24	0	285	0.0	5.4	23.8

		G	Min	FGM	FGA	Pct	FTM	FTA	Pct	Rebounds Off	Def	Tot	Ast	St	Blk	TO	Pts	Averages RPG	APG	PPG
73–74	Bos	18	811	199	411	.484	89	101	.881	28	88	116	108	24	6	—	487	6.4	6.0	27.1
74–75	Bos	11	464	83	192	.432	66	76	.868	18	39	57	51	16	1	—	232	5.2	4.6	21.1
75–76	Bos	15	505	80	180	.444	38	47	.809	18	38	56	51	12	5	—	198	3.7	3.4	13.2
76–77	Bos	9	375	62	167	.371	41	50	.820	15	34	49	62	8	4	—	165	5.4	6.9	18.3
Total		172	6,860	1,451	3,329	.436	874	1,046	.854	—	—	1,186	825	60	16	—	3,776	6.9	4.8	22.0

PERSONAL FOULS/DISQUALIFICATIONS: 1973–74, 43/0; 1974–75, 38/1; 1975–76, 204/1; 1976–77, 208/4; 1977–78, 185/2. Total: 3281/21.

NBA ALL-STAR GAME RECORD

Season	Team	Min	FGM	FGA	Pct	FTM	FTA	Pct	Reb	Ast	PF	DQ	Pts
1966	Boston	25	6	16	.375	6	6	1.000	6	1	2	0	18
1967	Boston	17	7	14	.500	0	0	—	2	1	1	0	14
1968	Boston	22	9	15	.600	8	11	.727	5	4	0	0	26
1969	Boston	31	6	14	.429	2	2	1.000	7	2	2	0	14
1970	Boston	29	7	15	.467	3	3	1.000	5	7	2	0	17
1971	Boston	24	6	12	.500	0	2	.000	3	2	3	0	12
1972	Boston	24	5	13	.385	5	5	1.000	3	2	2	0	15
1973	Boston	22	6	10	.600	2	5	.400	3	5	1	0	14

		Min	FGM	FGA	Pct	FTM	FTA	Pct	Rebounds			Ast	PF	DQ	St	Blk	TO	Pts
									Off	Def	Tot							
1974	Boston	18	5	10	.500	0	2	.000	0	0	0	2	2	0	1	0	—	10
1975	Boston	31	7	12	.583	2	2	1.000	1	5	6	1	2	0	2	0	—	16
1976	Boston	21	3	10	.300	3	3	1.000	1	1	2	2	0	0	1	0	—	9
1977	Boston	17	2	5	.400	0	0	—	0	1	1	1	1	0	0	0	—	4
1978	Boston	22	5	8	.625	0	0	—	0	3	3	1	2	0	0	0	4	10
Total		303	74	154	.481	31	41	.756	2	—	—	31	20	0	4	0	4	179

Chapter Three

ALLEN IVERSON—Guard

Courage

by John Smallwood

This time, not even those closest to him were sure that Allen Iverson was going to bounce right back.

During his first five seasons in the NBA, Iverson's teammates on the Philadelphia 76ers had seen the generously listed six-foot, 165-pound guard bounced around like a human pinball while he carved his niche as a little man in a big man's league.

Although they often wondered how Iverson could continually fight through the daily physical punish-

ment that his full-speed-ahead style put his slender body through, they just always knew he would, because he always did.

But this time it was different.

It was the 2001 NBA playoffs, and Iverson and the Sixers had just finished a grueling seven-game series with the Toronto Raptors to advance to the Eastern Conference Finals against the Milwaukee Bucks.

There were, however, costs to be paid. Point guard Eric Snow was playing with screws in his surgically repaired ankle. Forward George Lynch had broken his foot in Game 3 against Toronto.

And now Iverson was hurting, hurting so bad that he had actually sat out Game 3 of the conference Finals in Milwaukee.

In Game 7 against Toronto, Iverson took one of his patented drives into the Land of the Giants and got whacked hard by Raptors block of granite Charles Oakley.

The technical name for the injury was a sacroiliac joint contusion, but Iverson correctly diagnosed it in layman's terms by saying, "My ass hurts," even when he did something as simple as sitting down.

Iverson had played through the painful injury in Games 1 and 2 in the conference Finals, but the Sixers' medical staff finally convinced the ultracompetitive guard to sit out Game 3, for the betterment of himself and the team.

The Sixers lost Game 3 and trailed 2–1 in the best-of-seven series, with Game 4 in Milwaukee's Bradley Center. The situation was desperate. No matter the pain, if Allen Iverson could walk, he was going to play.

He played forty-seven of a possible forty-eight minutes. He scored twenty-eight points and dished out eight assists.

With about two minutes left in a tight game, Iverson took an inadvertent elbow to the jaw from Milwaukee Bucks guard Ray Allen. It split Iverson's mouth open, and the blood started to flow. By NBA rules, Iverson knew that if the officials saw the blood, he'd immediately have to leave the game.

Iverson knew he couldn't let that happen, but there was no time for stitches.

He improvised.

"I didn't think the refs were going to let me come back out because I kept spitting out so much blood," Iverson said. "My team-mates were telling me I had to get back on the floor.

"I was trying to stop spitting blood, but it wouldn't stop. I didn't want the [officials] to try and get me out of the games. So I kept my mouth closed, just swallowed the blood when it filled up."

The Sixers won 89–83 and eventually advanced to the NBA Finals before losing to the Los Angeles Lakers.

According to *Webster's Dictionary,* "courage" is defined as the mental or moral strength to venture, persevere, and withstand danger, fear, or difficulty.

But how do you define that in a basketball player, and how do you determine that one player above all others represents that characteristic?

Sure, other players have played hurt. Some of the NBA's greatest moments were testaments to players who overcame injury and illness to perform brilliantly.

There was Willis Reed limping back out onto the court in Game 7 of the 1972 NBA Finals against the Los Angeles Lakers; Michael Jordan leading the Chicago Bulls to victory against the Utah Jazz while playing with food poisoning; and Sean Elliott helping the San Antonio Spurs to the 1999 NBA title after receiving a kidney transplant.

Still, there's something about Iverson—something that makes him stand out among others, something others see.

"You could poke both of [Iverson's] eyes out, and he'd probably still be wandering around out there trying to play," former Sixers center Todd MacCulloch said of the teammate he towered over by a foot. "With Allen, there are no technical knockouts, no knockouts. He keeps getting up."

Maybe it's the "little guy syndrome." If Iverson were six-seven and 205 pounds, the things he does wouldn't look nearly as amazing.

But he's not.

He is what he is.

And when you see how he plays, his aggression, his passion, his drive to fight until the last ounce of energy has been expended, you can't help believing that 85 percent of whatever Iverson is, is heart.

"You can't discount how tough [Iverson] is because that's part of what defines courageous in sports," said 76ers radio commentator Tom McGinnis, who has seen virtually every whack, hit, and body shot Iverson has taken in his NBA career.

"To get knocked down and to know that when you go right back in there you're going to get knocked down again.

"When there is pain and potential for injury, it takes courage to go in there time after time. But Iverson does. This guy is barely six feet and weighs 160 pounds, and he goes in there against seven-footers and six-ten guys who are ready to lay the wood on him. That's courage and wanting to score.

"I always say things in a sports sense," McGinnis noted, "because to me real courage is being in a foxhole in a war, knowing you may be killed.

"Courage in sports is a little bit different, but I think with Iverson the fact that he plays hurt speaks of courage. Some guys are out for two weeks, and this guy is back the next game, and that's just one of his injuries.

"In the NBA you've got eighty-two games, and each night you've got to come back no matter if you are hurt or if you've fallen on your face. You have to have the courage to be there the next time," McGinnis concluded.

So where does this courage, this toughness, come from?

Iverson isn't Superman. He isn't invulnerable. His forays into the Land of the Giants and the beatings he's received for his brashness have often landed him on the injury list.

A miniature guard doesn't keep pounding into the likes of Shaquille O'Neal, Alonzo Mourning, Dikembe Mutombo, or even Greg Ostertag and not come away unfazed.

The laws of physics don't allow for that.

Still, as far as paying the price to play the game, Iverson, who is unquestionably new school in his style, defiance of authority, and attitude, is decidedly old school when it comes to his courage and toughness.

"That makes it more fun," Iverson said of the nightly beatings he

takes in NBA games. "Your mouth's all busted up, but you keep getting knocked down to the floor. That's when you know you're in a
real war. Honestly, it helps me concentrate better."

Iverson hears the talk. He knows what's in store for him every
time he takes the court, but it simply doesn't faze him when he hears
ex-Cleveland Cavaliers coach and former NBA tough guy Paul Silas
say, "What I would have done had I played against Iverson would
be to knock the crap out of him the first time he touched the ball.

"After that, I'd pick my spots and make judicious use of my six
personal fouls. Should he make a few shots in a row, *bang!* I'd clock
him again. Let him pick his little behind off the floor and make
some free throws."

It doesn't faze Iverson when he hears someone like Indiana Pacers enforcer Ron Artest say, "This guy's coming to the hole like he's
Shaq. I'm not trying to hurt him; I'm just trying to let him know I
can't let you keep coming to the hole.

"Someone has to do it. I don't want to be the only one getting fla-
grants, but if nobody else is going to step up and give a hard foul, I
guess I'm going to have to get suspended. I'm willing to make that
sacrifice."

Growing up as a two-sport star athlete at Bethel High School in
Hampton, Virginia, Iverson said, it was the physical nature of football that fueled his courage in basketball.

When you've grown up being tackled by defensive linemen and
linebackers, what's a little bit of contact from a power forward?

"Being an ex-football player, I'm used to the contact," Iverson
said. "That has enabled me to withstand everything that goes on in
basketball.

"I'm used to being banged up. You try to suck it up and not think
about it. You just play off your adrenaline.

"Now any little injuries I get here and there, I'm fine. I think football made me tough. It gave me a lot of the heart that I have because
I was always small. The guys were always bigger than me, and they
would always take a lot of shots at me, try to hurt me."

Still, having courage and being tough isn't about being fearless,
it's about overcoming that fear.

And while he'll never say he was afraid, Iverson did recall his first professional encounter with Shaquille O'Neal, the seven-foot-one, 335-pound behemoth who is one of the most dominant forces in sports history.

"Shaq was really big," Iverson recalled of playing against O'Neal and the Los Angeles Lakers during his rookie season. "But I really only know one way to play.

"I was going to play my game, regardless. You can't be intimidated. I've never been scared of anything. I wasn't going to let anyone change the way I play."

The immovable object put a hurting on the irresistible force. Iverson bruised his right thigh in a collision with O'Neal that affected him for several weeks.

"It just hurt the whole time for a while," Iverson said.

That was merely the first of several bruises and contusions Iverson has received in his encounters with O'Neal.

"That comes with the territory," Iverson said of his endless résumé of crashes with NBA big men. "I always take spills. Every game I play in, guys try and knock me down and I get right back up.

"I guess that's kind of the fun part of the game. You go through a whole game with no contact and then you fall asleep. Those shots sometimes wake you up."

In a sport where toughness is one of the most respected attributes, Iverson has more than earned his stripes.

"He's a throwback when you talk in terms of how tough Allen is, his willingness to play hurt," said former NBA player and Sixers television analyst Steve Mix. "There are a lot of things you can disagree with about Allen, but you can't ever question his courage. I've seen him take shots where I'd say there's no way he's getting up from that. Five minutes later he's right back in there doing the same thing, playing just as hard."

Is it hard to be courageous when failure is the only thing you are afraid of?

Iverson's story isn't unique. He grew up in poverty in Hampton, Virginia. He saw basketball as the ticket out for him and his family.

He was the only man in a family of four. His natural father had abandoned him and his mother when he was a toddler. The man he had come to know as his father was incarcerated for selling drugs.

Allen accepted the responsibilities of being the man of the house. He was only fifteen.

"When you're the oldest man in the house," Iverson once said, "and your mother is motherless and not much older than some of your friends, and your sister is shaking, and you don't know why you're living in a dark, freezing sewer hole, it occurs to you that there is a lot riding on you.

"People would say that's a million-to-one shot to make it to the NBA. I'd say, 'Not for me, it ain't.' If I didn't succeed, man, I don't want to think about it. I had a big picture of my life. I wasn't going back to the sewer."

Is it courage to be poor, to see those around you selling drugs to make money yet not succumb to the temptations tugging at you every day?

Is it courage that keeps you going when you've been jailed at sixteen and your entire future is threatened?

"It's all about always believing. I've seen the bad side of life and I survived," said Iverson, who was put in jail as a teenager for his role in a fight in a bowling alley. "Now I plan to enjoy the good side. And I don't plan to look back.

"My past has taught me a lot, and I'm not ashamed of it. It taught me how quickly things can be taken away from you. It taught me how important it is to believe in yourself even if others turn their back on you.

"It's hard to think when you're scared. I've never been scared of anything, just being from where I'm from. After all the crap I've seen, you think I'm going to feel pressure from a game?"

It was November 15, 1996, and Iverson was just a few games into his rookie season when in a game against the Cleveland Cavaliers he ran into a pick set by forward Danny Ferry and separated his left shoulder.

The doctors said that Iverson should sit out a minimum of two weeks.

Eight days later Iverson strolled into the Sixers home arena, which was then called the CoreStates Center, and told team president Pat Croce, head coach Johnny Davis, and general manager Brad Greenberg that his shoulder felt fine and that he intended to play that night against the New York Knicks.

With his teammates believing he was going to miss a few more games, Iverson scored twenty-six with nine rebounds, nine assists, and four steals in forty-two frantic minutes to lead the Sixers to a victory.

On the game's first play, New York intimidator Charles Oakley put a blow into Iverson's shoulder just to see if the rookie had the insides to stick it out with the big boys of the NBA.

"I said, 'Uh-oh, it might be one of those nights,' " Iverson recalled. "I just shook [the hit] from Oakley off. I didn't want to come out of the game, make all those guys think they were right in saying I shouldn't play."

That was the start of Iverson's reputation as the toughest little man in the NBA. You could knock him down and around, but you'd have to near kill him to stop him from playing.

From the beginning, Iverson understood that for a player of his size to make a name for himself as one of the top players in the league, he was going to have to sacrifice body and soul along the way.

It was a price he willingly accepted.

"That comes with the territory," he said. "A lot of times that will show what type of player you are, when you can play through injuries. It's a tough season, eighty-two games, when you're going to get banged up a little bit. It's just important for you to try and play through it."

So is it the courage gained from the sum of his life experiences that compels Iverson to play at breakneck speed, treating each game as if it might be the last one he plays?

"Where I grew up, street ball is played hard and physical," Iverson said. "I definitely believe that my environment helped to shape my attitude on the court and my style of play.

"In my hood, if you're soft or you can't produce on the court, then you never get a chance to play. These same rules pretty much apply to the NBA.

"That's what it's all about. What I try to tell young guys is that when an opportunity presents itself, you have to make the best of it. When you get the opportunity to play, you cherish the moment and play the game like it's your last."

After Iverson was selected ninth overall by the Sixers in the 2004 NBA Draft, one of the first things six-foot-six swingman Andre Iguodala said was, "I think it's going to be a great experience for me going out there and playing with a true warrior like Allen Iverson. That's going to rub off on me."

Less than halfway through his rookie season, Iguodala said that he learned that all the things he'd heard about Iverson's courage as a player were true, and then some.

"Obviously, I had watched him while I was growing up," the twenty-year-old Iguodala said of Iverson, who had just turned thirty. "Seeing him play on TV, you could always tell how tough he was.

"You could see that Allen came to play every game, so that's what I expected of him, that he was always going to come out and fight every night.

"When you see a teammate play with that much courage and heart, I think it brings out toughness in everybody. It has to, because when you've got the smallest guy on the court who is willing to do whatever it takes to win, it has to carry over to other guys.

"I, as a big guy, look at it like I can't let this little guy show me up by being tougher than me. Therefore you come out and work harder. Allen brings out more toughness from everybody."

It was during the 2001 Eastern Conference Finals that NBC television displayed the famous graphic of Iverson with a bright yellow dot positioned over each part of his body that had an injury he was playing through.

By the time the graphic image was complete, virtually no part of Iverson's body could be seen.

"I know I am [going to be sore], that's the way it goes," Iverson said. "My thing is, as long as I can run, I can play.

"God's been looking out for me with every injury I get. A lot of times people act like they're amazed when I come back early. There are a lot of doctors who say, he's going to be out this long and that long, but a doctor really can't tell you exactly. It's the person's body, the way you heal up. Obviously, I heal up a little faster than other people.

"If somebody bangs me or knocks me to the floor, I can deal with all of that. When it comes to the point where somebody can guard me, then I'll really feel I'm hurt."

As the favorite for the 2000–01 MVP, Iverson knew from the start of the playoffs that he was going to be the target of physical play.

"Yeah, I expect it," Iverson said before the Sixers opened the 2001 postseason with a series against the Indiana Pacers. "I expect it every night when I come on the basketball court.

"I didn't even play eighty-two games this season. But the games I did play, there was a lot of beatings going on.

"That's part of the game, though. I'm not concentrating on anything like getting hit or hurt. I feel I'm so mentally focused, I don't care if people tell me they're going to bang me, that's their game plan.

"I owe too much to myself and my teammates and the people of Philadelphia, the coaching staff, everybody that roots for the Sixers. I owe those people too much to let fear of getting hit affect how I play."

Perhaps that's why during that 2001 run to the Finals, Sixers guard Eric Snow played with screws inserted into his foot, reserve guard Aaron McKie played with a broken bone in his ankle, forward George Lynch came back early to play with a fractured foot, and center Dikembe Mutombo didn't even bother to complain about playing with a broken finger.

"Nothing Allen does surprises me," said Snow, who was Iverson's backcourt mate for five and a half seasons before being traded to Cleveland in 2004. "He's a special kid, a special player. That's why he's the best player in the league."

Added McKie, "When I get bumped and beat up during a game, it kills me the next day. My body is real sore.

"I don't know how Allen does it. He doesn't have much meat on his bones, but it's his heart. Some people are able to block out pain and still be able to perform."

Iverson's toughness in a game endears him to teammates and foes alike. It's allowed him to earn respect despite some questionable off-court behavior.

"What I like about Allen is, he's a tough kid," said Indiana Pacers legend Reggie Miller. "He plays hurt. He plays every single game. He's a gamer. When they say he's out a month, he comes back in a week. That's what I like most about him. I like tough kids."

The NBA is a man's league. Quarter is rarely asked, and quarter is never given.

"Allen is a product of his environment and what he had to go through while growing up," former Sixers coach Randy Ayers said. "He just displays a certain toughness that you'd like to see in some other players. No doubt his background has played a part in that.

"He's like a boxer. You can knock him down, but he'll keep coming back. Everyone is not going to be a big, strong athlete, but Iverson keeps coming at you and keeps coming at you. He's a survivor."

Gary Moore has known Iverson for virtually the Sixers star's entire life. As a coach, mentor, and friend, Moore has seen Iverson deal with the highest of highs and the lowest of lows.

"Courage and Allen Iverson are a perfect fit," Moore said. "Allen Iverson *is* courage.

"You throw a challenge his way, and he'll give all it takes to meet that challenge. That's his makeup.

"I heard a coach once say that you ought to get Iverson's DNA because it's got something in there that says, win—do not lose. His life story has been to win."

In a 2003 survey taken by NBA.com, the league's general managers were asked to name the toughest player in the league.

Iverson finished behind Detroit Pistons center Ben Wallace and Indiana Pacers forward Ron Artest.

The amazing thing about that is that Iverson is hardly the defensive intimidator that the six-nine, 240-pound Wallace is, nor is he the aggressive physical defender that the six-seven, 246-pound Artest is.

Respect for Iverson's toughness comes directly from his ability to take the pounding he does for playing the way he does without ever altering his style.

"He might be the toughest guy I've ever seen play this game," eleven-year NBA veteran Monty Williams said of Iverson. "He's not a guy who goes into a weight room to build himself up. He's just a freak of nature. He gets knocked down going to the hole and gets up like nobody's touched him.

"I know I've cracked him a few times. He's probably in a lot of pain, but he'll never show you."

And New Jersey Nets forward Richard Jefferson said Iverson is "easily the most amazing person I've ever seen. Iverson, for his size and what he can do, with his quickness and how much he gets beat up, he's amazing."

Early on it was frequently suggested that Iverson's aggressive mentality and recklessness with his body, his driving to the basket, would keep him on the injured list for the better part of his career.

"My question was with him hitting the floor so much. Would he survive and have a long career, a twelve- to fifteen-year career?" said ex-Orlando Magic coach Johnny Davis, who coached Iverson as a rookie. "But he has a high tolerance for pain. Injuries that most guys would be out a month with, he'll be out a game or two, if at all."

A quick inventory shows that Iverson has sustained a break, bruise, bump, strain, or sprain to virtually every part of his body. The list of Iverson's injuries reads like a medical dictionary—left knee synovitis, right elbow bursitis, left sacroiliac joint contusion—not to mention a long list of broken bones and contusions.

But his willingness to play despite pain never seems to fade.

"Allen will tolerate a lot of pain to keep playing," Ayers said. "If there's any way, he's going to play. I've seen him get up [after absorbing blows] a lot of times in the last six years. He really wants to show people he can step up and play, even in pain."

There are stories behind the scenes. Several Sixers said that sometimes coaches have hidden Iverson's jersey to keep him from trying to play with an injury. It hasn't worked.

"You know me—I get in this environment and I just want to play," Iverson said. "Sitting out has always been difficult for me. I always went against everybody else and played anyway."

During the 2004–05 season, Iverson bruised a bone in his right ankle and one in his right clavicle.

"I don't know which hurt worse," Iverson said.

When Iverson informed first-year Sixers coach Jim O'Brien that he was too hurt to play in the next game, O'Brien didn't have to think twice about sitting his player down.

"I didn't really have to make a decision," O'Brien said. "Allen said he didn't think that he'd be able to go. He never says that.

"I never question any player, let alone a guy that has shown over the years the willingness to play hurt the way Allen had."

But three days later O'Brien experienced firsthand the fiery side of Iverson's competitive nature.

Coming home after an eight-game road trip, Iverson was still hobbling when the Sixers faced the Portland Trail Blazers but decided he would play.

Iverson played thirty-five minutes, scoring twenty-one with nine rebounds and nine assists. But with ten and a half minutes left, the Sixers trailed by nineteen points. O'Brien decided to err on the side of caution and sub in Kevin Ollie for Iverson, guarding against his star guard aggravating his injuries in a game that seemed to be lost.

"I just didn't think I wanted to risk Allen with that type of deficit," O'Brien reasoned. "It was my decision. Just imagine what the questions would have been if I would've put him back in and he got hurt more."

Iverson didn't necessarily buy that logic.

"I was fine," Iverson said. "I fall down all the time. I wasn't hurt. Anybody that's been watching me play since grade school knows when I'm hurt, knows when I can't play. I was fine. I don't do the subbing. I'm not the coach. I'm just a player, just one of the soldiers.

"But I honestly felt that game was still winnable. I never gave up, [never] felt like we couldn't win it. I'm sitting over there on the bench, helpless. It was like I was injured or something."

Iverson has played a full eighty-two-game season only once in his career (2002–03), but he has played in a remarkably high percentage of his team's games considering the number of injuries he has suffered.

"Did they cut his heart out?" McKie responded once when asked if he was surprised that Iverson would play through another injury. "I've seen him come into this locker room dragging his leg, barely able to straighten his right arm fully, and then he goes out and plays forty-eight minutes.

"Allen can be out there with one leg and would play. That's the kind of individual he is; that's the kind of heart he has. That's the way he grew up, playing the hand you're dealt, whether it's favorable or not. But that's what makes him Allen Iverson."

Of course, there have been injuries that were so severe that Iverson couldn't play through them.

Even in 2002–03, when he went the full eighty-two games, Iverson started the season fighting through an injury.

At the start of the preseason, Iverson was expected to be side-lined two to four weeks because of a right-finger fracture. He ended up missing only one game and played twenty-six or more minutes in each of the remaining preseason games.

"The guy is fearless, and he always has been. He's probably not the easiest guy to coach, but yet you'd want him on your side," Seattle scout Brian James told the *Philadelphia Daily News* about Iverson.

The respect Iverson has received for his fearless style has almost become mythical.

"Iverson goes out there and gives it his all," Seattle Supersonic guard Ray Allen said. "I think that's what people respect the most. The things he's able to conjure up seem unimaginable for somebody his size. I applaud his effort because he's a tough guy. A lot of guys through the league, because of injuries like he gets, would sit down."

But Iverson's toughness has also become a detriment.

NBA basketball is not a noncontact sport. And when a player has demonstrated time and time again that he can take the physical punishment associated with the game, it sometimes gets taken for granted.

Iverson gets contact virtually every time he drives into the lane, but he doesn't always get the fouls called for him that he feels he deserves.

Maybe in some situations his courage works against him. Even though he's always among the league leaders in free-throw attempts, there are times when it seems his numerous forays into the lane have caused officials to look the other way unless he really gets clobbered.

"I'm not going to cry over spoiled milk, but sometimes I honestly believe that," Iverson said. "In some games the official says that I initiate the contact. Look, I'm 160 pounds soaking wet. The last thing I want to do is create a whole lot of contact.

"I'm just trying to get my shot off. I'm not going in there trying

to get an And1 every time. I'm just going in trying to make a layup.
As far as me going in trying to make a lot of contact, that's crazy.
I'm trying my hardest *not* to hit the floor."

Iverson said his reputation for refusing to stay down for the count
has raised the bar for the amount of punishment that can be dished
out to him.

"I do feel that way," he said. "It's like, Iverson is tough, he can
take it. He can do it. We've seen him get hit and get back up. He can
take the contact and still make the shot because we've seen him do
it before.

"I'll ask a referee if there was contact on a play, and a lot of times
they'll say, 'Yeah, he got a piece of you, but I don't think it was
enough to call a foul.' "

"What's that mean? A foul is a foul. Contact is contact. When is
it enough? Not until I fall and break down or hurt myself. You call
a foul when it's a foul. You don't let them go."

The cautious player might adapt his style to avoid the punishment. The courageous one accepts it as a part of life.

"I don't know, but I'm going to keep going in [to the lane]," Iverson said. "I never stop going in there, and I won't ever stop going in
there because that's the way I play the game.

"Hopefully, I'll get calls when I get hit, but if I don't, I'll just keep
playing the game the way I do."

Since he entered the league as the number-one overall draft pick
in 1996, no player has had his team lean on him as much as the
Philadelphia 76ers have used Iverson for a crutch.

That he is a six-footer, not a seven-footer, just reinforces the
strength of the man's will to succeed.

"I've been blessed to have been around the NBA for sixteen
years," Sixers director of player personnel Courtney Witte said,
"and I've never seen a bigger competitor than Allen in such a small
frame.

"He gives you everything he can. He's willing to take on any challenge at any moment for forty-eight minutes. I've been around some
great players before at this level that have taken challenges, but to be
honest, they couldn't do it on a nightly basis. [Iverson] does it on a
nightly basis in a six-foot frame. That's incredible to me, especially
to see the abuse his body takes."

Is it courage that wills you to become the shortest scoring champion in NBA history?

Is it courage that allows you to become the smallest Most Valuable Player in NBA history?

"The way you can judge a guy is, does he help you win or lose," Houston Rockets coach Jeff Van Gundy said. "Man, does Iverson help them win. He's one of those guys who is a difference maker.

"Most guys who have taken as many blows as he has would have slowed down. Iverson hasn't. His competitive nature is as good as anybody's in the league."

It takes courage to average 27.0 points in your career while shooting just 42.0 percent from the floor.

"One thing I've always admired about [Iverson], regardless of how he shoots or how many times he shoots in the first three quarters, it seems like when the game is on the line, he kicks into another gear, both physically and mentally," Seattle scout James said.

It takes courage to absolutely believe that when the game is on the line, the next shot you take is going in, even if you've missed the previous eight.

"That's what I get paid for, to play in the fourth quarter," said Iverson, who has barely shot 40 percent for his career but annually is near the top of the league in field goal attempts. "That's when my teammates look for me to make things happen.

"That's not just scoring, but just being aggressive. Regardless whether I'm hitting my shots or not, it makes it easier for my teammates."

Is it courage that forces you to lead at those moments when others are most looking for you to lead?

"I definitely feel that way—I always feel that way," Iverson said. "That's what my team usually needs, that energy, that spark. My whole thing is to get down and dirty, get on the floor, scar my knees up, go to the basket, get banged up, get knocked on the floor, get right back up. They see that from you, then they feed off it, and they're able to make things happen themselves.

"That's my heart. That's how I play the game. I'd rather play with heart than talent any day. I try to trust my teammates as much as I can because they trust me in game situations. Everything in life, fighting as the game goes on."

In his first 540 NBA games, Iverson, as impossible as it may sound, had never sunk a shot to win a game as time expired on the clock.

But on November 12, 2004, in a game at Indiana, Iverson and the Sixers found themselves tied with the Pacers as time was running down in overtime.

Going into the final seconds, Iverson had missed eighteen of his previous twenty-two shots. Still, when clutch time came, Iverson calmly drained a jumper to give the Sixers a 106–104 victory.

"It's going to go in," Iverson said when asked what he was thinking before he shot. "That's what I always think when I shoot the basketball. I could miss twenty shots in a row, but I always feel the next shot is going to go in. I'm never going to be afraid to take the next shot or the last shot."

Two weeks later, with the Sixers tied in the closing seconds with the Washington Wizards, Iverson stole an inbounds pass from Jarvis Hayes and cruised in for a game-winning layup.

"I figured they were trying to get the ball to [guard Gilbert] Arenas," Iverson said of why he took the gamble. "It seemed like Hayes couldn't get the ball in.

"I didn't want to go for it if I couldn't get it, because they would've had a wide-open shot. But sometimes, if you see a chance, you can't be afraid to take it. Once he threw it, my eyes lit up."

There was a time early in his career when Iverson was singled out as a representative of all that was going wrong with the NBA.

But through the courage of his conviction to make a place and a name for himself in the NBA, he has turned that perception—from fans as well as other players—around.

"When you hear other players say you play with courage or you're tough on the court," Iverson said, "it makes me feel great, because that's coming from your peers, other players who have made it in this league.

"People don't always understand exactly how hard it is to make it in this league. Then, if you have a name, and people talk about you all of the time, the critics talk about you all of the time, kids talk about you all of the time, it's that much harder because you have to do so much more to produce and meet expectations.

"You have to be that much better than other guys. It's been an ongoing process for me, and I'm just trying to play every game like it's my last."

It takes courage to always fight to live up to expectations.

ALLEN IVERSON'S PERFECT TEAM

That's a bad team, the one in this book. It doesn't have Wilt Chamberlain on it. I'm not sure where I'd put him, because I think Shaq has to stay as dominant, but Wilt has got to be on there somewhere, anywhere.

You're starting out with the three guys who absolutely have to be on any great team—Michael Jordan, Magic Johnson, and Larry Bird. Michael could go in two or three places, for competitive drive, confidence, and mental toughness. Larry Bird I would probably just say, "winner."

I like myself for courage, but I think Willis Reed can also be there to represent that. I think I'd put me down for hustle too.

You could say it's missing some other players like Charles Barkley, Patrick Ewing, and Isiah Thomas, but it's still a strong team.

Maybe if I was looking at some of the current players and guys I played with, I could put in some different people, like for clutch I'd pick Reggie Miller, and for confidence I think Kobe Bryant has to be there. Oscar Robertson basically created the triple-double, so he's there, but I think LeBron James has to be there for versatility too.

Jason Kidd has to be there for self-sacrifice and team play, without question. You know, honestly, for someone who people might not think of, I'd really like [Detroit Pistons guard] Lindsey Hunter for hustle. Man, he's always going, but it is hard to place him on a nice list like this.

You're talking about the general manager, so you have to take Red Auerbach, but I'd have a different coach. Phil Jackson is a great coach, and you have to be able to motivate players to have won all of those championships, but honestly, I'd go with Larry Brown as the coach of my team, I honestly would. The man can just coach.

Starters
Guard—Oscar Robertson
Guard—Magic Johnson
Center—Shaquille O'Neal
Forward—Larry Bird
Forward—Michael Jordan
Sixth Man—Wilt Chamberlain

Bench
Center—Bill Russell
Forward—LeBron James
Forward—Kobe Bryant
Guard—Allen Iverson
Guard—Jason Kidd
Guard/Forward/Center—Jerry West

General Manager
Red Auerbach

Coach
Larry Brown

ALLEN IVERSON—GUARD

PERSONAL: Born June 7, 1975, in Hampton, VA . . . 6–0/165 (1.83 m/75 kg).
HIGH SCHOOL: Bethel (Hampton, VA).
COLLEGE: Georgetown.
TRANSACTIONS/CAREER NOTES: Selected after sophomore season by Philadelphia 76ers in
first round (first pick overall) of 1996 NBA draft.

COLLEGIATE RECORD

NOTES: *The Sporting News* All-America first team (1996).

Season	Team	G	Min	FGM	FGA	Pct	FTM	FTA	Pct	Reb	Ast	Pts	Averages RPG	APG	PPG
94–95	Georgetown	30	966	203	520	.390	172	250	.688	99	134	613	3.3	4.5	20.4
95–96	Georgetown	37	1,213	312	650	.480	215	317	.678	141	173	926	3.8	4.7	25.0
Total		67	2,179	515	1,170	.440	387	567	.683	240	307	1,539	3.6	4.6	23.0

THREE-POINT FIELD GOALS: 1994–95, 35-for-151 (.232); 1995–96, 87-for-238 (.366). Total: 122-for-389 (.314).

NBA REGULAR-SEASON RECORD

RECORDS: Shares NBA record for most seasons leading league in steals—3 (2001, 2002, 2003). . . . Holds career record for most consecutive seasons leading league in steals—3 (2000–01 through 2002–03).

HONORS: NBA Most Valuable Player (2001). . . . NBA Rookie of the Year (1997). . . . All-NBA first team (1999, 2001). . . . All-NBA second team (2000, 2002, 2003). . . . NBA All-Rookie first team (1997). . . . MVP of Rookie Game (1997).

NOTES: Led NBA with 2.51 steals per game (2001), 2.80 steals per game (2002), and 2.74 steals per game (2003).

									Rebounds								Averages		
Season	Team	G	Min	FGM	FGA	Pct	FTM	FTA	Pct	Off	Def	Tot	Ast	St	Blk	TO	Pts	RPG	APG	PPG
96–97	Phil	76	3,045	625	1,504	.416	382	544	.702	115	197	312	567	157	24	337	1,787	4.1	7.5	23.5
97–98	Phil	80	3,150	649	1,407	.461	390	535	.729	86	210	296	494	176	25	244	1,758	3.7	6.2	22.0
98–99	Phil	48	1,990	435	1,056	.412	356	474	.751	66	170	236	223	110	7	167	1,284	4.9	4.6	26.8
99–00	Phil	70	2,853	729	1,733	.421	442	620	.713	71	196	267	328	144	5	230	1,989	3.8	4.7	28.4
00–01	Phil	71	2,979	762	1,813	.420	585	719	.814	50	223	273	325	178	20	237	2,207	3.8	4.6	31.1
01–02	Phil	60	2,622	665	1,669	.398	475	585	.812	44	225	269	331	168	13	237	1,883	4.5	5.5	31.4
02–03	Phil	82	3,485	804	1,940	.414	570	736	.774	68	276	344	454	225	13	286	2,262	4.2	5.5	27.6
03–04	Phil	48	2,040	435	1,125	.387	339	455	.745	34	144	178	324	115	5	209	1,266	3.7	6.8	26.4
Total		535	22,164	5,104	12,247	.417	3,539	4,668	.758	534	1,641	2,175	3,046	1,273	112	1,947	14,436	4.1	5.7	27.0

THREE-POINT FIELD GOALS: 1996–97, 155-for-455 (.341); 1997–98, 70-for-235 (.298); 1998–99, 58-for-199 (.291); 1999–2000, 89-for-261 (.341); 2000–01, 98-for-306 (.320); 2001–02, 78-for-268 (.291); 2002–03, 84-for-303 (.277); 2003–04, 57-for-199 (.286). Total: 689-for-2226 (.310).

PERSONAL FOULS/DISQUALIFICATIONS: 1996–97, 233/5; 1997–98, 200/2; 1998–99, 98/0; 1999–2000, 162/1; 2000–01, 147/0; 2001–02, 102/0; 2002–03, 149/2; 2003–04, 87/0. Total: 1178/10.

NBA PLAYOFF RECORD

NOTES: Holds single-game playoff record for most steals—10 (May 13, 1999, vs. Orlando). . . . Shares NBA Finals single-game record for most free throws made in one quarter—9 (June 10, 2001, vs. Los Angeles Lakers).

Season	Team	G	Min	FGM	FGA	Pct	FTM	FTA	Pct	Off	Def	Tot	Ast	St	Blk	TO	Pts	RPG	APG	PPG
										Rebounds								Averages		
98–99	Phil	8	358	88	214	.411	37	52	.712	14	19	33	39	20	2	24	228	4.1	4.9	28.5
99–00	Phil	10	444	91	237	.384	68	92	.739	14	26	40	45	12	1	32	262	4.0	4.5	26.2
00–01	Phil	22	1,016	257	661	.389	161	208	.774	15	89	104	134	52	7	63	723	4.7	6.1	32.9
01–02	Phil	5	209	45	118	.381	51	63	.810	1	17	18	21	13	0	12	150	3.6	4.2	30.0
02–03	Phil	12	557	137	329	.416	87	118	.737	11	41	52	89	29	1	47	380	4.3	7.4	31.7
Total		57	2,584	618	1,559	.396	404	533	.758	55	192	247	328	126	11	178	1,743	4.3	5.8	30.6

THREE-POINT FIELD GOALS: 1998–99, 15-for-53 (.283); 1999–2000, 12-for-39 (.308); 2000–01, 48-for-142 (.338); 2001–02, 9-for-27 (.333); 2002–03, 19-for-55 (.345). Total: 103-for-316 (.326).

PERSONAL FOULS/DISQUALIFICATIONS: 1998–99, 19/0; 1999–2000, 24/0; 2000–01, 55/0; 2001–02, 8/0; 2002–03, 25/0. Total: 131/0.

NBA ALL-STAR GAME RECORD

NOTES: NBA All-Star Game Most Valuable Player (2001, 2005).

Season	Team	Min	FGM	FGA	Pct	FTM	FTA	Pct	Off	Def	Tot	Ast	PF	DQ	St	Blk	TO	Pts
									Rebounds									
2000	Phil	28	10	18	.556	4	5	.800	2	0	2	9	0	0	2	0	5	26
2001	Phil	27	9	21	.429	6	6	1.000	0	2	2	5	0	0	4	0	4	25
2002	Phil	25	2	9	.222	1	2	.500	1	3	4	3	0	0	0	0	2	5
2003	Phil	41	13	23	.565	8	9	.889	3	2	5	7	2	0	5	0	6	35
2004	Phil	23	1	6	.167	1	4	.250	0	1	1	11	3	0	0	0	4	3
2005	Phil	32	4	13	.308	7	7	1.000	0	4	4	9	0	0	5	0	7	15
Total		176	39	90	.433	27	33	.818	6	12	18	44	5	0	16	0	28	109

THREE-POINT FIELD GOALS: 2000, 2-for-2; 2001, 1-for-1; 2003, 1-for-3 (.333). Total: 4-for-6 (.667).

Chapter Four

MAGIC JOHNSON—Guard

Leadership

by Mark Heisler

Like, who else?

Although there are never enough to go around, there have been a lot of great point guards. However, such was the genius of Magic Johnson that there could be no debate about who was best. Only two other players would be accorded such respect. You might get an argument that Shaquille O'Neal or Wilt Chamberlain was better than Bill Russell, but whatever criteria anyone sets for the NBA's all-time starting five, Johnson, Larry Bird, and Michael Jordan will be on it.

Not that there weren't things some of the great points didn't do as well or better than Johnson. Bob Cousy's flair represented a break with the past, just as Magic's arrival did as the first six-nine point guard, the first big man to play with the same flair, grace, and agility as the classically smaller ball-handlers. Jerry West, who played the point late in his career, was a better shooter and scorer and in a class of his own in the clutch.

Oscar Robertson became the first point to dominate games from the top of the floor, running up incredible numbers of points and rebounds to go with all his assists; even in an era when teams took more shots, creating more rebounds, no one else ever averaged a triple-double for an entire season. And if you're looking for the classic point, the one who's excellent at everything, it would be John Stockton, who ran teams as well as anyone ever did, played dogged defense, and was a deadeye long-range shooter as well.

Classicism wasn't Johnson's thing. He was marginal (30 percent on threes lifetime) from distance and didn't even shoot a jumper.

Magic was all anomaly, all the time. Like the greatest of the great, he transcended everything: his position, form, whatever.

You could put him anywhere on the floor, and he would still dominate. At six-nine, 220, when he entered the league, and 240 in his prime, he was as big as full-size power forwards and just as hardnosed under the hoop as any of them.

But size was just what people saw. What Johnson had that no one could ever match was the ability to lead, the sine qua non of the position.

"He grew up leading people on the court," said Lakers teammate Kurt Rambis. "He didn't turn himself into a leader or someone who could guide a team. It was already there. He'd grown up doing those kinds of things."

Centers are supposed to dominate, to get close-in shots, like a Shaq dunk, or keep opponents from getting them, like Russell. Power forwards are crosses between centers and forwards. Small forward and big guard are scoring positions.

Point guards are supposed to make sure everything goes as it should, that everyone is in the game and where he should be. And then—and if the point is really special—he can step in and take over the game if no one else on his team can. Point guards lead, whatever that takes at a given moment.

And no one led like Magic.

When he arrived in L.A. as a fresh-faced teenager in 1979, he was already the leader of the Lakers. Even though they were a veteran team anchored by then five-time-MVP Kareem Abdul-Jabbar, everyone knew Magic was in the driver's seat.

"I was the leader even if it was Kareem's team," said Magic. "I still made sure I called out all the defensive and offensive sets. They deferred to me when there were things to do out on the court.

"Kareem was a quiet leader. He led by example. My voice was the one they heard all the time. That's why I was the leader."

As the years went on and Magic's legend grew, he still deferred to his center.

"Even when Magic got to the point where he was obviously an established All-Star, he was still saying it was Kareem's team," said Rambis. "Everybody knew it wasn't, but he kept saying it.

"It was just a way to keep the Big Fella happy, and it kept everyone else's egos in check. We'd say, 'Hey, we think Magic is the best guy on the team, but if he says Kareem is the guy, then obviously I can't be the guy.' "

Pat Riley actually had to convince his point guard to become the primary offensive option before the Lakers' championship '86–87 season. As usual, Magic did not want to step on Kareem's toes.

"Pat Riley said, 'You gotta score more points, and I wanna turn the offense over to you,' " said Magic. "And I said, 'Are you sure about that?' And he said, 'Yeah.' I said, 'Did you ask Kareem?' And he said, 'Yeah, Kareem's okay with that.' I said, 'Well, let me go up and ask Kareem about taking more of the shots.'

"So I went up and asked Kareem, 'Can I take more shots because the coaches asked me to take more shots?' He said, 'I'm fine with it.' So I said, 'Okay. So now instead of taking ten or twelve shots a game, I have to take twenty shots a game.'

"But I didn't have enough shots in my repertoire to be a good scorer. So I decided to go to Kareem and learn the baby hook. I decided to work on my drop stop and things down low. So this would be the first time in my career I would post up as a big guard."

Pat Riley's decision would prove to be the difference when the Lakers matched up with the Celtics in the Finals that year. In the closing seconds of Game 4 at Boston Garden, Magic would show off one of his newly acquired low-post moves.

"What happened was, Kevin McHale came out on me on a switch, and I only had seven seconds," said Magic. "And I looked up and said, 'Well, I gotta beat him to the hoop.' So I took him to the hoop, and just as I got to the middle of the lane, Robert Parish jumped out at me and here comes Larry Bird. So I said, the only shot I could get up was the baby hook. So I got it up, and I made it, and we ended up winning the game. It put us up 3–1, and we ended up winning the series."

Everything about him spelled l-e-a-d-e-r-s-h-i-p. It was a reflection of his personality, as were his teams. You couldn't mistake the way a Magic team played, the way it got up and down the court, the dunk shows it put on, the way it could also grind it out in the half-court when necessary.

He had an exuberant, infectious, unfailingly buoyant personality, an iron will, and the preternatural maturity to understand from the get-go that winning was what counted, not point totals, highlight plays, fame, or money.

"My approach was to make sure that I helped my team and that I put them in a position to win," said Magic. "That meant not only getting on them when they made a mistake but also patting them on the back when they did something real well.

"I also made sure I was the first one to get to practice and the last one to leave. Leadership doesn't start in the game. It starts in practice."

This workmanlike attitude did not go unnoticed among his "Showtime" teammates.

"He worked hard, he practiced hard, he was a winner, he was poised in difficult situations, he was always positive, he was unselfish," said Rambis. "I don't know of anything negative I could say about him in terms of him being a leader. I can't think of anything he didn't bring."

At the root of Magic's leadership was his large, stable family. Even though he grew up watching heroes like Jerry West and Wilt Chamberlain, it was his father—Earvin Johnson Sr., who worked two jobs to support Magic and his six brothers and sisters—who left the biggest impression.

"I really had a good time idolizing guys like Bill Russell and Oscar Robertson," said Magic of his childhood, "but my ultimate hero was my dad. He led by example."

Magic might have still been a great basketball player without the support of his family, but it's doubtful he would have become one of the game's greatest leaders without them.

"My family really shaped my career," he said. "I got the support and the love from my parents, brothers, and sisters. They gave me all the values I have today, and they helped me to shoot balls every day. We did a lot as a family. I was brought up in a strong family that taught me love and respect."

People who knew him—teammates, coaches, fans, press people—adored him. It wasn't a chore to play with Magic—which meant doing what Magic wanted—it was a privilege.

Better than that, it was fun.

"He was the first person I can remember who brought the enthusiasm element to the game of basketball," said Greg Kelser, his old Michigan State teammate. "It was not hard to tell that he loved the game and got a great deal of joy out of playing it. And I could see that at age sixteen when I first met him. . . .

"Earvin is one of those people, among the very few who come along, who is tremendously gifted, blessed. I mean, everybody is blessed in different ways, but he's one of the special people that come around once every generation or so. Nothing he has done really amazes me because I have seen it from its roots, but I'm thrilled for him and for all that he has accomplished. I just feel fortunate that I was around to be a part of it."

Everywhere Johnson went, it was the same story. He came, he saw, he took over. He was a Michigan State star as a freshman, won an NCAA title as a sophomore, then went directly to the NBA (without benefit of controversy, despite the fact that only a few undergraduates had ever jumped to the league at that point, since everyone understood this guy was ready), arriving at age twenty and taking over a Laker team loaded with veterans, telling old hands like Abdul-Jabbar, Jamaal Wilkes, and Norm Nixon what to do. Not that anyone considered doing it any other way.

Nixon, a Johnson intimate, had famously mixed feelings, which was one reason he was sent away four seasons later. Abdul-Jabbar and Wilkes resented the favoritism that new owner Jerry Buss lavished on Magic—remember that $25 million "lifetime" contract—but on the floor it worked like a dream.

"There was a uniqueness about that whole [first] year, and that started in the summer pro league," said Michael Cooper, who broke in alongside Johnson in 1980. "They were playing that summer pro league at Cal State L.A. And all of a sudden they said, 'Hey, Magic's going to come play with us on a Friday night.' They opened up the top. And that had never been open the whole summer.

"And you could see the magicalness of it all. The place was full, it was hot. I remember that game so well. That was the time when we got our first Coop-a-Loop. We went over the top, and I got a dunk. You could tell there was going to be something special, not only that young man but what he was bringing to the game of basketball."

The exuberance of those preseason games set the stage for Magic's very first regular season game on October 12, 1979, in San Diego. The Lakers were locked in a tight battle with the Clippers when Kareem Abdul-Jabbar scored his patented sky-hook at the buzzer to give the Lakers a 103–102 victory. While his teammates were definitely glad to escape with a victory, Magic took the celebration to a whole different level.

"Kareem hit a hook shot from the free-throw line to beat the Clippers in San Diego," said Magic. "World B. Free had an unbelievable game for the Clippers, so when Kareem hit that shot at the buzzer for the Lakers to win, I ran up and jumped in his arms. I started choking him and I rode his back. I was jumping from the free-throw line all the way to the locker room.

"When we finally got to the locker room, he pulled me aside and said, 'Look, young fella, we still got eighty-one more games. Don't ever do that again.'

"I said to him, 'If you hit that shot eighty-one more times, I'm gonna jump in your arms eighty-one more times.' I think, at that moment, he realized I was a guy who loves the game of basketball and who loves to show people that I love the game. It wasn't a gimmick or something to get attention. That enthusiasm kept Kareem around for a few more years. He was ready to retire before that. He stayed around because we were having so much fun."

His youthful energy was a jolt for the Lakers franchise, and it made his teammates and the fans look forward to the games.

"That's the way Magic approached it," said Cooper. "Every game was fun. And in turn, when the players are having fun, the fans are having fun. He brings them out on the court, even though they can't physically be out there. . . .

"He made them part of Lakers Showtime, and I think that was the specialness and uniqueness about Magic Johnson. It's very rare that a player can do that, to get everybody excited about playing."

The Lakers won two titles in Johnson's first three seasons, blew one in his fifth (the '84 Finals against Boston, in which they led going into the last minute of Games 1 through 4 but went 2–2), then won three more titles in the next four seasons.

Add it up—it was five titles and seven Finals appearances in nine seasons, nine in twelve. As Johnson wasn't shy about saying, he was "all about winning." Since it was so patently true, no one seemed to mind the braggadocio.

The Lakers weren't just good, but entertaining, the last high-octane elite team the NBA would ever see. It was a marriage made in basketball heaven, the glamorous Lakers, the Hollywood mystique . . . and Magic, with his big smile and flashy game. No teams got up and down the floor like his teams. When he got the ball, everyone turned and hightailed it to the other end for all they were worth (well, everyone but Abdul-Jabbar, whose fast-break days were behind him), because they knew (a) Magic would be along directly, (b) he was already looking for them, and (c) if they didn't, he would definitely let them know about it.

"I just made sure I kept the game at a tempo that we liked to play at," said Magic. "We had to play fast, and we had to keep it moving.

"I also made sure everyone got their shots. The most important thing about being a leader is understanding what everybody needs to do for the team to be successful. Some nights James Worthy needs twenty shots. Some nights Byron Scott would need ten or fifteen shots to help us win."

Magic's approach kept everyone, from All-Stars like James Worthy to role players like Kurt Rambis, implicitly involved in the Showtime offense.

"If you get out and run, you know you're going to get the ball," said Rambis. "It's the simplest formula in the world.

"You don't have to hover around—'Well, am I going to get the ball? Do I do this?' No, you just put your head down, take the six fastest steps you can take, and look over your shoulder because by then you'd have the ball and you'd already have taken one dribble because he's already thrown it up to you."

Every night Magic would bring something different to put his team over the top. Each team had its weaknesses, and he was sure to take full advantage.

"A leader makes adjustments every night," he said. "What do we need to do to win? Who do I need to do to help us to win the game?

"Different teams are weak in different areas. If they didn't have any big guys, that means I'm going into Kareem a lot. If they did have a lot, maybe it was gonna be James Worthy's night or Byron Scott's. Maybe I needed to grab twenty rebounds that night. So I went out to do that."

Magic's teammates always felt compelled to follow their leader's example.

"Body language with Earvin during the game was contagious," said Lakers teammate James Worthy. "When he got on the floor and he got more physical, we knew that meant, pick it up. When he was in a mode where he was running nonstop, we knew we needed to run more. We knew when he went in and grabbed two, three offensive rebounds in a very bullish way, that meant we needed to rebound."

As West, then the laker GM, noted ruefully at the end, in the somber days following Johnson's 1991 announcement that he was HIV-positive:

"I think somewhere out there, there's a young little kid who'll be as great as Magic Johnson as a player. But he won't be as great as a leader."

Magic's leadership was never more evident than in Game 6 of the 1980 Finals against Philadelphia.

"Game 6 was probably my greatest game," said Magic. "It was probably my greatest moment. It was a great moment in Lakers history as well."

Although the Lakers had a 3–2 lead as they boarded the plane to the East Coast for Game 6, spirits were low. Kareem Abdul-Jabbar had sprained his ankle so badly in Game 5 that he couldn't even make the flight. At the airport, coach Paul Westhead informed his six-foot-nine point guard that he would be filling in for the Big Fella, even jumping center against the six-eleven Caldwell Jones. Young Buck, as his teammates called him, decided to get into character right away.

"Everybody was kind of down the next day when we got to the airport," Magic recalled. "I decided I had to bring the guys up. I went and sat in Kareem's seat up front, first one on the left. When the guys came down on the plane, I said, 'Have no fear, the Big Fella's here!' That cracked 'em up."

Even as a twenty-year-old rookie, Magic's positive attitude was contagious.

"Buck wouldn't let anybody have negative thoughts," said Michael Cooper. "He kept telling us we were going to win this game, no doubt about it. That's the way he was, the way he is. He thinks he's going to win every game."

The Philly newspapers played right into Magic's hands, predicting a Game 6 Sixers victory against the shorthanded Lakers.

"When we got to the airport in Philly," Magic said, "I got the papers, and it was all about, 'Okay, we're going back to L.A. for Game 7. We got this one in the bag with Kareem out. We're gonna kill 'em.'

"That's all I needed. I took all the papers to the guys and said, 'Can you believe this? They're giving us no shot! They think they've already won this game. Hey, all we gotta do is keep the pressure up. They can't keep up with us.' "

Later that night Magic kept the optimism rolling.

"I had a meeting the night before the game," said Magic. "And we had another meeting the day of the game to make sure that the guys understood that we're gonna win this game tonight and this is how we're gonna do it.

"We had one great individual defender in Cooper, but the rest of us played great team defense. That's what people don't realize when they talk about the Showtime days. It was our defense that started everything. We figured out what the other team wanted to do and shut that down. That got our break going, and everything flowed from there."

The next day the Lakers stayed true to this vision and took the series with a 123–107 win. Magic, the series MVP, overwhelmed the Sixers in the backcourt and the frontcourt with fifteen rebounds, seven assists, three steals, and a block. The pace was so frenetic that he didn't even realize he had also poured in forty-two points.

"They all came in the flow of the game," he said. "It wasn't like we were concentrating on getting me the ball. A lot of it was in transition, just getting out and running. We were just gone. They were like, 'Oh, man, what are we gonna do about this?' "

Asked what he would do for an encore, Magic didn't hesitate.

"Win it again next year," he said. "Then win another and another and another. I never get tired of winning."

In Johnson's time, the All-Star Game was more than the desultory exhibition it has become, since Magic would always be woofing about winning, which would fire up his pal Isiah Thomas—and then, of course, there was Bird's mouth—so that the guys actually competed.

In Johnson's time, U.S. pro teams didn't get carried out of international competitions feet first, as the 2002 team did in Indianapolis and in 2004 in Athens. Nor did they go down to the wire with Lithuania and France, like our 2000 Olympic gold medalists.

Johnson's 1992 team, the one and only real Dream Team, was the greatest collection of players ever put together (Magic, Jordan, Bird, David Robinson, Patrick Ewing, Charles Barkley, Karl Malone, John Stockton, Scottie Pippen, etc.), but they didn't get full of themselves (well, aside from Barkley) or yawn their way through it. They blew away all opponents. In between, they went after each other as their coaches marveled at the pre-tourney scrimmages in Monte Carlo, which some called the highest-level basketball ever played.

"Those practices were the greatest basketball I've ever participated in, in my life," said Magic. "We went at each other like it was the seventh game of the world championship.

"That's what made the games so much fun. When we got to the games, it was easy because we had practiced so hard. Our mission was to blow everybody out and show them that the best basketball in the world was played in the United States."

Johnson was thirty-three and officially retired, but his personality still towered above everyone, even Jordan. No player has so dominated any of the other U.S. teams, nor have any of those teams played as hard, or as well, or looked like they were having any fun at all.

Careers were planned around Johnson. When Pat Riley was coaching the Lakers in the '80s, he used to say he'd leave when Johnson did. Riley, of course, is still on the job, but he meant it at the time. And he never did win a championship, as a coach, without Magic on his team.

It wasn't just the intangibles. Johnson could put up tangibles with the best of them.

"He was unique in almost every way, okay?" West said. "I've said, I've seen guys have size advantages—and the Heat have one now in Shaquille—but he probably had the greatest size advantage playing his position of anyone I've ever seen. . . .

"He just had such a confidence about his ability to make other people better, to make 'em play hard. . . . He started every season with an incredible optimism. More importantly, he started every season an improved player, 'cause he worked so hard on his game in the off-season.

"When I look back at him, my God, what a treat for the city of Los Angeles."

Johnson wasn't fast, or quick, and as he noted at his Hall of

Fame induction, holding his fingers an inch apart, he couldn't jump. Nevertheless, his ability to play the point at his immense height, to keep defenders from stealing the ball when he dribbled it, something never seen before in a player of his size, made all his matches mismatches. Opposing point guards, usually around six-foot-one, rarely over six-five, were too small. The opposing shooting guard, who was usually six-four or six-five, couldn't handle Johnson. The opposing small forward was almost always smaller too.

Opposing coaches could put their power forwards, who were usually Johnson's size, on Magic, but they rarely did, since few fours are any good playing in the middle of the floor.

Passes into Abdul-Jabbar in the post were easy for Johnson. His defender just wasn't tall enough to stop them, so Magic could wait for Kareem to get as close as he could to the hoop and then toss him the ball. It was no coincidence that a revitalized Kareem won his sixth MVP during Magic's rookie campaign.

That astounding vision and playmaking ability paid off in all sorts of ways. The Lakers seemed to get endless layups every game when Johnson would start running a play on the right side of the floor, and suddenly James Worthy, who was on the low post on the other side, would flash into the lane, and Magic would throw him the ball.

"I thought I was a pretty good transition player when I came here, but playing with him stepped it up so much," said Worthy. "He was such an incredible passer. He saw things other people didn't see."

It didn't make any difference who they sent after Johnson. In the wars with the Pistons in the late '80s, Detroit's Chuck Daly began putting Dennis Rodman, pound for pound arguably the greatest defender the NBA would ever see, on Magic, but Dennis couldn't do much with this tricky behemoth either.

"Magic played hard," said Worthy. "A lot of people didn't realize that was where we used to get a lot of our toughness from. That's why he had the nickname Buck. He was like a bull, and he was really physical."

With his ball-handling ability, size, and strength, Johnson went where he wanted to go on the floor. By the Lakers' last two titles of the Showtime era, in 1987 and 1988, Riley had deliberately moved him ahead of the aging Abdul-Jabbar as the number-one option, and Magic began putting up points, by any means necessary: the occasional set shot, runners in the lane, post moves.

Then there was his nonpareil knack for drawing fouls. He would get a step on his defender, which was easy enough for him since he could go left and right, get his shoulder in front, veer into him, cause contact, and go shoot his free throws.

For such a sunny guy, Johnson was always barking at the referees. Opponents complained that he might as well have his own whistle since he was making all the calls. Mentally, physically, spiritually, Johnson had the whole package—as a discipline-transcending genius, as a playmaker, with people whom he met by the thousands, as a man.

He had his share of vices, including the womanizing that led to becoming HIV-positive. He often seemed like a kid in the candy store of life, breathlessly awaiting his next sweet, but he was a stand-up guy too.

His image took a beating when he announced he had acquired the virus; a he's-no-hero backlash in the press erupted anew when he described his sexual exploits in his autobiography. But the fact remains: he acknowledged being HIV-positive when only a few intimates knew and he could have made up a cover story. As commissioner David Stern would note, at a time when Ryan White was being kicked out of a school in Indiana for acquiring the virus, Johnson going out front changed everything.

His bitter-rivalry-turned-friendship with Larry Bird became one of the nicest things the NBA ever saw. From the time they did that Converse commercial together in French Lick and discovered they were just city/country versions of the same guy, there was mutual admiration in those Laker-Celtic hate-a-thons.

It couldn't get any better. One or both of these glamour teams with popular stars from major markets appeared in every Finals from 1980 to 1987. They met head to head three times. Everyone talked trash. The series were all competitive, even in '87, when the younger Lakers went 3–0, 4–1, 4–0 in the first three rounds, and the older Celtics, who'd just survived the Pistons' challenge, were out on their feet.

Johnson and Bird were brothers who weren't quite in arms, revitalizing the NBA in a golden moment that lasted a decade.

When Bird retired, Johnson flew to Boston for his going-away ceremony, tore off his Laker warm-ups on the floor, and revealed that he was wearing a Celtic jersey. Bird told him, and the Garden crowd, "Magic, get outta my dreams!" Johnson had Bird present him when he went into the Hall of Fame.

"Larry and I take a personal pride in everything regarding the game today, the salaries, everything," Johnson said that day in Springfield, Massachusetts. "Because if we don't do what we do, the TV contracts wouldn't be what they are and the salaries wouldn't be what they are. We take pride in the fact that it's covered worldwide. . . .

"But when you look at us, you look at us as winners. Guys don't understand, they want to be a star in this league, but a lot of them have never won. And to be a star in this league and then to be a superstar, you have to win. And all of us cared about winning. We didn't care about commercials, we didn't care about shoe deals, all that. We wanted to win.

"Even today, I saw Larry, he saw me, I saw the look in his eye, he could see the look in my eye—if these people weren't in here [the Hall of Fame's new building], we'd probably be playing horse right now. . . .

"He looks good. I'm up here looking good. That's guys who care about their bodies. Two crazy, possessed guys, even at our age."

One of a kind, times two. It ain't bragging if it's fact, and it was.

MAGIC JOHNSON'S PERFECT TEAM

Starting Five

Point Guard—Isiah Thomas: He was the meanest, toughest, most competitive point guard that ever played this game. In my opinion, he was the greatest point guard. And he was a winner.

Shooting Guard—Michael Jordan: He was the greatest ever. He was a winner, and he understood how to play the game.

Small Forward—Julius Erving: He won a championship, and he was unselfish. He knew how to make people better.

Passing Forward—Larry Bird: He could pass, dribble, and shoot. He was an awesome big man that could play all over the court. He was one of the most fundamentally sound players who ever played, and he was my toughest opponent on the court.

Center—Bill Russell: Even though I love my man Kareem, you have to defer to Bill because he won eleven championships. He was fundamentally sound. He didn't block the shot out of bounds. He blocked it where he could control it.

Sixth Man—Oscar Robertson: He's a versatile player and he made people better. Triple-double man. When I was growing up, he was my number one role model.

Bench

Forward—James Worthy: He was the sweetest, most beautiful player I've ever seen. He was very versatile too. He can move from the three to the two.

Forward—Kevin McHale: Also versatile. McHale can play center and power forward. If you're gonna win, you gotta be versatile.

Forward—Charles Barkley: Charles was unstoppable. He played so hard. Also, his size made him a hard person to actually stop and cover.

Center—Wilt Chamberlain: The Big Dipper was the strongest player who ever played this game. I used to love to watch him when he was with the Sixers and he used to have that ugly finger roll. It would go in all the time. He was just unbelievable. He used to grab thirty rebounds a night. But he was also a finesse player as much as he was strong and physical. Wilt was also a good human being.

Guard—Jerry West: He's the greatest clutch shooter of all time. Also had a great outside shot, and he's a winner. You don't have to worry whether he starts or comes in off the bench. You know he's gonna give you all that you want.

Center—Shaquille O'Neal: He's a winner and he's dominant.

Head Coach

Pat Riley: He was a coach that demanded excellence. Riley expects you to come out and play 100 percent every night. Also, he prepares you offensively and defensively. He puts you in a position to win every night.

General Manager

Jerry West: He's a winner. He chooses the best players—he not only chooses superstars, but he also chooses guys who you would never expect to be superstars who turn out to be great players.

MAGIC JOHNSON—GUARD

PERSONAL: Born August 14, 1959, in Lansing, MI . . . 6–9/255 (2.05 m/102.1 kg) . . . full name: Earvin Johnson Jr.

HIGH SCHOOL: Everett (Lansing, MI).

COLLEGE: Michigan State.

TRANSACTIONS/CAREER NOTES: Selected after sophomore season by Los Angeles Lakers in first round (first pick overall) of 1979 NBA draft. . . . On voluntarily retired list (November 7, 1991–January 29, 1996). . . . Activated from retirement by Lakers (January 29, 1996). . . . Announced retirement (May 14, 1996). . . . Rights renounced by Lakers (July 16, 1996). . . . Broadcaster, NBC Sports (1992–94). . . . Vice president, Los Angeles Lakers (1994–95–present). . . . Analyst, Turner Sports.

CAREER HONORS: One of the 50 Greatest Players in NBA History (1996). . . . Selected to Naismith Memorial Basketball Hall of Fame (2002).

MISCELLANEOUS: Member of NBA championship team (1980, 1982, 1985, 1987, 1988). . . . Member of gold-medal-winning U.S. Olympic team (1992). . . . Los Angeles Lakers franchise all-time assists leader with 10,141 and all-time steals leader with 1,724 (1979–80 through 1990–91 and 1995–96).

COLLEGIATE RECORD

NOTES: *The Sporting News* All-America first team (1979). . . . NCAA Division I Tournament Most Outstanding Player (1979). . . . Member of NCAA championship team (1979).

| | | | | | | | | | | | | | | Averages | | |
Season	Team	G	Min	FGM	FGA	Pct	FTM	FTA	Pct	Reb	Ast	Pts	RPG	APG	PPG
77–78	MSU	30	—	175	382	.458	161	205	.785	237	222	511	7.9	7.4	17.0
78–79	MSU	32	1159	173	370	.468	202	240	.842	234	269	548	7.3	8.4	17.1
Total		62	—	348	752	.463	363	445	.816	471	491	1,059	7.6	7.9	17.1

NBA REGULAR-SEASON RECORD

RECORDS: Holds career record for highest assists-per-game average—11.2. . . . Shares career record for most consecutive seasons leading league in steals—2.

HONORS: NBA Most Valuable Player (1987, 1989, 1990). . . . IBM Award for all-around contributions to team's success (1984). . . . Citizenship Award (1992). . . . All-NBA first team (1983, 1984, 1985, 1986, 1987, 1988, 1989, 1990, 1991). . . . All-NBA second team (1982). . . . NBA All-Rookie team (1980). . . . J. Walter Kennedy Citizenship Award (1992).

NOTES: Led NBA with 3.43 steals per game (1981) and 2.67 steals per game (1982).

Season	Team	G	Min	FGM	FGA	Pct	FTM	FTA	Pct	Off	Def	Tot	Ast	St	Blk	TO	Pts	RPG	APG	PPG
79–80	LAL	77	2,795	503	949	.530	374	462	.810	166	430	596	563	187	41	305	1,387	7.7	7.3	18.0
80–81	LAL	37	1,371	312	587	.532	171	225	.760	101	219	320	317	127	27	143	798	8.6	8.6	21.6
81–82	LAL	78	2,991	556	1,036	.537	329	433	.760	252	499	751	743	208	34	286	1,447	9.6	9.5	18.6
82–83	LAL	79	2,907	511	933	.548	304	380	.800	214	469	683	829	176	47	301	1,326	8.6	10.5	16.8
83–84	LAL	67	2,567	441	780	.565	290	358	.810	99	392	491	875	150	49	306	1,178	7.3	13.1	17.6
84–85	LAL	77	2,781	504	899	.561	391	464	.843	90	386	476	968	113	25	305	1,406	6.2	12.6	18.3
85–86	LAL	72	2,578	483	918	.526	378	434	.871	85	341	426	907	113	16	273	1,354	5.9	12.6	18.8
86–87	LAL	80	2,904	683	1,308	.522	535	631	.848	122	382	504	977	138	36	300	1,909	6.3	12.2	23.9
87–88	LAL	72	2,637	490	996	.492	417	489	.853	88	361	449	858	114	13	269	1,408	6.2	11.9	19.6
88–89	LAL	77	2,886	579	1,137	.509	513	563	.911	111	496	607	988	138	22	312	1,730	7.9	12.8	22.5
89–90	LAL	79	2,937	546	1,138	.480	567	637	.890	128	394	522	907	132	34	289	1,765	6.6	11.5	22.3
90–91	LAL	79	2,933	466	976	.477	519	573	.906	105	446	551	989	102	17	314	1,531	7.0	12.5	19.4
91–92	LAL									Did not play—retired										
92–93	LAL									Did not play—retired										
93–94	LAL									Did not play—retired										
94–95	LAL									Did not play—retired										
95–96	LAL	32	958	137	294	.466	172	201	.856	40	143	183	220	26	13	103	468	5.7	6.9	14.6
Total		906	33,245	6,211	11,951	.520	4,960	5,850	.848	1,601	4,958	6,559	10,141	1,724	374	3,506	17,707	7.2	11.2	19.5

THREE-POINT FIELD GOALS: 1979–80, 7-for-31 (.226); 1980–81, 3-for-17 (.176); 1981–82, 6-for-29 (.207); 1982–83, 0-for-21; 1983–84, 6-for-29 (.207); 1984–85, 7-for-37 (.189); 1985–86, 10-for-43 (.233); 1986–87, 8-for-39 (.205); 1987–88, 11-for-56 (.196); 1988–89, 59-for-188 (.314); 1989–90, 106-for-276 (.384); 1990–91, 80-for-250 (.320); 1995–96, 22-for-58 (.379). Total: 325-for-1074 (.303).

PERSONAL FOULS/DISQUALIFICATIONS: 1979–80, 218/1; 1980–81, 100/0; 1981–82, 223/1; 1982–83, 200/1; 1983–84, 169/1; 1984–85, 155/0; 1985–86, 133/0; 1986–87, 168/0; 1987–88, 147/0; 1988–89, 172/0; 1989–90, 167/1; 1990–91, 150/0; 1995–96, 48/0. Total: 2050/5.

NBA PLAYOFF RECORD

NOTES: NBA Finals Most Valuable Player (1980, 1982, 1987). . . . Holds NBA Finals single-series records for highest assists-per-game average—14.0 (1985); and highest assists-per-game average by a rookie—8.7 (1980). . . . Holds NBA Finals single-game records for most points by a rookie—42 (May 16, 1980, vs. Philadelphia); most assists—21 (June 3, 1984, vs. Boston); most assists by a rookie—11 (May 7, 1980, vs. Philadelphia); and most assists in one half—14 (June 19, 1988, vs. Detroit). . . . Shares NBA Finals single-game record for most assists in one quarter—8 (four times). . . . Holds career playoff record for most assists—2,346. . . . Holds single-series playoff record for highest assists-per-game average—17.0 (1985). . . . Shares single-game playoff records for most free throws made in one half—19 (May 8, 1991, vs. Golden State); most assists—24 (May 15, 1984, vs. Phoenix); and most assists in one half—15 (May 3, 1985, vs. Portland).

| Season | Team | G | Min | FGM | FGA | Pct | FTM | FTA | Pct | Rebounds | | | Ast | St | Blk | TO | Pts | Averages | | |
										Off	Def	Tot						RPG	APG	PPG
79–80	LAL	16	658	103	199	.518	85	106	.802	52	116	168	151	49	6	65	293	10.5	9.4	18.3
80–81	LAL	3	127	19	49	.388	13	20	.650	8	33	41	21	8	3	11	51	13.7	7.0	17.0
81–82	LAL	14	562	83	157	.529	77	93	.828	54	104	158	130	40	3	44	243	11.3	9.3	17.4
82–83	LAL	15	643	100	206	.485	68	81	.840	51	77	128	192	34	12	64	268	8.5	12.8	17.9
83–84	LAL	21	837	151	274	.551	80	100	.800	26	113	139	284	42	20	79	382	6.6	13.5	18.2
84–85	LAL	19	687	116	226	.513	100	118	.847	19	115	134	289	32	4	76	333	7.1	15.2	17.5
85–86	LAL	14	541	110	205	.537	82	107	.766	21	79	100	211	27	1	45	302	7.1	15.1	21.6
86–87	LAL	18	666	146	271	.539	98	118	.831	28	111	139	219	31	7	51	392	7.7	12.2	21.8
87–88	LAL	24	965	169	329	.514	132	155	.852	32	98	130	303	34	4	83	477	5.4	12.6	19.9
88–89	LAL	14	518	85	174	.489	78	86	.907	15	68	83	165	27	3	53	258	5.9	11.8	18.4
89–90	LAL	9	376	76	155	.490	70	79	.886	12	45	57	115	11	1	36	227	6.3	12.8	25.2
90–91	LAL	19	823	118	268	.440	157	178	.882	23	131	154	240	23	0	77	414	8.1	12.6	21.8
95–96	LAL	4	135	15	39	.385	28	33	.848	8	26	34	26	0	0	12	61	8.5	6.5	15.3
Total		190	7,538	1,291	2,552	.506	1,068	1,274	.838	349	1,116	1,465	2,346	358	64	696	3,701	7.7	12.3	19.5

THREE-POINT FIELD GOALS: 1979–80, 2-for-8 (.250); 1981–82, 0-for-4; 1982–83, 0-for-11; 1983–84, 0-for-7; 1984–85, 1-for-7 (.143); 1985–86, 0-for-11; 1986–87, 2-for-10 (.200); 1987–88, 7-for-14 (.500); 1988–89, 10-for-35 (.286); 1989–90, 5-for-25 (.200); 1990–91, 21-for-71 (.296); 1995–96, 3-for-9 (.333). Total: 51-for-212 (.241).

PERSONAL FOULS/DISQUALIFICATIONS: 1979–80, 47/1; 1981–82, 50/0; 1982–83, 49/0; 1983–84, 71/0; 1984–85, 48/0; 1985–86, 43/0; 1986–87, 37/0; 1987–88, 61/0; 1988–89, 30/1; 1989–90, 28/0; 1990–91, 43/0; 1995–96, 3/0. Total: 524/3.

NBA ALL-STAR GAME RECORD

NOTES: NBA All-Star Game Most Valuable Player (1990, 1992). . . . Holds career records for most assists—127; and most three-point field goals made—10. . . . Holds single-game record for most assists—22 (1984, OT).

Season	Team	Min	FGM	FGA	Pct	FTM	FTA	Pct	Rebounds Off	Def	Tot	Ast	PF	DQ	St	Blk	TO	Pts
1980	LAL	24	5	8	.625	2	2	1.000	2	0	2	4	3	0	3	2	2	12
1982	LAL	23	5	9	.556	6	7	.857	3	1	4	7	5	0	0	0	1	16
1983	LAL	33	7	16	.438	3	4	.750	3	2	5	16	2	0	5	0	7	17
1984	LAL	37	6	13	.462	2	2	1.000	4	5	9	22	3	0	3	2	4	15
1985	LAL	31	7	14	.500	7	8	.875	2	3	5	15	2	0	1	0	3	21
1986	LAL	28	1	3	.333	4	4	1.000	0	4	4	15	4	0	1	0	9	6
1987	LAL	34	4	10	.400	1	2	.500	1	6	7	13	2	0	4	0	1	9
1988	LAL	39	4	15	.267	9	9	1.000	1	5	6	19	2	0	2	2	8	17
1989	LAL							Did not play—injured										
1990	LAL	25	9	15	.600	0	0	—	1	5	6	4	1	0	0	1	3	22
1991	LAL	28	7	16	.438	0	0	—	1	3	4	3	1	0	0	0	3	16
1992	LAL	29	9	12	.750	4	4	1.000	3	2	5	9	0	0	2	0	7	25
Total		331	64	131	.489	38	42	.905	21	36	57	127	25	0	21	7	48	176

THREE-POINT FIELD GOALS: 1980, 0-for-1; 1983, 0-for-1; 1984, 1-for-3 (.333); 1986, 0-for-1; 1988, 0-for-1; 1990, 4-for-6 (.667); 1991, 2-for-5 (.400); 1992, 3-for-3. Total: 10-for-21 (.476).

NBA COACHING RECORD

Season	Team	Regular Season W	L	Pct.	Finish	Playoffs W	L	Pct.
94–94	LAL	5	11	.313	5th/Pacific Division	—	—	—

NOTES: 1994—Replaced Randy Pfund (27–37) and Bill Bertka (1–1) as Los Angeles Lakers head coach (March 27), with record of 28–38 and club in fifth place.

Chapter Five

MICHAEL JORDAN—Guard

The Will to Win and Competitive Spirit

by Paul Ladewski

S o who do we blame for *this* exactly?

For the better part of fourteen-plus seasons, Michael Jordan abused opponents with his speed and quickness and hops and smarts and touch like few players before or since. But what about the cast-iron will? Wasn't that what separated Jordan from the other poor souls? The basketball gods couldn't possibly be so unfair, so inconsiderate to the mental and physical health of others, as to give one person all that talent and all that athleticism *and* such a desperate desire to succeed, could they?

Leroy Smith, this is all your fault.

You see, Smith and Jordan were close friends at Lamey High School in Wilmington, North Carolina, the rural town where Jordan was raised. Smith might have been better than his buddy at a few things, but Jordan didn't consider basketball to be one of them. When it came time to pick the varsity team, though, his opinion didn't count. Smith made the cut. Guess who didn't.

Jordan couldn't have been crushed more if he had been stood up on prom night. "When I got cut from my varsity team, that's when everything began," he said. "If you don't think that I'm good enough, but my friend Leroy—who I don't think is as good as me—is on that team, then you're going to see . . ."

Hell unleashed.

From that point on, the dark day served as a supersized source of motivation for Jordan in the decades to come. Whether the slights were real or imagined, it didn't matter. He turned virtually every one of his teams into a personal confrontation designed to elevate his game and that of those around him.

"Once I got to the pros, no one felt like I would make a difference in Chicago in terms of turning the team from a nonplayoff team to a playoff team," Jordan said. "Then no one thought a scoring champion could win a championship. Then it went to 'He can only score, but he can't make his teammates better.' Those types of challenges continued to come and created an inner drive for me, an appetite to prove everyone wrong."

The son of Deloris and James Jordan grew up in a rural, middle-class family in Wilmington, North Carolina, 987 miles from Chicago. As the youngest of three children, Michael felt like something of an outcast. "I had a very tough childhood in the sense that I didn't feel like I fit into the family," he said. "It wasn't anything that my mother or father did knowingly, but them seeing that I was more or less the troublesome one." Jordan wasn't a problem child exactly, but he was defiant to the point that he was suspended from grade school on more than one occasion.

While Jordan was an above-average student, he was an even better athlete in baseball, basketball, football, and track. But because of his free spirit and wide range of interests—BB guns, motorcycles, and the opposite sex, among others, not necessarily in that order—

Jordan felt that he wasn't always taken seriously. His rep was in stark contrast to that of his older brother Larry, whose athleticism and work ethic made him the easy pick as the most likely to succeed in the Jordan household.

Big bro cast a large shadow over Michael, not the least of which was on the basketball court. As the far stronger and physical of the two, Larry didn't dominate Michael so much as scare the heck out of him. "We had fights, outright fights," Michael said of the backyard brawls. "I wouldn't *compete* compete, because I was afraid of his aggressiveness." Heck, if Dad hadn't intervened, the Jordan boys might still be out there.

The frequent whuppins brought out a desperate desire in Jordan to be accepted and to prove any doubters wrong in the process. The more Michael had his bloody nose rubbed in it, it seemed, the more intent he was on payback. He began to practice more, and his confidence grew by leaps and bounds. When his body started to come of age as well and he got bigger, the score was about to be settled.

"Once I became dominant, I wasn't going to let it go," Jordan said. "Because my mother and my father saw that Larry was a better player, I felt like it was me against them. I was going to prove them wrong."

Okay, maybe Leroy Smith doesn't deserve *all* the blame.

After three seasons under head coach Dean Smith at North Carolina—Jordan's buzzer-beater clinched the 1982 national championship—the Bulls made Jordan the third overall pick in the NBA draft two years later. They did so largely on the basis of his outrageous athleticism and potential to become a big-time scorer. "We envisioned someone who could average as many as twenty-five points eventually," said Rod Thorn, the Bulls general manager at the time. "But we had no idea what kind of competitor he was when he arrived at camp. I doubt that anybody could have known."

Imagine the surprise—nay, shock—of Bulls coaches and team officials when Attila the Hun showed up disguised as a skinny twenty-one-year-old kid with a forty-six-inch vertical. So passionate was

Jordan in his desire to succeed, so cocksure was he in his ability to pull it off, that not a day went by that Thorn and his coaches didn't have to pick up their jaws off the floor.

"My leadership qualities had to come to the forefront," Jordan said. "Once you show that, then other guys gain that same type of confidence. 'We're gonna win this game. We're gonna do everything we can. We're gonna dive on the floor for loose balls. We're gonna come up with loose rebounds. We're gonna make our free throws. We're gonna play hard defense.' And that has to start with my leadership on the basketball court."

Consider it done in a matter of . . . hours?

"After about one practice, it was obvious to us that Michael was our best player," Thorn said. "But what surprised us was his drive to succeed. He set the tone immediately to the point that, by the time we played our first regular-season game, he already was the team leader. Almost every great player is a great competitor, but I've never seen anyone more competitive than Michael before or since then."

Training camp was all of one day old when Thorn and company witnessed Jordan at his obsessive best. In a routine scrimmage—the loser would have to run laps—Team Jordan had a comfortable lead as usual. In an attempt to level the field and extend the competition—a near-impossible task as long as Jordan was part of the mix—head coach Kevin Loughery instructed him to switch sides. Jordan would have been more thrilled to have foot fungus, especially after he was required to sprint with the losers moments later.

"Michael didn't think the decision was fair and was very vocal about it," Thorn recalled. "He didn't storm out of practice, but he was pissed off. At that point, we knew that we had a young guy who was different than any we had seen before."

Different? Jordan didn't treat every practice as though the future of Earth was at stake, mind you. He treated *every freaking drill* that way. When the players shot free throws, Jordan had to make at least one more than the next guy. When the players sprinted the lines, Jordan had to be the first to finish. Not only that, but he did so with almost impeccable fundamentals *and* demanded to know his exact time afterward.

Then again, if there had been a race to see which player could put on his uniform the fastest, then one guess as to who would have been the odds-on favorite to lap the field.

"Michael brought a sweeping confidence into the drills and competitions," recalled Johnny Bach, who spent eight seasons with him as a Bulls assistant coach. "I'm talking about the three-on-three, four-on-four, and buildup drills that are routine to a lot of players. Michael was so highly competitive in *any* drill that he grabbed your attention as a coach. He wanted to perform well and win. His was the kind of thirst that you didn't see in young players particularly."

It wasn't enough for Jordan to beat the hell out of an opponent physically either. Everyone in the same zip code had to damn well know about it. In sprint drills, for instance, Jordan liked to poke fun at the bigger lugs in particular. "You can't run!" Jordan would break out in a broad grin while they ate his dust. After scrimmages it was more of the same. "See the score?! I did it! You lost!" he was quick to remind them.

And you thought a water pump was the best way to loosen earwax.

Yet if Jordan hadn't shot the shot as well as he talked the talk, his words wouldn't have amounted to squat. If Jordan was the captain of the All-Smack Team, then he also was on the very short list of most talented players ever. And not even Donald Trump could close a deal like Jordan routinely did in close games.

Or as Jordan put it, "As long as I got the ball and we got a chance to win, we'll always be able to succeed."

It took Bulls head coach Doug Collins all of four days—common theme alert!—to realize that Jordan was a different animal with the game on the line. In the 1986–87 season opener in New York, his first as Bulls boss, Collins started a lineup of Jordan and Steve Colter in the backcourt, Earl Cureton and Charles Oakley on the wings, and Granville Waiters in the middle. Not exactly the 1966–67 Philadelphia 76ers. But Jordan was so stoked for the new season, so intent on beating a more talented Knicks team at Madison Square Garden, his favorite road stop in the league, that Collins actually had to advise him to tone it down in the first half.

In the midst of a time-out in the final minutes, Collins was about to address his team in the huddle. Sport coat soaked in sweat, face worn to a frazzle, the coach looked as though he had spent the previous two hours in a car wash with the top down. Collins had chewed his gum down to a powder, the film of which was visible around his lips.

Suddenly Collins saw a hand with a cup of water flash in front of him. "I looked up, and it was Michael," Collins said. Strange, but Jordan was as dry as desert heat. "As calm as he could be, Michael looked me in the eyes and said, 'Coach, take a drink of water and get that crap off your mouth,' " Collins said. " 'I won't let you lose your first game.' " Then Jordan put the final touches on a 108–103 victory in which he scored fifty big ones.

The Bulls traveled to Cleveland, where they met the Cavaliers the next day. Jordan went off for forty-one points in a 94–89 triumph. After a day off, the team returned home—and promptly fell behind by seventeen points against the San Antonio Spurs in the first half. Once again, Jordan would have none of it. He drained thirty-four points to trigger a 110–104 comeback.

"After three games, I said to myself, 'Whoa!' " Collins said. "I told my friends, 'This guy is in another world.' I played with and against some of the greatest players ever, but Michael had the kind of insatiable appetite to win that I had never seen before."

Only days later, Collins discovered a very different competitive side to Jordan at practice. A former All-Star guard and U.S. Olympic team member himself, Collins was a hyper-intense competitor in his own right. Yet Collins was no match for Jordan in that regard—not that anyone ever could be.

At a practice early in the 1986–87 season, Collins inadvertently lost track of the score and shorted Jordan and his team. An honest mistake, right? Well, to Jordan the oversight was a felony punishable by life in prison. He vented on his coach while teammates looked on in stunned silence.

"It was one of those moments when you feel that you're frozen in time," Collins said. "Here I was, a young coach, and I had to think immediately about how I would handle the situation. Michael realized that, because of the impact that he had on our team, he had made a mistake. But Michael was such a strong-willed person, the worst thing I could have done was challenge him.

"So I asked myself, who does Michael respect the most? Dean Smith came to mind. So I asked him, 'Would you say that to Dean

Smith?' Michael said, 'No, I wouldn't, but I'm leaving anyway.' 'But, Michael, you're our leader,' I said."

No matter. Jordan grabbed his bag and bolted the place. Rather than confront Jordan about what had taken place the next day, when the team had a preseason game at Minnesota, Collins allowed both sides to cool off for a while. But after word leaked out about the stormy affair, the Chicago media staked out the two of them at a practice at the Multiplex in suburban Deerfield the next day.

While Collins was in the midst of a television interview outside the building, who should happen to walk out an adjacent door but Mr. Intensity himself. "I told the person who interviewed me, 'Hey, everything's great. I love Michael and Michael loves me, and I'll show you,' " Collins said. Then Collins walked over and planted one on his cheek. Jordan looked at his coach and smiled. Neither mentioned the incident again.

"Michael knew that he was far more important than me, and I knew it too," Collins said. "At the same time, Michael understood that, in order for us to be successful as a team, he had to listen to me like every other player. From that point on, not once did he disrespect me as a head coach. Ever."

In the 1990s, when the question was asked, "Which team will win the NBA title?" the correct answer was, "Which team does Jordan play with?" In each of the six seasons in which Jordan played from start to finish, the Bulls carted off the big prize. But while his career is remembered best for its glory days, easily forgotten is the fact that it took Jordan a full seven seasons to finally reach the mountaintop.

If not for the Detroit Pistons, Jordan and his supporting cast almost certainly would have reached the promised land sooner. As if the fact that the Pistons beat the Bulls on the scoreboard wasn't bad enough, it was the manner in which they did it that ate away at Jordan like some sort of cancer. Bill Laimbeer, Dennis Rodman, Isiah Thomas, and the rest of the so-called Bad Boys didn't merely outscore the Bulls. They left bruises on their bodies and welts on their psyches along the way.

"They were bullies to us, and I didn't like being bullied," Jordan said. "I didn't like being told, 'You guys can't beat us no matter what.' We're going to beat you on the basketball court, we're going to beat you physically, we're going to beat you mentally, we're going to beat you all kinds of ways."

Like it or not, that's exactly what the Pistons did to Jordan and the Bulls in three consecutive postseasons. But while the near-misses only served to strengthen the Jordan resolve, the same couldn't be said for many of his teammates. In his mind, the question wasn't one of talent as much as it was desire. *Did his teammates want it bad enough?*

Then again, could any mere mortal ever want it as badly as Jordan did?

"At first, I felt like guys accepted that," Jordan said. "I didn't. And when I saw that the guys accepted it, that bothered me. It was like, 'I can't believe that I'm going out there every day busting my butt, and everybody else doesn't have the same focus.' I wanted them to see that I was tired of it. I didn't accept it from day one, and I won't accept it now. It's up to you to either get into that hole and fight with me, or get out of that hole and go somewhere else."

The volcano that smoldered inside Mount St. Michael for years finally erupted after the decisive game of the 1990 Eastern Conference Finals. The Bulls had extended the Bad Boys to seven games, a sign that they had closed the gap after five- and six-game eliminations the previous two seasons. But to Jordan at least, only the score mattered—Bad Boys, 93, Bullieds, 74. Not even his 36.7 points and 6.8 assists per game in the playoffs were good enough this time.

Alone in his thoughts, Jordan broke down and cried on the team bus after the game. "You know, I was going to be with these guys again next year," he said. "If they didn't want to have the same attitude that I had, then I didn't want to be a part of it. One of us couldn't be there, and either I wasn't going to be here or they weren't going to be here." James Jordan took a seat alongside him, but no one person, no amount of words, could console Jordan after the biggest letdown of his career.

One misconception about Jordan is that he entered the NBA as a ready-made player. Closer to the truth is that his game was a work-in-progress in the early years. But while players of lesser ability would pack it in each summer, Jordan treated the downtime as something of a pre-preseason. True, Jordan enjoyed casinos, golf courses, and the like as much as the next guy, but he never allowed pleasure to get in the way of what mattered most to him.

Each summer Jordan set out to hone his game, even add another weapon to his arsenal. Of particular interest was his jump shot, which lacked range and fundamentals at the outset. Eventually Jordan became so confident in his ability as a jump shooter that he would frequently challenge Steve Kerr, B. J. Armstrong, Craig Hodges, and John Paxson, teammates who ranked among the best distance shooters in the league. Of course, any Jordan-inspired competition had to include a, ahem, friendly wager of some kind.

The instant Jordan arrived at preseason camp each fall, the message was clear. "Every season I got dressed for a game, I wanted to win," Jordan said. "That didn't change."

To hear team members tell it, few if any preseason camps were more intense than the one in advance of the 1995–96 season.

The previous spring Jordan had returned to action after retiring for a year and a half from basketball. With Jordan at something less than his physical and mental best—the comeback took place sixty-four games into the regular season—the Bulls had been eliminated by the Orlando Magic in the Eastern Conference Semifinals.

To say that the early tee times didn't sit well with Jordan would be like suggesting that he sold a few sneakers once. In the next four months, fully intent on reclaiming his title as the preeminent player in the game, Jordan prepared like he had never done before in his career. Even while Jordan filmed the movie *Space Jam* in Los Angeles, he practiced on a makeshift court that he had built on location, where he routinely took on any and all comers until the wee hours. When Jordan arrived at the Berto Center in October, he was loaded for bear. And Knicks. And Magic. "A man possessed," teammate Steve Kerr called him.

This return to the game marked the second time in the decade that the Bulls bid for three consecutive league championships. But in style if not substance, this was a much different group than the one that Jordan had led to a third NBA championship nearly twenty-seven months earlier. Unlike the early 1990s, when Jordan's supporting cast featured playoff-hardened types such as Scottie Pippen, B. J. Armstrong, Bill Cartwright, Horace Grant, Stacey King, John Paxson, and Will Perdue, a core group that had been required to pay their dues against the Detroit Pistons in the playoffs, this group wasn't nearly as tough physically and mentally. The immediate task for Jordan was to determine who would be up for the challenge in his own locker room, where Pippen was the only teammate he recognized from the first three-peat champions.

In scrimmages head coach Phil Jackson usually had Jordan play opposite Pippen, the teammate closest to him in talent and attitude. But he also would pair others against Jordan on occasion, a change designed to give Pippen a breather and test the mettle of new teammates in particular.

At practice one day the unenviable assignment went to Kerr, a six-foot-three guard with Opie-like looks. The reserves were suffering another embarrassment at the hands of the starters, and as Jordan was known to do, he was burning their ears in the process. Except that Kerr did something out of character for most Jordan teammates. He actually mustered enough testosterone to talk smack right back. After Jordan laid down the hammer moments later, push came to shove. Before their teammates knew what hit them, a Bulls fight broke out.

"Steve started to get favorable treatment from Phil, and that started to bother me," Jordan said. "So I became more aggressive with Steve. I said, 'You call that a foul? Okay, I'll show you a foul the next time we come down the court.' And I just wiped him out. Steve was like the innocent bystander, because I played my games with Phil in a sense. *You know how aggressive I like to be in practice, but now you make it more passive.* Steve was just a piece of the puzzle in this game between Phil and me."

Yeah, a piece of the puzzle, all right.

"Everybody grabbed us and pulled us apart, which was good for me, or else I might be dead by now," Kerr said. "It was a good, clean fight—and I got whupped." He sported a nasty black eye for weeks to prove it, although the original excuse was that his face had blindly kissed a door that his kid opened at home.

Jordan was kicked out of practice for his troubles, but it was a small price to pay for a message sent. "I think Phil understood how practice should be and that there was no way that he should put me against Steve Kerr from that point on," Jordan said. "Phil realized that my practices are serious practices. That's how I get better, and that's how the team gets better. If you try to tone it down, it's better for me to sit on the sidelines and not practice, or I can make it worse."

As difficult as it was for him at times, Jordan understood that not all athletes are created equal, that some possess more natural ability than others. What Jordan could not and would not accept was less than a 100 percent effort from anyone at any time. If one wanted to get on his bad side, then all it took was to wimp out in the face of a challenge. A root canal was more enjoyable than to be *there*.

While Kerr called the confrontation "one of the stupidest things I ever did as a player" in one breath, he referred to it as "one of the best things that I ever did as well" in the next. Because not only did Kerr receive an apology from Jordan in person at a team shoot-around the next day, but he earned something far more significant—Jordan's respect and trust.

"Michael subscribed to the philosophy that if you couldn't face his wrath at practice, there was no way you could face the pressure of Game 7 in a playoff series," Kerr said. "He picked on players to see if they could handle it. That was his way to weed out some people and toughen up others. When I didn't back down from Michael, I earned his respect. He left me alone after that."

Yet what made Jordan the greatest player of his generation—perhaps the greatest player ever—wasn't only the fact that he could jump higher, shoot straighter, and react quicker and smarter than almost everyone else. No, what separated Jordan from the rest of the poor slobs was that he played the game within the game better than anyone before or since. "You ain't got no chance while he's playing," then Minnesota Timberwolves guard Stephon Marbury said early in his career. "He overtakes people with his mind. He's not out there playing basketball with his skills and his God-given talent. He's playing with *his mind.*"

Indeed, if there was an edge to be had, then Jordan was on it like lint on Velcro. Player, coach, media, or referee, it didn't matter. If Jordan could spindle, fold, or intimidate somebody—anybody—to improve his chances to succeed between the lines, then said person was fair game.

"He looks at you crazy," Marbury said. "He just gives you this look like, 'You know you can't stop me.' Don't get me wrong—I don't fear anyone. But he comes on the court with so much fanfare that he already has a mental edge over you. He says things like, 'I own you,' and, 'I own The Man,' and, 'I own the team,' and, 'I own the ball,' and, 'I own everything around me,' and 'When I get in my groove I can't be stopped.' He goes with that every night. That's the makeup of Michael Jordan."

As Jordan was well aware, nobody was easier prey than a naive young opponent. Jordan wasn't merely the best player on the planet to the youth of the world. He was a walking, breathing global icon, a basketball god who dominated the corporate world off the court as thoroughly as he did the competition on it. For a young player to have Jordan so much as smile at him was considered to be the thrill of a lifetime, a Kodak Moment that he could share with his grand-kids years later.

If a kid really made a good impression, Jordan might even put in a good word for him with Nike or another one of his dozens of cor-porate sponsors. Who knows? The young fella might even get a sneaker contract out of it. "I was a nervous wreck the first time that I played against him," Denver Nuggets forward Bryant Stith re-called. "I wasn't sure whether to kiss him or hug him or just play basketball." What number did Stith wear on his back? Twenty-three, natch.

More than one Jordan worshiper was so excited about playing against Jordan in the flesh for the first time that Port-a-Potties were almost required near the bench. They were players such as Danny Fortson, who still had the Jordan gum cards that he collected as a kid even after he entered the league.

A physical defender-rebounder who never saw a hard foul that he couldn't take, Fortson quickly earned the reputation as a tough guy who backed down from no one. But as a wide-eyed rookie, the kid melted like margarine at the mere sight of Jordan on the court.

"There's no question that it was very difficult to play against him," Fortson said. "It was like being in the same room with Presi-dent Clinton. People respected Michael Jordan more than they did the president. When you played against him, it was hard to concen-trate on the game, because you started to think about other stuff."

Young players were in such awe of Jordan that they found it difficult—sometimes impossible—to function properly in his presence. When one considered the influx of young players in the league at the time, that was a big chunk of the competition that Jordan had at his feet. So concerned became rival coaches such as Jeff Van Gundy that they warned their players not to accept candy from Jordan under any circumstances on or off the court.

While his team was in Chicago for a game midway through the 1996–97 season, Van Gundy called out Jordan in an interview with a Chicago radio station. "He sucks them into thinking that he wants to see them develop," Van Gundy charged. "He talks about young players. He invites people to be in his movies. It's all a con. Once people realize it's a con and you have to go as hard at him as he's going to go at you, then you have a chance [to be successful]. But only a chance, because he's still a great player."

Regardless of which version one believed at the time, it was difficult to argue that Van Gundy could have chosen a worse time or person with whom to pick a fight. As if he didn't already have enough motivation to prove the doubters wrong in his comeback season, now Jordan had another excuse to fan his internal flame.

"That's a crock," Jordan told reporters hours later. "[Van Gundy] never played the game, so he doesn't know. He's playing a con game with his own team, trying to get them motivated.

"C'mon, when I'm off the court, I have friends in the game. I know young players. I try to help them out with the way they approach the game. But when I step on the court, it's not a con game. I'm out there to win, and I'm not trying to win friendships. I can separate the two."

Sure enough, Jordan dropped fifty-one points on Van Grumpy and the Knicks in an 89–88 victory only hours later. *Con this!*

Nobody was off-limits to Jordan in his attempt to gain a competitive edge, least of all those who made the calls. The MO usually included a pat on the fanny or a few lighthearted words at the start. If that didn't work, then Jordan would try an icy stare at the ref in question, maybe even a verbal reminder about who was mostly responsible for the size of his paycheck. Remember, these were many of the same referees whose kids, wives, friends, and relatives idolized

Jordan at every turn, wore his brand of sneakers, ate his brand of cereal, gulped his brand of sports drink, wore his brand of cologne, and drove his brand of wheels.

For the most part, opponents were reluctant to make an issue of the favorable whistle that Jordan received lest he abuse them even more the next time they met, but if you had polled 100 of them off the record, 101 would have agreed that he was at an unfair competitive advantage in that regard.

"I mean, his first step is a walk every time," Marbury once said. "It's a walk. That's his move, though. That's how he plays, but he has earned that. He's Michael Jordan. He's God. He's Black Jesus."

In a game at Portland in the 1997–98 season, the Bulls trailed by nineteen points in the second quarter. At that point, Black Jesus parted the waters and carried his team to an easy victory. The daggers were three fadeaway jumps in the fourth quarter, after each of which Jordan turned and stared at the home-team bench. Finally, after Jordan got away with an obvious foul call, a helpless Trail Blazers coach Mike Dunleavy could only scream at the referees with palms spread upward, "Where's the holy water?!"

Of course, Dunleavy made sure to call Jordan "the greatest ever to play this game from the standpoint of intelligence, competitiveness, and athleticism" in the postgame news conference.

On the morning of Game 5 of the 1997 NBA Finals in Salt Lake City, Jordan felt lower than a manhole cover. The official word was that Jordan had a case of viral gastroenteritis, which was one way to say that he had eaten some bad room-service pizza at the team hotel the previous night. Could the kryptonite have come at a worse time for Jordan and his team? The Utah Jazz had already pulled even in the best-of-seven affair with victories in Games 3 and 4 at the Delta Center, and a third consecutive triumph would put them *this close* to the league championship.

Next came one of the defining moments of his career, one that Jordan would call "the most difficult thing that I've ever done."

Clearly, Jordan wasn't himself at the outset. Neither was his team. The Utah Jazz bolted to a 36–20 lead, and better yet for them, a listless Jordan was no factor. Heck, the guy didn't even have enough energy to burn the ears of his teammates.

The thing about Jordan, though, was that his reserve tank was the size of the Grand Canyon. In the second quarter he sensed that the game—the series?—had begun to slip-slide away. Jordan mustered enough energy to score seventeen points in the second quarter— eight in a row at one point—to pull his team within four points, 53–49, at halftime.

At halftime Jordan still felt like junk. He ate applesauce and sipped juices. Didn't matter. Jordan started the second half with cotton mouth and shortness of breath. "In the third quarter I really felt like I couldn't catch my wind and get my energy level up," he said. "I just tried to get myself through it." At one point he nearly passed out.

The NBA Finals? No, more like ER.

With Jordan on the verge of dehydration, team medical personnel were ready to hook him up to an IV. Finally, in a desperate attempt to jump-start the only person who could bail his team out of the mess, Jackson gave Jordan a blow with three minutes left in the quarter. "I cooled down a little bit," Jordan said. "I didn't know if I could get a sweat going again, because I was really low on energy, but I kept pushing."

In the fourth quarter Jordan didn't recover physically as much as he willed his team to victory mentally. He scored fifteen points in the quarter—including a drop-dead three-pointer in the final minute— as the Bulls escaped with a dramatic 90–88 victory. Jordan finished with thirty-six points, seven rebounds, and five assists.

And the team never stayed at the same hotel again.

"It's something about desire," Jordan said afterward. "We wanted it really bad. I wanted it really bad. If we had lost, I would have been devastated."

If there was a body of work that defined the Jordan will to win, then it was the tumultuous 1997–98 campaign, his last in a Bulls uniform. Even before the start of preseason camp, there were indications that the Bulls dynasty was about to write its final chapter. At the root of the breakup was the contemptuous relationship between head coach Phil Jackson and general manager Jerry Krause, massive egos in their own right who had clashed on several fronts for years.

Finally convinced that they could no longer coexist, Jackson made it known that, unless changes were made and made soon, he had no intention of returning after his contract expired at the conclusion of the season. When the team owners showed no inclination to pull the switch, it became clear that this was a match that Jackson simply could not and would not win.

In effect, the imminent departure of Jackson would become the first big domino to topple the dynasty. At thirty-four, Jordan had no desire to play for any head coach other than Jackson, under whom he had played for seven seasons and experienced his greatest success. Once Jackson and Jordan were out the door, there would be no reason for team management to shell out big bucks to re-sign the thirty-one-year-old Pippen, yet another soon-to-be free agent. And so the season began, not with the anticipation of another glorious championship in the months ahead but with the bleak expectation that this could be the last time for the Rolling Stones of basketball.

Not surprisingly, the Bulls opened the season with an emotional hangover *this* big. On Halloween night they dressed up as the Los Angeles Clippers and dropped the regular-season opener in Boston. After three consecutive victories at home, they lost three of their next four games. Two wins were followed by a forgettable 2–3 road swing. One month into the season the Bulls could do no better than an 8–7 record, hardly the stuff of which championship teams are made.

So this was how the greatest dynasty in modern NBA history would end? Like chihuahuas, not pit bulls?

"You know, if you've never really experienced it before, then you're going to need a push," Jordan said. "That's what I was saying. 'We're 8–7, and you guys feel like you accomplished everything, that you were focused the same way I was focusing on that season, and that's not the approach I came back for.' I came back with the intention of doing this twice, three times in a row, you know, and I just wanted to wake up a few people and make them focus on that season."

Yet the master plan proved to be easier explained than executed. After Jordan had returned to the game two years earlier, the Bulls experienced almost instant success. The next season saw them post a league-record seventy-two victories in the regular season en route to their fourth league crown in six years. As a result, only a few of his new teammates had experienced any adversity to speak of. Even fewer were aware of what it would take to win a third consecutive title, a feat that only the Bulls and the Boston Celtics had accomplished in league history.

Only weeks into the season, it was obvious that Jordan and many of his teammates didn't read from the same page, let alone the same book, a division of purpose that left him thoroughly frustrated, even mad as hell at times. "You know, I was so angry because I was trying to get the guys to understand it from my standpoint," Jordan said. "None of the guys had done things three times in a row other than Scottie, myself, and Phil."

To compound matters, Pippen sat out the first thirty-five games of the season after foot surgery the previous summer, an absence that left Jordan with no one to ride shotgun. "Scottie was out, so it was even more difficult," Jordan said. "My voice had to be the loudest as well as Phil's. Phil's going to push but so much, and then a leader has to take his push, take it to the locker and take it to the court and take it to the practices and take it on the bus. Those were the things that were my responsibility.

"I felt like the guys were not creating that hunger again. You know, the hunger to do something for the third time. Being that I had been through it already, I knew how difficult it was. I let my anger try to motivate the players by saying, 'Hey, I want this. I still want this third championship in a row. Do you guys want it?' "

God help the poor soul who dared to say no. If this was to be the last season for Jordan, then there would be no other way for him to go out but on top. He prodded some of his teammates and pushed the others. When he was done, he prodded and pushed some more. If a few egos were bruised along the way, frankly, Jordan didn't give a hoot.

"Basically, that's what I was doing," Jordan said. "If people now look back, they can understand it, but maybe at the time they didn't. I had to keep pushing. I had to push to the brink of where people were offended by what I was doing. But I knew by going through it once before that everybody needs this push. I'm self-motivated. I can get myself to that point. Phil can get me to that point. But it was up to me as well as Phil to get the rest of the guys to believe that it could be done. You just have to push them to do it."

Nobody was pushed harder than forward Scott Burrell and swingman Toni Kukoc, chronic underachievers who had to step up at small forward with Pippen in dry dock.

Acquired in a trade with the Golden State Warriors the previous summer, Burrell possessed obvious skills. In fact, the onetime pitcher was the first athlete ever to be drafted in the first round of two major sports. But at that point his career had been marked by injuries and indifference. When Burrell arrived at Chicago, little did he know that certain demands and expectations would greet him there.

"I let him know that, when Scottie was with the team, we had won a few championships," Jordan said. "And I'm saying, 'Well, you've got to earn your keep around here. You just can't come in laughing and joking around and not work, fall on the fruits of our labor. You've got to fit in. You've got to do something. You've got to make a difference.'"

Worse yet, Burrell had the kind of demeanor that Jordan didn't care for. Burrell wore a permanent smile, and win or lose, he acted as though every day was a paid holiday. It was the lose part that Jordan loathed, of course.

"That's the thing that bothered me the most with him—his personality was outgoing," Jordan said. "He was a funny guy, never had a bad day in his life, always smiled, always joked. He didn't show disappointment, you know, he didn't show pain that much. And for you to understand what the attitude of this franchise is, you've got to show it. You've got to make an impact on this team."

Jordan ridiculed teammates in public only as a last resort. After all, to do that would be to admit a weakness, which could only give an edge to an opponent. Instead, Jordan preferred to toughen them up behind closed doors at practice. It was there that Jordan attacked Burrell at both ends of the court the way a Doberman would a filet.

"Every day that he backed down, I'd just hit him harder," Jordan said. "I would chastise him a little harder. I would ridicule him a little harder. You know, 'C'mon, man, show me when you're going to fight back. Because when we need you to play against Detroit, this is what they're going to do. If you respond with a laugh and a giggle, I can't go in a foxhole with you, because you're going to laugh at me. I can't count on you because you're not really taking it with the same passion that I'm taking it.' "

Drafted in the second round of the 1993 NBA Draft, Kukoc had been the best player in Europe for years. And general manager Krause made sure that everyone knew it. Even before Kukoc arrived at Chicago amid the hype, he wore a very large bull's-eye, and Pippen and Jordan immediately set out to challenge him.

Kukoc proved to be a rather easy target. For one, he often played passively, especially at the defensive end. What's more, Kukoc had a low pain threshold and often begged out of practices and games because of various ailments. "Initially, I felt like Toni took the easy way, took shortcuts," Jordan said. "I felt like he had the talent to be better defensively, had the talent to be more physical, had the talent to be a better basketball player."

In time, Jordan grew to admire Kukoc for his ability, but questions about his desire remained.

"I needed a firmer, stronger partner with Scottie down," Jordan said. "I felt that he didn't want it as badly as I wanted it, so I pushed him. I challenged him in practice, and to some degree I would ridicule him about his defense. If he lined up in front of me, I would attack him and I would talk trash to him. I tried to get him mad to the point where he would want to fight me."

One can argue with the method to the Michael madness, but it's difficult to argue with the results. Burrell and Kukoc capably filled the void while Pippen was away, and after he returned, they made the bench that much deeper in the championship drive.

At thirty-eight years of age, Jordan came out of his second retirement to play with the Washington Wizards for two seasons. Physically, there was only a faint resemblance between this Jordan and the vintage model. His first step lacked the burst of old. He couldn't elevate or change directions the way he once had. For the first time in his career he struggled to get through two-hour practices and the last of back-to-back games. Jordan was still a twenty-point threat and better-than-adequate defender, all right, but he did it on memory more than anything else.

Yet there was one part of Jordan that never changed, that he would never allow to change regardless of the circumstances. The old man still demanded a lot of himself and those around him, even if many of the young Wizards didn't bother to answer his call. And nobody outworked him at practices or in games, which at least in part explained why the team failed to earn a playoff berth both seasons.

"The Michael we saw at twenty-three years old had the youth and the exuberance and energy to match his will to win," Collins said. "I also coached the man at forty, when he didn't have the energy and legs that he once had. But the one thing that never left him was his competitive spirit. Even on nights when he didn't feel well, Michael somehow could get himself in the frame of mind necessary to compete at a high level."

In his two seasons as Wizards head coach, Collins and his wife Cathy lived in the same building as Jordan in Washington, D.C. Several times each week Cathy would take part in a 7:30 A.M. fitness class. By the time she arrived, Jordan and his personal trainer would already be well into their strength and conditioning program. It was a sight often seen only hours after Jordan *had played a game the previous night,* for God's sake.

Jordan owns or shares numerous league records, but the most remarkable one of all cannot be found in the *Official NBA Guide:* with the possible exception of Wilt Chamberlain, nobody did more on less sleep in league history.

After the 2002–03 season, Jordan left the game again, for good this time. But even in retirement the challenges were no less great for him. How does one so addicted to competition find a fix after he calls it quits? Will he ever find it? Where?

"I can't channel it anywhere, not the way that I did on the court," Jordan said. "Even in business, even in ownership of a team, you can't. There's no way you can give it to someone else. It's tough each and every day. It's like a dependency, you know? You want to get over it, but you can't really get over it, because it's always gonna be part of you until you can pass it on."

Yet while Jordan may be gone, he will be heard from for years, decades, perhaps even centuries to come. Go ahead, listen closely. Hear the echoes in the background?

Didn't think I could play all those years?! I whipped your butts! Losers! Where's Leroy Smith now?!

MICHAEL JORDAN—GUARD

PERSONAL: Born February 17, 1963, in Brooklyn, NY . . . 6–6/216 (1.98 m/98 kg) . . . full name: Michael Jeffrey Jordan.

HIGH SCHOOL: Emsley A. Laney (Wilmington, NC).

COLLEGE: North Carolina.

TRANSACTIONS/CAREER NOTES: Selected after junior season by Chicago Bulls in first round (third pick overall) of 1984 NBA draft. . . . On voluntarily retired list (October 6, 1993–March 18, 1995). . . . Activated from retirement (March 18, 1995). . . . Announced retirement (January 13, 1999). . . . Signed as free agent by Washington Wizards (September 25, 2001). . . . President of basketball operations, Washington Wizards, and minority owner, Washington Wizards Sports and Entertainment (January 19, 2000, through September 25, 2001).

CAREER HONORS: NBA 50th Anniversary All-Time Team (1996).

MISCELLANEOUS: Member of NBA championship team (1991, 1992, 1993, 1996, 1997, 1998). . . . Member of gold-medal-winning U.S. Olympic team (1984, 1992). . . . Chicago Bulls all-time leading scorer with 29,277 points, all-time leading rebounder with 5,836, all-time assists leader with 5,012, and all-time steals leader with 2,306 (1984–85 through 1992–93 and 1994–95 through 1997–98).

COLLEGIATE RECORD

NOTES: *The Sporting News* College Player of the Year (1983, 1984). . . . Naismith Award winner (1984). . . . Wooden Award winner (1984). . . . *The Sporting News* All-America first team (1983, 1984). . . . Member of NCAA Division I championship team (1982).

													Averages		
Season	Team	G	Min	FGM	FGA	Pct	FTM	FTA	Pct	Reb	Ast	Pts	RPG	APG	PPG
81–82	NC	34	1,079	191	358	.534	78	108	.722	149	61	460	4.4	1.8	13.5
82–83	NC	36	1,113	282	527	.535	123	167	.737	197	56	721	5.5	1.6	20.0
83–84	NC	31	915	247	448	.551	113	145	.779	163	64	607	5.3	2.1	19.6
Total		101	3,107	720	1,333	.540	314	420	.748	509	181	1788	5.0	1.8	17.7

THREE-POINT FIELD GOALS: 1982–83, 34-for-76 (.447).

NBA REGULAR-SEASON RECORD

RECORDS: Holds career record for most seasons leading league in scoring—10; highest points-per-game average (minimum 400 games or 10,000 points)—30.12; most seasons leading league in field goals made—10; and most seasons leading league in field goals attempted—10. . . . Shares career records for most consecutive seasons leading league in scoring—7 (1986–87 through 1992–93). . . . Holds single-game records for most free throws made in one half—20 (December 30, 1992, vs. Miami) and most free throws attempted in one half—23 (December 30, 1992, vs. Miami). . . . Shares single-game records for most free throws made in one quarter—14 (November 15, 1989, vs. Utah, and December 30, 1992, vs. Miami); and most free throws attempted in one quarter—16 (December 30, 1992, vs. Miami).

HONORS: NBA Most Valuable Player (1988, 1991, 1992, 1996, 1998). . . . NBA Defensive Player of the Year (1988). . . . NBA Rookie of the Year (1985). . . . IBM Award for all-around contribution to team's success (1985, 1989). . . . Slam Dunk Championship winner (1987, 1988). . . . All-NBA first team (1987, 1988, 1989, 1990, 1991, 1992, 1993, 1996, 1997, 1998). . . . All-NBA second team (1985). . . . NBA All-Defensive first team (1988, 1989, 1990, 1991, 1992, 1993, 1996, 1997, 1998). . . . NBA All-Rookie team (1985).

NOTES: Led NBA with 3.16 steals per game (1988), 2.77 steals per game (1990), and 2.83 steals per game (1993).

									Rebounds								Averages		
Season	Team	G	Min.	FGM	FGA	Pct	FTM	FTA	Pct	Off	Def	Tot	Ast	St	Blk	TO	Pts	RPG	APG	PPG
84–85	Chi	82	3,144	837	1,625	.515	630	746	.845	167	367	534	481	196	69	291	2,313	6.5	5.9	28.2
85–86	Chi	18	451	150	328	.457	105	125	.840	23	41	64	53	37	21	45	408	3.6	2.9	22.7
86–87	Chi	82	281	1,098	2,279	.482	833	972	.857	166	264	430	377	236	125	272	3041	5.2	4.6	37.1
87–88	Chi	82	3,311	1,069	1,998	.535	723	860	.841	139	310	449	485	259	131	252	2868	5.5	5.9	35.0
88–89	Chi	81	3,255	966	1,795	.538	674	793	.850	149	503	652	650	234	65	290	2633	8.0	8.0	32.5
89–90	Chi	82	3,197	1,034	1,964	.526	593	699	.848	143	422	565	519	227	54	247	2753	6.9	6.3	33.6
90–91	Chi	82	3,034	990	1,837	.539	571	671	.851	118	374	492	453	223	83	202	2580	6.0	5.5	31.5
91–92	Chi	80	3,102	943	1,818	.519	491	590	.832	91	420	511	489	182	75	200	2404	6.4	6.1	30.1
92–93	Chi	78	3,067	992	2,003	.495	476	569	.837	135	387	522	428	221	61	207	2541	6.7	5.5	32.6
93–94	Chi								Did not play—retired											
94–95	Chi	17	668	166	404	.411	109	136	.801	25	92	117	90	30	13	35	457	6.9	5.3	26.9
95–96	Chi	82	3,090	916	1,850	.495	548	657	.834	148	395	543	352	180	42	197	2491	6.6	4.3	30.4
96–97	Chi	82	3,106	920	1,892	.486	480	576	.833	113	369	482	352	140	44	166	2431	5.9	4.3	29.6
97–98	Chi	82	3,181	881	1,893	.465	565	721	.784	130	345	475	283	141	45	185	2357	5.8	3.5	28.7
98–99	—								Did not play—retired											
99–00	—								Did not play—retired											
00–01	—								Did not play—retired											
01–02	Was	60	2,093	551	1,324	.416	263	333	.790	50	289	339	310	85	26	—	1375	5.7	5.2	22.9
02–03	Was	82	3,031	679	1,527	.445	266	324	.821	71	426	497	311	123	39	—	1640	6.1	3.8	20.0
Total		1,072	41,011	12,192	24,537	.497	7,327	8,772	.835	1,668	5,004	6,672	5,633	2,514	893	2,924	32,292	6.2	5.3	30.1

THREE-POINT FIELD GOALS: 1984–85, 9-for-52 (.173); 1985–86, 3-for-18 (.167); 1986–87, 12-for-66 (.182); 1987–88, 7-for-53 (.132); 1988–89, 27-for-98 (.276); 1989–90, 92-for-245 (.376); 1990–91, 29-for-93 (.312); 1991–92, 27-for-100 (.270); 1992–93, 81-for-230 (.352); 1994–95, 16-for-32 (.500); 1995–96, 111-for-260 (.427); 1996–97, 111-for-297 (.374); 1997–98, 30-for-126 (.238); 2001–02, 10-for-53 (.189); 2002–03, 16-for-55 (.291). Total: 581-for-1778 (.327).

PERSONAL FOULS/DISQUALIFICATIONS: 1984–85, 285/4; 1985–86, 46/0; 1986–87, 237/0; 1987–88, 270/2; 1988–89, 247/2; 1989–90, 241/0; 1990–91, 229/1; 1991–92, 201/1; 1992–93, 188/0; 1994–95, 47/0; 1995–96, 195/0; 1996–97, 156/0; 1997–98, 151/0; 2001–02, 119/0; 2002–03, 171/1. Total: 2,783/11.

NBA PLAYOFF RECORD

NOTES: NBA Finals Most Valuable Player (1991, 1992, 1993, 1996, 1997, 1998). . . . Holds NBA Finals career records for most three-point field goals made—42; and most consecutive games with 20 or more points—35 (June 2, 1991, through June 14, 1998). . . . Holds NBA Finals single-series record for highest points-per-game average—41.0 (1993). . . . Holds NBA Finals single-game record for most points in one half—35 (June 3, 1992, vs. Portland). . . . Shares NBA Finals single-game records for most field goals made in one half—14; most three-point field goals made in one half—6 (June 3, 1992, vs. Portland); most free throws made in one quarter—9 (June 11, 1997, vs. Utah); and most free throws attempted in one half—15 (June 4, 1997, vs. Utah). . . . Holds career playoff record for most points—5,987; highest points-per-game average (minimum 25 games or 625 points)—33.4; most field goals attempted—4,497; most free throws made—1,463; most free throws attempted—1,766; and most steals—376. . . . Holds single-game playoff records for most points—63 (April 20, 1986, vs. Boston); and most free throws made in one quarter—13 (May 21, 1991, vs. Detroit). . . . Shares single-game playoff records for most field goals made—24 (May 1, 1988, vs. Cleveland); most field goals attempted in one half—25 (May 1, 1988, vs. Cleveland); and most three-point field goals made in one half—6 (June 3, 1992, vs. Portland).

										Rebounds								Averages		
Season	Team	G	Min.	FGM	FGA	Pct	FTM	FTA	Pct	Off	Def	Tot	Ast	St	Blk	TO	Pts	RPG	APG	PPG
84–85	Chi	4	171	34	78	.436	48	58	.828	7	16	23	34	11	4	15	117	5.8	8.5	29.3
85–86	Chi	3	135	48	95	.505	34	39	.872	5	14	19	17	7	4	14	131	6.3	5.7	43.7
86–87	Chi	3	128	35	84	.417	35	39	.897	7	14	21	18	6	7	8	107	7.0	6.0	35.7
87–88	Chi	10	427	138	260	.531	86	99	.869	23	48	71	47	24	11	39	363	7.1	4.7	36.3
88–89	Chi	17	718	199	390	.510	183	229	.799	26	93	119	130	42	13	68	591	7.0	7.6	34.8
89–90	Chi	16	674	219	426	.514	133	159	.836	24	91	115	109	45	14	56	587	7.2	6.8	36.7
90–91	Chi	17	689	197	376	.524	125	148	.845	18	90	108	142	40	23	43	529	6.4	8.4	31.1
91–92	Chi	22	920	290	581	.499	162	189	.857	37	100	137	127	44	16	81	759	6.2	5.8	34.5
92–93	Chi	19	783	251	528	.475	136	169	.805	32	96	128	114	39	17	45	666	6.7	6.0	35.1
94–95	Chi	10	420	120	248	.484	64	79	.810	20	45	65	45	23	14	41	315	6.5	4.5	31.5
95–96	Chi	18	733	187	407	.459	153	187	.818	31	58	89	74	33	6	42	552	4.9	4.1	30.7
96–97	Chi	19	804	227	498	.456	123	148	.831	42	108	150	91	30	17	49	590	7.9	4.8	31.1
97–98	Chi	21	872	243	526	.462	181	223	.812	33	74	107	74	32	12	45	680	5.1	3.5	32.4
Total		179	7,474	2,188	4,497	.487	1,463	1,766	.828	305	847	1,152	1,022	376	158	546	5,987	6.4	5.7	33.4

THREE-POINT FIELD GOALS: 1984–85, 1-for-8 (.125); 1985–86, 1-for-1; 1986–87, 2-for-5 (.400); 1987–88, 1-for-3 (.333); 1988–89, 10-for-35 (.286); 1989–90, 16-for-50 (.320); 1990–91, 10-for-26 (.385); 1991–92, 17-for-44 (.386); 1992–93, 28-for-72 (.389); 1994–95, 11-for-30 (.367); 1995–96, 25-for-62 (.403); 1996–97, 13-for-67 (.194); 1997–98, 13-for-43 (.302). Total: 148-for-446 (.332).

PERSONAL FOULS/DISQUALIFICATIONS: 1984–85, 15/0; 1985–86, 13/1; 1986–87, 11/0; 1987–88, 38/1; 1988–89, 65/1; 1989–90, 54/0; 1990–91, 53/0; 1991–92, 62/0; 1992–93, 58/0; 1994–95, 30/0; 1995–96, 49/0; 1996–97, 46/0; 1997–98, 47/0. Total: 541/3.

NBA ALL-STAR GAME RECORD

NOTES: NBA All-Star Game Most Valuable Player (1988, 1996, 1998). . . . Holds career record for field goals (110), field goal attempts (233), and steals (37). . . . Shares record for most field goal attempts in one game—27 (2003). . . . Recorded only triple-double in All-Star Game history (February 9, 1997).

Paul Ladewski

Rebounds

Season	Team	Min	FGM	FGA	Pct	FTM	FTA	Pct	Off	Def	Tot	Ast	PF	DQ	St	Blk	TO	Pts
1985	Chi	22	2	9	.222	3	4	.750	3	3	6	2	4	0	3	1	1	7
1986	Chi							Selected but did not play—injured										
1987	Chi	28	5	12	.417	1	2	.500	0	0	0	4	2	0	2	0	5	11
1988	Chi	29	17	23	.739	6	6	1.000	3	5	8	3	5	0	4	4	2	40
1989	Chi	33	13	23	.565	2	4	.500	1	1	2	3	1	0	5	0	4	28
1990	Chi	29	8	17	.471	0	0	—	1	4	5	2	1	0	5	1	5	17
1991	Chi	36	10	25	.400	6	7	.857	3	2	5	5	2	0	2	0	10	26
1992	Chi	31	9	17	.529	0	0	—	1	0	1	5	2	0	2	0	1	18
1993	Chi	36	10	24	.417	9	13	.692	3	1	4	5	5	0	4	0	6	30
1996	Chi	22	8	11	.727	4	4	1.000	1	3	4	1	1	0	1	0	0	20
1997	Chi	26	5	14	.357	4	7	.571	3	8	11	11	4	0	2	0	3	14
1998	Chi	32	10	18	.556	2	3	.667	1	5	6	8	0	0	3	0	2	23
2002	Was	22	4	13	.308	0	0	—	0	4	4	3	1	0	2	0	—	8
2003	Was	36	9	27	.333	2	2	1.000	2	3	5	2	3	0	2	0	—	20
Total		382	110	233	.472	39	52	.750	22	39	61	54	31	0	37	6	42	262

THREE-POINT FIELD GOALS: 1985, 0-for-1; 1987, 0-for-1; 1989, 0-for-1; 1990, 1-for-1; 1991, 0-for-2; 1993, 1-for-2; 1998, 1-for-1; 2003, 0-for-2. Total: 3-for-11 (.273).

Chapter Six

JASON KIDD—Guard

Selflessness and Sacrifice

by Steve Popper

It was the moment that you dream of when you're on a playground or in a driveway as a child. The defining moment, the seventh game, and Jason Kidd finally faced it in a noisy Palace of Auburn Hills.

But the dreams never happened like this. Kidd, whose career had been built on speed, on outracing the opposition from end to end on sprints, was hobbled. He had injured his knee in the opening game of the season and fought his way through the regular

season, pushing off surgery for the summer and trying every way possible to heal his knee enough to get on the court.

The 2004 Eastern Conference Semifinals had come down to one last chance for Kidd. He had seen the Nets fall short in the NBA Finals in each of the two years prior, and he was determined to do whatever he could this time. And in the postseason he persevered, gritting his teeth through the pain and playing an average of thirty-nine minutes in every one of the first ten playoff games, including a fifty-seven-minute epic earlier in the series against the Detroit Pistons.

And now he could barely make it onto the court. His knee ached. He was hiding a back ailment that arose from trying to compensate for the knee. The Pistons knew what Kidd was struggling through and ran him endlessly through brutal picks, piling on and punishing him every single minute he played.

This story does not end with a magical performance. It ends with reality. Kidd was a decoy at best, and as the minutes wore on, not a good one. He endured the first scoreless postseason game of his career, taking eight shots and missing them all. The Nets called timeout with two minutes and twenty-six seconds remaining in the game and the season—in what would be the last moments of the Nets' run at the top of the Eastern Conference—and Lawrence Frank called Brandon Armstrong into the huddle.

Kidd left the floor and went to the bench unceremoniously, without hugs or high-fives from his teammates. But when the game was over, what he had earned was a level of respect that a high-flying dunk or even his own breathtaking passes would not have earned him.

"Jason Kidd is the toughest freaking guy you'll ever meet," Frank said. "He gave it everything he had, and it doesn't matter about the points. The guy does so many other things. He's a Hall of Fame player. As a team, it just wasn't our night."

For Kidd, it was the night he had waited for, and it turned out to be the harshest night of his career.

"The whole year, after the first game, I was on one leg," Kidd explained. "But just knowing I could play gave my teammates the sense of security. They all knew the situation I was in, but I was going to go out there and play—maybe not score, but I knew I could try to help in other ways so we would have a chance.

"I'll take the criticism of not playing my best. I'll take that criticism knowing that my teammates understand the situation and I understand. The bigger picture is if I take that criticism, then one of my teammates can go out there without that and play hard."

And that, not the game-winning shot, was really the defining moment for Kidd. That he carried his team one more time when he could hardly hold himself up was little surprise to anyone who knew him. Kidd was scoreless on that night, but points are not what he's really ever been about.

Kidd has lifted his team in so many ways that the Nets seemed shocked afterward that he had not somehow shrugged off the reality of the situation and poured in points or whatever it was that his team needed.

"He's borderline Superman, but he's not Superman," Frank said. "The bottom line is this—you do whatever it takes to help the team win. Sometimes that means you sacrifice your shot-making because you're doing so many other things. That's what the great players do. You look at many of the great players in the history of this game— it was their commitment to winning and sacrificing and doing whatever it took."

There was a time when Kidd won games in other ways. He was thirteen years old, so young, but a big man playing the game. He was scoring at a prolific rate, topping forty points a game and drawing crowds already, dominating the game on the inside and flashing the sort of high-wire acrobatics that deserted him before he ever made it to the National Basketball Association.

But his game turned, slowly starting with defensive rebounds that would lead to length-of-the-court outlet passes. Then there was a prescient coach who saw the skills in the big man and moved him to point guard. Almost immediately a steady growth began, and he was transformed into a player who now has become the visible presence of the team game, one who sees the floor and brings players with him on an unselfish and hardworking path to victory.

"I think he gets more thrill out of rebounding, playing defense, and making a pass than anything else," said Willis Reed, a Hall of Fame player who was with the Nets organization when Kidd arrived.

"Those are the things that really excite him in the game. You see some of the passes he throws—they're phenomenal. I think what he brought to that team was his ability to work hard on the defense, create opportunities out of the defensive end for the offensive end. I think he is a throwback kind of player. We don't have many like him.

"He can dominate without having to score, but I'll tell you what: I really think that in the fourth quarter I would not bet against him when he comes down and needs a big shot. I've seen him too many times take a big shot in order for them to win big games."

"I'll sacrifice an MVP award for us to win," Kidd said. "If I could only average ten points for the rest of my career, I would do that to win. Whatever it takes to win. Whatever the team needs. If they need me to rebound more, then I'll try to go in and rebound more. If it's shoot more, or pass more, whatever. If it's to be a decoy, that's the name of the game, to be able to give yourself up for the sake of the team. That's what I want to give to these other guys. Some nights you've got to give yourself up—it's not your night. And you know what, that'll make you a better player at the end of your career. You're going to pass that on to somebody else."

Growing up in Oakland, Kidd might have been more famous than he is now. He has said that in high school at St. Joseph's of Notre Dame he was shoulder to shoulder with Joe Montana as the most famous athlete in the Bay Area. Before LeBron, before nonstop highlights played across television screens of increasingly younger and younger players, Kidd was a superstar draw carrying the hopes of a city.

Playing in youth league tournaments, he would have to be slipped out the back door of the gymnasium with autograph seekers, teenage girls, and street agents fighting for a piece of him. His high school games were moved to various colleges and then to the Oakland Coliseum Arena, where a crowd that rivals NBA game crowds filed in to see the phenom, the attention and applause following his every move.

"It was for everything," Kidd said. "For the passes, for the scoring, dunking. It came with whatever I did. As I got older, in high school, it became bigger and bigger. So whatever I did, anytime I took the floor, a lot of people would express themselves, I guess."

"At the time you're going through it you think it's normal," Jason's mother Anne said. "It didn't happen overnight. He was excelling in sports from the get-go, and you get used to it. Then you get used to the next level. But it got bigger and bigger. Still, it always seemed like this is how it should be. He sold out the Coliseum in high school for games. You get used to it."

Gordon Johnson, now head coach at the University of California at Santa Cruz, was an assistant coach at St. Joseph's during Kidd's time there and saw him come up through elementary school.

"The first thing you saw was that he was very dominating, but he had an awareness that you didn't see in a lot of kids," Johnson said. "You saw that he really enjoyed the game, really had a passion for playing, always played with a smile. The way he played the game you could see it was something that he loved to do.

"He played five positions back then in the CYO league, and the funny part was, he never started the game. Every kid had to play, so Jason wouldn't start, but then he'd play the final three quarters. He'd come in the game, and you'd see the game change. They were blowing kids out, and he could have scored forty anytime he wanted, but what caught my attention was that he enjoyed distributing the basketball."

When the staff at St. Joseph's got him at the high school level, it was little surprise that state championships followed. But the task for the coaches was twofold: to continue Kidd's growth as a player and a leader, while also trying to keep him focused on the floor.

"It was crazy," Johnson said. "The big thing that we had to do, the hardest thing, was trying to shelter him from the people with their hands out, trying to get stuff, to befriend him, so he understood who were his real friends.

"A lot of times I would take him home after practice—I worked at the naval base as athletic director, and I would bring him with me and make him do his homework. Then after that we'd reward him with playing on the floor. I took him to every Stanford game his freshman year. They had Todd Lichti, who was my former player, and Jason was being chased by every person, but he would stand there and study the game. He would ask questions—why did they make this pass, why was that done, constantly absorbing stuff.

"Then he'd come over to my house on the weekend. I have a son who was a few years younger than Jason, and they'd play video games, but usually Jason would say, 'Coach, can you put the game film on?' He'd study things going on on the floor, and the good thing was he was continually asking questions, asking me to run it back, constantly absorbing. Then you'd see him in practice doing those things."

Joe Nelson, who would go on to become a major league pitcher, played beside Kidd in the backcourt at St. Joseph's.

"He worked real hard at his craft," Nelson recalled. "Jason had God-given ability, but nobody was in the gym more than he was. The dedication, for a guy like that to have it when you're going to be an eight-time All-Star, whatever he is, that all started when he was a kid. Jason worked his ass off, and he didn't need to. But he treated everybody the exact same way whether they were a student or his teammates. He's the type of guy you wanted your daughter to bring home. He treats people—and the game—with respect.

"He's a better player now—he's a man—but he hasn't changed his game. He's still about open passes and running. He physically thinks he can run you down for four quarters just like he did in high school. And he's proven that. You watch forty-eight minutes a game, there is no one working harder on both ends. He doesn't take off on defense. He doesn't take off on that end. Foul line to foul line, he runs as good as anyone I've ever seen. That hasn't changed. That's the thing you can say—he hasn't changed as a person."

But his lessons were not learned only at St. Joseph's. When those games were done, when the AAU tournament schedule allowed a moment, Kidd was on a court learning the other sides of the game. A child a little bigger than most, able to jump a little higher, scoring at pinball-like rates, Jason Kidd would find a game wherever he could. He would walk down the hill from his Oakland, California, home, and kids from other towns and cities would come to the court, knowing that was where the game was.

"They would find a schoolyard that had a good hoop that wasn't broken," Jason's mother Anne recalled. "We lived in an area that was available, so kids would come. Grass Valley School—everybody knew that was where the game was.

"We were on the outside of Oakland, and he'd go looking for competition. He was maybe twelve, thirteen years old, and he'd go to where the kids were playing street ball. He'd go to the middle of Oakland, maybe five miles away. He always found a way to get to where he wanted to go. We drove him to a baseball game in the morning, then a basketball game in another city in the afternoon. And then he'd want to play more, and he'd always find a way to get there."

Most of the lessons learned came from a man Jason still refers to with a smile as Mr. Mean—Al Payton, the father of Gary Payton. A few years older than Jason, Gary Payton was everything that Jason aspired to be, an unstoppable point guard who dominated the game on both ends of the court.

"Jason patterned himself after Gary, wanted to be as good as Gary," Jason's mother said. "And he played as hard and long as he did until he was."

But Jason never could really be like Gary. The younger Payton was an effusive, trash-talking tough guy built into a string-bean body. Jason was quiet—his actions spoke loudly, but his voice was barely audible. Since neither of his parents had been athletes, they hadn't provided him with any hint or preparation for what was to come, but his late father, Steve, did anything he could to facilitate Jason's path. He accompanied his son to every sporting event he could. But he wasn't a basketball man. So he placed Jason in the hands of Al Payton.

"My father might have played a little football, but that was it," Jason said. "He was a cowboy. He enjoyed the horses, that was his background. He understood horses better than anybody. He probably did ask Mr. Payton, if my son was going down this road, if he could help in any way. Mr. Mean could do that."

Jason's father approached him "around the fourth or fifth grade," Al Payton recalled. "His father was very fond of the kid. He used to film all the games. He filmed; me and another coach coached the games. Jason was a little different kid than the other kids on the team. He wasn't on the streets. Wherever he went, his father was with him. That's the way I was too.

"When Jason played basketball, going on traveling trips, he would room in my room with my son Gary. He didn't talk a lot. He never got angry. On the court, I don't care how he got fouled, he was the All-American boy. No matter what happened, he wasn't a fighter. I used to get on him about being tough. He was a soft kid, wasn't like the rest. He didn't talk. He just played basketball. He was very respectful. To this day he's a very nice young man."

But between Gary and Al Payton, he learned.

"I was sort of a trash-talker myself," the elder Payton added. "I talk a lot of trash. In Oakland you have to talk trash. I used to get on Jason about that. The only time he'd talk was when I'd make him. Kids would pick on you. His dad wanted him with me to learn. I did the talking for him. I had three boys, and they knew to talk, to speak up for themselves. Jason's father wasn't like that.

"Jason wanted to be Gary in being tough. He always played against Gary. In the summer he always came and played with Gary. They played at camp. He had a lot of respect for Gary and would hang out with Gary. They ran around together, but I told him, 'You can't be Gary. Gary is different.' "

Kidd had lessons to learn not just in his demeanor and in his play, but in handling the hype that surrounded him.

"He was a kid who, after each game, we had to slip him out the back," Payton said. "When he was in high school, kids would be crowded around him for his autograph. I couldn't believe it. The only way we'd get him away was slip him out the back door. He couldn't go to a game. People in the stands, they wore that number 5. Kids wore his jersey when he was in high school. He was like Michael Jordan already."

Jason grew tougher at the hands of Al Payton—not louder, but steely in his resolve. He still showed his teammates by playing harder, by not backing down. His game grew, and as strange as it may sound, while schoolmates were wearing his jersey and applauding him, Kidd learned by slipping on a pair of sneakers and dreaming that he was the player whose name was scripted onto the side of the shoe.

"One of the things then was to be able to wear shoes of a different player," Kidd said. "Like Magic Johnson, the Weapon with Converse, the New Balances were James Worthy. Whoever's shoes I had on, that's who I felt I was. If it was New Balance, I thought I was James Worthy. If you had on the Nikes, you thought you were Jordan. The Converse, you thought you were Magic or Larry Bird. So that's what I really tried. When I had those different types of shoes on, I tried to emulate those guys."

But during his high school days Kidd put away the dreams of being the next James Worthy or Kareem Abdul-Jabbar. He had been the big man all his life, a player who dominated the boards and scored inside, with a flourish.

"He was the only kid in the seventh, eighth grade who was dunking," Al Payton said. "He dunked everything. When he'd get the ball on the breakaway, he was the man. He could flush it real hard. He was way over the rim. You knew it was a dunk. He would tear the rim down."

You hear the stories and you wonder—is this the same player who gently lays the ball in now, whose teammates tease him about his inability to dunk?

"I've known Jason since I was eleven years old growing up in California," said Jason Collins, his New Jersey Nets teammate. "I used to go to AAU tournaments, and he would be in high school and I'd be in the same tournament, obviously in a younger division, but I remember going to his games and just seeing what a great player he was. Back then he could jump, I always kidded him, he was doing reverse double-pumps, throwing it off the backboard, so he was crazy. As athletic as he is now, he was even more athletic back then."

"I would do everything that people do today," Kidd said. "I don't know where it went. It left in a hurry. The thing was, playing down there, playing against the best players in California, being able to throw it off the backboard, being a point guard and having somebody throw me an alley-oop, was something that I enjoyed doing. Playing above the rim, that was fun. Those are the type of things I love, used to love to do."

"He hasn't changed. He can dunk on anybody," Nelson said. "Guaranteed, he could go up anytime he wants on the baseline and put it down. He chooses not to. He finishes with his left hand still now because our coach in high school put that into him."

But Kidd brought his game from the pits to the perimeter, moving from the frontcourt to point guard. It was a simple decision in eighth grade. The team's point guard moved on and the position was open, so the athletic player who ran the floor and dunked, who tossed length-of-the-court outlets, got the ball in his hands.

When the lessons weren't coming in the gym, Kidd, like so many others, watched on television, learning by osmosis as he scouted the best players a generation ahead of him.

"I grew up watching Magic," he said. "I hope I don't make him feel old, but Mark Jackson too. I'd watch *Big Monday* on ESPN. It would be four-thirty on the West Coast. Being able to watch Georgetown and St. John's play, being able to watch those guys play, trying to emulate what they did, and at the same time watching Magic and being able to go to Golden State games, watching Tim Hardaway and those guys play. It was not so much picking up their shooting or anything other than watching a point guard, how they played."

The natural evolution of a lineage running from Bob Cousy through Oscar Robertson and Magic Johnson, Kidd emerged almost immediately as something unique and precious—a true point guard. He could score, a point that he'd already proven as a youth. But as he began to pass the ball, he quickly became a special talent, and the fans still jumped out of their seats, scouts and agents joining in the frenzy. Standing out in a world full of scorers, Kidd quickly found he could dominate the game without scoring a point.

"I think everybody was doing that, looking to score as many as they could and catch someone's eye," Kidd said. "Everybody felt that if they scored or were the best scorer, they would be picked first, so I kind of went the other way. I was the one who said, somebody has to get those guys the ball at some point. That's just the way I went. Those guys were older than I was, so that's the only way I thought I could get into the game was by being able to pass to the 'A' player. And at times, with the passing came something else—they thought I would always pass the ball, so then I would be able to get layups. Then guys really felt I could play with those guys."

The transition from youth to the NBA began on those playgrounds and in the uniform of St. Joe's, but what Kidd showed at that time were hints of what was to come. Nets' president Rod Thorn remembers the first time he saw Kidd play.

"It was on television," Thorn said. "He was a senior in high school, and he was playing in a game that was on national TV from someplace in Arkansas. Corliss Williamson was on the other team, and Jason's team lost. But the thing I remembered was, he never made a jump shot and he was all over the place, stealing balls, making assists, getting rebounds, making some layups. He was very athletic, but his energy level is what stood out. He was constantly in motion."

While the hops may have abandoned him, that speed never really did. Even as his knees have succumbed to the pounding and grind of a schedule that has spanned from season to postseason to international competition, he is still a fearsome sight barreling across the court with the ball in front of him and moving at a pace no other player can touch. But somehow he is always in control too, seeing things as if they are frozen in time.

"You could see in high school what a great point guard he was," Collins said. "Playing for the same club team, at a younger age group, you'd always hear stories about how unselfish he was and what a great player he was. Then having him as my point guard now, knowing if you run the floor, if you get open, if you work, you set screens, he's going to find you. He followed Magic Johnson's role of looking to pass first.

"He's the best point guard in the NBA, and it's because of his intangibles, his court vision, his court awareness. Playing with him, you appreciate that even more. What he sees out there on the court, his court awareness, is the best I've ever seen. He's the kind of player who just makes everybody around him better."

If it wasn't on that first flickering image on the television, Thorn remembered when he knew that he had to bring Jason Kidd to New Jersey. It wasn't anything that he saw Kidd do as much as what he saw others around him do. Not yet the Nets president, Thorn was serving as the chair of the U.S. Senior Men's Basketball Committee for USA Basketball, overseeing the Team USA men's basketball team prepping for the 2000 Sydney Olympics. As he accompanied the team and helped put together trips to Puerto Rico and Hawaii for tournaments to prep the team for the 2000 Olympics, Thorn saw a common theme developing among the players.

"I don't say he was the most talented player in terms of offensive ability on the team," Thorn recalled. "But he was the guy that you had to have in the game. Everybody wanted to play with him."

"Why wouldn't you?" said Kenyon Martin, Kidd's former Nets' teammate who joined him on Team USA in the qualifying tournament in 2003. "Really, he's a great guy. On and off the court, he's a great teammate. He's the ultimate teammate. He sacrifices everything. He's all about winning. He plays hard every day. Knowing that, if you have those same goals, he's easy to play with. I don't see how anyone couldn't play with him."

After two years at the University of California at Berkeley, Kidd moved on to the NBA. The common denominator when you speak to anyone who saw him from those early days in the church leagues through St. Joseph's High School and then on to Cal and to the Dallas Mavericks, where his professional career began, is that there was very little difference in what you saw from the early product until he arrived.

Even as his skills sharpened and his knowledge of the game grew, the intent was the same from the very start—to make his team better, to make the game simpler, and to win.

"I'll give you a good example," said Johnson, who has seen Kidd from those early steps and remains close to him today. "We had a kid on the team who came off the bench. He wasn't real fast. He was really a slow kid, but he handled the ball well. Jason would tell us, 'Move me to the two,' so that he could make sure that this kid got on the floor. He'd move wherever he could to make certain kids got the chance and could give the team something it would flourish from.

"He understood the different strengths of players and the team. I still see that stuff today. With Jason, everybody gets something. He doesn't like to see somebody not get something."

Early in the 2004–05 season, Kidd was on a break in Atlanta, alone ahead of the pack. The easy two points would be adding on to his career totals, numbers for the Hall of Fame to post under his bust. But he waited and handed the ball off to Jabari Smith, a player who seemed unlikely to finish the season with the Nets, or even to finish the season in the league at all.

"He's always giving love to his teammates," Frank said. "It just lifts your teammates. Everyone wants to play with a guy who makes them better. Why do people want to play with Jason Kidd? Because he makes them better.

"It goes back to Jordan passing the ball to Paxson, Jordan passing the ball to Kerr. Those were the biggest situations you could have, but they passed the ball. Why? Because the defense told them to. So it's trust in your teammates. That's just contagious, when your best players trust everyone else. Everyone likes to be loved."

"It's just to make the game easy," Kidd said. "I never try to change because of who the guy is. Just play one way so I don't confuse my teammates or send them any different messages. As much as I believe in Vince Carter, I believe in Jabari Smith. If they can sense that, they'll go out and bust their butt."

His star had already risen by the time he was traded to the New Jersey Nets in July 2001. He was already a four-time All-Star, a three-time All-NBA first-teamer, and an Olympian. But he was still growing. Even if the physical part had been in place and the unselfishness was the main weapon in his arsenal, there was still something missing.

There were still some gripes and problems in his stops in Dallas and Phoenix. When he left them behind with the trade to New Jersey, he arrived in the Garden State as the purest leader the franchise had ever known, the one player who could turn around an organization plagued by a history of dysfunction and disarray.

Kidd arrived in New Jersey, flying cross-country immediately after the birth of his twin daughters, just in time to settle in for the team dinner the night before the start of training camp. The team gathered at the Renaissance Meadowlands Hotel across from Continental Airlines Arena. Some of the players and the entire coaching staff were left over from a 26–56 season, the latest disaster in a history in which that had been the norm.

"I think in Dallas I was too young," Kidd said. "In Phoenix I was learning, and I was surrounded by a lot of great players, Kevin Johnson, Danny Manning, Wayman Tisdale, guys I respected, so there was no room for me. This was my training ground to become a leader. That's why when I came here, there was an emptiness. Where does this team want to go? I wanted to keep winning. I believed when the trade happened that we could be a successful team, but if these guys didn't believe that, it wasn't going to work. Those guys believed it after that first meeting we had before the first day of training camp. Those guys were on board."

And that was it really. Not in a fiery speech, not in a physical confrontation, and not in the fire of a game. In a dinner that is usually an uneventful opportunity for coaches to wish-list the season to come, Kidd took a franchise on his back and changed what no coach or star before him had been able to.

"Our first meeting, Joumana gave birth to the twins, and he flies in for the first team meeting, and what he does, he goes around the room and introduces himself to everybody—like we don't know who he is," said Nets coach Lawrence Frank, who was an assistant at that time. "He introduces himself to everyone, goes one by one to everyone in the room. Then he talked at the dinner, a couple things, and he set the tone for how we were going to be as a team."

The Nets had assembled a team that was built around Kidd but included three key players coming off of injuries—Kenyon Martin, Kerry Kittles, and Keith Van Horn had all missed significant time—and a quartet of rookies who carried few expectations of immediate success. Kidd told the team—and then the media the next day—that the team would win at least forty games and be a contender for a playoff berth. In the Nets world that was akin to Joe Namath sitting in the lounge chair poolside predicting a Super Bowl III victory. That the team actually won fifty-two games and the first Eastern Conference title in team history was a show that materialized before disbelieving eyes even within the organization.

"I think I was putting myself out on a limb to see who was going to jump on board," Kidd said, now laughing at the recollection. "The thing was that they had talent. It was just a matter of knowing how to win. Letting it be contagious that winning is fun, that with fun comes success, and with success you get everything you want to accomplish. For them to believe meant, one, I had to be respected, because anybody can get up and say anything, but if you're not respected, then it's not going to happen. I thought I *was* respected, that I had paid my dues. It was going to work or it wasn't going to work. There was no in between."

And when he made his prediction, Kidd wasn't so sure that he was right, having never seen this newly revamped team in action.

"I was nervous the first practice because I didn't know what to expect," he admitted.

He *was* right, though. Even though they were rookies, he knew Jason Collins from California and had met Richard Jefferson when he ran camps in Arizona and Jefferson had worked them. He put the pressure on the team, sure, but what he really did was put it on himself. That was a big difference. And the pressure didn't faze him.

"He went public with the amount of wins we'd get," Frank said. "Basically just saying, 'We're going to be together, we can do this together, we have to trust each other.' That was the biggest point—trust."

"Just coming in, predicting how many wins we'd get, that we were going to make the playoffs, it showed that he cared," Kenyon Martin said. "It showed that he cared about winning—no matter what it took, it was all about winning.

"When he was in Dallas, I was in high school and I saw him all the time. I knew how good he was. But I didn't know the kind of guy he was. Lucious Harris told me when I first heard about the trade, 'You will love playing with him.' Lu let me know, but I had no idea. That first year he just made everybody play so much harder. That was R.J.'s rookie year, along with [Collins and Brian Scalabrine]. We had some new faces, but guys knew what it was going to take. Guys knew that they had to play hard. Everybody came into training camp and worked hard. We knew from then what it was going to be."

It actually started before that meeting. When a trade goes down in any sport—and particularly one like this one, which culminated after bitter feelings between the Suns and Kidd had boiled over—it would never be a surprise if the player involved sulked over the deal and hid away from the press and his new team.

But when the trade was made, Kidd set about starting something in New Jersey where few believed he could. He spoke with Gordon

Johnson, picking apart the Nets roster and finding promise where few had. And why would anyone believe it? The Nets, to acquire Kidd, had surrendered their own franchise talent, Stephon Marbury, a point guard who was among the most skilled offensive players in the game. Why would things be any different simply by exchanging star players who manned the same position?

Kidd settled that question quickly by quietly inviting Lawrence Frank out to Phoenix. Unable to come to New Jersey with his wife facing a difficult pregnancy, he instead brought the unheralded assistant to his home and began his indoctrination into the Nets system.

"I went up there, spent five days with him when we traded for him," Frank said. "I stayed at his house, and we worked out every day, and right there I knew how special he was because it's September, not too long after September 11, and I went there, and he just worked his tail off. You're just going on, I knew he was all-pro. He studied film and we did drills, really worked. But his approach to do that, plus just how giving he was dealing with all the people, you learn a lot about people when you stay with them and see how they deal with their family and friends. Just how giving [he is], and his demeanor and how people responded to him, I got a feel for him there."

When Kidd arrived in New Jersey, the cast was set as soon as he walked into the first dinner.

"From day one," Byron Scott said. "The day he walked in our meeting, that day everybody knew he was the leader of this team. Everybody accepted that. Not only did they accept that—he accepted it. Some people don't want to be leaders in his position. Some guys run away from that leadership role. I thought he embraced it, and when he did that, the other guys were right behind him.

"That's what you need. If your best player is a guy who works his butt off in practice, plays hard every single game, that's all you need, because that's your example right there. You don't have to, as a coach, preach to these guys about going out and practicing hard, working hard in a game, because they see it on an everyday basis. As long as they see it in him, half your job is done."

Scott Skiles, who coached Kidd in Phoenix and burns with a visible passion as both a player and a coach, saw the change coming from the time Kidd began with the Suns until he departed. He saw little emerge in New Jersey that he didn't believe was already in place.

"Early on in Phoenix, when he first got there," Skiles said, "he was not that great of a practice player. But he gradually became one. He was still a young player at that point, and he started realizing the importance of leadership, and to his credit it was nothing that anyone did with the Suns. He did it, and he really became a guy that you could depend on and a guy that you had to pull back, tell him not to practice sometimes.

"Everybody grows as people, and people always want to force leadership on a certain guy. It just has to happen naturally. I think that what happened with Jason is over time he's just sort of naturally developed into one of these guys.

"And he can also play at that crazy level, and now you do have to pay attention to what he's saying," Skiles added. "He can take it to a level in instances that few people can take it to from an energy standpoint and a competitive standpoint. When he really turns it up, there just aren't that many guys that can take it to that level against him. So when you're playing with him and you see him go there, you can't help but lift your own level of play."

Vince Carter had already made his own place in the game when he was traded to the Nets. He'd already been an All-Star, an Olympian, a prolific scorer. But he was also saddled with his own labels and warts.

The best player ever paired with Kidd, Carter had never quite lived up to the accolades he earned in Toronto. In New Jersey he had damage control to navigate, and there was no better player to guide him through it than Kidd.

"If you go on reputation, a lot of people wouldn't want to be playing or coaching or shouldn't be in the league," Kidd said. "You find out personally, firsthand, and you can make your own decision about somebody. Most of the time it turns out to be the opposite of what people say."

Kidd took Carter into his confidence, into the Nets family—a team that had made its own way over the previous three seasons experiencing more success than Carter had ever seen—and dipped out of the spotlight himself. He made room for Carter to score—surrendering the attention but never the leadership.

His task as the team captain and the heart and soul of his team has always been to make the universe revolve around him—to bring the players together. He has done it with young players like Richard Jefferson, Kenyon Martin, and Shawn Marion, with veterans like Kerry Kittles and Lucious Harris, and with stars like Carter. And he has had to make it all work together.

"It's just trial-and-error to find out what you have to put in different situations to see how people respond," Kidd said. "That's one way to find somebody's character, and it could be good or bad. I think to be a good teammate you have to think first about the team, and then you try to make the game as easy as possible, as stress-free as possible."

There is little argument that Kidd is a great teammate—maybe the greatest teammate of his era. But he has found himself in the crosshairs of the media at times as he has sought out the best players to ride beside him. His goal is the title that has eluded him throughout his career, and he has shuttled through three franchises trying to find it.

But while he might have lusted for a Tim Duncan or a Kevin Garnett to finish his passes off, he has embraced the Brian Scalabrines and Lucious Harrises, the same way he embraced the lesser talents on his high school team and brought them along for the ride.

"You don't lose confidence because you need everybody," Kidd said. "No matter what the situation is, you'll find out that you're going to need somebody when it becomes crucial. If you've already made that person feel like you don't believe in him, then things won't work out. That's the first step—make sure you make your teammates feel welcome and that you believe in them as much as you believe in the stars.

"I think it's a lot of little things—being able to communicate, talk to your teammates. When things are going bad, you have to find a positive. Never give up until the game is over. All those little things make a good teammate."

"He's just a leader," Carter said. "In games, in practice, period. He works hard. In games he gets respect from the players because of who he is, but he does extra things. I knew that before, but playing with him, it's unreal."

It is not just the stars of the NBA who saw it. In high school he played the game the same way.

"Jason would steal the ball in the frontcourt, and he would just wait, let the guy hound him a little bit, and give it up," Nelson said. "He would find a way to make the crowd come to life, and it didn't have to be his doing. A guy like me, if I was filling the lane and he's got twenty-seven points and I've got two, he'd stop, feed it to me, and then he'd follow me just in case I missed because he wants the team to win. He would do that to everybody. Jason is the only player in the country—then and now—who can dominate a game and score six points. He will do that, and you will walk away from the arena saying, 'I've just seen the best basketball player I've ever seen.' Amazing."

If the dream did not come true for Jason Kidd in that seventh game against Detroit, it was one of the few times in his life that it hadn't. Just a year earlier, Kidd calmly stood at the top of the key, dribbling the ball and not even looking at the action unfolding in front of him. He was just waiting.

It was the first game of the 2003 Eastern Conference Finals in Detroit, and the sound was deafening at the Palace of Auburn Hills as the clock ticked down to ten seconds remaining in the game. Byron Scott, the Nets coach, waved for the play to begin and the bodies began to shift into motion. Richard Jefferson cleared out of the right corner. Kenyon Martin appeared momentarily, posting up Mehmet Okur, and then he left too.

Everyone departed, clearing out the right side of the court. The play, the game, maybe the season, was going to end in Jason Kidd's hands. He drove to the right, blowing by Detroit's Chauncey Billups and approaching Okur, who drifted out toward him in the corner. By the time Kidd reached the baseline, he was leaning backward, lofting a prayer over the outstretched arms of the seven-foot Okur, and Kidd could not even see where the shot landed. What he could see were his young teammates celebrating, and he could hear the groan of the entire crowd at the Palace.

"We knew he was going to make it all along," Jefferson said. "I wasn't even trying to rebound. J-Kidd is unbelievable. That's why he's one of the greatest players in the NBA. That's why he is a future Hall of Famer. When you need him, no matter how he's been shooting all night, he's going to knock down the big one for you."

But Kidd did not join any of the celebrations but quietly headed back on defense. And then when the game was over, he changed the subject.

"You want the ball down in crunch time, to be involved, if not with the shot, then passing to someone who is open," Kidd said. "The opportunity presented itself, and I finally made one."

When Kidd arrived in New Jersey, Byron Scott had seen this before. He had played alongside Magic Johnson in Los Angeles, winning championships propelled by Johnson's charisma as well as his talent. It was different and it was the same somehow—Kidd never displayed the ebullient demeanor of Johnson, but led just the same.

"Just playing with Earvin showed me a lot about his character," Scott said. "Jason has a lot of the same characteristics. Jason has a knack for hitting big shots and taking them. He doesn't mind being a goat or the hero. It takes a special player to be like that, because sometimes you're not going to make that shot. He has a way of helping his teammates become better basketball players because he's willing to sacrifice a part of his game for the betterment of not only the players but the team. I saw those things very early. I saw it when he was in college, saw it when he was in high school, and obviously when he got to the pros.

"They are not much different, to be honest. Magic and Jason have a lot in common, especially on the court, because they do make people better. Magic was a lot more vocal, maybe even more animated than J-Kidd. J-Kidd sometimes is mild-mannered. But you'll still see him bring guys to the side. It could be Kenyon or Richard or it might be Brian Scalabrine or Zoran [Planinic]. They make guys better, and they make guys aware of what's going on on the basketball court."

Frank, who took over the Nets for Scott, agreed, adding: "I think everywhere he's been he's done that. Shawn Marion—look what he did to him. He understands what a job being a leader, not only a veteran, is, taking young guys under his wing because they look to him. They respond to him. He's the pied piper. They're going to follow him. He sets such good examples. Think about it, as a coach—your best player is your hardest worker, and he's your most unselfish player. You're going to be good."

Part of Kidd's leadership lies in his love of the game, love of all the games really. It is early in the afternoon at Continental Arena, and the place is nearly empty, with only a few workers preparing for the game to come more than two hours later. Still, a half hour before players are required to arrive, Kidd is on the court shooting, going through drills with the assistant coaches and a handful of other players who constitute the injured reserve list and the end of the bench. But he is working as hard as those who are trying to catch a coach's eye.

His influence runs from his emerging-star teammates to the end of the roster, and there is not a player on the team who dissents when it comes to acknowledging Kidd's leadership.

"I think it comes down to understanding, at the end of the day, it's just about winning," Kidd said of his own leadership style. "No matter how many points you score. There are a lot of examples. You could be 1-for-10, but if I see you're open, you're going to get the ball, and I believe you're going to make it no matter what those other nine shots were or what you've done beforehand. And if you dropped the ball and you're wide open, I'm going to throw it right back to you if you're open again.

"I think the confidence, that's what I always want to share with my teammates. I have just as much confidence in those guys as they have when they're relying on me to do something, and it becomes contagious. Making them better, it goes hand in hand with confidence. If they don't catch the ball, then they don't make me look good. If I don't have confidence in those guys, they won't have the confidence in me, and that's where it all starts."

And where did that start?

"I think it's just Jason's makeup," his mother said. "That's his personality. He was born with it. He definitely knows what he wants. Winning is what he wants. He would want everyone to want it as much as he wants it. He finds his own way by performing on the court. He puts out over 100 percent every game, so how could a player not try to match that and survive in the league?

"I think players help Jason stay that way. He sees the accomplishments. I watch him now, and it reminds me of when he was in grade school. They just enjoyed playing with each other. Then in high school, not everyone is a superstar, but in their minds, for that game when they were playing together, they were."

From grade school to the NBA, Kidd has done that. If you look for the trait that makes him great, it is not an infallible shot, the ability to soar, or the destructive force of a Shaquille O'Neal. It is simply that he makes those around him better.

"I think Bob Cousy, Magic Johnson, and Oscar Robertson, in the pantheon of the game, are guys that really stand out," Thorn said. "I think Jason is right up there. Magic was so big and so charismatic and his team did so great, he rightfully got a bunch of credit. Cousy was the first of the guys who were creative, [who] could do things off the dribble. He was precursor to the great smaller points. Oscar, he did everything, he was in another category.

"Kidd, everywhere the guy goes the team gets a lot better because he brings to the table those things he brings. He's not the best shooter in the world, but he scores when you need it. He can defend, particularly when the game is on the line. He's one of the best rebounding guards. He does all those intangible things. He just does everything."

"I just try to make the game easy," Kidd countered. "Maybe that's where I get in trouble—a lot of the hard stuff looks easy and maybe I should make it look hard. But that's the thing, make it simple, that's always been my MO, never try to do anything that you don't want to do. It's kind of like Barry Sanders—you never see him celebrate. When he scored a touchdown, he gave the ball to the ref and went back and sat down. That's just the way I am."

When Jason Kidd was deciding on a college to attend, he was wooed by every major program, and at the eleventh hour he shocked observers by deciding to stay close to home and join Cal's Golden

Bears. It was a school without a hint of the history or prestige that every other finalist held.

It was a lesson to be learned, one in which history could have foreshadowed the future. In the summer of 2003, Kidd was faced with a decision. After leading the Nets to the NBA Finals in each of his two seasons in New Jersey, he was a free agent and was being recruited hard by the team that had just bested him for the championship, the San Antonio Spurs. Tim Duncan, his friend and arguably the best big man in the game, was pitching him on San Antonio the same way the college recruiters had come at him.

And when everyone was convinced that Kidd was being fitted for a Spurs uniform, Kidd gave the word. He was staying in New Jersey.

"The underdogs," he said, summing up his reasoning in staying home to help a team like Cal burst onto the national scene and his decision to remain in New Jersey and pursue a chance to finish what he'd started. "I enjoy the underdog. I like to do that, like to do it on my own, not so much on my own, but with my team. Going to Cal, I thought they had the right pieces and we had a pretty good run. The last two years here we've had a great run, we've come so close, it would hurt me more to leave and go somewhere else and win than to try to accomplish it here."

JASON KIDD'S PERFECT TEAM

Starters

Guard—Magic Johnson: He revolutionized the point guard position. Magic made the assist as exciting as the slam-dunk. He controlled the game like nobody could and did it with a flair that nobody else had. Magic was such a complete player that he could have led the league in scoring instead of assists all those years. Everyone wanted to play with Magic. He was a true leader and winner.

Guard—Allen Iverson: Allen is the quintessential scorer. To do what Allen does at his size night in and night out is a truly remarkable feat. His quickness and ability are unmatched. Allen has a heart as big as his game, which is why he is such a tremendous player.

Small Forward—Michael Jordan: When you combine the most

talented player with the best work ethic with a hatred for losing, you get the best player to ever play the game. This is what Michael Jordan was to basketball. He simply did things that no other player was capable of doing and did it within the confines of a team concept. Michael was able to dominate a game on both ends of the floor. You are truly special when you are the best player in the league both offensively and defensively. You could not build a perfect team without the perfect player.

Forward—Larry Bird: Every team needs a shooter, and Larry was the best ever. And since my team needs a shooter, I might as well take one that can rebound, pass, and even defend with the best of them. Larry was one of the best clutch players. You could always count on him to make the big basket in the big game. Larry is truly one of the all-time greats and a must for any team. Larry was a proven winner and leader. He made the players around him better.

Center—Bill Russell: He was the first player to truly be able to change the course of the game on defense. He was the ultimate team player and a true champion. Bill Russell was as dominant mentally as he was physically. Opposing players were actually scared when they stepped on the same court with him. Every great team needs that player who gives them that intimidation factor.

Bench

Sixth Man—Scottie Pippen: Mr. All-Around. Scottie was a great player who could do anything you asked him to do on the court. Score, rebound, pass, and defend. He was a true team player who excelled at being a complete player.

Forward—Dennis Rodman: Dennis played the game with such energy and enthusiasm. Dennis was the type of player who you loved to play with and hated to play against. You could always count on Dennis to come up with the big play in a big game. Dennis had a nose for the ball and could lock down the other team's best post player every single night. There are not many players who have played this game who can defend any player on the floor and grab you fifteen rebounds night in and night out.

Guard—John Stockton: John Stockton played the game the right way. John always got the job done and got the ball to the right person. John was known for his passing ability, but he always seemed to hit the big shot when his team needed it. That is the sign of a great floor leader. John simply was the textbook definition of a point guard: an extension of the coach actually playing the game on the court.

Forward—Alonzo Mourning: Alonzo plays with such heart and fire when he is on the floor. A true leader who will do whatever it takes to win. He was the enforcer, the intimidating presence every great team needs. He can anchor your defense and also get you twenty a night. You know you are going to get 100 percent every time Alonzo steps on the court.

Center—Wilt Chamberlain: No all-time team is complete without Wilt on it. Nobody could score and dominate a game like Wilt was able to do. He was a man among boys at times. Wilt was not just a scorer but a terrific rebounder and leader.

Center—Tim Duncan: Most complete post player in the NBA today. Tim combines superior talent with incredible fundamentals, making him a dominant force in the paint. Tim is the player every point guard would love to play with.

Center—Kevin Garnett: Kevin redefined the small forward position with his outstanding athleticism and skill level for a seven-footer. Kevin is a true all-around talent who can control an entire game on his own. There is not a position on the floor he could not play and play extremely well.

General Manager

Jerry West: Not everyone can build a winner, a team that is both talented and plays together as a cohesive unit, but Jerry has an eye for finding those players who have that innate quality of knowing how to win and not wanting to lose. Jerry is just as great as a GM as he was as a player, which is truly something spectacular.

Coach

Larry Brown: Larry is the ultimate coach. He is a true teacher who understands basketball better than anyone else and puts players in the best position to succeed as a team. Larry's teams always perform to the best of their ability and in most cases beyond. Larry blends individuals together to build a cohesive unit that plays as one.

JASON KIDD—GUARD

PERSONAL: Born March 23, 1973, in San Francisco . . . 6–4/212 (1.93 m/96 kg) . . . full name: Jason Frederick Kidd.

HIGH SCHOOL: St. Joseph of Notre Dame (Alameda, CA).

COLLEGE: California.

TRANSACTIONS/CAREER NOTES: Selected after sophomore season by Dallas Mavericks in first round (second pick overall) of 1994 NBA draft. . . . Traded by Mavericks with guard Tony Dumas and center Loren Meyer to Phoenix Suns for guard Sam Cassell, forward A. C. Green, forward Michael Finley, and 1997 or 1998 conditional second-round draft choice (December 26, 1996). . . . Traded by Suns with center Chris Dudley to New Jersey Nets for guard Stephon Marbury, forward Johnny Newman, and center Soumaila Samake (July 18, 2001).

MISCELLANEOUS: Member of gold-medal-winning U.S. Olympic team (2000).

COLLEGIATE RECORD

NOTES: *The Sporting News* All-America first team (1994). . . . Led NCAA Division I with 3.8 steals per game (1993). . . . Led NCAA Division I with 9.1 assists per game (1994).

Season	Team	G	Min	FGM	FGA	Pct	FTM	FTA	Pct	Reb	Ast	Pts	Averages RPG	APG	PPG
92–93	California	29	922	133	287	.463	88	134	.657	142	222	378	4.9	7.7	13.0
93–94	California	30	1,053	166	352	.472	117	169	.692	207	272	500	6.9	9.1	16.7
Total		59	1,975	299	639	.468	205	303	.677	349	494	878	5.9	8.4	14.9

THREE-POINT FIELD GOALS: 1992–93, 24-for-84 (.286); 1993–94, 51-for-141 (.362). Total: 75-for-225 (.333).

NBA REGULAR-SEASON RECORD

RECORDS: Shares single-game record for most turnovers—14 (November 17, 2000, vs. New York).

HONORS: NBA Co-Rookie of the Year (1995). . . . All-NBA first team (1999, 2000, 2001, 2002, 2004). . . . All-NBA second team (2003). . . . NBA All-Defensive first team (1999, 2001, 2002). . . . NBA All-Defensive second team (2000, 2003, 2004). . . . NBA All-Rookie first team (1995).

NOTES: Led NBA with 8.9 assists per game (2003).

| | | | | | | | | | Rebounds | | | | | | | | Averages | | |
Season	Team	G	Min	FGM	FGA	Pct	FTM	FTA	Pct	Off	Def	Tot	Ast	St	Blk	TO	Pts	RPG	APG	PPG
94–95	Dal	79	2,668	330	857	.385	192	275	.698	152	278	430	607	151	24	250	922	5.4	7.7	11.7
95–96	Dal	81	3,034	493	1,293	.381	229	331	.692	203	350	553	783	175	26	328	1,348	6.8	9.7	16.6
96–97	D-P	55	1,964	213	529	.403	112	165	.679	64	185	249	496	124	20	142	599	4.5	9.0	10.9
97–98	Pho	82	3,118	357	859	.416	167	209	.799	108	402	510	745	162	26	261	954	6.2	9.1	11.6
98–99	Pho	50	2,060	310	698	.444	181	239	.757	87	252	339	539	114	19	150	846	6.8	10.8	16.9
99–00	Pho	67	2,616	350	855	.409	203	245	.829	96	387	483	678	134	28	226	959	7.2	10.1	14.3
00–01	Pho	77	3,065	451	1,097	.411	328	403	.814	91	403	494	753	166	23	286	1,299	6.4	9.8	16.9
01–02	NJN	82	3,056	445	1,138	.391	201	247	.814	130	465	595	808	175	20	286	1,208	7.3	9.9	14.7
02–03	NJN	80	2,989	515	1,244	.414	339	403	.841	110	394	504	711	179	25	296	1,495	6.3	8.9	18.7
03–04	NJN	67	2,450	368	959	.384	206	249	.827	85	343	428	618	122	14	214	1,036	6.4	9.2	15.5
Total		720	27,020	3,832	9,529	.402	2,158	2,766	.780	1,126	3,459	4,585	6,738	1,502	225	2,439	10,666	6.4	9.4	14.8

THREE-POINT FIELD GOALS: 1994–95, 70-for-257 (.272); 1995–96, 133-for-396 (.336); 1996–97, 61-for-165 (.370); 1997–98, 73-for-233 (.313); 1998–99, 45-for-123 (.366); 1999–2000, 56-for-166 (.337); 2000–01, 69-for-232 (.297); 2001–02, 117-for-364 (.321); 2002–03, 126-for-370 (.341); 2003–04, 94-for-293 (.321). Total: 844-for-2,599 (.325).

PERSONAL FOULS/DISQUALIFICATIONS: 1994–95, 146/0; 1995–96, 155/0; 1996–97, 114/0; 1997–98, 142/0; 1998–99, 108/1; 1999–2000, 148/2; 2000–01, 171/1; 2001–02, 136/0; 2002–03, 127/0; 2003–04, 110/0. Total: 1,357/4.

NBA PLAYOFF RECORD

										Rebounds								Averages		
Season	Team	G	Min	FGM	FGA	Pct	FTM	FTA	Pct	Off	Def	Tot	Ast	St	Blk	TO	Pts	RPG	APG	PPG
96–97	Pho	5	207	21	53	.396	10	19	.526	4	26	30	49	11	2	13	60	6.0	9.8	12.0
97–98	Pho	4	171	22	58	.379	13	16	.813	5	18	23	31	16	2	12	57	5.8	7.8	14.3
98–99	Pho	3	126	18	43	.419	5	7	.714	1	6	7	31	5	1	9	45	2.3	10.3	15.0
99–00	Pho	6	229	22	55	.400	7	9	.778	8	32	40	53	11	1	23	59	6.7	8.8	9.8
00–01	Pho	4	166	22	69	.319	9	12	.750	9	15	24	53	8	0	12	57	6.0	13.3	14.3
01–02	NJN	20	803	147	354	.415	80	99	.808	42	122	164	182	34	8	67	391	8.2	9.1	19.6
02–03	NJN	20	852	137	341	.402	94	114	.825	36	118	154	163	36	4	79	402	7.7	8.2	20.1
03–04	NJN	11	474	43	129	.333	43	53	.811	16	57	73	99	25	6	43	139	6.6	9.0	12.6
Total		73	3,028	432	1,102	.392	261	329	.793	121	394	515	661	146	24	258	1,210	7.1	9.1	16.6

THREE-POINT FIELD GOALS: 1996–97, 8-for-22 (.364); 1997–98, 0-for-7; 1998–99, 4-for-16 (.250); 1999–2000, 8-for-22 (.364); 2000–01, 4-for-17 (.235); 2001–02, 17-for-90 (.189); 2002–03, 34-for-104 (.327); 2003–04, 10-for-48 (.208). Total: 85-for-326 (.261).

PERSONAL FOULS/DISQUALIFICATIONS: 1996–97, 11/0; 1997–98, 13/0; 1998–99, 12/0; 1999–2000, 14/0; 2000–01, 13/0; 2001–02, 40/0; 2002–03, 46/0; 2003–04, 15/0. Total: 164/0.

NBA ALL-STAR GAME RECORD

									Rebounds									
Season	Team	Min	FGM	FGA	Pct	FTM	FTA	Pct	Off	Def	Tot	Ast	PF	Dq	St	Blk	TO	Pts
1996	Dal	22	3	4	.750	0	0	—	2	4	6	10	1	0	2	0	2	7
1998	Pho	19	0	1	.000	0	0	—	0	1	1	9	2	0	0	0	2	0
2000	Pho	34	4	9	.444	0	0	—	0	5	5	14	0	0	4	0	6	11
2001	Pho	30	4	6	.667	0	0	—	0	4	4	2	3	0	1	0	5	11
2002	NJN	18	1	2	.500	0	0	—	0	1	1	3	0	0	1	0	1	2
2003	NJN	33	4	9	.444	2	2	1.000	1	4	5	10	0	0	5	0	2	11
2004	NJN	22	4	6	.667	3	4	.750	0	3	3	10	1	0	2	0	3	14
Total		178	20	37	.541	5	6	.833	3	22	25	58	7	0	15	0	21	56

THREE-POINT FIELD GOALS: 1996, 1-for-2 (.500); 2000, 3-for-6 (.500); 2001, 3-for-4 (.750); 2002, 0-for-1; 2003, 1-for-4 (.250); 2004, 3-for-4 (.750). Total: 11-for-21 (.524).

Chapter Seven

BILL LAIMBEER—Center

Intensity

by Bryan Burwell

Every single night he was always right there, in your face, in your chest, in your jock, in your head.

"Call the foul on him, dammit!!"

Every single night, he was always right there, toying with you, aggravating you, annoying you, frustrating you. He was this creeping, insidious, infuriating menace to hoop society who could turn forty-eight minutes of basketball into an excruciating mental and physical chamber of horrors.

"Dammit, he's floppin' . . . I tell you that SOB's floppin'. WHY CAN'T YOU SEE THAT?!?!?!!!"

Every single night, he was always right there, pounding on you with his sizable hips, elbows, and forearms. And just when he was beginning to wear you down physically—right at that very point where he knew your flesh was weak—that was only half of the torment. Now the real fun and games could begin, because when the flesh is weak, the mind is vulnerable. And so began his particular barrage of mental games that would exasperate you to the point of distraction and self-destruction.

There was Bill Laimbeer flat on his behind, sliding across some gleaming hardwood floor, flopping around like some six-foot-eleven, 260-pound bull elephant seal on a slippery rock. He had just inflicted every manner of devious old-school trickery on you. He'd hip-checked you like a hockey defenseman; he'd tugged on your jersey like a nervous three-year-old clinging to his daddy; he'd grabbed every crucial rebound, made every smart pass, set all these perfect, teeth-rattling picks. And, oh yes, he'd also just agitated and battered you like a thug in a dark alley, yet now there he was lying on the floor and somehow . . . some way . . . *he* was the victim, not you.

"JEEZUHS!!!!!! WHAT!!!! You're calling a foul on ME!???!!! What about HIM, DAMMIT!!??? Didn't you see what the $%&@ did to ME?!!?"

Time and place never mattered. Neither events nor circumstances altered his approach. It could have been an emotionally charged playoff game with serious championship hardware on the line. Then again, it could have just as easily been a mundane, mid-December regular-season contest with absolutely nothing at stake. Regardless of time or condition, it was always the same for Bill Laimbeer: the Detroit Pistons center was the absolute epitome of athletic intensity. For fourteen rugged, controversial, and championship-filled seasons, he was always right there, in your face, in your chest, in your jock, in your head. He was always stalking the sidelines, with his ice-blue eyes glaring, or marching down-court with that funny but very familiar tip-of-the-toes gait, fuming like some enraged, preying big cat.

The look of those cold, blue, penetrating eyes was as unmistakable as any of his signature bone-jarring picks. The look was an odd cross between the perpetually eerie, glazed stare of a serial killer, the seething glare of a madman, and the calculated gaze of a diabolical genius. You knew there was something powerful going on behind those glaring, deep-set eyes as he kept sticking his head into the huddle.

So if you want to know how Bill Laimbeer has found his way onto the Perfect Team, it begins and ends with this:

The unfiltered potency of Laimbeer's athletic life came from his intensity.

Heck, everyone knew there were stone statues that ran faster than Laimbeer. On a Perfect Team full of graceful, gravity-defying acrobats, hang gliders, and aesthetically pleasing improvisational stallions, Laimbeer was an improbable, thick-legged Clydesdale. His vertical jump might not have taken him any higher than a phone book. For a man who nearly topped seven feet, he will be remembered far more for drilling in a three-point jumper dancing off his tiptoes than for a vicious, rim-rattling dunk that would bring the house down.

Yet there was an emotional flame that raged inside Laimbeer's competitive soul that transformed him from a player with obvious athletic limitations into one of the league's finest big men throughout the 1980s and into the early 1990s. That flame was his intense approach to competition. And that is what allowed him to become a four-time All-Star and the nineteenth player in league history to amass more than ten thousand points and ten thousand rebounds. He won the NBA rebounding title with 13.1 boards per game in 1985–86, snapping Moses Malone's five-year streak as league leader. From 1982 to 1990, no player in the league grabbed more defensive rebounds than Laimbeer.

"Games are all about mental focus, discipline, and intensity," Laimbeer said from his suburban Detroit office at the Palace of Auburn Hills. He is the head coach of the WNBA's Detroit Shock now, but eleven years after retiring, the forty-seven-year-old Bad Boy for life is still fueled by intense competitive instincts. "I don't care what you're playing, if it's a game I was involved in—basketball, baseball, golf—there's a consistent way I have to play and approach a game. It wasn't a conscious thing. It wasn't like some special moment in my life happened that turned me into this. I couldn't help myself. This is who I am. This is what I've always been. This is who I'll always be. I don't have a choice. To me, it was always about mental intimidation in every game I play."

We can transport you back in time, and it still feels the same. It seems like only yesterday, and you can still hear his unmistakable rumbling voice piercing through the incredible din of fifteen thousand crazed spectators inside ancient Boston Garden, one of basketball's most hallowed halls. It was midway through the fourth quarter of a first-round duel with Boston in the 1989 Eastern Conference playoffs, and the Pistons were finally on the verge of shoving the Celtics out the postseason door.

You are a witness to four years' worth of frustrating, maddening, gut-twisting emotion being purged from deep in Laimbeer's competitive soul. The Celtics had consistently found a way to make life a living hell for Laimbeer and the Pistons in the late '80s. Every year, every playoff series, Larry Bird and the Celtics found new and more profound ways to teach the Pistons how demanding the road to championships would be.

Every spring the damned Celtics would conjure up something that was more twisted, more hurtful, more galling than the year before. These splendid and agonizing postseason lessons had come along when the Boys were still learning how to be so Bad. So now the lessons had been learned, and it was time for the students to shove the teachers out the door. They had all the talent they needed to complete the job. They had the perfect blend of playoff-tested veterans and wide-eyed youthful exuberance. They had experienced enough of the agony of defeat and had finally figured out what it took to win. Laimbeer and his teammates finally were ready to show Boston what kind of attentive students they had become.

So lean your head into the huddle and listen:

"Do it now!" he screamed, as his eyes blazed with a controlled rage. *"DO IT NOW! DO IT NOW!"*

It was still a two-point ball game with seven minutes, fifty seconds left in the fourth quarter of this series-clinching fifteen-point victory. At the time, the Pistons were holding only a slim 79–77 lead, but the more you watched Laimbeer's behavior during this time-out—eyes blazing, voice screaming, emotions bubbling—it was like he just knew something significant was about to transpire.

In much the same way a predator can pick up the scent of a wounded animal, Laimbeer had gotten a strong whiff of the vulner-ability of the aging Celtics. And if he sensed it, he wanted to make sure that every other Piston could pick up the same scent too.

Laimbeer was a cold-blooded competitive killer, and he de-manded that anyone who wore his team's uniform play with the same voracious thirst for victory. So it was time to not only plunge the knife into the Celtics' chest but stomp on their necks and suffo-cate them for extra emphasis. Laimbeer wanted to make sure this was a thorough kill. He saw that the carcass was heaving its last faint breath, but he felt it was his job and responsibility to make sure that his teammates understood what had to be done. It hardly mat-tered that he would not be on the floor during this critical stage of the game. Laimbeer always had an impact on a contest with his burning, infectious, competitive fire. So he urged, he screamed, he hollered, he prodded, he encouraged.

"End it now!" he screamed. *"Do it RIGHT NOW!!"*

And that is exactly what the Pistons did. Within a blink of an eye, the Pistons turned that two-point lead into a five-point lead. Then the killer drive built steadily. Over the final seven minutes, Detroit would go on a 21–7 run, win the game, and complete the first step on the way to its first NBA title. Laimbeer would have only nine points and one rebound in the victory, yet on this night—just as on so many others—his greatest contribution to the Pistons was impos-sible to measure on a stat sheet.

This is a man who was comfortable in his role as the creator of commotion and emotion. "I would say this about what I did," Laim-beer said, reflecting on his Bad Boy days and intense ways. "I was watching TV the other day, and the former [White House] budget director was talking about how he knew when he was doing his job the right way. 'You can always tell by how much screaming and yelling is coming from the other side of the aisle.' "

Laughter filled the air when Laimbeer told that story. "Now, I have to agree with that," he said. "Particularly when it was noise from opposing fans. Man, when I had eighteen thousand people screaming at me, booing me, cursing me, well, that just meant I'm successful. How many times did you see me standing in the middle of the floor waving my hands and arms for them to keep it coming? I always figured if I had their fans thinking about me that much, then I'm sure their players were thinking about me too. That was perfect."

So now that you have heard him firsthand, are you surprised at what you hear? Did you always think that maybe his intensity was created out of some calculated competitive necessity, as if Laimbeer decided this was something he needed to develop, like a left-handed jumper, a better free-throw technique, or Spanish as a second language?

Well, now you ought to know better. He did not just think this up after a long process of self-examination. There was nothing premeditated about his passion. This was a guy who came out of the womb with that competitive rage already deeply implanted in his gut. Maybe for some folks intensity is a learned trait, but not for Bill Laimbeer. It was all part of his DNA code, as natural as his hair color, as apparent as a birthmark. "It didn't just start up one day in high school or college," Laimbeer laughed. "I've been this way as long as I can remember. If it was a game, I had to win. If it was a game, I had the same approach every time. If I can't win, why in the hell would I play?"

And isn't that part of what has always intrigued us about him? It was never enough to just know that he was the Baddest of the Bad Boys. We also wanted to know how and why he turned out this way.

How many times have we checked into his personal background in search of an answer, yet instead come away with even more questions? How in the world does a kid who was raised in the affluent Chicago suburb of Clarendon Hills, the son of a highly successful business executive, turn into one of the meanest, toughest, most intense competitors in NBA history?

For so many years the joke in hoop circles about him was that he was the only man in the NBA who made less money than his father. But this joke had a wicked, insulting little socioeconomic edge to it. Where else but in the world of big-time sports—or the rap-music industry—could a background of privilege be considered a detriment to professional success?

Rich is bad? Poor is good?

What sort of strange, Kafkaesque world was this?

Oh yeah, Laimbeer gets the joke. A wicked laugh seemed to stir up from somewhere deep in his belly soul as he tried to dispel the myth that a kid from affluence cannot become an ornery, competitive SOB. But the laughter quickly changed to indignation, because Laimbeer has heard this stuff all his life. He was the kid born with a silver spoon stuck in his mouth, and that was supposed to be his greatest liability on the NBA landscape. It was worse than all those derisive stares he used to get for being a thick-legged white boy who couldn't jump over a phone book but always found a way to come up with a handful of rebounds. It was a far worse indignity than being outsourced to Italy for a season by the pitiful Cleveland Cavaliers when he was a rookie third-round draft pick. Those eyebrow-raising skeptics had made up their minds about him long before he even came through the NBA's door, and that ticked him off.

After an unspectacular college career at Notre Dame, where he averaged a little over seven points and six rebounds, the Cavaliers made him the sixty-fifth pick in the 1979 NBA Draft. And if his draft position didn't convince him that the sorry, no-account Cadavers had little interest in him, then not getting a contract offer until the middle of August certainly did. By then, he had already decided to play for Pinti Inox of Brescia in the Italian League, and no one in America's pro basketball circles tried to revoke his passport either.

Yet even after starring for Pinti Inox in his only season in Europe (21.1 points and 12.5 rebounds), the only person who believed Bill Laimbeer was going to be a true success in the NBA was Bill Laimbeer. "I think I got my confidence reenergized overseas," he recalled. "Playing in college, we had a really good team, with quite a few guys who ended up playing in the pros. So [Irish coach] Digger [Phelps] never played us a lot of minutes. No one played any more than twenty-five minutes a game. That affected my minutes and my statistics. I could have scored more and grabbed more rebounds, and so could everyone on our team, but Digger wouldn't let us. But when I went over to Italy, I became a star again, just like in high school. I never came out of the game. The fate of the team was on my shoulders every night, and I loved it, I needed it. I've never been short on confidence anyway, but being over there and being a star again sure did reenergize me."

Too bad no one on this side of the Atlantic Ocean shared that same confidence in him. Back here in America, they all had him pegged as a pedestrian baller; they had him scripted to be a bit player. Unspoken in their low assessment of him were certain cultural and social biases. Remember now, the world is full of songs about the hard-knock life *("Life sure ain't easy when you're a ghetto child . . ."),* and Laimbeer never would be mistaken for any of the urban soldiers who populated the NBA.

No one has ever seen any poetic romance in the plight of an upper-crust white boy from a well-heeled, suburban cul-de-sac heaven, have they?

So the pop psychologists lined up to figure him out when he finally got into the league and started to produce immediately. They saw a rich suburban kid who eventually turned into a notorious, intense Bad Boy, playing like he was the one with something to fight for. They saw him thrusting a hip, landing a well-placed elbow, or flopping to the ground like he'd been mugged when in fact he had been doing all the mugging. And they kept scratching their heads. What the hell was *he* so mad about?

They would soon find out. You see, this poor little rich kid hated losing.

Let's repeat that with the proper emphasis so that there is no misunderstanding.

Bill Laimbeer *hated* losing.

He hated it so much that he would do anything and everything to make sure he didn't do a lot of it. The only problem was, when he returned to the States for the 1980–81 season, he was with the Cavaliers, which means there was a lot of losing going on. The year he returned from Italy and signed with the Cavaliers, Laimbeer was a quiet, unassuming rookie who didn't try to wield his emotional influence over anyone. He came into a bad situation, and no matter how hard he played, it only got worse.

"We were awful," he recalled. "But what was even worse than the losing was that we had a team full of veterans who didn't give a damn that we were losing. It was a terrible environment, and because I was just a rookie, I didn't say anything. They didn't care about practicing hard. They didn't care about playing hard. It was the worst year of my life as an athlete."

In February 1982, Laimbeer was traded to Detroit, along with Kenny Carr, for Phil Hubbard, Paul Mokeski, and two draft picks. At the time, he couldn't know this would be the best move of his life. Waiting for him in Motown was his former Notre Dame teammate Kelly Tripucka and a twenty-year-old point guard from Indiana named Isiah Thomas.

On paper, Laimbeer and Thomas look like the oddest couple in the history of organized sports. Thomas was the scrappy, inner-city brother whose momma once stood on their front porch with a loaded shotgun to keep the gangsters of Chicago from recruiting her baby boy. With his clean-shaven, choirboy face, the six-foot-one Thomas looked like a sweet little angel.

But looks can be deceiving.

His new partner in crime was a tall, lumbering child of suburban privilege. The only danger Laimbeer's parents probably had to save him from was the first time his Fortune 500 executive daddy once taught him the importance of saving par. Oh yes, this was some unlikely pair, all right. On the surface, they were two socioeconomic polar opposites, but they turned out to be fierce competitive soul mates because they both carried an intense fear and loathing of losing.

"We were not going to lose—period," Laimbeer said. "It didn't matter where we were raised or what our upbringings were like, because it has nothing to do with social or economic situations. Isiah wasn't motivated by the projects. He just wanted to win. No, he had to win. And it was the same with me. Isiah used to call it gambling. We were gambling our physical and mental well-being on these games. If you knew us, you saw that our entire mental and physical psyches were wrapped up in winning."

So they bonded because of their competitive similarities instead of separating because of their many differences. "A winning environment is created; it doesn't just happen," Laimbeer said. "When I got traded, I made it clear to myself that I wasn't going to let what happened in Cleveland happen again. I didn't exert any leadership ability there. I let things happen that never should have continued, and I promised myself that would never happen again. And I met

Isiah, and as soon as we were paired, we knew immediately I was just like him and he was just like me. I kept thinking, *This is great.*"

So Laimbeer's leadership manifested itself in Detroit the same way it did when he was a kid playing board games with his big sister. Winning was all that mattered. Of course, his passion for the thrill of victory did have a few rough edges to it. The more intense Laimbeer got, the more unpopular he became outside his home arena.

They booed him relentlessly. They called him a thug. They called him "the Prince of Darkness." They called him "His Heinous." And he would stand there in the middle of all those NBA arenas soaking it all in. He would stalk around enemy arenas with his arms and hands outstretched, begging for more angry bile from all the cursing, ranting spectators. The louder they booed and the more they cursed him, the more he waved his hands as if he were trying to usher a delicious aroma into his nose.

How could they know that he loved it? How could they know that he craved it? How could any of these people understand that he fed off the antagonism? You would see him standing out there with all their hatred cascading down on him, and only then did anyone figure out that he was actually bathing in the animosity.

His ice-blue eyes stared into the heavens. There was always a dark red or purple welt under his eye. There were always welts or scratches on his arms, back, or neck. Occasionally, there would be a bloody red chevron gash on the bridge of his nose. You would look at him and swear he had been on the wrong end of a barroom brawl.

Yet when all the commotion was over, there was Laimbeer, surveying the spoils of his own private basketball war with a devious smile on his face. The bumps and bruises were just more conclusive evidence that he was winning the war, because he'd been able to provoke some of the league's best players, like Larry Bird, Charles Barkley, Robert Parish, or Bob Lanier, to lose their cool and take a swing at him.

And the more accomplished he became at aggravating everyone's last nerve, the more all the amateur shrinks tried to figure out what the hell he was doing out there. The picture still didn't quite fit the way we wanted it to. But now, after all this time, it's fairly clear what we had in this crazy, intense tough guy:

Is it possible that maybe, just maybe, Bill Laimbeer is the National Basketball Association's greatest test case for the merits of nature versus nurture?

We all thought it was impossible for someone from his comfortable background to become the epitome of a take-no-prisoners approach. But Laimbeer never allowed his environment to define him. He always did what came naturally to him. If you don't believe me, listen to him.

I broached the familiar subject of the apparent shortcomings of his pampered upbringing.

"Why, when considering your background . . ."

"*Why??!!!*" he said, abruptly cutting me off before the words got halfway out of my mouth.

"Why?" he grumbled. "*Why?* How about, *Why not?* What's your background got to do with anything? What does it matter where I grew up? City? Suburbs? Rich or poor? Who cares? It's not about money. You know what it's all about? It's about, are you driven to win? There are lots of ways to be the best. There are lots of ways to get to the top, and it doesn't matter whether my dad was a successful businessman or not. What matters is, do you have that burning drive to win? And I've always had it. Always."

The words came out of his mouth with an urgent emphasis. I had heard this speech several times before, the first time maybe fifteen years ago. Back then, the words had a scolding, defiant tone to them. But time has tempered the defiance. Now the words sounded more like a lecture; they were more instructive, more enlightening. He wanted you to understand exactly where he was coming from. He wanted you to appreciate who he is and how he became this hard-as-nails competitive dynamo.

This is definitely about nature, not nurture.

You want to know how Laimbeer turned into one of the most intense and competitive players in the history of the NBA?

"Let me tell you something," he said, his voice picking up steam. "I've always been like this, from the day I was born. Hey, I remember when I was a little kid, it didn't matter what the game was—heck, it could be a simple game of chess or checkers with my sister—and as long as I was winning, things were pretty cool. But oh brother, if she started winning—and particularly if I saw there was no way I could possibly win the game—well, there was only one thing left to do."

A diabolical chuckle came gurgling out of his belly as he recalled when he was just a bad boy, not a Bad Boy.

"I wouldn't . . . no, I guess it was more like I *couldn't* let her beat me," Laimbeer said.

And how exactly would you prevent her from winning? he was asked.

"Oh, that's easy. I'd just break up the game once she built up too big a lead. Seriously, I'm talking about slamming all the game pieces off the board. It was a very simple strategy, really. Can't win? No way out? Okay . . . destroy the damned game!"

Forty-odd years later, and nothing could dull the glorious sensation of young Bill's first forays into the not-so-subtle art of infuriating the opposition.

"Well, it all made perfect sense to me," Laimbeer cackled. "If you can't win, why on earth would you continue to play?"

So you see, the genius of Laimbeer's petulant competitive nature was no overnight sensation. There is no way anyone could have that much intense energy unless it has built up over time.

Anyone who saw the way he played, particularly during his stormy, but mostly successful, twelve seasons in Detroit, where Laimbeer became the Pistons' all-time leader in rebounds and second in games played, had to realize that he had been auditioning for the role of head villain for the Bad Boys all his life.

Anyone who saw the fire in his eyes, heard the rage in his voice, saw the way he enthusiastically embraced the role as the emotional eye of the stormy reign of intimidation that characterized Detroit's back-to-back championships (1989 and 1990), surely has to understand this.

"THIS IS OURS!!!! STAY FOCUSED!!! DON'T LET UP!!! IT'S NOT OVER, DAMMIT, IT'S NOT OVER!!!"

He was always the emotional voice of the Detroit franchise in the heat of battle. He was the one who always stalked around like some fierce madman, stirring up the emotional forces that turned the Pistons into a hard-edged dynasty. As Game 6 of the 1989 NBA Finals against the Los Angeles Lakers began to wind down, you always saw Laimbeer standing on the edge of the team huddles, a big white towel wrapped around his neck. He would lean into every huddle, and even as Chuck Daly frantically scribbled all the intricate Xs and Os, Laimbeer bellowed a far more impressionable emotional game plan.

"We're FIVE MINUTES from a championship!!! DON'T LET UP!!"

"We're THREE MINUTES away . . . KEEP PUSHING!!!"

"Look! LOOK! We're TWENTY-EIGHT SECONDS AWAY FROM A CHAMPIONSHIP . . . BUT IT'S NOT OVER, DAMMIT!!! IT'S NOT OVER!!!! DON'T LET UP!!!"

"I could never understand players who would just go sit on the end of the bench when they came to the sidelines," he said. "Why in the hell would you do that, just go sit down and not stay into it mentally? I wanted to be in the game all the time. I wanted to know what was going on every second of every game. I felt it was my job to put that sort of fire into us. That was my role, to make sure we all played like that all the time. We knew if our team would play with intensity for forty-eight minutes, no one could beat us."

During the late 1980s, not many teams could beat the Pistons, and much of that had to do with Laimbeer's intense influence. He was always a demented combination of Dennis the Menace and Bart Simpson with a thyroid condition. He was the basketball player from hell if you were the opposition. He was six feet, eleven inches' and 260 pounds' worth of passion, covert hoop activities, and underappreciated basketball skills.

He had a special talent for defensive rebounding, and he could pump in outside shots and hit free throws with an almost carefree ease. Despite his frequent injuries, Laimbeer was an iron man (his consecutive-game streak of 685 remains among the longest in NBA history). Even though trying to appreciate his best gifts was always difficult on a team filled with dazzling offensive artists, there was something absolutely brilliant in Laimbeer's unsightly cleverness. Exhibit A of Laimbeer's hidden ability had to be Game 3 of the

1990 NBA Finals, when the Pistons beat the Portland Trail Blazers. A lot of people that night were talking about the three-guard attack of Isiah Thomas (twenty-one points, eight assists, five rebounds), Joe Dumars (thirty-three points), and Vinnie Johnson (twenty-one points off the bench).

But what I remember most about that night was Laimbeer's impact on the outcome of the Pistons' victory. It could not be measured on the box score (eleven points, twelve rebounds). But the game tapes should have been immediately sent to the "old school" hall of fame, where down-and-dirty old heads such as Wes Unseld, Maurice Lucas, Paul Silas, and Tom Heinsohn could observe and cackle in admiration.

I approached him in the visitors' locker room after the game and informed Laimbeer that I thought he had just played one of his best games ever, and he immediately contradicted me.

"Oh no, I disagree," he said. "That wasn't one of my best games. I didn't score all that much."

"I wasn't talking about that," I told him when he began talking about his point and rebound totals. "I was talking about what you *really* did to the Blazers. How you ticked them off, how you got them all so frustrated."

"Ohhhhhhhhhhh," he said. His eyes lit up, and a decidedly devilish grin dominated his broad face. "Ohhhh yes, in *that respect,* yes. Absolutely. Definitely. You gotta do what you gotta do."

This contest was the ultimate highlight reel of his intense gamesmanship. This was one of his finest masterpieces of mental intimidation and manipulation. Somehow, all by himself, he created a colossal mental mismatch between himself and the entire Portland frontcourt. From the starters all the way down to the bench, all the Blazers' big men had Laimbeer's mental imprint on their brains by the end of this series.

Laimbeer was so effective in throwing all the Blazer big men off their games that they completely forgot they were in the NBA Finals and instead behaved like they were foolish hoop neophytes on the playground playing against some wise hoop oldhead. Laimbeer climbed in their heads with all sorts of mind games. He flopped, he tugged, he bumped and thumped, and none of the Blazer big men knew how to handle it.

Laimbeer once told *Sports Illustrated,* "I don't fight. I agitate, then walk away."

This game was the definitive manifestation of that philosophy. The more Laimbeer agitated, the more the Blazers engaged him in his game of tricks. Ah, but they were sadly and dramatically out of their element. He was the international jewel thief, and they were but overmatched dime-store pickpockets. While most of Laimbeer's crimes were exposed only by instant replay's delayed eyes, the Blazer big men always seemed to be tossing elbows, shoving forearms, and displaying other sorts of frustrating retaliation in broad daylight with all three referees staring right at them.

Now, some folks might say that what Laimbeer did that night was more closely related to professional rasslin' than to pro basketball at its highest level. Most of those folks would be either exasperated opponents or fans of a team the Pistons had just defeated. "Most of the same people who curse him now would love him for the things he does if he were on their team," Memphis Grizzlies head coach Mike Fratello once said about Laimbeer. "For some odd reason, the guys who always beat you are the guys you always hate."

And a lot of people hated Laimbeer during his Bad Boy days.

"I wouldn't say fans hate him," his Hall of Fame teammate Isiah Thomas once said. "I'd say they love to hate him. It's a love-hate relationship. Tell you the truth, if I didn't know Bill, I wouldn't like him either."

But on this particular night of Game 3 of the 1990 Finals, Thomas surely loved Laimbeer and his intense and aggravating ways. Of the thirty-eight team fouls called against Portland that night, at least fourteen of those fouls—a whopping 36 percent— were called as a result of a Blazer big man either bumping into or being baited by Laimbeer.

His intensity not only fueled the Pistons but burned up the Blazer big men, driving them beyond distraction and all the way to self-destruction. Of the six Blazer big men, only backup center Wayne Cooper (one foul) avoided foul trouble. Reserves Cliff Robinson (five fouls in only fourteen minutes) and Mark Bryant (three fouls in seven minutes) were lured into their trouble trying to hack at Laimbeer. Starting center Kevin Duckworth spent all night—and for that matter, the entire series—stomping around the floor, flummoxed by

Laimbeer's antics. Three of Duckworth's five fouls were offensive charges. And who was the guy who flopped to the ground drawing the referees' attention?

Laimbeer, of course.

"Damned man," said Duckworth, the words spitting out of his mouth like sour milk. "I don't know who to blame. The whole thing is all screwed up. I was goaded. I didn't see the fouls like that. He just flopped. But I respect him for using it. If I was good at it, I'd use it too. We all got carried away and lost our heads, especially me."

Late in the game, Buck Williams received his sixth foul when he retaliated against Laimbeer grabbing his jersey on a rebound by elbowing Laimbeer square on the chin. Of course, the refs never saw the jersey tug.

But for some reason, they all managed to catch Williams flinging the elbow.

All these years later, Laimbeer still revels in the moment. "Oh well," he giggled. "Such is life. It's all part of the game. There are many ways to win the game, and everyone does it differently. One of the great traits of our team was mental intimidation of the other team. One of my tasks was to be that guy who went out there and got the other team off their game. It's how I got by. It made me valuable because I honestly didn't care what other people thought of us.

"What I remember most about that game was that it got us over the hump in Portland. We hadn't won in Portland in years. We played the first two games of that series at home, and the Blazers won one of those games. So now we had to go out there and play three straight games. I needed to set the tone of the game."

So Laimbeer decided that during the pregame warm-ups he would do what he always did—instigate some mischief with the opposition. He was trying to come up with some sort of tactic that would mess with the Portland players, and so, after much careful thought and planning with several unnamed teammates, the plot was hatched.

"We would come out on the court and start our layup lines, and we picked the side of the court that was down near where they would come out of the locker room," said Laimbeer. "That meant, when they came out onto the court, we'd be in their way and they'd probably have to cut through our layup line. And when they did, I was going to run one of their guys over. I was going to just bowl right over somebody and cause a big stir."

So sure enough, everything went right according to plan. The Pistons came out onto the court first. And a few minutes later, the Blazers came onto the court, and Laimbeer grabbed a ball and began a mad rampage like an angry bull. He dropped his head, lowered his shoulder, and bolted toward the basket . . .

"But I missed," Laimbeer howled. "I somehow managed to miss their guys, and instead all I did was run over a photographer who was standing under the basket."

When the rest of the Piston players saw the plot disintegrate, the sight of a photographer flying into the cheap seats from the blunt force trauma of a Laimbeer body slam seemed to inspire them all the same.

"The whole team just started laughing," said Laimbeer. "And we all kind of looked at each other and we knew. We were ready."

A day later, as the Trail Blazers went to practice and still kept grumbling about Laimbeer's antics, former NBA star Spencer Haywood stood out on the practice court catching rebounds as the Portland players worked on their jump shots. Haywood was working as an analyst for one of the Detroit TV stations at the time, and as an "old school" fanatic, he admired the Pistons' handiwork.

"See, the trouble is that half of these Blazers don't know to play 'old school' ball," Haywood said. "That's their biggest problem. Hell, there ain't nothing wrong with the way Laimbeer's playing. That's how it was always played in the old days. Guys like [Wes] Unseld? Man, they'd beat the hell out of you. Now all these guys are playing what I call 'highlight basketball.' You know, it's TV basketball. All they can do is make those moves they see on the eleven o'clock news highlights. Then you watch Bill doing all that dirty work. Then you say to yourself, 'Yeah, now that's basketball. That's smart basketball.' "

The kid was an NBA neophyte. He had seen Laimbeer only from a distance on television and remembered that what he'd seen on TV did not exactly present a favorable impression of his new professional teammate.

But now young Cliff Levingston was in the same gym with him, and now he was getting an inspirational NBA tutorial from the master of mind games. "Without a doubt, Laimbeer was one of those guys who did all the intangible things on the court to help his team win games," Levingston recalled. A longtime league veteran who won an NBA title with the Chicago Bulls and spent two years in Detroit, Levingston said the lessons he learned from Laimbeer about those intangible things stuck with him for the rest of his basketball life. Now a head coach for the St. Louis Flight of the minor league American Basketball Association, Levingston remembered those lessons.

"He'd actually show us how to play the mind games with the other team," said Levingston. "It was like he had this vast mental book on every team and every player around the NBA. He knew what would get inside everybody's head. But he also knew how to play mental games with his own guys to get us all upset with the other team. It didn't matter if it was true or false. If he thought it would work, he'd tell you something—anything."

Levingston remembered watching Laimbeer work his psychological warfare one day after practice. "We had a big game coming up, so he calls a bunch of reporters over to his locker and starts making stuff up that he 'heard' that the other team said about us. He was telling them that they said our bench was weak. He told them that the other team said we all sucked and that half the guys on our bench didn't need to be in the league.

"Well, the next day we come in, and before the shootaround he's walking around the locker room with the sports pages in his hands, and he's showing all of us the story. 'Ohhh, man, look what they said about us! Can you believe this? Look, Cliff, they said you suck. Hey, Walker [Russell] and Ricky [Pierce], they said you guys are soft.' It was all BS, it was all a lie, but it got all of us fired up."

Laimbeer offered no apologies for his deceptions. "Look, I told you, that was my job, to make sure everyone was ready to play," he said. "It was basically how we do business. This is an intense business, and this is how we expect you to do business, because what we strived for was perfection. We tried to take the execution of our offense and defense to the nth degree, and we preached that to everyone on the team."

That often meant that when a new player showed up, Laimbeer and Thomas would sit them down and explain the Piston Way of playing basketball. "We laid all those ground rules. We told them how we expected them to play, to practice, to compete. We gave them a speech when they first arrived, then another one just before the playoffs began to explain how we conducted ourselves in the playoffs. And we dismissed [teams and players] who didn't approach basketball the same way. We'd talk about them, we'd look at them as great basketball players but not champions. And if you were on our team and didn't buy into what we were preaching, we'd dismiss you too. We were driven to succeed. With me, it was always a fear of failure. Isiah was the same way.

"If you didn't compete like we did, if you weren't smart, dedicated, and tough mentally, you weren't around here very long. It was peer pressure. We'd drive you away if you couldn't do what we expected."

The Piston Way was a common thread that ran all the way through the organization, from general manager Jack McCloskey (a hard-nosed tough guy who, like a feisty Bad Boy, competed in Senior Olympic basketball competitions into his sixties and played in pickup games with men half his age) to the head coach Chuck Daly (a master motivator), all the way down to the last man on the roster.

But whenever the mood needed to be set, whether in the midst of a high-stakes playoff game or a mundane January practice, Laimbeer was usually the man to spark up the needed intensity.

"We had our ways of turning a bad practice session into a good one," Laimbeer said.

And how would you do that? he was asked.

"Oh, perhaps an extra-hard screen on somebody, just to let a guy know," he snickered.

Levingston cackled when someone asked him about Laimbeer's hard picks in practice. "Oh man, he'd always lay out one of the second unit guards. He'd just blast either Ricky Pierce or Walker Russell. I mean, just knock the crap out of them. And as they're getting up off the floor, rubbing their behinds or their ribs or their arms, they'd get pissed off at the second-unit big men because we didn't call out the pick and let them know what Bill was up to. See, then it was our fault, and this incredible, emotional chain reaction would start.

"He'd hit the second-unit guards. They'd get mad with us. Then we'd have to nail Isiah or someone else on the first group, and then all hell would break loose and it was like the seventh game of the NBA Finals. One Laimbeer pick would intensify everything."

Laimbeer chuckled again.

"Like I said . . . that . . . was . . . my job."

His job has changed now. But then again, it really hasn't. Eleven games into the 1993–94 season, with his back and knees aching and his competitive ego unable to handle losing or diminished skills, Laimbeer retired and went into private business until two years ago, when he was named the head coach of the WNBA's Detroit Shock. They were 0–10 at the time, and when he walked in the door, more than a few of the young ladies were a little nervous about what sort of approach he would take with them.

"They were all scared I was going to turn them into Bad Girls," Laimbeer cackled. "But once they realized I wasn't going to do that, it turned out to be pretty good. I like coaching the women, because they listen better. This is a smart team."

Smart enough to make a sudden midseason turnabout that led to the WNBA title in that first season. "They responded to my coaching because they're smart. Once they understood that I still have the same attitude I did as a player concerning intensity and effort—once they got it that when you walk onto the court, either at practice or in the game, this is how we do it every time—things changed rather quickly."

So now the orneriest man in basketball history is a leader of women, teaching them the Piston Way. But there is a part of his competitive soul that will never feel quite satisfied sitting there on the bench barking out instructions to players. "It's just not the same as playing," he said. "I miss the mental intensity of the competition. You can never duplicate that mental high of trying to figure out how to get five guys to win the game. That was the highest form of competition, and I will always miss it."

The coach still loves looking at the wall of his office and seeing the clock ticking down closer to 7:30 P.M. and feeling that Pavlovian response to go out and engage in another competitive contest of psyches and skills.

"If you talked to anyone who ever coached me, I'm hoping they'll say what I say: I was always there. I never went away," Laimbeer said. "If you got tired, I was there. If you missed a shot, I was there. If you made a mistake, yeah, I was there. That's why people got so frustrated with me, because I was always there. I was there to annoy people and throw them off their games. I was there every minute of every game. I was there to win."

BILL LAIMBEER—CENTER

PERSONAL: Born May 19, 1957, in Boston . . . 6–11/260 (2.11 m/118 kg) . . . full name: William Laimbeer Jr. . . . Name pronounced "lam-BEER."

HIGH SCHOOL: Palos Verdes (CA).

JUNIOR COLLEGE: Owens Technical (OH).

COLLEGE: Notre Dame.

TRANSACTIONS/CAREER NOTES: Selected by Cleveland Cavaliers in third round (65th pick overall) of 1979 NBA draft. . . . Played in Italy (1979–80). . . . Traded by Cavaliers with forward Kenny Carr to Detroit Pistons for forward Phil Hubbard, center Paul Mokeski, and 1982 first- and second-round draft choices (February 16, 1982). . . . Announced retirement (December 1, 1993). . . . Special consultant, Detroit Shock, WNBA (April 18–June 19, 2002). . . . Head coach, Detroit Shock (2002–present).

MISCELLANEOUS: Member of NBA championship team (1989, 1990). . . . Detroit Pistons franchise all-time leading rebounder with 9,430 (1981–82 through 1993–94).

COLLEGIATE RECORD

													Averages		
Season	Team	G	Min	FGM	FGA	Pct	FTM	FTA	Pct	Reb	Ast	Pts	RPG	APG	PPG
75–76	Notre Dame	10	190	32	65	.492	18	23	.783	79	10	82	7.9	1.0	8.2
76–77	Owens Tech					Did not play									
77–78	Notre Dame	29	654	97	175	.554	42	62	.677	190	31	236	6.6	1.1	8.1
78–79	Notre Dame	30	614	78	145	.538	35	50	.700	164	30	191	5.5	1.0	6.4
Total		69	1,458	207	385	.538	95	135	.704	433	71	509	6.3	1.0	7.4

ITALIAN LEAGUE RECORD

												Averages		
Season	Team	G	Min	FGM	FGA	Pct	FTM	FTA	Pct	Reb	Ast	Pts	RPG	APG	PPG
79–80	Brescia	29	—	258	465	.555	97	124	.782	363	—	613	12.5	—	21.1

NBA REGULAR-SEASON RECORD

										Rebounds							Averages		
Season	Team	G	Min	FGM	FGA	Pct	FTM	FTA	Pct	Off	Def	Tot	Ast	St	Blk	TO	Pts	RPG	APG	PPG
80–81	Cle	81	2,460	337	670	.503	117	153	.765	266	427	693	216	56	78	132	791	8.6	2.7	9.8
81–82	C-D	80	1,829	265	536	.494	184	232	.793	234	383	617	100	39	64	121	718	7.7	1.3	9.0
82–83	Det	82	2,871	436	877	.497	245	310	.790	282	711	993	263	51	118	176	1,119	12.1	3.2	13.6
83–84	Det	82	2,864	553	1,044	.530	316	365	.866	329	674	1,003	149	49	84	151	1,422	12.2	1.8	17.3
84–85	Det	82	2,892	595	1,177	.506	244	306	.797	295	718	1,013	154	69	71	129	1,438	12.4	1.9	17.5
85–86	Det	82	2,891	545	1,107	.492	266	319	.834	305	770	1,075	146	59	65	133	1,360	13.1	1.8	16.6
86–87	Det	82	2,834	506	1,010	.501	245	274	.894	243	712	955	151	72	69	120	1,263	11.6	1.8	15.4
87–88	Det	82	2,897	455	923	.493	187	214	.874	165	667	832	199	66	78	136	1,110	10.1	2.4	13.5
88–89	Det	81	2,640	449	900	.499	178	212	.840	138	638	776	177	51	100	129	1,106	9.6	2.2	13.7
89–90	Det	81	2,675	380	785	.484	164	192	.854	166	614	780	171	57	84	98	981	9.6	2.1	12.1
90–91	Det	82	2,668	372	778	.478	123	147	.837	173	564	737	157	38	56	98	904	9.0	1.9	11.0
91–92	Det	81	2,234	342	727	.470	67	75	.893	104	347	451	160	51	54	102	783	5.6	2.0	9.7
92–93	Det	79	1,933	292	574	.509	93	104	.894	110	309	419	127	46	40	59	687	5.3	1.6	8.7
93–94	Det	11	248	47	90	.522	11	13	.846	9	47	56	14	6	4	10	108	5.1	1.3	9.8
Total		1,068	33,956	5,574	11,198	.498	2,440	2,916	.837	2,819	7,581	10,400	2,184	710	965	1,594	13,790	9.7	2.0	12.9

THREE-POINT FIELD GOALS: 1981–82, 4-for-13 (.308); 1982–83, 2-for-13 (.154); 1983–84, 0-for-11; 1984–85, 4-for-18 (.222); 1985–86, 4-for-14 (.286); 1986–87, 6-for-21 (.286); 1987–88, 13-for-39 (.333); 1988–89, 30-for-86 (.349); 1989–90, 57-for-158 (.361); 1990–91, 37-for-125 (.296); 1991–92, 32-for-85 (.376); 1992–93, 10-for-27 (.370); 1993–94, 3-for-9 (.333). Total: 202-for-619 (.326).

PERSONAL FOULS/DISQUALIFICATIONS: 1981–82, 296/5; 1982–83, 320/9; 1983–84, 273/4; 1984–85, 308/4; 1985–86, 291/4; 1986–87, 283/4; 1987–88, 284/6; 1988–89, 259/2; 1989–90, 278/4; 1990–91, 242/3; 1991–92, 225/0; 1992–93, 212/4; 1993–94, 30/0. Total: 3,633/63.

NBA PLAYOFF RECORD

NOTES: Shares NBA Finals single-game record for most points in an overtime period—9 (June 7, 1990, vs. Portland).

Season	Team	G	Min	FGM	FGA	Pct	FTM	FTA	Pct	Off	Def	Tot	Ast	St	Blk	TO	Pts	RPG	APG	PPG
												Rebounds							Averages	
83–84	Det	5	165	29	51	.569	18	20	.900	14	48	62	12	4	3	12	76	12.4	2.4	15.2
84–85	Det	9	325	48	107	.449	36	51	.706	36	60	96	15	7	7	16	132	10.7	1.7	14.7
85–86	Det	4	168	34	68	.500	21	23	.913	20	36	56	1	2	3	8	90	14.0	0.3	22.5
86–87	Det	15	543	84	163	.515	15	24	.625	30	126	156	37	15	12	20	184	10.4	2.5	12.3
87–88	Det	23	779	114	250	.456	40	45	.889	43	178	221	44	18	19	30	273	9.6	1.9	11.9
88–89	Det	17	497	66	142	.465	25	31	.806	26	114	140	31	6	8	19	172	8.2	1.8	10.1
89–90	Det	20	667	91	199	.457	25	29	.862	41	170	211	28	23	18	16	222	10.6	1.4	11.1
90–91	Det	15	446	66	148	.446	27	31	.871	42	80	122	19	5	12	17	164	8.1	1.3	10.9
91–92	Det	5	145	17	46	.370	5	5	1.000	5	28	33	8	4	1	5	41	6.6	1.6	8.2
Total		113	3,735	549	1,174	.468	212	259	.819	257	840	1,097	195	84	83	143	1,354	9.7	1.7	12.0

THREE-POINT FIELD GOALS: 1984–85, 0-for-2; 1985–86, 1-for-1; 1986–87, 1-for-5 (.200); 1987–88, 5-for-17 (.294); 1988–89, 15-for-42 (.357); 1989–90, 15-for-43 (.349); 1990–91, 5-for-17 (.294); 1991–92, 2-for-10 (.200). Total: 44-for-137 (.321).

PERSONAL FOULS/DISQUALIFICATIONS: 1984–85, 32/1; 1985–86, 19/1; 1986–87, 53/2; 1987–88, 77/2; 1988–89, 55/1; 1989–90, 77/3; 1990–91, 54/0; 1991–92, 18/1. Total: 408/13.

NBA ALL-STAR GAME RECORD

Season	Team	Min	FGM	FGA	Pct	FTM	FTA	Pct	Off	Def	Tot	Ast	PF	DQ	St	Blk	TO	Pts
											Rebounds							
1983	Det	6	1	1	1.000	0	0	—	1	0	1	0	1	0	0	0	1	2
1984	Det	17	6	8	.750	1	1	1.000	1	4	5	0	3	0	1	2	0	13
1985	Det	11	2	4	.500	1	2	.500	1	2	3	1	1	0	0	0	0	5
1987	Det	11	4	7	.571	0	0	—	0	2	2	1	2	0	1	0	0	8
Total		45	13	20	.650	2	3	.667	3	8	11	2	7	0	2	2	1	28

Bryan Burwell

WNBA COACHING RECORD

		Regular Season				Playoffs		
Season	Team	W	L	Pct	Finish	W	L	Pct
2002	Detroit	9	13	.409	8th/West	—	—	—
2003	Detroit	25	9	.735	1st/East	6	2	.750
Total (2 years)		34	22	.607		6	2	.750

NOTES: 2003—Defeated Houston, 2–1, in first round; defeated Connecticut, 2–0, in Eastern Conference Finals; defeated Los Angeles, 2–1, in WNBA Finals.

Chapter Eight

SHAQUILLE O'NEAL—Center
The Will to Dominate
by Tom Friend

He enters the arena through the security en-
trance—his password being a non-expressive
grunt—and while much of the city sleeps,
Shaquille O'Neal has come to fix his game.

He walks in with a basketball, an uncle, and a secret—the secret being, *I'm sick of missing foul shots.*
He's there to do some shooting, there because he's
tired of Hack-a-Shaq, there because the best things in
life are supposed to be free (throws). His critics say he
isn't dedicated enough, that he makes too many
movies, raps too many songs, tells too many one-

liners, rides in too many police cars. But they've never walked in his size 22s. They don't know how it feels, in the final two minutes of a game, to have an opposing coach point at you and say, "Foul Shaq! Foul Shaq! Foul Shaq!" They don't know what it's like to step your painted toenail up to the line and hear the opposing center shout, "Box out. It's coming off long." They don't know what it's like to re-lease your foul shot in Sacramento and see the fans along the base-line reaching for their hard hats.

So, every other week, he comes to an arena after midnight—al-ways after midnight—to put an end to it. Staples Center, American Airlines Arena in Miami, any arena will do. He shoots his two hun-dred free throws, his Uncle Jerome rebounds the two hundred free throws, and by 1:00 A.M., Shaquille O'Neal is absolutely certain he's Larry Bird. "I don't miss in private," he says. But in public he misses. In public he misses almost two-thirds of the time. He's shot more playoff free throws than anyone in NBA history—more than Jor-dan, Chamberlain, or Abdul-Jabbar—and it's all because teams love to foul him, love seeing him shoot a curveball at the rim. It's like a turnover.

And damn, that bothers Shaquille O'Neal. He has always wanted to be, in his words, the MDE—most dominant ever. He's wanted it as far back as when he was the MDF—most dominant fourth-grader. He's wanted it ever since a Little League parent demanded to see his birth certificate, ever since his stepfather read him an arti-cle about big bad Bill Russell. But the one place he's just never been able to dominate from is the foul line. The one place where his "Diesel" tattoo carries no weight is the foul line. The one place where he can't dunk on you or tell you a joke is the foul line. The one place where his coach, his teammates, his fans, his mother, his kids, his dentist, his accountant, his gardener don't want him to be . . . is the foul line.

God, he hates that.

So he doesn't get mad, he gets even. When the game's for real—not a past-midnight practice session—for every bricked free throw, there's a two-handed dunk from Shaquille O'Neal that sends the rim into convulsions. Say what you will about Shaquille Rashaun O'Neal, at least he knows what he is: a center. A legit center. The kind that's seven-foot-one and not an ounce less than 335 pounds. If he wanted to, he could head-fake and spin-move all day but instead he keeps things simple. Instead, he plants his ample butt in the lane, waits 2.88 seconds for the ball, steps out when people like Kobe won't hand it over, then steps back in. It's what makes him unique. It's why he calls himself the Last Big Man on Earth. It's why, even with his crooked free throws, he's right: he's the MDE.

"Even fat guys don't want to play inside nowadays," he said. "They want to shoot jumpers. That's why the game is b.s. now, because there ain't enough room for twenty dudes shooting jumpers. That's why the percentages are down.

"If I've got to step out and shoot jumpers, I'll just retire and go put my police uniform on. I'll go on patrol before I shoot jumpers."

No player's ever been this obsessed with all-out domination. He does it the old-fashioned way—by bullying you, by scaring the Nikes or And1s off of you. By getting inside your fearful little head.

"Yeah," Shaq said. "My college coach at LSU, Dale Brown, always told me, 'Dog them out before they dog you.' This game is 85 percent psychology, so most of these cats, if you play 'em for the first time and you 'bow 'em in their face, and you go in with a move, you got 'em for the rest of their career.

"I remember the '02 Finals when we played New Jersey. Dikembe [Mutombo] was talking in the paper how he was the best defender and all that. So right before Game 1, I'm in my game mode, I don't really want to talk to him, and I see him enter the building with his family. He's coming down the tunnel and he goes, 'Hey, Shaq, this is my family, I want you to meet my family.' Right then, I knew I had him. I *knew* I had him. I mean, I had my game face on like, 'Don't say nothing to me.' And now you're talking to me? After talking all that shit in the paper? Now you're saying [imitating Dikembe's Cookie Monster voice], 'Shaq, how you doing, man. I want you to meet my family. They want to take a picture with you'?

"I knew I had him! Because he stopped to take a picture. If he was serious, he would've believed all the stuff he said in the paper. He would've backed it up."

How dominant is Shaq? The only ones who have ever stopped him are himself (i.e., free throws) and the league office.

"Think about it," Shaq said. "They've changed the rules so many times since I've been here. For instance, when they legalized zone? That was because of me.

"And when they started with the excessive fouling rules? That's because of me too. Now whenever I foul, it's automatic flagrant.

"And morning shootarounds? Now the two teams can't walk in and out the same way. That's because of me. After I beat up [Greg] Ostertag at a shootaround, they changed that rule."

How dominant is he? Teams almost never guard him with one person.

"Actually, some cats have been able to put up a fight. Like [Alonzo] Mourning, I had to fight every time. Hakeem [Olajuwon], I had to fight every time. [Patrick] Ewing, I had to fight every time until he got older, and then he just kind of let me do what I wanted to do. But most of these regular centers, you just do what you do, and some of them are so weak that before they even come in, they already know what you can do . . . so you got 'em.

"Against Mourning, Hakeem, and Ewing, though, I had to work. Like, I'd come down and score. They'd score. Then I come down and score. It was actually a battle. However, none of those guys ever played me straight up. None of 'em. No, never. And I always guarded them straight up.

"Are some players easier to dominate than others? No. 'Cause they're all the same. That's why I know I'm the MDE. 'Cause nobody in this league will guard me one-on-one. Nobody in this league. Nobody. You name him, he won't, he won't play me one-on-one. Not [Tim] Duncan, not [Yao] Ming. Nobody will play me one-on-one. But I play everybody one-on-one. That's why sometimes it's funny that they try to make it a Shaq vs. Whatchamacallit. Like Shaq vs. Amare. Amare [Stoudemire] didn't play me at all. He'd just stand in front, somebody would come from behind, and he wasn't playing no defense at all. Then he'd run down, because he's faster than me, and he'd get dunks. But nobody can play me one-on-one. If they try, we'll demolish them.

"Actually, one time I do remember the 76ers guarding me straight up. With a big dude named Lang. Andrew Lang. And I had about fifteen dunks."

How dominant is he? The Pistons tried the Andrew Lang approach during the 2004 Finals—guarded him straight up and watched the eyes practically pop out of Shaq's head. He shot a torrid 63.1 percent from the field.

How dominant is he? In the playoffs he actually posts up harder, bangs harder, dunks harder.

"Everytime we go to the playoffs, I try to dominate more," he said. "Every time we played Sacramento in a series, I had to do something. One year, the first game in L.A., I think I had forty. The next game, I had forty-two. I got in their heads. So I think without me getting those forty and forty-two, we don't have the championship."

How dominant is he? Defenders have received Academy Award nominations trying to draw fouls on him.

"They flop," Shaq said. "And then they want sympathy from the officials. See, if the officials knew my game, and knew *the* game, I'm skilled enough to go around people. I don't really have to go through 'em. What I'm trying to do is bump you and get you off-balance, so I can go to my next move. But see, guys like Vlade Divac and Shawn Bradley, they're floppers. And the refs feel sorry for them.

"The refs don't feel sorry for me. I guess it's because I don't kiss their ass, I don't ask no questions. If they want to call that crap and try to take over the game, I just let 'em. I never complain, I never embarrass them, but there's some b.s. they let go out there. Other guys get to push and lean, and then when I make one little simple bump . . . whistle. Foul on me.

"But what it does, it evens out the game for them. If the refs didn't call those flops, I'd average forty, fifty. Without the free throws. Without making them."

He's so dominant that when defenders intentionally foul him (i.e., Hack-a-Shaq), they make sure to never foul him *too* hard.

"Shawn Bradley, every time he fouls me, says, 'You okay? You all right?' Because these guys know I'll fight 'em," Shaq said. "These guys know I don't care about getting fined and don't care about getting suspended. If you foul me, and I think you're being dirty, when I get up, these guys know I'm either gonna walk it off or I'm gonna mess you up.

"Like Brad Miller. He kept fouling me, and the refs wouldn't call it. So I told the ref, 'You better clean it up,' and the ref wouldn't want to clean it up. He'd want to let these guys think they're tough. So I told Miller, I said, 'Miller, you foul me again, and I'm messing you up.' So he fouled me again, and he kind of walked away. And I had a back-of-the-head shot, but you can't hit nobody in the back of the head. 'Cause I know I can mess 'em up that way. So I don't want to hit anybody in the back of the head. And if you look at the tape, you can tell I stopped. Because I wanted him to turn around. I just wanted him to turn around so I could hit him in the side of the face. And I swung and he moved and Charles Oakley tackled me. . . . So, like I said, if you're dirty, I'll mess you up."

How dominant is he? After he conquered a string of international centers such as Arvydas Sabonis, Vlade Divac, and Rik Smits, he said, "I'm the Big Deportator; I'm sending all the foreign centers home."

How dominant is he? When his son Shaqir was born during the 2003 playoffs, the newborn baby was afraid to cry and keep his daddy up at night.

"He knows better," Shaq said.

He was in the fourth grade when it happened, when the rest of the world woke up a sleeping giant.

Sweet, subdued ten-year-old Shaquille O'Neal was about to play a Little League basketball game . . . when he got called out of the gym.

"The parents were saying, 'He's not ten! I want to see his birth certificate!' " Shaq said. "I guess it was because I was a ten-year-old who'd just scored forty, fifty points. And the other parents wanted to actually try to fight my father. They'd be, 'I want to see his birth certificate now!' We'd have to come in, before we'd play in the Little League, and they'd tell my [step] dad, 'Sergeant Harrison, we need to talk to you.' And my [step]father would go off, 'I ain't showing you nothing.' And then they'd bring in the cops. They'd say, 'Before he plays, we need to see his birth certificate.'

"I'm serious, man. They'd bring in cops, the officials, the leaders. Everybody would have to come in. And I'd have to show them my birth certificate.

"I guess it was because I was real big and mean. My [step]father was in the military, and in football it used to be the regular kids against the officer's kids. So my [step]father used to tell me, 'That's the general's son. Get him.' And the general's son played quarterback, and I'd be the nose guard, and I'd get him. So I'd tackle him, and they'd go, 'He's not ten! He's six-foot. He's not ten!' "

But he *was* ten, and that has been bad news for Shaq's ensuing opponents. He's taken it out on all of them.

Of course, in a game like basketball, the referees weren't going to let him Bogart everybody, and Shaq needed to learn how to play with a certain finesse, needed to learn how to dominate in other ways. And that's why, when Shaq was a preteen, when Shaq was just an MDS (Most Dominant Sixth-Grader), he was taught how to play unselfishly.

"Started elementary school," Shaq said. "My father ran the high triple post offense. Throw the ball to me—because I was bigger than everybody—and guys just cut. I don't remember names, but I do remember nicknames. We had guys like Doogle who couldn't really play at all. And you know, Doogle would be all in glasses and he'd be a nerd, and people'd say, 'Doogle can't score.' So my dad would say, 'Throw the ball to Shaquille, cut, set a pick for Doogle. Doogle, we're gonna throw it to you.' We used to be up by so much that my father used to experiment like that. So I used to get the ball, guys used to cut, and I'd just hit 'em. My father always taught us to shoot it off the glass, don't even try to shoot it and hit the rim. We went undefeated for many, many years.

"And then Magic Johnson. Just watching Magic. Big guy, fancy passes. You can get the same oohs and aahs on a fancy pass as you can on a dunk. And when you're playing basketball, it's all about marketing, it's all about looking good. So I can look good many ways rather than just dunk all the time."

So, before Shaq was Shaq, he was the Great Imitator.

"Being in trouble a lot, I got to watch a lot of basketball on TV," he said. "What I mean is, my dad would send me to my room a lot. For not doing my work in school. You know the little dunce hat? They made that because of me. They'd say, 'You want to be a clown? Sit in the corner and wear this hat.' I used to have to wear that every day.

"But anyway, my father would say, 'Go to your room, do your homework, and don't come out until it's time to eat.' And at those times I'd watch basketball. I was able to watch a lot of my favorite players and what they did. So I stole what they did. I stole Magic's smile [he grins a toothy grin]. I stole Ewing's meanness, the scowl on the court. And I've always been a silly guy, so I knew if I added those two things I'd be cool. I don't talk a lot, but I'm very smart and funny.

"At the time, they only showed the big games on TV. So I used to always wait for when the Hawks played the Bulls, or the Lakers and the Celtics. Those are like the only games I really paid attention to. I used to sit down and watch. And knowing how the media is, I used to watch the ones that got in trouble too. So I used to sit there and say, 'I'm not doing that. I ain't doing cocaine.' They'd put it on TV, 'Darryl Strawberry did blah, blah, blah.' I'd sit and watch and know what not to do."

But make no mistake, the person he listened to most was his stepfather, Sgt. Philip Harrison. And the Sergeant, as Shaq calls him, used to always bring up three names. All the time, it was three names: Bill, Wilt, and Kareem.

"Yep, my father would tell me about Bill Russell, Wilt, and Kareem," he said. "We'd go to the park and just work on stuff. He'd say, 'Okay, I'm gonna go layup—block my shot like Bill Russell.' And I'm like, 'Who is Bill Russell?' And then he'd sit me down and show me. In books. And he said, 'I want you to develop a sky-hook like Kareem.' I was like, 'Who Kareem?' He'd say, 'You know what, I've got to go around the corner and try to get some tickets, I'll be back.' So we went to a Knicks game, way up at the top. Way up at the top. 'That's Kareem, that's the sky-hook you have to work on.' And then after we got a little team, that's a shot I used to shoot when I was little. I was the best. But as I got older and got in rec leagues, I said, 'Who's this too-mean mother from Georgetown, the dude with the bald head, Michael Graham. I'm gonna start doing what they're doing. Jump hook, jump hook. Okay. That's the move. The sky-hook, that's too old, I ain't doing it. The jump hook, the jump hook.' And then as I got older, coaches would say, 'You're six-eleven, you can shoot and you can do all that, but you need to dunk.' So I was shooting jumpers. Get mean. Dunk. Get mean.

Dunk, dunk, dunk, dunk, dunk. I kinda got away from my shooting touch a little bit.

"My junior year of high school, that's when I realized I could dominate physically. Before, I used to be like all the other big men they have now—shoot jumpers, do all that crap. And they used to tell me, 'Stop shooting jumpers, get inside.' So I used to get inside and start fighting and throw 'bows, and I'd see that people didn't like contact. That's when it all changed mentally for me. See, what most people don't understand about me is I started out as a football player. So I liked contact, and I like bumping, and I like pain and all that stuff. And then the psychology factor came in. The first time I played somebody, I tried to destroy 'em mentally. Like, for example, I played Shawn Bradley in a high school tournament, so I 'bowed him in the face, dunked on him, talked a little trash to him. Then I took it to college, and it worked in college. I took it to the pros, and it worked against everybody except Patrick Ewing.

"But I kept doing it to Patrick Ewing, and of course, he got older, and then it worked with Patrick Ewing. I averaged forty on the Knicks. Look it up. David Robinson, the same way. And it's been my style ever since. I 'bow a guy, talk a little trash, then I got him for the rest of his life."

And that's the Shaquille O'Neal we have today: opposing centers duck when he dunks, *and* they duck when he shoots a free throw.

"Well, when I was in college, I said, Okay, I'm gonna develop a style that's gonna get me to that next level. And I was doing what I do, just playing my game, and Dick Vitale says, 'Hey, this buck's gonna be the number-one pick, so I stayed with that style.' And when I got in the NBA, I stayed with that style. And it got me here, it got me through the rain, and I'm still staying with that style. Now you see guys shying *away* from that style, so that's why I always say, 'I'm the last big man left.'

"Because I am."

And then a player like Kobe Bryant shows up.

Kobe shoots first and learns his teammates' names last. Kobe's never told a joke in his life. Kobe's never been taught the *right* way to play.

"I've always been the type that if I take three shots and it ain't looking right or feeling right, I'm not gonna take a fourth shot," Shaq said. "I'll say, 'Screw it, Ricky Fox was open last time, let me see what he's gonna do. Ah, Ricky just hit a three. Let me do it again. Get everybody else going, and then you can get yourself going.' I've never been the type to just shoot until I get going. My jump hook is off, the next time I'm gonna act like I'm going to the jump hook, because people will probably think, 'Ah, Shaq's only got four points, he's gonna score now, he's gonna score.' So when I get it and they come, I'm, 'Hey, let me kick it out to Ricky right quick.' And I've always been known to make people better because I had to do that when I was little.

"Kobe thinks I'm jabbing at his game when I say *all this,* but I'm not. It's just that I've been on both sides. For a long time, it was always, 'Shaq, go out and score thirty every night. Shut up, just be quiet, you score thirty, and you don't ask no questions, you do it.' But *then* when I get two other Hall of Famers with me—Karl [Malone] and Gary [Payton]—I don't have to force shots anymore.

"I'm just saying, if I'm getting doubled, I got a Hall of Famer Malone out there who can hit the jumper, because he used to bust my ass with that same jumper. See, if I got two guys on me and he's by himself, the percentage for him is better because he's right there and there ain't nobody on him. If Gary's cutting to the basket, the closer you are to the basket, the better your percentage. And that's the basketball I was always taught. Pass, cut, pass, cut, pass, cut.

"And I know what I'm talking about because I've been on both sides of the fence. Starting off in high school, I wasn't always a scoring machine. So I had to rebound, block shots, and do all those other things. And after all the seniors left, 'Shaq, we need you to score. All-American, la la la.' I get to LSU, and I had to cut it back off again. We already got Chris [Jackson] and Stan [Roberts], so, 'We don't need you to get thirty points a game.' 'Okay, Coach Brown, whatever you need me to do, sir, I'll do that.'

"Chris and Stan leave, and it's 'Now, Shaq, show what you can do.' I get to Orlando—score, score, score, score, score. Get to the

Finals and lose to Hakeem. Don't like living in Orlando, I get to L.A.—score, score, score, score, score. Don't win. Score, score, score, score, score. Phil [Jackson] comes. Score, score, score a little bit, win, win, win. Lose one year. We get Karl and Gary.

"I mean, I can get twenty-seven and ten whenever I want. Couple of years ago [2002–03], I had a bad foot and really wasn't in the greatest shape and still averaged twenty-seven. I can get twenty-seven, period, every night. Six or seven points a quarter, I can do that. But it just don't make sense to do things when you have all this talent with you.

"So that's why, when I played with Kobe, I'd say Kobe doesn't have to shoot every time, doesn't have to score all the time. I'm not picking on him, it's just that I'm all about business and I'm all about winning. Ever since I was little, I've been getting triple-teamed. And if we wanted to win games, my father said, you know what, get the ball to Todd, he'll cut off you and throw it right to him. . . . Because, you know, as a kid, winning was everything. If you didn't win, you cried. I always used to hate to lose. So I learned how to give it up. In high school too. In high school I played with a whole bunch of white guys that could shoot. So we went 36–0 my last year. Throw it in, if they don't double, Shaq go to work. Stay in there. Make the ref call three seconds every time. Just get it and shoot your little jump hook. Bam, bam, bam. When they double, kick it out to guys that can shoot. College, same thing."

But in the pros, it wasn't always the same thing. If he kicked it out to Kobe, most of the time it never got kicked back.

Is that the way to become the most dominant ever?

"No, it isn't," Shaq said.

And so now you know why Shaq and Kobe never truly got along on the court. Now you know why Shaq's in Miami. Proving again how dominant he really is.

Needed to be said.

Ask Shaquille O'Neal if leadership is important, and he'll say, hell, yeah.

Ask Shaq if dealing with pressure is important, and he'll say, damn straight.

Ask Shaq if competitive drive is important, and he'll say, you betcha.

Ask Shaq if confidence is important, and he'll say, no doubt.

Ask Shaq if mental toughness is important, and he'll say, abso-bleeping-lutely.

But ask Shaq if there's a better intangible, something else that makes a team great, and he'll tell you exactly what that is:

Humor.

In NBA history, no superstar has ever been this much of a team clown. Not only does Shaquille O'Neal dominate in scoring and rebounding (career averages of twenty-seven and twelve, respectively), he also excels at keeping his teammates doubled over in laughter.

"I keep a team loose by being silly," he said. "I think when you concentrate too hard, you really can't do nothing. So I'm just always being silly, being myself. It's important for the team. Guys that are serious all the time, they can't concentrate. The only time to be serious like that is forty minutes before the game."

To put it mildly, Shaq is entertaining. He's obsessed with gaudy cars, Ice, tattoos, and Superman. But the way he keeps a team loose is simple. He just opens his mouth:

1. Shaq's comment when asked whether he had visited the Parthenon during his trip to Greece: "I can't really remember the names of the clubs that we went to."
2. Shaq's comment when asked why he didn't know the phone number to the Lakers' front office: "We, as humans, only use 8 percent of our craniums. Why fill it up with non-essential things?"
3. Shaq's comment after being told he'd offended women everywhere when he said George Karl looked like a woman coach: "Sorry, women."
4. Shaq's comment after he dove for a loose ball near the sideline and broke a reporter's computer: "I'll buy you a new one at Radio Shaq."
5. Shaq's comment when told Eddy Curry's nickname was

"Baby Shaq": "There already is a baby Shaq. My one-year-
  old."
6. Shaq's comment after dominating Yao Ming one night during
   the 2003–04 season: "That's why they call me the Big Diesel.
   I'm expensive, I'm built to last, and I'm stanky."
7. Shaq's comment when asked at his wedding if he took his
   bride Shaunie for richer or for poorer: "No. For richer or
   richer."
8. Shaq's comment after a game-winning dunk against Houston
   in the 2004 playoffs: "I'm no hero. A hero ain't nothing but a
   sandwich, and I'm trying to cut down on my carbohydrates."

Moral of the story: he's also the MFE—most funniest ever.

A lot of people say they've never seen anyone like him.

(Miami assistant Bob McAdoo, for instance, bumped into Shaq
at a restaurant, after Shaq had torched Alonzo Mourning in Miami,
and said, "Damn, big man, I didn't know you had all that. Spin
moves and all.")

On the other hand, a lot of people say they *have* seen someone
like him: Wilt Chamberlain.

Over and over again, Wilt is the one player Shaquille O'Neal is
compared with. Wilt weighed a ton; Shaq weighs a ton. Wilt was an
exquisite passer; Shaq is an exquisite passer. Wilt got traded; Shaq
got traded. Wilt was a Globetrotter; Shaq, in spirit, is a Globetrotter. Wilt's free throws were brutal; Shaq's free throws are brutal.

On the other hand, no one can ever remember Wilt dribbling a
basketball; Shaq can put it behind his back. Wilt shot a step-back
fadeaway; Shaq doesn't step back, he steps on you.

"I would've probably dominated him," Shaq said of Wilt. "Because Wilt was just power, power, power, and I'm more hip-hop
powerful. I've got some stuff with my power, you know what I'm
saying? It's 2005. It's like a 2005 Benz going up against a 1971 Benz.
Both of 'em are still great cars, but in these days, a 2005's got the
nice wheels, got the nice engine. Wilt's game looked good, it's a classic. But it's been over thirty years."

On the other hand, ask Shaquille O'Neal to analyze his own game, and he'll grab your tape recorder and be a little more humble than that. Here's what he said into my recorder:

"Shaquille O'Neal analyzing Shaquille O'Neal's game. On the court, very focused individual, very mean individual, plays very hard. Does not play dirty, plays real strong, likes to take the high-percentage shot. Doesn't do things out of his range. For example, even though he can shoot the fifteen-footer, he does not shoot the fifteen-footer. He stays in the painted area—that's why for his last twelve years in the NBA he's been top five in field goal percentage, because he's either taking a little jump hook or the shot off the glass or he's going for the dunk.

"Not a good free-throw shooter. Similar to Wilt. But when the game's on the line, you can put the ball in Mr. O'Neal's hands, anytime, and he will do it. Looking at the books, Mr. O'Neal is a historical player. He's one of three players to win regular-season MVP, All-Star MVP, and Finals MVP. One of the three players to win three Finals MVPs and a regular-season. Off the court, he's never been in trouble. Went back to college, graduated from college. Went to police academy, graduated from police academy. Is working on his master's. Has a wife and five children. Never been in the tabloids, never really done anything wrong. Soft-spoken. Really doesn't talk up a lot, and he's a real funny guy. So hopefully, Mr. O'Neal will go down as one of the top four or five big men in the game. . . . There's been a lot of great big men. Where does O'Neal rate himself among big men? He rates himself number four. Wilt number one, Mr. Russell number two, Mr. Kareem number three, and Mr. O'Neal number four.

"Why? Because those guys were here, and they put the blueprint for the game, and even though it's 2005, you really can't erase those guys out. Because without those guys, there'd be no me. If those guys weren't there, then you could say Shaquille O'Neal was the best ever in the game, but Shaquille O'Neal is just an updated hip-hop version of what has come before him."

SHAQUILLE O'NEAL'S PERFECT TEAM

Shaq is also not afraid to be candid when picking his all-time team:

"My point guard for leadership would probably be John Stockton. He's out there leading guys. By the pass, he's leading. My shooting guard? For dealing with pressure? I don't really believe in pressure, but Jerry West, I'd have to say Jerry West, because he hit a lot of big shots.

"Small forward with competitive drive? These days, I don't really know what competitive drive is, because I've been in the locker room with a lot of guys who act like that, but they'll be out there goofing. I guess I could be like everybody else and pick Michael Jordan, but I'll be different. My small forward would be James Worthy.

"Power forward with confidence? There're a lot of confident guys. But I'd say confidence goes to Mr. Barkley. Because he *thinks* he's the greatest player.

"The center with mental toughness? Bill Russell. Russell, yeah.

"A sixth man with versatility? I'll have to go with Vince Carter. An unselfish guy? Me. A guard with courage? Iverson. A forward with intensity? No, not Bill Laimbeer. Laimbeer is dirty. Probably Kobe. Someone with a will to dominate? Me. Always me.

"My general manager, I'd go with Jerry West. My coach, probably Phil. Phil Jackson."

But Shaq wasn't done. . . .

"Now, my all hip-hop team. The best point guard, I have to go with Jason Kidd. My hip-hop shooting guard, I'd have to go with Dale Ellis. My hip-hop small forward, I'll still have to go with James Worthy, because he was ahead of his time. My hip-hop four would be Larry Bird, because he was just bad. You knew what he was gonna do, and he was slow and he was all that, but you still couldn't stop him. When you know what a man's gonna do, and you still can't stop him, that means his game is nice. My hip-hop center goes to Hakeem Olajuwon, because he was the only guy I couldn't break. My hip-hop Sixth Man would probably be Bobby Jackson.

"And I have a new millennium team: new millennium point guard: Mike Bibby. New millennium shooting guard: Allen Iverson. New millennium small forward, probably be Tracy McGrady. New millennium power forward, Elton Brand. And my new millennium center would be me."

And his new millennium free-throw shooter?

"Not me."

Not you?

"Well, I'm gonna keep working. . . . Millennium ain't over yet. Is it?"

John Stockton (leadership)

Jerry West (dealing with pressure)

Bill Russell (mental toughness)

James Worthy (competitive drive)

Charles Barkley (confidence)

Vince Carter (versatility)

Allen Iverson (courage)

Kobe Bryant (intensity)

Shaquille O'Neal (will to dominate)

Shaquille O'Neal (unselfish)

Coach: Phil Jackson

General Manager: Jerry West

SHAQUILLE O'NEAL—CENTER

PERSONAL: Born March 6, 1972, in Newark, NJ . . . 7–1/315 (2.16 m/143 kg) . . . full name: Shaquille Rashaun O'Neal . . . nickname: Shaq . . . name pronounced "shuh-KEEL."

HIGH SCHOOL: Cole (San Antonio, TX).

COLLEGE: Louisiana State.

TRANSACTIONS/CAREER NOTES: Selected after junior season by Orlando Magic in first round (first pick overall) of 1992 NBA draft. . . . Signed as free agent by Los Angeles Lakers (July 18, 1996). . . . Traded by Lakers to Miami Heat for forward Lamar Odom, forward Caron Butler, forward Brian Grant, a first-round draft choice, and a second-round draft choice (July 14, 2004).

CAREER HONORS: NBA 50th Anniversary All-Time Team (1996).

MISCELLANEOUS: Member of NBA championship team (2000, 2001, 2002). . . . Member of gold-medal-winning U.S. Olympic team (1996). . . . Member of gold-medal-winning U.S. World Championship team (1994). . . . Orlando Magic all-time leading rebounder with 3,691 and all-time blocked shots leader with 824 (1992–93 through 1995–96).

COLLEGIATE RECORD

NOTES: *The Sporting News* All-America first team (1991, 1992). . . . Led NCAA Division I with 14.7 rebounds per game (1991). . . . Led NCAA Division I with 5.2 blocked shots per game (1992).

Season	Team	G	Min	FGM	FGA	Pct	FTM	FTA	Pct	Reb	Ast	Pts	RPG	APG	PPG
													Averages		
89–90	LSU	32	901	180	314	.573	85	153	.556	385	61	445	12.0	1.9	13.9
90–91	LSU	28	881	312	497	.628	150	235	.638	411	45	774	14.7	1.6	27.6
91–92	LSU	30	959	294	478	.615	134	254	.528	421	46	722	14.0	1.5	24.1
Total		90	2,741	786	1,289	.610	369	642	.575	1,217	152	1,941	13.5	1.7	21.6

NBA REGULAR-SEASON RECORD

RECORDS: Holds single-game record for most free throws attempted, none made—11 (December 8, 2000, vs. Seattle).

HONORS: NBA Most Valuable Player (2000). . . . NBA Rookie of the Year (1993). . . . IBM Award for all-around contributions to team's success (2000, 2001). . . . All-NBA first team (1998, 2000, 2001, 2002, 2003, 2004). . . . All-NBA second team (1995, 1999). . . . All-NBA third team (1994, 1996, 1997). . . . NBA All-Defensive second team (2000, 2001, 2003). . . . NBA All-Rookie first team (1993).

Season	Team	G	Min	FGM	FGA	Pct	FTM	FTA	Pct	Off	Def	Tot	Ast	St	Blk	TO	Pts	RPG	APG	PPG
										Rebounds								Averages		
92–93	Orl	81	3,071	733	1,304	.562	427	721	.592	342	780	1,122	152	60	286	307	1,893	13.9	1.9	23.4
93–94	Orl	81	3,224	953	1,591	.599	471	850	.554	384	688	1,072	195	76	231	222	2,377	13.2	2.4	29.3
94–95	Orl	79	2,923	930	1,594	.583	455	854	.533	328	573	901	214	73	192	204	2,315	11.4	2.7	29.3
95–96	Orl	54	1,946	592	1,033	.573	249	511	.487	182	414	596	155	34	115	155	1,434	11.0	2.9	26.6
96–97	LAL	51	1,941	552	991	.557	232	479	.484	195	445	640	159	46	147	146	1,336	12.5	3.1	26.2
97–98	LAL	60	2,175	670	1,147	.584	359	681	.527	208	473	681	142	39	144	175	1,699	11.4	2.4	28.3
98–99	LAL	49	1,705	510	885	.576	269	498	.540	187	338	525	114	36	82	122	1,289	10.7	2.3	26.3
99–00	LAL	79	3,163	956	1,665	.574	432	824	.524	336	742	1,078	299	36	239	223	2,344	13.6	3.8	29.7
00–01	LAL	74	2,924	813	1,422	.572	499	972	.513	291	649	940	277	47	204	218	2,125	12.7	3.7	28.7
01–02	LAL	67	2,422	712	1,229	.579	398	717	.555	235	480	715	200	41	137	171	1,822	10.7	3.0	27.2
02–03	LAL	67	2,535	695	1,211	.574	451	725	.622	259	483	742	206	38	159	196	1,841	11.1	3.1	27.5
03–04	LAL	67	2,464	554	948	.584	331	676	.490	246	523	769	196	34	166	195	1,439	11.5	2.9	21.5
Total		809	30,493	8,670	15,020	.577	4,573	8,508	.537	3,193	6,588	9,781	2,309	560	2,102	2,334	21,914	12.1	2.9	27.1

THREE-POINT FIELD GOALS: 1992–93, 0-for-2; 1993–94, 0-for-2; 1994–95, 0-for-5; 1995–96, 1-for-2 (.500); 1996–97, 0-for-4; 1998–99, 0-for-1; 1999–2000, 0-for-1; 2000–01, 0-for-2; 2001–02, 0-for-1. Total: 1-for-20 (.050).

PERSONAL FOULS/DISQUALIFICATIONS: 1992–93, 321/8; 1993–94, 281/3; 1994–95, 258/1; 1995–96, 193/1; 1996–97, 180/2; 1998–99, 155/4; 1999–2000, 255/2; 2000–01, 256/6; 2001–02, 199/2. Total: 2,745/37.

NBA PLAYOFF RECORD

NOTES: NBA Finals Most Valuable Player (2000, 2001, 2002). . . . Holds NBA Finals records for most points in a four-game series—145; most free-throw attempts—68; and most free throws made—45 (2002, vs. New Jersey). . . . Holds NBA Finals single-game record for most free throws attempted in one quarter—16 (June 9, 2000, vs. Indiana; June 5, 2002, vs. New Jersey); most free throws made in one half—13; and most free throws attempted in one game—39 (June 9, 2000, vs. Indiana). . . . Shares NBA Finals single-game records for most free throws made in one quarter—9 (June 9, 2000, vs. Indiana); and most blocked shots—8 (June 8, 2001, vs. Philadelphia). . . . Holds single-game playoff record for most free throws attempted—39 (June 9, 2000, vs. Indiana); most free throws attempted in one half—27; and most free throws attempted in one quarter—25 (May 20, 2000, vs. Portland).

											Rebounds								Averages		
Season	Team	G	Min	FGM	FGA	Pct	FTM	FTA	Pct	Off	Def	Tot	Ast	St	Blk	TO	Pts	RPG	APG	PPG
93–94	Orl	3	126	23	45	.511	16	34	.471	17	23	40	7	2	9	10	62	13.3	2.3	20.7
94–95	Orl	21	805	195	338	.577	149	261	.571	95	155	250	70	18	40	73	539	11.9	3.3	25.7
95–96	Orl	12	459	131	216	.606	48	122	.393	49	71	120	55	9	15	44	310	10.0	4.6	25.8
96–97	LAL	9	326	89	173	.514	64	105	.610	38	57	95	29	5	17	22	242	10.6	3.2	26.9
97–98	LAL	13	501	158	258	.612	80	159	.503	48	84	132	38	7	34	43	396	10.2	2.9	30.5
98–99	LAL	8	315	79	155	.510	55	118	.466	44	49	93	18	7	23	18	213	11.6	2.3	26.6
99–00	LAL	23	1000	286	505	.566	135	296	.456	119	236	355	71	13	55	56	707	15.4	3.1	30.7
00–01	LAL	16	676	191	344	.555	105	200	.525	91	156	247	51	7	38	57	487	15.4	3.2	30.4
01–02	LAL	19	776	203	384	.529	135	208	.649	67	172	239	54	10	48	62	541	12.6	2.8	28.5
02–03	LAL	12	481	121	226	.535	82	132	.621	63	115	178	44	7	34	35	324	14.8	3.7	27.0
03–04	LAL	22	917	182	307	.593	109	254	.429	91	200	291	55	7	61	55	473	13.2	2.5	21.5
Total		158	6,382	1,658	2,951	.562	978	1,889	.518	722	1,318	2,040	492	92	374	475	4,294	12.9	3.1	27.2

NBA ALL-STAR GAME RECORD

NOTES: NBA All-Star Game Most Valuable Player (2004). . . . NBA All-Star Game Co-Most Valuable Player (2000).

Season	Team	Min	FGM	FGA	Pct	FTM	FTA	Pct	Off	Def	Tot	Ast	PF	DQ	St	Blk	TO	Pts
1993	Orl	25	4	9	.444	6	9	.667	3	4	7	0	3	0	0	0	0	14
1994	Orl	26	2	12	.167	4	11	.364	4	6	10	0	2	0	1	4	1	8
1995	Orl	26	9	16	.563	4	7	.571	4	3	7	1	2	0	3	2	2	22
1996	Orl	28	10	16	.625	5	11	.455	3	7	10	1	3	0	1	2	2	25
1997	LAL							Selected but did not play—injured										
1998	LAL	18	5	10	.500	2	4	.500	2	2	4	1	2	0	0	0	2	12
2000	LAL	25	11	20	.550	0	2	.000	4	5	9	3	2	0	0	3	4	22
2001	LAL							Selected but did not play—injured										
2002	LAL							Selected but did not play—injured										
2003	LAL	26	8	14	.571	3	5	.600	3	10	13	1	3	0	2	1	3	19
2004	LAL	24	12	19	.632	0	1	.000	5	6	11	1	3	0	2	2	4	24
2005	Miami	25	6	11	.545	0	3	.000	0	6	6	1	2	0	0	3	0	12
Total		203	67	127	.528	24	53	.453	28	49	77	9	22	0	9	17	18	158

(Rebounds: Off / Def / Tot)

THREE-POINT FIELD GOALS: 1995, 0-for-1; 2005, 0-for-1. Total: 0-for-2.

Chapter Nine

OSCAR ROBERTSON—Guard

Versatility

by Lyle Spencer

They came into the NBA together, having won gold medals for the United States in Rome as teammates in the 1960 Summer Olympics. Fourteen years later, they left together, their stamp on the game indelible. Through all that time, Oscar Robertson was always on Jerry West's mind, motivating him, driving him, inspiring him. The Big O, in a fascinating way, was Mr. Clutch's enduring role model, his personal measuring stick.

"Oscar was the best of the best," West, the legendary Los Angeles Lakers guard, said. "I have enor-

mous respect and admiration for him as a player and person, and he knows how I feel about him. That's what matters most to me.

"I always said he's the best I ever played against. I loved to compete, and I was always trying to get to his level. It took me a long time to get to where I was skilled enough and confident enough to believe I could compete with him on an even playing surface.

"He was just so incredibly good, so skilled and so smart. It's hard for people to understand how great he was unless you played against him. His versatility was unequaled, and he was incredibly competitive. There was just no weakness in his game. None."

In the Swinging Sixties, when goliaths and legends roamed the NBA landscape, nobody—not the Big Dipper in Philadelphia and San Francisco, not the goateed wonder in Boston—commanded more profound respect among his peers than Robertson, the stone-faced Cincinnati assassin.

"He could make you look silly," longtime rival Jerry Sloan said. "But he never showed you up, never got in your face. Oscar just scored on you, then ran to the other end to defend. You couldn't stop him—and that was a pretty sickening feeling. There was nothing he couldn't do on a basketball court."

The O in Big O, as he came to be known universally, stood for a variety of qualities in Robertson throughout his amazing basketball life: Original. Overpowering. Overwhelming. Olympian. Omnipresent. Omniscient. Omnipotent. Otherworldly.

One of a kind.

What comes shining through in the final character analysis is his uncompromising nature. Oscar never gave an inch of ground, on or off a basketball court. He stood firm and straight, unyielding in his beliefs, fully committed to doing what he felt was right on his way to becoming the best basketball player who ever lived.

There are those who will tell you he succeeded in his grand goal, for in versatility, in a full complement of skills taken to the highest level, there has been no match for the Big O from Indianapolis's Crispus Attucks High School to the University of Cincinnati to the Cincinnati Royals and, finally, to the Milwaukee Bucks.

"Oscar Robertson is, in my opinion, the best all-around player in the history of basketball," said Kareem Abdul-Jabbar, the Big O's gifted young sidekick with the Milwaukee Bucks during their 1970–71 NBA title run.

What distinguished Oscar from all the others, in Kareem's mind, was his total impact, physically, mentally, and emotionally. It goes beyond his statistical legacy: the full-season triple-double of 1961–62, the 26,710 points, 9,887 assists, and 7,804 rebounds, the league MVP award in '64 and three All-Star Game MVPs, and the nine first-team all-league selections.

It was the way he played the game, the way he inspired and elevated teammates, the way he carried himself.

He was as hard and impenetrable as pavement.

"Am I the greatest?" Robertson said, repeating a question during the NBA's fiftieth anniversary celebration in 1996, when he was named one of its all-time fifty greatest players. "I think I could have played against anybody, played very well against anybody.

"No one's going to ever know who's the greatest basketball player. I think I'm the greatest, 'cause look at my record."

Those numbers speak volumes. An artist in reflection, recalling his colorful palette of talents, Oscar sees subtleties, intricacies, essential components that add up.

"They look at a guy who dunks the ball today," he said. "They think that's great. You dunk the ball and can't make a free throw . . . can't make a play . . . can't set up an offense. You don't know when to slow the ball down or speed it up. You don't know who's hot. You don't know who can't guard from the other side. . . . You don't know the intangible things about basketball.

"I played as well as I could. I tried to conduct myself the way I was taught, by my coaches, my parents. That's all you can give—and let the cards fall where they lay."

He never dunked, he out-rebounded centers, he twice led the league in foul shooting, and he retired in 1974 as the league's number-two career scorer (behind Wilt Chamberlain) and all-time assist leader.

He seemed in complete control of every game he ever played, dictating tempo and tone with the force of his personality and the breadth of his skills.

"The biggest thing was his knowledge," West said. "He had more than skill; he had an instinctive ability to know where everybody was on the floor and how to make the right play. He had a gift to play the game, and he took that gift to the highest level you can imagine. He played every night the same way, a tremendous competitor who was incredibly consistent.

"People who look for the spectacular play—the dunk, the behind-the-back pass, that kind of thing—probably didn't comprehend how great he was. All he did was fill up the stat sheet every night."

West labored night after night to match those numbers, Oscar in his head.

"When somebody's that good, you're always measuring yourself, gauging what you can and can't do," West said. "With Oscar, you'd say, 'Can I run him left? No. Can I take him right? No.' I can try to do this or that, but he'll have the answer, because he's so smart.

"Our careers evolved. When we first started competing, I felt there was such a difference between us. When I became more experienced and confident, at least I felt I was able to challenge him. Every night he made you push yourself."

Robertson clearly prided himself on his fundamental ability to break down an opponent, physically and mentally.

"I don't think you have to be flashy in sports," Robertson said. "If you're a real good pro, you don't have to be flashy, because the name of the game is to be consistent, to be able to get on the court every game and perform."

Rivals speak of the man in reverent tones. They've never forgotten the first time they bumped chests with him. Facing Robertson in the flesh, the anticipation and then the experience itself, left indelible impressions on hardened old pros as well as young, overmatched dreamers.

"I was matched up with Oscar in his first NBA game," Utah Jazz announcer and former All-Star Rod Hundley said, a smile creasing his face as he revisited that 1960 meeting between his Lakers and Robertson's Royals.

"Jerry West had played with Oscar on the Olympic team that won the gold medal. Jerry was a rookie, like Oscar, and what people might not remember is that Jerry didn't start right away. Frank Selvy and I were the starting guards, and I drew Oscar.

"I went to Jerry before the game and said, 'You've played with the guy; you know all his moves and everything. What can you tell me about Robertson?'

"Jerry just looked at me and said, 'You're about to play against a guy who might be the greatest player of all time.' "

Hundley, the number-one overall pick in the 1957 draft out of West Virginia and a two-time All-Star, grinned.

"I'm not so sure to this day Jerry wasn't right," he continued. "Oscar was great from that first night on. He was just unlike anybody else, completely unique. I can still see him taking me to a spot about fifteen feet away, backing in, backing in, finally just jumping over me and scoring. There was nothing I could do about it—and I made the All-Star team that year.

"Jerry also made the All-Star team as a rookie, even though he wasn't starting on his own team. But it took him a while to get to where he felt totally confident as a pro. Oscar was there that first night. A great, great basketball player—maybe the greatest ever."

The Royals beat the Lakers that October 19, 1960, night at Cincinnati Gardens, 140–123, ushering in an exciting new era.

Hot Rod didn't feel so hot as he checked the stat sheet. Dominating the court in a fashion that was to become his norm, Robertson had authored the first of his 181 career triple-doubles that night, although nobody was calling them triple-doubles yet. Next on the all-time list: Magic Johnson, at 138.

"What I remember," Robertson's teammate, Jack Twyman, recalled through laughter, "was Rod saying, 'Switch!' all night."

Robertson loved to run off a screen by mammoth Wayne Embry at the high post, creating space to shoot that deadly jumper or deal to an open man.

Twyman, at 25.3 points per game, was the league's fifth-leading scorer during Oscar's rookie year behind four legends: Wilt Chamberlain, Elgin Baylor, Oscar, and Bob Pettit. The year before, Twyman had averaged 31.3, second behind Chamberlain—but his team had lost fifty-six games.

Formerly the Rochester Royals, Cincinnati would make the playoffs six consecutive seasons with Robertson in charge, starting in 1961–62.

"Before Oscar, the offense revolved around me," Twyman said.

"In effect, I became a supporting player to him. But you could see right away that Oscar was a franchise player."

"That first game he played," West said, "Oscar looked like he'd been in the league ten years. He was just so far advanced, in his skills and his understanding of the game. I don't think anyone's come into the league at that age who was that good right away."

Hundley understood what it was like to be overwhelmed by the Big O.

"He was so strong, he just went to a spot on the floor where he felt comfortable and either shot over you or found somebody open," Hundley said. "He had that ability to use his body to protect the ball while he was figuring out what he wanted to do.

"Oscar was in complete control of the game. There was nothing he couldn't do: dribble, pass, score, rebound, defend. He just did whatever he wanted to do basically."

Taking a Royals team that had won nineteen games the previous season to thirty-three wins while tripling home attendance, Robertson was the NBA's third-leading scorer as a rookie, averaging 30.5 points per game while shooting 47.2 percent, fourth best in the league. No guard had ever approached that scoring level.

In his uncomplicated view, he simply was continuing what he'd done in college, where he set a record averaging 33.8 points as three-time scoring champion and consensus national player of the year.

Robertson had nine games with forty or more points as a rookie, five with fifteen or more assists. His 9.7 assists average established a league record, eclipsing a mark set by another legend, Bob Cousy, who would come into Oscar's life a decade later as Cincinnati's coach.

The league's Rookie of the Year, the Big O was named Most Valuable Player of the All-Star Game for leading the West to a 153–131 triumph with twenty-three points, nine rebounds, and fourteen assists.

The East, featuring Chamberlain and Bill Russell, was overrun again the following season, with Robertson providing twenty-six points, seven rebounds, and thirteen assists in a 150–130 West decision.

That was the year Robertson produced the first and only NBA season triple-double: 30.8 points, 12.5 rebounds, and 11.4 assists. He narrowly missed repeating the act the following season, averaging 31.4 points, 11 assists, and 9.9 rebounds for a team that improved by another ten wins. In two other seasons, he came within one rebound or one assist per game of authoring a season triple-double.

"There are nights when even the great players just don't shoot the ball well," West said. "But they still can have a great impact on games, rebounding, defending, passing, doing all the intangible things that help a team win.

"That's when you really see a great player, when he's shooting poorly but still helping his team. The great players make poor players better. That's what Oscar did, throughout his career."

Robertson's do-whatever-it-takes approach first became clear to West when they were co-captains of the 1960 U.S. Olympic team coached by Pete Newell. Oscar and Jerry Lucas, his future teammate in Cincinnati, shared the team scoring lead at 17 per game, with West third at 13.8.

Rolling to the gold—Russia's twenty-four-point loss was the closest anyone came to them—the Americans were considered the finest team ever assembled. Some observers still call it the best of all the Olympic squads, with Robertson and West, Lucas and Terry Dischinger, Walt Bellamy and Darrell Imhoff, Bob Boozer, Adrian Smith, and Jay Arnette. A perfect team led by a great coach, Newell, and matchless floor leader, Robertson.

"It was just a special time for me to be able to play with him," West said. "I consider it a real privilege. We had a great team that really played together. As men get older, they appreciate times like that more."

Reunited with Robertson during the All-Star Game their first two NBA seasons, West thoroughly enjoyed being his teammate again.

"People always talked about this incredible rivalry we had, but I never looked at it that way at all," West said. "We were friends. I had so much respect for him, I just admired the way he played, his selfless nature. Everyone would get the ball. It was that simple."

The Royals were moved to the Eastern Conference in 1962–63, and there was Robertson again in control of the midseason classic, directing a 115–108 East victory with twenty-one points and six assists.

This was becoming a showcase for the Big O, who also claimed

All-Star MVPs in '64 and '69. His teams won eleven of the twelve All-Star Games he played in, eight in the East, four in the West.

Meantime, he continued to rack up unprecedented individual numbers as a versatile virtuoso in the regular season. A model of consistency, he averaged between 28.3 and 31.4 points in his first eight NBA seasons.

One of the league's premier coaches for seventeen seasons in Utah, Jerry Sloan was a fresh-faced kid out of Evansville when he came face-to-face with the Cincinnati floor leader for the first time.

Averaging a triple-double through his first five seasons—30.3 points, 10.6 rebounds, and 10.4 assists—Robertson was known to crush the spirit of rookies when Sloan debuted with the Baltimore Bullets in 1965.

"I remember taking a cab to Cincinnati Gardens, thinking about what I was up against," Sloan said. "I'd heard about Oscar Robertson, of course. I'm from Illinois and he's from Indiana; everybody knew Oscar Robertson. But I'd never seen him play in person. So this was going to be my introduction."

Sloan experienced some anxiety about the assignment when he learned that the Bullets' starting guards, Kevin Loughery and Don Ohl, both were sick that night. He'd be on Oscar, and he sensed that school was about to be in session.

"I was never intimidated by anybody, so that wasn't an issue," Sloan said. "I was trying to make a living, and you can't do that if you're going to play scared.

"I didn't really have a clue, and we got beat pretty bad. I got a good lesson. He took advantage of the situation. I remember thinking that when he was dribbling the basketball, it was like he had it under his arm. He was that comfortable with the ball. You weren't going to take it away from him. That just didn't happen.

"He could take a basketball and tell you where he was going, and he'd go there and do what he wanted. That's how good he was. He was so strong, and so quick and agile, he could just take you anywhere he wanted. And keep in mind, those were the days when you could hand-check guys all over the floor. With most guys, you could put your hands on their waist and kind of slow their progress.

"That never worked with Oscar. People say he used his off hand to keep you away, but he didn't need to do that. I can't imagine how unstoppable he'd have been without the hand-check rule, the way it is now."

Even as Robertson was exploiting the raw rookie, Sloan appreciated Oscar's demeanor. Known for his businesslike style, Robertson didn't verbally target the kid defending him, nor did he rub it in when he dropped one of his familiar one-handed jumpers over him. Nobody ever duplicated that jumper, cocked over his right shoulder in his right hand, released so purely and accurately.

"You had to respect him—I don't know anybody who didn't have total respect for Oscar's professionalism, the way he played," Sloan said. "He played the game on the floor, the way Magic and Bird did. You see guys today in the air all the time, but what do they accomplish? Oscar never did anything without a purpose. He had the ball all the time and could have scored a lot more than he did.

"He easily could have scored as many points as Michael Jordan. Oscar could score from anywhere on the floor, anytime he wanted. But he was the dictator, getting the ball to the right guy. He could see the game so much better than anybody else, because of his height and vision. That was a huge advantage."

There was in Sloan's voice a genuine awe as he flashed back to prime-time Robertson, carving up defenders, as serious and expressionless as a surgeon.

"I gave it everything I had, but I never had much success with Oscar," said Sloan, four times a first-team all-NBA defender. "It was the same with Jerry West. They were different players—West a little quicker with his shot, Oscar stronger. But the results were the same. Those were great, great players, as great as anybody who's played. And I've been in this game a long time."

Abdul-Jabbar had vivid memories of Sloan going at it with the Big O when Jerry was with the Chicago Bulls and Robertson was running the show for Kareem in Milwaukee.

"Oscar was a master of the three-point play (before the arc), and he was at his best against guys who played him tough," Kareem said. "Oscar versus Jerry Sloan was always a great matchup, because Jerry played very physical defense.

"Jerry would get great position, allowing no movement, no first step to the hoop, and then let his man run into him and be charged with the foul. Oscar loved that, because it played right into his hands. Oscar would always let Jerry set, then fake as if to go around him. Jerry would react, and as soon as he started Oscar would bowl Jerry over, go up, and hit the jumper—and he'd be on his way to the foul line as the whistle was blowing and the ball was hitting the net. Oscar was so subtle he'd never get called for it.

"Meanwhile, Oscar was a truck. It was like getting hit by Jim Brown. But Sloan would bounce up, complain to the refs, and get on with his game. I loved to watch them."

While West was widely viewed as Oscar's only equal in the backcourt during their time, the Lakers star rarely defended Oscar in the early years, generally deferring to backcourt partners such as Hundley, Selvy, or Dick Barnett.

"I was 177 pounds when we came into the league, and Oscar was about 210, 215," West said. "I look at myself, and I was so weak then in comparison. He was the long-armed, strong, classic athlete, powerfully built."

"We didn't want to wear Jerry out or get him in foul trouble," Hundley said. "I don't think he minded not guarding Oscar. He always held Oscar in the highest esteem, as if he was on a level above everyone else. Even at his peak, I'm not sure Jerry ever really felt he was as good as Oscar."

While Robertson's fundamental genius set him apart and was best appreciated by pros of his era, closer to Robertson in style than West or anybody else was Jerry's teammate Elgin Baylor.

Even though they played different positions and rarely guarded each other, Oscar and Elgin held each other in the highest regard, Robertson unfailingly mentioning Baylor and West as two of the game's premier players.

If Baylor was the NBA's answer to Willie Mays—boldly innovative, spectacular, breathtaking in every way—then Robertson was Henry Aaron, a quiet master of his craft, never seeking attention, relentlessly consistent.

"I played with Elgin and learned so much from him," West said, "and I learned an awful lot from Oscar Robertson. I learned different things from the two of them.

"Depending on your physical gifts, you try to combine the best elements of what you see in players. You figured it out for yourself. There weren't any training aids out there. I'd always say, 'Can I physically do this, or not?' I learned a lot from watching how controlled Oscar was.

"I just marveled at Oscar's skill level and the level he competed on every night. Elgin was the same way, a great player who came at you with everything he had."

Baylor is flattered by comparisons with Robertson.

"When I played, I knew every position, what every guy on the floor was supposed to do," said Baylor, vice president of basketball operations for the Los Angeles Clippers since 1986. "Oscar was the same way. He didn't hold anything back; he let his teammates know how he felt about things. He was really a perfectionist, and a leader.

"Oscar had great basketball skills and an extremely high basketball IQ. He was as smart as anybody I ever played against. You always knew you were going up against a finely tuned athlete and basketball mind.

"It was really interesting for me watching Oscar, how he never rushed anything, just took his time. He was always in complete control of everything he was doing, a real master of the game."

Baylor played up front, defending Robertson only on occasion. But he saw enough of the Big O on both ends of the floor to know the regal Royal was a vastly underrated defender.

"We were the same size, both six-five," Baylor said. "I weighed 225, and he was a little less than that. Oscar was a good defender. He played smart and had strong hands to go with everything else. He could put those hands on guys and stop them.

"There are certain rules now that benefit offensive players, especially in going to the basket. We didn't have that area under the hoop marked off, so it was a charge when you knocked a guy down in there. Now you go to the free-throw line. I think Oscar and myself would have benefited from that rule."

West, formerly a highly successful executive with the Lakers and now the Memphis Grizzlies, thinks the offensive stars from his era would have benefited from liberalized interpretations of the palming rule.

"When we played, you dribbled on top of the ball," West said. "They began dribbling on the side of the ball, and now they're dribbling underneath the basketball. If you're a good offensive player and put up numbers, they let you do some things we never did. You can carry the ball anywhere you want.

"If you gave Oscar any more advantages besides what he had already with his talent and size and strength, it would've been ridiculous."

Baylor, at Seattle University, made it to the NCAA title game, losing to Kentucky while winning the tournament's Most Outstanding Player award. It was a frustration he would share with both West and Robertson.

His sophomore year, Kansas State knocked off Oscar's Cincinnati Bearcats in overtime in the Midwest Regional in spite of Oscar's thirty points and fourteen rebounds. Taking out his frustration on Arkansas in the regional third-place game, Robertson produced a tournament-record fifty-six points.

There would be more of the same disappointment in his junior and senior years: California knocked off Cincinnati both times in the semifinals. In his final college game, Oscar had thirty-two points and fourteen rebounds in a third-place victory over NYU. Having averaged 33.8 points and 15.3 rebounds across his career, he was Mr. Consistency to the end.

"I saw him in college but never got a chance to play him until he came to the pros," Baylor said. "Everybody knew he was going to be great when he came into the league, and he didn't let anybody down.

"We were good friends, and we loved competing against each other. We had some great games when he was in Cincinnati. I think we usually won, though."

Baylor smiled as he recalled his Lakers taking the measure of Oscar's Royals in those days when scores in the 130s were commonplace.

An unsparing critic, never easily impressed, Baylor doesn't believe there's such a thing as a perfect player.

"How could there be?" he said. "A perfect player would be one who never made a mistake. Everyone makes mistakes.

"But I will say this: Oscar, at his position, was as close to perfect as perfect could be."

Sloan agreed with that assessment wholeheartedly.

"He'd always make the right play, the correct decision, whether it was on the break or in the set offense," Sloan said. "That's why players like to play with guys like that. They know they'll get the ball if they're open."

Twyman, a perennial All-Star forward, was one of the lucky ones on the receiving end of Robertson's perfect passes for seven seasons in Cincinnati.

"What set Oscar apart was purely and simply his great athleticism coupled with his tremendous strength," Twyman said. "I guarded Elgin Baylor, and I'd have to say Oscar was at least as strong as Elgin. Baylor was a great player, don't get me wrong. That's a fair comparison, with Oscar. But I think I'd have had more trouble guarding Oscar, because of his size, strength, and skills.

"Oscar was so strong, he could control the ball against a double team and find the open man. He had great vision, just a remarkable ability to find somebody in a good position. We had laid the foundation when he came to us in 1960, and he made a good team a great team, in my opinion. We just couldn't beat the Celtics."

In 1964 Boston was on its way to a fifth straight NBA title when the Royals stretched Red Auerbach's club to a Game 7 in the East Finals.

"Our management, in its infinite wisdom, booked Cincinnati Gardens for the Shrine Circus during the playoffs," Twyman recalled. "We had to play our home games in Schmidt Fieldhouse at Xavier University, and it wasn't much of a home-court advantage. The Celtics won two games there. But we won twice in Boston Garden [Games 1 and 3] to force a Game 7.

"That was a real heartbreaker, losing that one. It was the closest we came."

Robertson, disqualified on fouls only once all season, recalled that getting four personals in the first quarter of that Game 7 inhibited his aggressiveness. The Celts prevailed, 140–131, and went on to beat the Lakers in six games in the Finals.

Robertson became a legend in Cincinnati whose image would appear—against his wishes initially—on a nine-foot bronze statue outside the east concourse of the University of Cincinnati's Shoemaker Center in 1994.

At the statue's unveiling, Robertson spoke through tears about the sacrifices of Jackie Robinson in breaking baseball's color barrier and about the first African American players in the NBA and what they went through. It was a rare public display of emotion by a man always in control.

He'd been involved in trying to create social change for years. As president of the Players Association for more than a decade, starting in 1963, he was an outspoken advocate and helped forge free agency. The "Oscar Robertson suit" surfaced in 1970, when he was a driving force in a lawsuit challenging a proposed merger between the NBA and the American Basketball Association.

His greatest sacrifice would come later, when he donated a kidney to his ailing daughter, Tia, in 1997. Oscar always brushed aside the suggestion that this was a noble gesture, claiming that he did what any father would do for his child.

His work with the Players Association was monumental, by all accounts. He compared himself with Curt Flood, the baseball player who lobbied hard for a union and was blackballed by his sport, in his judgment, as a consequence.

"In anything you're involved in," Robertson said, "there has to be movement upward; you can't stay on a level plane, or else you become stagnant. The game of basketball had to change. The owners knew that, but they resisted."

The players' suit challenging the legality of the college draft and the NBA's reserve clause prohibiting free agency finally was settled after he'd retired, but from a player's standpoint, it was the greatest assist of his career. He remained active as president of the NBA Retired Players Association at the same time that he ran several businesses in Cincinnati.

"These players today have no clue what he did, what went before them," Twyman said. "They don't understand what went on in the '50s and '60s to get the game to where it is now.

"Oscar did so many things outside the game. When [Royals star] Maurice Stokes was sick, he was always there to help. I consider Oscar a good pal; we see each other from time to time in Cincinnati."

Despite his greatness and popularity, Oscar was on the verge of being remembered as the NBA's Ernie Banks, spending his life on also-ran teams. The Royals had endured three consecutive losing seasons without making the playoffs, and he was getting in a no-win position, feeling the heat if he shot too much or didn't shoot enough.

"No matter what I did, every loss was Oscar Robertson's loss," he said. "I did the best I could to win every game, but if you shoot over fifteen, sixteen times a game, the guys on the team wouldn't like it, [and] management wouldn't like it, [saying] we don't have a team concept.

"But they want you to perform as an individual to win the games. Sure, you must have stars on your team in order to win. Somebody has to put the ball in the basket. But still, it's a team game. And as a guard, I wanted to get the other guys involved in the offense. That was my chore."

Cousy, the NBA's first great floor general in Boston, became the Royals' coach in 1970 with the idea of reinventing them, in the image of his Celtics, as a fast-break team. He didn't feel Oscar's style was conducive to his design and began shopping his superstar. A trade with Baltimore was struck, but Robertson rejected it.

When another deal was reached with Milwaukee, Oscar took a good look at the roster—featuring a seven-foot-two reigning Rookie of the Year in the pivot named Alcindor, later to be Abdul-Jabbar—and decided it made sense.

Journeymen Flynn Robinson and Charlie Paulk became the answer to a trivia question: who did Milwaukee swap for the legendary Big O on April 21, 1970?

"That was one of those deals where you said, 'Oh, oh—there's a missing ingredient there, and Oscar was exactly what that team needed,' " said West, whose Lakers were still trying to claim an elusive first title in L.A. "Getting Oscar, with everything he could offer, was like getting two or three players. He gave the Bucks all the intangibles they were missing.

"He certainly was not in the prime of his career. He'd started to get muscle pulls. But he had enough left to make that team dangerous."

The impact on the Bucks was immediate and dramatic. Cincinnati, meantime, collapsed, falling sixteen games under .500 without Robertson.

"Oscar was even more valuable as a leader than as a scorer," Kareem recalled. "He was thirty-two years old [during the 1970–71 season] and had lost maybe a step, but his total mastery enabled him to be just as effective as when he was averaging thirty points a game. By directing and inspiring the rest of us, he enabled the Bucks to play the game the way it was supposed to be played."

Kareem wasn't the only young Buck who flourished under Robertson's guidance in Milwaukee. Forwards Bobby Dandridge and Greg Smith instantly catapulted onto higher ground, and Jon McGlocklin and Lucius Allen enjoyed the fruits of Oscar's generosity in the backcourt. The team raised its field goal percentage from .488 to a league-best .509 under Robertson's steady hand.

With all the pieces in place, the Bucks reeled off winning streaks of twenty and sixteen games over the course of the season. They steamrolled into the playoffs, winning the Midwest Division handily with sixty-six wins.

"What the Big O did for me that gave a quantum jump to my game was get me the ball," Kareem said. "It sounds simple, and it was—for him. Oscar had this incredible court vision and a complete understanding of the dynamics of the game. Not only did he see guys open on the periphery for a jumper; he knew when each of us would fight through a pick or come open behind a screen, and the ball would arrive and be there like you were taking it off a table."

Abdul-Jabbar recalled one game late in the season, against San Francisco and former Royals teammate Jerry Lucas, when Oscar turned back the clock.

"For some reason, Oscar shed ten years and brought out the Big O one last time," Kareem said. "That night, maybe because he was challenged, maybe because he was angry, maybe simply because he wanted to, Oscar just dominated the floor. He crushed everyone who opposed him on the court, threw hard, precise passes, rebounded with a passion, made 70 percent of his shots, and scored thirty-seven points before he was lifted. Total mastery. I envy the guys who played with him in his prime.

"Playing with Oscar was like working with Thomas Edison."

At thirty-two, his prolific days behind him, Oscar tied for tenth in the league in field goal percentage (.496) and was second in free-throw shooting (.850) and third in assists (8.2), averaging 19.4 points.

In the playoffs the Bucks knocked off San Francisco and Los Angeles, four games to one each, then swept Baltimore in the Finals. Young Bullets guard Fred Carter, Kareem recalled, made the mistake of getting a little overconfident early in the Finals—and Oscar made him and the Bullets pay.

Carter, as Kareem remembered it, was running down the floor in Game 1, shouting, "I've got Oscar! I'll score easy!"

Taking it as an insult, Robertson used every opportunity to school Carter from that point forward.

"Oscar took him down on the baseline and misused him," Kareem said. "He'd pump, get Carter up in the air, jump into him to draw the foul, hit the two, and make the free throw. He had Carter in foul trouble, talking to himself."

It was a mismatch, and it was over quickly, Robertson finally climbing back to the top of the mountain. It had been a long time since he'd celebrated a championship.

Born November 24, 1938, in Charlotte, Tennessee, Oscar Palmer Robertson moved to a housing project in Indianapolis with his family as a child. He began attending Crispus Attucks High, an all-African American school in Indianapolis, in 1952. It was a different America then. In his teens, Oscar and his friends wouldn't consider eating in a downtown restaurant or going to a movie there.

From two older brothers Oscar learned how to be strong to survive on a basketball court, and from his mother, who would work several jobs to support them, he inherited a work ethic that drove him to be the best-conditioned player wherever he competed.

"When I was a freshman in high school, I was five-eight," Robertson said. "Over the summer I went to see my grandparents outside of Nashville, Tennessee, and I grew maybe six or seven inches. But I still had guard skills and kept the guard skills throughout high school."

A National Honor Society student, Robertson was an immediate sensation in high school, taking Crispus Attucks to the state tournament as a sophomore in 1954 before losing to Milan, the school made famous in the movie *Hoosiers*.

There was no stopping Oscar after that. As a junior, his team was the first from Indianapolis to claim the prestigious Indiana state title, and when it repeated during his senior year, it was the first ever to go undefeated in the state. Oscar was Mr. Basketball, the most prestigious title in the state for a teen.

"It's a tremendous game," Robertson said. "It teaches you a lot of things about life. It teaches you about different people. I was told by my coach [Ray Crowe] when I was in high school that I was expected to do certain things for the team as a guard, and I just tried to keep those things within myself—and not let other guys on the team know how I was truly feeling, other than trying to win the game.

"Basketball was a way of life where I was from, [being] very poor. It was a social thing to do to play sports, because you had nothing else to do other than steal and get in trouble. People talk about basketball as a black kids' sport, but it's not. I think it's a matter of timing and what you have. I think people who are without certain things are going to have more drive, more determination, than people who are more affluent."

His great high school triumphs were tempered by city officials. Unlike other state champions who traditionally paraded through town, Crispus Attucks was asked to celebrate in a park in the minority section.

"Were they ever proud of the championship?" Oscar asked rhetorically. "No, because we were all black. When we won, it was almost like, 'So what?' "

Yet Indianapolis historians give Robertson's Crispus Attucks teams credit for helping force integration in the city's schools. It seems there was a fear that all-black schools would dominate the state tournament in Crispus Attucks's wake, so African American students began to be distributed throughout previously all-white schools.

Robertson had wanted to play for Indiana University but didn't feel accepted there during a recruiting visit. Widely recruited, and with the grades to go almost anywhere, he selected the University of Cincinnati, where he became the second African American athlete and first to play basketball.

Freshmen didn't play varsity then, but the legend of Oscar Robertson spread nonetheless. Half the arena would empty after Oscar's freshmen played. The show was coming, but it would have to wait until his sophomore year.

Twyman was a senior at Cincinnati when Robertson was a sophomore in high school. They met for the first time on the campus, when Twyman was asked by the school to assess Oscar's talents in a one-on-one game.

"My first contact with Oscar was at the university," Twyman said. "It wasn't against the rules at the time, so they asked me to go and shoot around and play a little one-on-one with him. The intent was to see what kind of player he was.

"My report was that this guy was a franchise player. That was 1955."

It didn't take Robertson long to justify Twyman's scouting report. In the eleventh game of his sophomore season, Oscar made his first trip to New York and stunned the Big Apple with fifty-six points—a Madison Square Garden record, and two more than Seton Hall managed against his Bearcats.

If that was an official christening of sorts, Robertson didn't let up, finishing his sophomore year with a 35.1 scoring average—and the NCAA record 56 in the season finale against Arkansas.

"I was put in at forward at the University of Cincinnati," Oscar said, "but I still had the guard skills. There were a lot of guys who were just as tall as I was or taller. But they didn't have the skills I had with the basketball. I didn't go out in the game to shoot initially. I went out to run the offense, to get our team going as a team no matter what level of ability we might have had. You're only going to win as a team."

Robertson and West had a shared experience in the NCAA tournament. Both were victimized by the man who would coach them in the '60 Olympics, Pete Newell. California's esteemed coach led his Golden Bears to victories over West and West Virginia, 71–70, in the 1959 championship game after eliminating Cincinnati, 64–58, in the semifinals.

It was more of the same in 1960 for Oscar, who shot poorly (4-for-16) in another semifinal loss to Cal, 77–69.

"Those are the losses that stay with you forever," West said.

The most underrated aspects of Robertson's game, the areas where many experts give the edge to Michael Jordan, were his athleticism and defense. Oscar was second in the state in the high jump in high school, and he had speed to go with his great strength.

Those physical qualities, coupled with his anticipation, made him a versatile defender, capable of clamping down on guards and forwards alike. Former NBA center Bob Ferry recalled the night in college when he was wearing out the nets for St. Louis University until the Bearcats put Robertson, five inches shorter, on him. Ferry didn't see much of the ball the rest of the game.

"Believe me, Oscar was a terrific defender," West said. "He took great pride in everything he did."

West's feelings about Robertson—his extraordinary game and his place in the game's history—are mutual.

"We came up at the same time," Oscar said. "We were on the [1959] Pan American team together [which won a gold medal]. We were on the Olympic team together. He is a very good friend of mine. He came from the same type background—very, very poor. He went to West Virginia, of course, and I came from Indianapolis, and here again, I think it was destiny. I think it really helped the league."

Robertson drew a parallel with the Magic Johnson and Larry Bird era in the impact that he and West had coming into the NBA, Oscar as a $22,000 territorial pick, West as a $16,500 addition by the Lakers as the number-two overall choice in that 1960 draft.

"Everyone wants to make it a white-black situation all the time," Robertson said. "But it wasn't true. Jerry was a great basketball player. I was more of an inside player, penetrating. He was a tremendous shot. He was very, very smart. He worked his game. He led his team.

"When the game was on the line, they called on Jerry West. I think you've got to be in critical situations in a championship arena in order to make you a great player. And he was a tremendous player during the clutch time. Mr. Clutch."

Robertson feels West ought to own a league MVP trophy to

match his own, referring to 1970, when Chamberlain was hurt and West carried the Lakers on his back.

"He should have been the MVP that year, but he was denied that," Oscar said.

It was fitting that Robertson and West, who both retired after the 1973–74 season, were elected into the Naismith Memorial Basketball Hall of Fame the same year, 1979, entering the shrine together. Oscar has had three numbers retired: 12, by the University of Cincinnati; 14, by the Sacramento Kings (formerly the Cincinnati Royals); and 1, by the Milwaukee Bucks. Number 44 out in Los Angeles thought that final jersey number was significant, venturing the opinion that Oscar was, and always will be, number one.

"In those early years I'd look at Oscar and think, 'Man, I have a long way to go if I'm ever going to be that good,' " West said. "That was one of the things that drove me. It was always substance above style with Oscar. He wasn't there to put on a highlight show; he was out there to win games.

"It was such a different time when we played. It had nothing to do with money. I used to get so nervous before games. We'd play three games in three nights, traveling tourist class on planes, sleeping in places no one today would consider sleeping in. Medical care was the best it could be, but it was nothing like it is today. We played hurt, sometimes really hurt. We just loved the game, the competition."

And a special few stood above all the rest. For his part, Oscar feels that the stamp of approval from contemporaries such as West is what matters most in the grand scheme.

"What's important to me is that the guys I played against, they have respect for me and I have respect for them," Oscar said. "That means more to me than anything."

Mission accomplished.

The late Wilt Chamberlain once said that if he could take his pick of any player in the game, it would be the Big O. Red Auerbach, with his nine titles in ten years in Boston, said Robertson scared him with his multiple skills.

"Oscar was a giant among men," Jerry West said. "Of all the players I ever played against, Oscar deserved everything that was ever written about him."

OSCAR ROBERTSON—GUARD

PERSONAL: Born November 24, 1938, in Charlotte, TN . . . 6–5/220 (1.96 m/99.8 kg) . . . full name: Oscar Palmer Robertson . . . nickname: Big O.

HIGH SCHOOL: Crispus Attucks (Indianapolis).

COLLEGE: Cincinnati.

TRANSACTIONS/CAREER NOTES: Selected by Cincinnati Royals in 1960 NBA draft (territorial pick). . . . Traded by Royals to Milwaukee Bucks for guard Flynn Robinson and forward Charlie Paulk (April 21, 1970).

CAREER HONORS: Elected to Naismith Memorial Basketball Hall of Fame (1979). . . . NBA 35th Anniversary All-Time Team (1980) and One of the 50 Greatest Players in NBA History (1996).

MISCELLANEOUS: Member of NBA championship team (1971). . . . Member of gold-medal-winning U.S. Olympic team (1960). . . . Sacramento Kings franchise all-time leading scorer with 22,009 points and all-time assists leader with 7,731 (1960–61 through 1969–70).

COLLEGIATE RECORD

NOTES: *The Sporting News* College Player of the Year (1958, 1959, 1960). . . . *The Sporting News* All-America first team (1958, 1959, 1960). . . . Led NCAA Division I with 35.1 points per game (1958), 32.6 points per game (1959), and 33.7 points per game (1960).

														Averages	
Season	Team	G	Min	FGM	FGA	Pct	FTM	FTA	Pct	Reb	Ast	Pts	RPG	APG	PPG
56–57	Cincinnati	13	—	151	—	—	127	178	.713	—	—	429	—	—	33.0
57–58	Cincinnati	28	1,085	352	617	.571	280	355	.789	425	—	984	15.2	—	35.1
58–59	Cincinnati	30	1,172	331	650	.509	316	398	.794	489	206	978	16.3	6.9	32.6
59–60	Cincinnati	30	1,155	369	701	.526	273	361	.756	424	219	1,011	14.1	7.3	33.7
Total		88	3,412	1,052	1,968	.535	869	1,114	.780	1,338	—	2,973	15.2	4.8	33.8

NBA REGULAR-SEASON RECORD

RECORDS: Shares single-game record for most free throws attempted in one quarter—16 (December 27, 1964, vs. Baltimore).

HONORS: NBA Most Valuable Player (1964). . . . NBA Rookie of the Year (1961). . . . All-NBA first team (1961, 1962, 1963, 1964, 1965, 1966, 1967, 1968, 1969). . . . All-NBA second team (1970, 1971).

| | | | | | | | | | | | | | Averages | | |
Season	Team	G	Min	FGM	FGA	Pct	FTM	FTA	Pct	Reb	Ast	PF	DQ	Pts	RPG	APG	PPG
60–61	Cin	71	3,012	756	1,600	.473	653	794	.822	716	690	219	3	2,165	10.1	9.7	30.5
61–62	Cin	79	3,503	866	1,810	.478	700	872	.803	985	899	258	1	2,432	12.5	11.4	30.8
62–63	Cin	80	3,521	825	1,593	.518	614	758	.810	835	758	293	1	2,264	10.4	9.5	28.3
63–64	Cin	79	3,559	840	1,740	.483	800	938	.853	783	868	280	3	2,480	9.9	11.0	31.4
64–65	Cin	75	3,421	807	1,681	.480	665	793	.839	674	861	205	2	2,279	9.0	11.5	30.4
65–66	Cin	76	3,493	818	1,723	.475	742	881	.842	586	847	227	1	2,378	7.7	11.1	31.3
66–67	Cin	79	3,468	838	1,699	.493	736	843	.873	486	845	226	2	2,412	6.2	10.7	30.5
67–68	Cin	65	2,765	660	1,321	.500	576	660	.873	391	633	199	2	1,896	6.0	9.7	29.2
68–69	Cin	79	3,461	656	1,351	.486	643	767	.838	502	772	231	2	1,955	6.4	9.8	24.7
69–70	Cin	69	2,865	647	1,267	.511	454	561	.809	422	558	175	1	1,748	6.1	8.1	25.3
70–71	Mil	81	3,194	592	1,193	.496	385	453	.850	462	668	203	0	1,569	5.7	8.2	19.4
71–72	Mil	64	2,390	419	887	.472	276	330	.836	323	491	116	0	1,114	5.0	7.7	17.4
72–73	Mil	73	2,737	446	983	.454	238	281	.847	360	551	167	0	1,130	4.9	7.5	15.5

| | | | | | | | | | Rebounds | | | | | | | Averages | | |
		G	Min	FGM	FGA	Pct	FTM	FTA	Pct	Off	Def	Tot	Ast	St	Blk	TO	Pts	RPG	APG	PPG
73–74	Mil	70	2,477	338	772	.438	212	254	.835	71	208	279	446	77	4	—	888	4.0	6.4	12.7
Total		1,040	43,866	9,508	19,620	.485	7,694	9,185	.838	—	—	7,804	9,887	77	4	—	26,710	7.5	9.5	25.7

PERSONAL FOULS/DISQUALIFICATIONS: 1973–74, 132/0.

NBA PLAYOFF RECORD

| | | | | | | | | | | | | | | | Averages | | |
Season	Team	G	Min	FGM	FGA	Pct	FTM	FTA	Pct	Reb	Ast	PF	DQ	Pts	RPG	APG	PPG
61–62	Cin	4	185	42	81	.519	31	39	.795	44	44	18	1	115	11.0	11.0	28.8
62–63	Cin	12	570	124	264	.470	133	154	.864	156	108	41	0	381	13.0	9.0	31.8
63–64	Cin	10	471	92	202	.455	109	127	.858	89	84	30	0	293	8.9	8.4	29.3
64–65	Cin	4	195	38	89	.427	36	39	.923	19	48	14	0	112	4.8	12.0	28.0
65–66	Cin	5	224	49	120	.408	61	68	.897	38	39	20	1	159	7.6	7.8	31.8
66–67	Cin	4	183	33	64	.516	33	37	.892	16	45	9	0	99	4.0	11.3	24.8
70–71	Mil	14	520	102	210	.486	52	69	.754	70	124	39	0	256	5.0	8.9	18.3
71–72	Mil	11	380	57	140	.407	30	36	.833	64	83	29	0	144	5.8	7.5	13.1
72–73	Mil	6	256	48	96	.500	31	34	.912	28	45	21	1	127	4.7	7.5	21.2

| | | | | | | | | | Rebounds | | | | | | | Averages | | |
		G	Min	FGM	FGA	Pct	FTM	FTA	Pct	Off	Def	Tot	Ast	St	Blk	TO	Pts	RPG	APG	PPG
73–74	Mil	16	689	90	200	.450	44	52	.846	15	39	54	149	15	4	—	224	3.4	9.3	14.0
Total		86	3,673	675	1,466	.460	560	655	.855	—	—	578	769	15	4	—	1,910	6.7	8.9	22.2

PERSONAL FOULS/DISQUALIFICATIONS: 1973–74, 46/0.

NBA ALL-STAR GAME RECORD

NOTES: NBA All-Star Game Most Valuable Player (1961, 1964, 1969). . . . Shares career record for most free throws attempted—98. . . . Shares single-game record for most free throws made—12 (1965).

Season	Team	Min	FGM	FGA	Pct	FTM	FTA	Pct	Reb	Ast	PF	DQ	Pts
1961	Cin	34	8	13	.615	7	9	.778	9	14	5	0	23
1962	Cin	37	9	20	.450	8	14	.571	7	13	3	0	26
1963	Cin	37	9	15	.600	3	4	.750	3	6	5	0	21
1964	Cin	42	10	23	.435	6	10	.600	14	8	4	0	26
1965	Cin	40	8	18	.444	12	13	.923	6	8	5	0	28
1966	Cin	25	6	12	.500	5	6	.833	10	8	0	0	17
1967	Cin	34	9	20	.450	8	10	.800	2	5	4	0	26
1968	Cin	22	7	9	.778	4	7	.571	1	5	2	0	18
1969	Cin	32	8	16	.500	8	8	1.000	6	5	3	0	24
1970	Cin	29	9	11	.818	3	4	.750	6	4	3	0	21
1971	Mil	24	2	6	.333	1	3	.333	2	2	3	0	5
1972	Mil	24	3	9	.333	5	10	.500	3	3	4	0	11
Total		380	88	172	.512	70	98	.714	69	81	41	0	246

Chapter Ten

BILL RUSSELL—Center

Pride

by Frank Deford

"Bill Russell" was always, to him, an alias. All the time he played, the Bill Russell of the box score or the long, lean man with the cackle for a laugh whom his teammates called "Russ"—neither was him. He was William Russell. You cannot stop people from calling you what they will. Willie Hartack, the great jockey, all but went berserk always telling people to stop calling him Willie. Dammit, he was Bill. William Russell never bothered. He let them call him Bill; he let them call him Russ. He knew he was William himself, and that was good enough.

That was because his mother told him that he was William—
William Felton Russell—and that he should never be anything other,
anything less. In fact, Katie Russell said that she would "wring his
neck" if her son ever let himself be anything but William.

It seems like a small thing, but all these years later, to himself and
to his wife and to the people closest to him, Russell is still and only
William. It does not matter much, perhaps. It's just a point of pride.
But then, you have to start somewhere with pride.

Ultimately, of course, this led the way to something that was
called Celtic Pride. Lou Gehrig was, famously, called "the Pride of
the Yankees," but it does not seem that any whole team except for
the Boston Celtics ever has been so associated with pride. There
was the coach, Red Auerbach, and the team leader, Bob Cousy, already long established in Boston, but Celtic Pride stemmed from
Russell's arrival after the Melbourne Olympics of 1956. The team
won its first championship that season, lost in the finals the next
(when Russell was injured), ran off the next eight in a row, and ten
of the next eleven . . . and then Russell rested. There has never
been anything like it in sport, not with the Yankees, not with the
Canadiens, not with any other team anywhere in the world.

It is impossible, of course, to accurately measure the ingredients
of a championship. How much is simply talent? Or coaching—organization? Leadership? Plain old Lady Luck plays some part. And attitude, of course. But how much? After all, teams have won titles
even though the teammates couldn't abide one another. Pride itself is
tricky, and probably hardest of all to define. It is often difficult even
to see. As Russell said: "The main thing about pride is that you can't
preach it or talk it." And we must never forget that the thing we are
most familiar with about pride is a negative—that, as the Bible says,
it "goeth before a fall." The majesty—and the utility—of the Celtic
Pride that Russell infused his team with was that it tiptoed right up
to the point of arrogance but never tipped over. It never fell. For the
man and his team, it simply was a force for good. It worked.

More so even than with most people, Bill Russell was shaped by his
family and his life. Pride was infused into him to take the place of

other things that, by historical circumstance and fate, were denied him. He was born in Louisiana, not only deep in the Jim Crow South but in the midst of the Depression, which left African Americans even more deprived. His mother instructed him: "It doesn't matter who you meet, William, just remember: there is no one better than you." But then she added: "But just know that you're no better than anyone else either."

And early on, his father, Charlie, inculcated the pride of accomplishment in him. "You know, if you decide to dig ditches, that's okay," he told the boy. "But I want you to be the best damn ditch-digger in the state of Louisiana."

Charlie Russell was largely untutored. He had grown up knowing people who had been slaves. He also knew the Ku Klux Klan. Yet somehow he and Katie managed to both protect their youngest son from the dangers of an oppressive society and exhibit dignity in the midst of their situation, which otherwise would have denied them so much dignity. Russell still remembers well an occasion when his father took him to an icehouse to purchase a block of ice. The white attendant simply ignored the black man, but as soon as a white customer appeared the attendant rushed to wait on him. Charlie Russell then simply turned his back and left. Infuriated, the attendant followed him outside, screaming: "Boy, don't you ever do what you just started to do."

Russell then watched as his father picked up the crank from the old car and raised it to the attendant. It was a dangerous thing to do. Maybe he wouldn't have done it if his son hadn't been there. But it was important for him to show young William that there was a point beyond which he simply could not countenance any more intolerance. There was a point at which pride could not be checked. Even now, when Charlie Russell is dead and the son himself is seventy-one, Russell said: "I try not to do anything that my father would not be proud of."

The Russells moved to Oakland, California, when William was nine. It was a far better place for a black family, but a scant three years later Katie Russell's kidneys failed, and she died. Her final request to her husband was to make sure that her two sons got a college education. As his high school years neared their end, William Russell figured that if he could get a job at the shipyards, he could pay his way through college, taking classes at night. He had not been, you see, a particularly outstanding high school player. Only one college, the little University of San Francisco (which didn't even have its own gymnasium), recruited him, and even then he was almost an afterthought. Maybe that was a blessing, though. Russell did not know what it was like to be spoiled and fussed over, the way so many young stars are. He was a student first, an athlete a distant second.

Years later, in fact, when Russell was traveling with John Havlicek, a stranger, noting their height, inquired of Russell if they were basketball players.

"No," Russell replied.

When the man left, a puzzled Havlicek asked Russell why he had said that. "Because, John," Russell replied, "I'm not a basketball player. I'm a man who plays basketball."

The advantage to being the ugly duckling is that you don't know you're going to become a swan till it happens. Russell's identity was not grounded on the court. It was easier for him to take pride in the success of the team than in individual glory. Indeed, he said that "team pride is really team ego." The individual must subordinate himself to the group. Likewise, Russell, for all his fame, has never enjoyed the attention that comes with celebrity. Whereas it is well known that Russell doesn't sign autographs, which are a representation of personage, he is often quite willing to chat with those same autograph seekers, person to person. Russell's daughter, Karen, said: "I still think he's a shy mother's son, and even now he's uncomfortable being in the spotlight by himself."

So, unlike many young stars who grow up suffering the team as a necessary evil, Russell found refuge and happiness within that embrace. His teammates remark on how different a creature he was alone with the team and then when some outsider intruded on that privacy. John Thompson, the former Georgetown coach who backed Russell up at center for a couple of seasons in Boston, even remembered Russell as being "playful" with his teammates.

Even as Russell emerged as a star at USF, his experience in college strengthened his feelings about the glory—even the sanctity—of the team. First of all, the simple matter of race came into play.

At a time when African Americans have so long dominated basketball, it is perhaps hard to imagine a time when blacks were a distinct minority, often perceived as interlopers in a white sport. Russell was one of the very first outstanding black players to appear on the national scene, but USF had two other black starters, K. C. Jones and Hal Perry, and this was, in many precincts, considered downright revolutionary. Whites snickered that the Dons were the Globetrotters; behind his back, the coach who dared start the three black players, Phil Woolpert, was called "Abe Saperstein"—after the Globetrotter owner. When the Dons ventured as far south as Oklahoma, the citizens there threw coins at the USF players when they practiced, laughing that it must be a minstrel show.

Much has been made of the Texas Western team, which won the national championship in 1966 with an all-black starting team, but it was Russell (with Jones and Perry) who had really trod that path a full decade before. Even after his junior season, when Russell had led USF to the national championship, had won the MVP at the Final Four, and was obviously the outstanding college player in the country, the local writers could not bear to acknowledge that, voting a white center player-of-the-year honors in Russell's conference.

Russell was supposed to be a good sport about it. Instead, he seethed. It convinced him even more that all that mattered was victory. "I might have been a little naive up till then," he said. "But I decided then that I would not let these people, whose judgment I did not trust, critique my career. I would just try to win every game, and then there was nothing anyone could say. Win a championship, and it is not a matter of opinion."

Russell also found in college that he had to contend with an orthodoxy that sought to restrict him on the court. Whereas he admired Woolpert for his courage in not being cowed by racists, Russell was frustrated by his coach's inability to accept the innovations that Russell brought to the game. At that time, for example, it was basketball dogma that a defensive player should not leave his feet. Russell, on the other hand, keyed his defense on knowing when to leave his feet at exactly the right moment. This was, after all, what allowed him to block shots and change the very way the game was played. But even as Russell succeeded as a defender right before

Woolpert's eyes, the coach persisted in upbraiding Russell for his contrary tactics. "You can't do that," Woolpert would say.

"But I just did," Russell would answer.

Happily, when he got to the Celtics, Russell found much more of a kindred spirit in the pragmatic Auerbach. In 1958, when K. C. Jones tried out for Boston, he was considered something of a long shot to make the squad, inasmuch as he was not an outstanding shooter. Cousy even told Auerbach that friends of his who had seen Jones playing in the army had advised him that it was a waste of time even bringing Jones to camp. But in exhibition games Auerbach began to notice something . . . curious. Whenever Jones was in the game, the Celtics improved in the score. There was nothing demonstrable that Auerbach could see in Jones's performance. No, he didn't shoot pretty. But the results spoke for themselves. Auerbach did not have an ego that required him to know why Jones helped the team. It was enough that—somehow—he did. Jones made the club (and ultimately, of course, the Hall of Fame).

Russell understood early on that just as many players possess an exaggerated pride in their own individual skills, so do many coaches suffer a misplaced pride in their knowledge. They deal in stereotypes and seek players who fit some idealized physical package rather than take the players who succeed despite their idiosyncrasies. And, of course, it is so very often those types who infuse a team with greater pride.

No one suffered more from the Celtics than the Lakers of Elgin Baylor and Jerry West. Russell (cackling) remembered one off-season encountering West, who bewailed: "Bill, I know we had a better team."

Replied Russell: "Jerry, the best team always wins."

Contrary to that hoary old cliché, though, is the fact that in basketball the team with the best players does not always win. More than any other sport, basketball often requires even the best players to subjugate their individual talents to the quest of the unit. Sometimes the way to win is to have the potential sum of the parts equal more than the whole. One time, for example, Russell refused to accept a raise when Auerbach made it contingent on Russell leading the league in rebounds.

"No, I won't take it, Red," Russell replied, "because if I change my game to be closer to the basket so I can get more rebounds, I'd end up hurting the team, because that would too often take me out of the positions where I'd be best for the team."

Russell, in fact, believes that pride in all aspects of American life today is undermined because we tend to place too much dependency upon the resident superstar. "What we've developed," he said, "is somewhat of a dysfunctional obsession with superstars. I'm not talking just about sports. It's true in business, entertainment, politics—even our personal lives. I believe that forgetting team ego actually robs teams and organizations of the rhythm of winning. The cult of the superstar distorts organizational structure, forcing everything and everybody to evolve around them."

Russell pointed out that whereas basketball may have been born and bred in the United States, the European style is focused on the team rather than the star. "And isn't it interesting," he noted, "that this team-oriented approach creates higher-scoring teams who play faster basketball and give the spectators a more exciting game?"

Probably no player in any sport is identified more with individual superstardom than Russell's great rival, the late Wilt Chamberlain. The two dueled in the pivot for a decade, Russell forever in Celtic green, Chamberlain in the various attire of the Warriors, 76ers, and Lakers. While many of Wilt's critics accused him of placing his personal achievements above team victory, Russell was sympathetic and even defended Chamberlain. As he told the big man once: "I'm probably the only person on the planet who knows how good you really are."

"I cannot begin to describe how good a player he was," said Russell. "He was six inches taller than me. He was a whole lot stronger. He was the fastest guy on every team he played on. He was extremely smart, and he possessed limitless skills. If he wanted to lead the league in scoring, he did. Assists—he did. Rebounds—he did."

To Russell's mind, though, Chamberlain's problem was not that he was selfish but that he was, in effect, so good that he got lost differentiating between self and team. "Listen, Wilt wanted to win as much as anybody who ever played," Russell said. "He played so hard he always had to change jerseys at halftime. They were that soaked in sweat. But here is the way his thought process worked: 'I am the best player ever. Therefore, if I play as well as I can, then we must win.' And it's just not that simple a correlation.

"Now, if I had ever approached our matchups as a test of manhood to see who was really better man on man, I do feel that I could have held my own, but I also feel that in the process our team likely would have lost. So my strategy—our strategy—was simple. It was okay if Wilt got even forty-five or fifty points in a game, so long as we won. What I would do is, I would let Wilt get comfortably into his rhythm and then slowly and imperceptibly begin to edge him a few inches out from his starting point. There is a place on the floor where every player is most comfortable. As I'd force Wilt away from that spot—just five, six, seven inches out—he'd have to work harder to achieve what he could away from his original spot, and this would take him—and then, in turn, his whole team—out of their rhythm."

One time not long before he died, Chamberlain called Russell up, "outraged" that *Sports Illustrated* had praised Dennis Rodman as the champion rebounder. Russell's response was direct: "You're the best rebounder ever, Wilt. You averaged more than me. Hell, one time you got fifty-five against me. I spent the whole evening ducking."

Then Chamberlain volleyed back: "No, you're the best rebounder ever, because you hold all the records in the playoffs. You never took a night off when it mattered."

Notwithstanding this mutual admiration, there was one occasion when Russell brutally criticized Chamberlain—and he regrets his intemperance to this day. This happened in the summer of 1969, after the Celtics had defeated the Lakers in what was Russell's swan song. The seventh and deciding game was especially emotional. Sam Jones, who was also retiring after this game, came into the locker room at the Forum with an actual script of the ceremonies that Jack Kent Cooke, the Laker owner, had planned for after the game, when—not if, when—Los Angeles won.

The USC band—not just a few drums but the whole damn marching band—was there, ready to parade onto the floor and play "Happy Days Are Here Again," while ten thousand balloons, predominantly yellow and purple, were going to be released. (Well, Cooke didn't like the word "purple," so he always called his Lakers' purple "Forum blue.") Sixty bottles of champagne would be popped for the principals, while Chick Hearn, the Lakers' voice, would interview the winners in gold and Forum blue at center court. Cooke had even spelled out the exact order of the interviews.

While it is doubtful that the Celtics needed any more incentive, Russell was furious. "Now there is not even a remote possibility that the Lakers are going to win this game!" he said. So, fired up all the more, he changed the game plan, having the Celtics run the Lakers ragged. Sure enough, Boston built to a large lead. It was at this point, early in the fourth quarter, that Chamberlain was injured and took himself out of the game. With Mel Counts replacing him at center, the Lakers began to eat into the Boston lead, and when Chamberlain told the coach, Butch van Breda Kolff, that he was ready to return, van Breda Kolff waved him off. Cooke stormed down to the bench and ordered the coach to put Wilt back in. Van Breda Kolff refused—an action that would cost him his job. Amid this chaos, Boston held on to win, 108–106, in what would be Russell's glorious valedictory.

That summer, on a speaking tour, Russell disparaged Chamberlain's effort, saying that given the importance of the game, no injury short of decapitation should have led Wilt to remove himself from the fray. The accusation was clear: Chamberlain had shown a distinct lack of heart.

On reflection, as his words were played back to him, Russell grew furious with himself. He called up Chamberlain and apologized. In fact, just so there could be no mistake, he apologized three times. What is especially interesting, though, is how Russell explained why he had so harshly criticized Chamberlain. It was hubris. "Wilt," he said, "it really had nothing to do with you. It was only false pride on my part."

And on the other side of the coin from exhibiting too much pride, did Russell ever have his own pride pricked? "Well, not really," he said. "But I'll tell you: if ever Red had told me that he wanted someone else to guard Wilt, that would have hurt. I honestly don't know what I would have done if Red had ever told me that."

While, wisely, Auerbach never called for such a move, in fact there was one occasion when Russell, the coach, took Russell, the center, off of Chamberlain. This was in 1968, the year preceding the Laker showdown when Chamberlain was still with the 76ers. Philadelphia

had whipped the Celtics in the playoffs the year before and held a
3–1 lead in the Eastern championship, with two of the remaining
three games scheduled in Philadelphia. Boston came back then, and
not only tied the series but played the 76ers tight in the deciding
game at Convention Hall. Only Chet Walker, the Philadelphia forward, was keeping the 76ers in the game.

Wayne Embry had spent his career at Cincinnati, where he had
played Chamberlain often, despite a half-foot height deficiency.
Auerbach had brought him over to Boston the year before, in a ma-
neuver he had perfected—importing wise old warriors who were de-
lighted to play a lesser role in Boston just for the chance to put on
the Celtic green. Arnie Risen, Clyde Lovellette, Willie Naulls, and
Emmette Bryant were some of the other oldsters who had been rein-
vigorated by the Auerbach AARP plan.

Now Russell called on Embry to come in and defend Chamberlain for a few precious minutes while he waylaid Walker. The ploy
worked: Embry held off Wilt, Russell shut down Walker, Boston
won 100–96, and the Celtics went on to win another title, the first
for Coach Russell.

The comfort and support that Russell found with his team was perhaps heightened in Boston because of the racial situation there.
Russell was the first African American star to play on any Boston
team. The hockey Bruins were an all-white team in virtually an all-
white sport, and the Red Sox were the last team to be integrated in
major league baseball, not fielding a black player till Pumpsie Green
made the club in '59. (Boston had no football team at that time.)
Chuck Cooper, the first African American drafted in the NBA, had
worn Celtic green as early as 1951, but he was no more than a jour-
neyman and had long since moved on. Before Russell arrived late in
1956, the Celtics were, like the Sox and Bruins, an all-white team.
Moreover, they had a glamorous and beloved star, Bob Cousy, who
had been a local All-American at Holy Cross.

Even when it was understood within basketball circles that Russell was the bulwark of the Celtics, most Bostonians still believed
that Cousy was the team's eminence. As the Celtics began to win

championships, adding black players—first Sam Jones, then K.C., then Tom Sanders and Naulls—the woebegone Bruins continued to easily outdraw them. Moreover, outside Boston Garden, Russell and the other African Americans found little acceptance. In the most horrific instance, intruders broke into Russell's suburban house when he and his family were away, rampaging throughout, destroying his trophies, even defecating in his bed. The white players had no idea how much he suffered. There was a reason. "Russ had too much pride to let people know," Tommy Heinsohn said.

Cousy had once nobly ushered Chuck Cooper home from an exhibition trip in the segregated South. Yet he still feels tremendous guilt about being insufficiently sensitive to what his black teammates were suffering. Indeed, on one occasion when I was interviewing Cousy on television on this subject, he broke down so completely in anguish that we had to stop the taping session until he could recover his composure. "I wish I'd done more to support Russ," Cousy said. "We were so close as teammates, but we all should have been more aware of his anger. But you know jocks—all into the macho thing. Always afraid to let the conversation be anything more than superficial. We mature so much later than anybody else."

Even if Cousy criticized himself, Russell found him an easy and early colleague-in-arms. "Within a week Bob and I knew we were friends," he said. A couple of seasons after Russell arrived, a writer from *Sport* magazine, doing a profile on Cousy, asked Russell in what ways Cousy had improved him on the court. Russell answered, simply enough, "None." After all, Cousy was a guard, and Russell a center; there was no reason either would "improve" the other's game. But when the story appeared, the writer caustically noted that whereas all the other Celtics appreciated Cousy, Russell was obviously jealous of him and unwilling to extend him any credit.

That night, at the game, Cousy's wife approached Russell's, commiserating with her. "It must be tough for Bill to have to hear this nonsense," Mrs. Cousy said. The message was clear: Cousy understood and would not let any misunderstanding created by others come between them.

And so, as Russell began to assume command of the team, he melded those elements of pride that had been instilled in him as a child in Louisiana, and nurtured by his growing-up in California, into what Auerbach and Cousy had already fashioned of Celtic Pride. Trying to sum it up, Russell defined pride in these terms, especially as it relates to the basketball court: "Pride is faith, plus confidence. It is about taking the responsibility that faces you, accepting what honor comes to you, and always working hard to prove how good you are."

But, of course, there are different subsets of pride. Russell noted some of them:

Take pride in who you are and what you look like

Especially when Russell was growing up, it was fashionable to make fun of exceptionally tall guys, to call them "goons." Russell learned to be proud of his height, to literally stand tall.

And, of course, from his earliest moments he had to face racial prejudice. Here too, he did not shrink. Long before the expression "black pride" came into common usage, Russell had lived it. With some other prominent black athletes of his generation, like Jim Brown, Oscar Robertson, and Arthur Ashe, Russell was outspoken as a visible African American celebrity. In fact, at a time when the word "Negro" was generally applied to someone of his race, Russell was among the first to use the straightforward word "black."

Take pride in what your strength is

Russell made the ironic point that one of the major elements of team play is selfishness. That may sound paradoxical, but it is counterproductive not to concentrate on what you do best; at the same time, you should appreciate what your teammates do best and applaud them for it—and help them achieve it.

The Celtics, of course, were a premier fast-break team. Indeed, it was often Russell's rebounds or blocked shots that initiated a break. The classic fast break features the ball-handler in the middle, "pushing" the ball upcourt, as they say, with a teammate on either wing—leading to the three-on-two surge. To make that work, the man with the ball—usually Cousy in Russell's first years—needs to have two other teammates moving fast, with him, on either side. Heinsohn would, more often than not, cheat back when he saw a shot go up and lead the charge down one side. Russell knew too that Cousy was inclined to go to Heinsohn, who finished exceptionally well on the break. And who would get the credit? Cousy for his artistic pass, Heinsohn for his thrilling, mad dash layup.

But none of that would work unless there was the anonymous guy on Cousy's other side—"filling the lane," in the vernacular. Russell, then, as soon as he snared the rebound, would often rush out to the side and be the third man, filling the lane, even though he was pretty sure that he would not get the ball, the basket, or the acclaim.

In many ways, taking that role was the ultimate in taking pride in team play—doing something that virtually no one else even noticed, much less appreciated.

As Russell pointed out, at the time he entered the NBA there were no true defensive individual statistics kept. There were no official categories for blocked shots or steals, and no differentiation was made between offensive and defensive rebounds. Especially more than most players, Russell had to be secure in his own estimation of his work, because nobody tabulated it. In a way, he needed self-pride more than players who were more offensively inclined. Also, probably because Russell had to appreciate his own unnumbered efforts, he learned to recognize those efforts in his teammates' play that weren't celebrated with statistics.

Auerbach famously lived by this credo. When Celtics came in for salary review, he never dealt in statistics of any nature.

Take pride in your job

It's easy to be the star. Celtic pride was based on players being "honest with themselves, understanding their limits," and thereby accepting whatever position was given them. Of course, as Russell pointed out, a little applied psychology from the coach and teammates doesn't hurt. It was Auerbach who created, with Frank Ramsey, the term "Sixth Man." Before that, it had never really occurred to anyone that the sixth man, or the seventh, the eighth, and so on, was anything but a substitute. "Now, all of a sudden," Russell said, laughing, "Frank wasn't just second-string. He was the Sixth Man—and now he played like he was on a mission."

One of the clichés that Russell thought is ridiculous is the declaration, when the playoffs begin, that "it's time to step up." To try to suddenly do something different and beyond your natural scope, he felt, creates pressure and is bound to end in failure. The same formula of balance that worked for a team in the regular season should be maintained. "The only change," Russell said, "would be for everybody to play with more determination—because, after all, in the playoffs you're meeting only good teams."

Take pride in looking out for each other on the team

Actually, in Russell's view, this starts at the highest level. "An organization must be built on pride," he said. "If an atmosphere isn't created in which players can function naturally and easily, then it's going to be hard for the players' own pride to overcome that."

After Rick Pitino left as coach of the Celtics, when the team was in bad spirits, Russell met with the two stars of the team, Antoine Walker and Paul Pierce, and he told them that, more than ever, they, as the leaders on the team, had to look out for each other. The next day Walker, the captain, went to the new coach, Jim O'Brien, and told him he wanted Pierce to serve as co-captain with him. Whenever Cousy and Russell called team meetings, the two leaders would begin by citing their own faults—not those of others. That would set the atmosphere for others to step forward and speak candidly, yet without rancor. Russell even boasted, "In my whole career, I never once yelled at a teammate of mine."

"Teams like to talk about what great fans they have," Russell said, "and obviously, you're helped when you play in front of enthusiastic home crowds. But I'll tell you, in all my years in Boston, our greatest fans were whoever was sitting on the bench."

He paused and added, "To be metaphysical for a moment, basketball is an activity played in a box that is limited by time and space. And in this environment, pride is the tiebreaker."

BILL RUSSELL'S PERFECT TEAM

Starting Five

Oscar Robertson: No one was greater than Oscar. Unlike anyone before or after him, Oscar could play any tempo and control it better than anybody. His range of talent allowed him to be effective in either a half-court game or a fast-break game. There haven't been too many players who, like Oscar, made the triple-double part of their game. He was a scorer, passer, and rebounder.

Michael Jordan: Very competitive. He was big enough not to be overwhelmed and could take a smaller guard down low and overpower him. He was an exceptionally good passer. He was an outstanding defensive player and would bring a range of options to his teammates. He could defend anyone anyplace on the court.

William Felton Russell: Winning was my life. There was nothing subjective about that. And how I contributed to that achievement or helped others succeed was the only goal. I believe I was the best player on this list to play without the ball. I didn't have to have the ball to be effective, or help others be effective, because it was what I did that was invisible that made the greatest contribution.

Magic Johnson: The same could be said about Magic that I said about Oscar, but he would be more relaxed with an up-tempo game. Beyond talent—and his was enormous—Magic was a great player because of his endless amount of passion. He had so much fun being great. It didn't matter whether he was rebounding, running, passing, or shooting . . . he was enjoying himself. Of all the players I ever saw, he had the best court awareness. I put him at small forward because he was strong, tough, and able to handle any small forward that played the game.

Larry Bird: Larry would do whatever it took to win. I would place him at power forward for pretty much the same reason I would put Magic at small forward, but Larry's outside shooting would make him unstoppable. Most folks don't realize that Larry was one of the greatest passers in the history of the NBA. Great teams need as many passers as possible to create options. But it was Larry's completeness that made him one of my favorite players of all time.

Sixth Man

John Havlicek: No one was ever more ideally suited than John Havlicek to be the Sixth Man. The Sixth Man has to have a special type of attitude. Havlicek never thought of himself as second team, as many Sixth Men have. When John hit the floor, he was ready to play. There has never been anyone who was better than John coming off the bench ready to play. I attribute that to his intelligence and passion for the game. He knew we expected him to deliver as soon as he touched the ball . . . and he did, always.

Bench

Jerry West: Jerry was a six-foot-four-inch Michael Jordan. As outstanding a defensive player as has ever played the game. Confident shooter and great scorer. I don't think I have ever seen anyone more confident and at ease in tough situations than Jerry. When Jerry took that final dribble and had that look in his eye, it was time to head back down the court. A great competitor.

Sam Jones: In my opinion, Sam was the best shooter I have ever seen. For twelve straight seasons, I watched him play and got to know how good he really was. Sam defined the word "clutch." In our championship seasons, five times Sam was asked to take the shot that would make or break the season. Five times he didn't blink or hesitate with the burden of that responsibility, and five times he made the shot.

Wilt Chamberlain: Wilt was big, fast, extremely smart, and a giant of an athlete. He epitomized my belief that the greatest players are outstanding athletes who can play basketball. He could lead the league in anything he wanted to. He led in scoring, he led in rebounds, he led in assists. He could do anything. Hey, he was so good that he even got fifty-five rebounds against me.

Shaquille O'Neal: Shaq is one of the greatest centers ever, for many reasons, but he was more effective than Wilt was without the ball. About five or six years ago he asked me, "Bill, what can I do to become better?" I told him, "Become a great passer." Today Shaq has evolved into one of the best passing big men in the league, creating many opportunities for his team. I also believe that he is one of the absolute smartest players around today. And from the outside looking in, I find him to be an incredibly hardworking big man with an outstanding work ethic.

Bob Pettit: In my thirteen seasons, Bob was probably the most competitive of all the players I've ever played against. His timing, his sense for the ball and the moment, and his desire to win at all costs made him such a tough opponent. He also had an enormous amount of dignity. There have only been one or two other players who achieved Bob's twenty points and twenty rebounds single-season average. In the final game of the championships in '57, Bob scored fifty-one points, had more than twenty rebounds against the Celtics, and had nineteen of St. Louis's last twenty-one points.

Elgin Baylor: I have never seen a better player than the young Elgin Baylor. Before his knees gave out, I remember almost wanting to just sit courtside watching him play. He could do it all. Scoring, rebounding, passing—and he did all of those things with a competitive passion. He could not only do the right thing but do it effortlessly, with flair. Before Jerry joined the team, Elgin single-handedly got his team to the NBA Finals on his shoulders alone.

Head Coach

Red Auerbach: Great mind constructed on the logic of mathematics. In the history of the NBA, there hasn't been anyone who won nine championships with the same team besides Red. That is a remarkable achievement because it dramatizes how well he related to one team. Red was one of the greatest listeners I have ever met. He knew how to motivate each player individually and the group as a team. He also taught us to be better listeners. We were beginning a new season when Red started giving us a pep talk. I remember looking at him and saying, "Three seasons ago, you gave us that same talk. . . . If you want us to win you have to come up with something new, none of that old bull——."

General Manager

Red Auerbach: What can you say about a GM who drafted three Hall of Famers in one season . . . the year he drafted K. C. Jones, Tommy Heinsohn, and myself? Or a GM who gave up his first-round draft pick to acquire Kevin McHale and Robert Parish in the same year? Red knew talent and was extraordinarily shrewd. His acquisition of Dennis Johnson proved that. Red also drafted John Havlicek as the last pick of the first round. In all of our years together in building the Celtics' unchallengeable record, he made only one trade. And what I was most impressed with was how he brought retired guys back for one, two, or three years because he knew how to utilize them in his system.

BILL RUSSELL—CENTER

PERSONAL: Born February 12, 1934, in Monroe, LA . . . 6–10/220 (2.08 m/100 kg) . . . full name: William Felton Russell.

HIGH SCHOOL: McClymonds (Oakland, CA).

COLLEGE: San Francisco.

TRANSACTIONS/CAREER NOTES: Selected by St. Louis Hawks in first round (third pick overall) of 1956 NBA draft. . . . Draft rights traded by Hawks to Boston Celtics for forward/center Ed Macauley and draft rights to forward Cliff Hagan (April 29, 1956).

CAREER HONORS: Elected to Naismith Memorial Basketball Hall of Fame (1975). . . . Declared Greatest Player in the History of the NBA by Professional Basketball Writers' Association of America (1980). . . . NBA 25th Anniversary All-Time Team (1970), 35th Anniversary All-Time Team (1980), and One of the 50 Greatest Players in NBA History (1996).

MISCELLANEOUS: Member of NBA championship team (1957, 1959, 1960, 1961, 1962, 1963, 1964, 1965, 1966, 1968, 1969). . . . Member of gold-medal-winning U.S. Olympic team (1956). . . . Boston Celtics all-time leading rebounder with 21,620 (1956–57 through 1968–69).

COLLEGIATE RECORD

NOTES: NCAA Tournament Most Outstanding Player (1955). . . . Member of NCAA championship teams (1955, 1956).

													Averages		
Season	Team	G	Min	FGM	FGA	Pct	FTM	FTA	Pct	Reb	Ast	Pts	RPG	APG	PPG
52–53	SF	23	—	—	—	—	—	—	—	—	—	461	—	—	20.0
53–54	SF	21	—	150	309	.485	117	212	.552	403	—	417	19.2	—	19.9
54–55	SF	29	—	229	423	.541	164	278	.590	594	—	622	20.5	—	21.4
55–56	SF	29	—	246	480	.513	105	212	.495	609	—	597	21.0	—	20.6
Total		79	—	625	1,212	.516	386	702	.550	1,606	—	1,636	20.3	—	20.7

NBA REGULAR-SEASON RECORD

RECORDS: Holds single-game record for most rebounds in one half—32 (November 16, 1957, vs. Philadelphia).

HONORS: NBA Most Valuable Player (1958, 1961, 1962, 1963, 1965). . . . All-NBA first team (1959, 1963, 1965). . . . All-NBA second team (1958, 1960, 1961, 1962, 1964, 1966, 1967, 1968). . . . NBA All-Defensive first team (1969).

														Averages		
Season	Team	G	Min	FGM	FGA	Pct	FTM	FTA	Pct	Reb	Ast	PF	DQ	Pts	RPG	APG	PPG
56–57	Bos	48	1,695	277	649	.427	152	309	.492	943	88	143	2	706	19.6	1.8	14.7
57–58	Bos	69	2,640	456	1,032	.442	230	443	.519	1,564	181	181	2	1,142	22.7	2.9	16.6
58–59	Bos	70	2,979	456	997	.457	256	428	.598	1,612	222	161	3	1,168	23.0	3.2	16.7
59–60	Bos	74	3,146	555	1,189	.467	240	392	.612	1,778	277	210	0	1,350	24.0	3.7	18.2
60–61	Bos	78	3,458	532	1,250	.426	258	469	.550	1,868	268	155	0	1,322	23.9	3.4	16.9
61–62	Bos	76	3,433	575	1,258	.457	286	481	.595	1,790	341	207	3	1,436	23.6	4.5	18.9
62–63	Bos	78	3,500	511	1,182	.432	287	517	.555	1,843	348	189	1	1,309	23.6	4.5	16.8
63–64	Bos	78	3,482	466	1,077	.433	236	429	.550	1,930	370	190	0	1,168	24.7	4.7	15.0
64–65	Bos	78	3,466	429	980	.438	244	426	.573	1,878	410	204	1	1,102	24.1	5.3	14.1
65–66	Bos	78	3,386	391	943	.415	223	405	.551	1,779	371	221	4	1,005	22.8	4.8	12.9
66–67	Bos	81	3,297	395	870	.454	285	467	.610	1,700	472	258	4	1,075	21.0	5.8	13.3
67–68	Bos	78	2,953	365	858	.425	247	460	.537	1,451	357	242	2	977	18.6	4.6	12.5
68–69	Bos	77	3,291	279	645	.433	204	388	.526	1,484	374	231	2	762	19.3	4.9	9.9
Total		963	40,726	5,687	12,930	.440	3,148	5,614	.561	21,620	4,100	2,592	24	14,522	22.5	4.3	15.1

NBA PLAYOFF RECORD

NOTES: Holds career playoff record for most rebounds—4,104. . . . Holds NBA Finals records for highest rebounds-per-game average—29.5 (1959); and highest rebounds-per-game average by a rookie—22.9 (1957). . . . Holds NBA Finals single-game records for most rebounds—40 (March 29, 1960, vs. St. Louis, and April 18, 1962, vs. Los Angeles); most rebounds by a rookie—32 (April 13, 1957, vs. St. Louis); and most rebounds in one quarter—19 (April 18, 1962, vs. Los Angeles). . . . Shares NBA Finals record for most free throws attempted in one half—15 (April 11, 1961, vs. St. Louis).

														Averages		
Season	Team	G	Min	FGM	FGA	Pct	FTM	FTA	Pct	Reb	Ast	PF	DQ	Pts	RPG	APG	PPG
56–57	Bos	10	409	54	148	.365	31	61	.508	241	32	41	1	139	24.4	3.2	13.9
57–58	Bos	9	355	48	133	.361	40	66	.606	221	24	24	0	136	24.6	2.7	15.1
58–59	Bos	11	496	65	159	.409	41	67	.612	305	40	28	1	171	27.7	3.6	15.5
59–60	Bos	13	572	94	206	.456	53	75	.707	336	38	38	1	241	25.8	2.9	18.5
60–61	Bos	10	462	73	171	.427	45	86	.523	299	48	24	0	191	29.9	4.8	19.1
61–62	Bos	14	672	116	253	.458	82	113	.726	370	70	49	0	314	26.4	5.0	22.4
62–63	Bos	13	617	96	212	.453	72	109	.661	326	66	36	0	264	25.1	5.1	20.3
63–64	Bos	10	451	47	132	.356	37	67	.552	272	44	33	0	131	27.2	4.4	13.1
64–65	Bos	12	561	79	150	.527	40	76	.526	302	76	43	2	198	25.2	6.3	16.5
65–66	Bos	17	814	124	261	.475	76	123	.618	428	85	60	0	324	25.2	5.0	19.1
66–67	Bos	9	390	31	86	.360	33	52	.635	198	50	32	1	95	22.0	5.6	10.6
67–68	Bos	19	869	99	242	.409	76	130	.585	434	99	73	1	274	22.8	5.2	14.4
68–69	Bos	18	829	77	182	.423	41	81	.506	369	98	65	1	195	20.5	5.4	10.8
Total		165	7,497	1,003	2,335	.430	667	1,106	.603	4,104	770	546	8	2,673	24.9	4.7	15.1

NBA ALL-STAR GAME RECORD

NOTES: All-Star Game Most Valuable Player (1963).

Season	Team	Min	FGM	FGA	Pct	FTM	FTA	Pct	Reb	Ast	PF	DQ	Pts
1958	Bos	26	5	12	.417	1	3	.333	11	2	5	0	11
1959	Bos	27	3	10	.300	1	1	1.000	9	1	4	0	7
1960	Bos	27	3	7	.429	0	2	.000	8	3	1	0	6
1961	Bos	28	9	15	.600	6	8	.750	11	1	2	0	24
1962	Bos	27	5	12	.417	2	3	.667	12	2	2	0	12
1963	Bos	37	8	14	.571	3	4	.750	24	5	3	0	19
1964	Bos	42	6	13	.462	1	2	.500	21	2	4	0	13
1965	Bos	33	7	12	.583	3	9	.333	13	5	6	1	17
1966	Bos	23	1	6	.167	0	0	—	10	2	2	0	2
1967	Bos	22	1	2	.500	0	0	—	5	5	2	0	2
1968	Bos	23	2	4	.500	0	0	—	9	8	5	0	4
1969	Bos	28	1	4	.250	1	2	.500	6	3	1	0	3
Total		343	51	111	.459	18	34	.529	139	39	37	1	120

HEAD COACHING RECORD

BACKGROUND: Player/head coach, Boston Celtics (1966–67 through 1968–69). . . . Head coach/general manager, Seattle SuperSonics (1973–74 through 1976–77). . . . Head coach, Sacramento Kings, 1987–88.

		Regular Season				Playoffs		
Season	Team	W	L	Pct	Finish	W	L	Pct
66–67	Bos	60	21	.741	2nd/Eastern Division	4	5	.444
67–68	Bos	54	28	.659	2nd/Eastern Division	12	7	.632
68–69	Bos	48	34	.585	4th/Eastern Division	12	6	.667
73–74	Sea	36	46	.439	3rd/Pacific Division	—	—	—
74–75	Sea	43	39	.524	2nd/Pacific Division	4	5	.444
75–76	Sea	43	39	.524	2nd/Pacific Division	2	4	.333
76–77	Sea	40	42	.488	4th/Pacific Division	—	—	—
87–88	Sac	17	41	.293	—	—	—	—
Total (8 years)		431	290	.540	Total (5 years)	34	27	.557

NOTES: 1967—Defeated New York, 3–1, in Eastern Division Semifinals; lost to Philadelphia, 4–1, in Eastern Division Finals. 1968—Defeated Detroit, 4–2, in Eastern Division Semifinals; defeated Philadelphia, 4–3, in Eastern Division Finals; defeated Los Angeles, 4–2, in NBA Finals. 1969—Defeated Philadelphia, 4–1, in Eastern Division Semifinals; defeated New York, 4–2, in Eastern Division Finals; defeated Los Angeles, 4–3, in NBA Finals. 1975—Defeated Detroit, 2–1, in Western Conference First Round; lost to Golden State, 4–2, in Western Conference Semifinals. 1976—Lost to Phoenix, 4–2, in Western Conference Semifinals. 1988—Replaced as Sacramento head coach by Jerry Reynolds (March 7).

Chapter Eleven

BILL WALTON—Center

Precision

by Sam Smith

There really is no signature play to define the career of Bill Walton like there is for most of the best players in NBA history.

Michael Jordan has that final shot and pose against the Utah Jazz in the 1998 Finals, among many, all geared to his scoring, like the switch-hands layup in the 1991 Finals or the game-winning shot against the Cleveland Cavaliers in 1989 to start the Bulls' run. Larry Bird has that steal against Isiah Thomas and the Detroit Pistons and the walk-off three-pointer in the All-Star exhibition long-distance shooting contest.

There are sky-hooks for Kareem Abdul-Jabbar, power slams for Shaquille O'Neal, and lookaway passes from Magic Johnson.

Perhaps the waning seconds of the biggest moment of his brief NBA playing career best symbolizes Walton.

It is the very end of what would be the last game of the 1977 Finals between Walton's Portland Trail Blazers and the—until then—thought to be invincible Philadelphia 76ers. Philadelphia was awash in All-Stars, future Hall of Famers, and legends, with Julius "Dr. J" Erving, George McGinnis, Darryl Dawkins, Doug Collins, Henry Bibby, Lloyd "World" Free, Joe Bryant, and Mike Dunleavy. It was supposed to be the NBA crowning for Dr. J, and the 76ers had won the first two games at home. The Trail Blazers, never even a playoff team before, won the next two back on their home court, returned to Philadelphia, hung on for a 3–2 lead, and then were back in Portland for Game 6.

The 76ers had come clawing back from a twelve-point halftime deficit. They were within two with the clock running out. Free shot and missed. McGinnis went up for the rebound, and the ball seemed to hang in the air as a welter of arms and elbows also sprang up toward it, big men and bruisers like Maurice Lucas and McGinnis, willowy leapers like Caldwell Jones and Erving.

Let Johnny Davis, the Blazers guard and later the Orlando Magic coach, tell it:

"It seemed like everyone was going for it," recalled Davis. "If Philly tips it in or gets it back and scores, it's overtime. If we secure it, we win. With all these bodies banging and arms and hands going for the ball, there's Bill. No one could grab it, so he pushed the ball out to me, and I was able to run it down and get it and dribble out the clock.

"Years later I asked Bill if he knew I was out there and where I was," said Davis. "He said, 'Yes.' He saw it amongst everything that was taking place. Even then, he had the mind to know where everyone was on the floor in the critical part of the game, and rather than snare the rebound, maybe losing it in traffic, maybe getting fouled, he pushed it out to me to end the game."

Anything to win.

"I had one dream," said Walton, "and that was to be part of a special team and have a chance to be out there when the game was on the line. Like that. You always know where the ball is going. The unpredictability is in the player who has the ball. So you watch his eyes. While I'm doing that, I'm consistently taking mental pictures of where all my teammates are at. Because I know I'm going to get the ball some way. I'm watching the eyes to see what they are thinking. The eyes telegraph what the mind is thinking. When the guy is coming to the hoop, I can see in his eyes what he's trying to do, and then I try to put myself in position where I can make the play because I know from his eyes where the ball is going to go."

Getting that tip to Davis to end the game was a precise move and an unselfish move, and one that defines the Haley's Comet career of the player who, if healthy, could have been the best player ever in the NBA. At his best, he was the perfect basketball player.

No, Bill Walton never would have been as great a scorer as Wilt Chamberlain or Jordan. He wouldn't have been the passer that Johnson was, or the shooter that Bird was. Nor did he have the force of Shaq. But he played the game perfectly. He was a player whom the textbooks could be modeled after.

Walton never took a shot in practice that he wouldn't use in a game. His positioning was from a coaching manual: legs spread for balance, butt back, arms out and up, fingers extended, the perfect target for a pass, the ideal balance for a move, all backed up by quickness, intelligence, instincts, and passion for the game. It was the complete package, a coach's fantasy.

"For those two years," recalled then Blazers coach Jack Ramsay with a sigh, "I don't know how you could play the center position better."

Walton had twenty points, twenty-three rebounds, and seven assists in that final game, but appropriately, statistics could never define him. There was no statistic for the final play, just what was best for the team. In that series Walton twice had seven assists in a game, nine in another, figures virtually unheard of for a center. For those who have only faded memories and grainy highlight films, it's a shame. No one ever played the game in its purest form like Bill Walton.

"If you took all the great centers who ever played," said John

Wooden, Walton's UCLA coach and perhaps the premier basketball figure of the twentieth century, "and you took seven, eight, nine fundamentals and rate each one to ten and add those up, Bill Walton would rate number one over all of them. Counting everything—rebounding, passing, defense, free-throw and field goal shooting, every little fundamental for a post man, with the physical, mental, and emotional balance he had, never losing control—he'd be number one."

David Halberstam, perhaps the premier nonfiction author of his generation, who has written best-selling books on baseball and basketball, including one on Michael Jordan, agrees.

"For those two seasons," he said, "I don't know that anyone ever did it better."

Of course, Bill Walton's legacy, though he is a member of the Naismith Memorial Basketball Hall of Fame, is what could have been as much as what was. Walton was part of the best college team in history, UCLA's eighty-eight-straight-win juggernaut. He won an NBA championship with Portland, and in one magical season when he wasn't nearly what he had been, he came off the bench for the championship team many regard as the best ever in the NBA, the 1985–86 Celtics. But it was less the feats for Walton than the feet. He didn't suffer defeat as much as he had to deal with da feet.

He said he never knew everyone didn't have pain in their feet until ankle fusion surgery in 1990 finally relieved the lifetime of agony. Both Ramsay and Lenny Wilkens, Walton's first coach in Portland, talk of their first meetings with Walton in hospitals. Walton said he spent the better part of his twenties and thirties in them. He has had thirty-two surgeries. Ramsay said the Trail Blazers the season *after* the championship were his best team—they started the year 50–10. Then Walton was hurt again, and the Trail Blazers fell apart. He left Portland in anger, with lawsuits flying back and forth over his injuries. He signed back home in San Diego, where the Clippers were based then, but played very little over six anguished seasons until catching on with the Celtics and playing eighty of eighty-two regular-season games and all but two playoff games.

In Boston Walton had the time of his life once again: back with a great team, he was able to play a role, if not the starring one anymore. The first day he got there, Larry Bird recalled, the players gathered around and Kevin McHale said, "Hey, Bill, okay, you can tell us now. Did you have Patty Hearst in your basement?"

"I never met Patty Hearst," Walton says emphatically, as he's still often asked. His Portland home was sort of a village commune for many of the radical figures of the 1970s: activist Jack Scott lived with him for a time, and well-known antiwar protesters like Daniel Berrigan and John Froines were frequent guests. At UCLA, Walton was a liberal figure during the '70s campus protests, and by the time he went to progressive Portland, a bearded six-foot-eleven (he'd refuse to admit to being over seven feet tall for the freakish connotation he felt it gave), his iconoclastic image was enhanced by his unselfish lifestyle. (Even to this day his San Diego home is open year-round to friends.) He's stumbled across people in trouble who have become caretakers on his property; he's quietly endowed college scholarships, frequently for friends and former teammates who haven't fared as well. Walton developed, early on, a passion for giving, and not only the basketball. He was so upset when he got all the attention and the MVP in the 1977 Finals that he had a huge photo of teammate Maurice Lucas prepared and sent to Lucas as thanks. When he was being recruited in high school, instead of showing off for the recruiters, Walton constantly passed to teammates to give them a chance to show better and get scholarships. His high school coach used to call time-outs just to tell Walton to shoot. Being able to support the great Celtics of the mid-1980s was one of the moments in his life he most treasures.

"Kevin used to ride Bill all the time at practice. And Kevin used to kill him. I think Bill beat him once," laughed Bird. "But when we needed him, he was there to make the play for us."

It happened to be the one to clinch the last game of the 1986 Finals over the Houston Rockets.

It was not the Bill Walton of UCLA or Portland, but rather one who was perhaps 60 to 70 percent of that, although Bird used to say that every one of the guys coming off the bench with Walton was better because of Walton. Celebrated as a great reserve corps at the time, none of the bench players ever accomplished much after they stopped playing with Walton, though Scott Wedman was at the end of a solid career. It was not unlike the crew Stu Inman had assembled in Portland—refugees from the ABA, rookies and journeymen, with his one star who worked for the team and his teammates.

"People felt we had the greatest players in the world," recalled Portland's then-general manager. "They were peripheral players, and Bill made them what they were. Not that they weren't good players with talent, but a lot of these guys were picked up because they were given up by other teams."

Lionel Hollins was a third-year guard who would play for five teams in eleven seasons and never have a higher scoring average than he did with Portland in 1976–77. Johnny Davis was a second-round pick who would play for four NBA teams. Larry Steele was a third-round pick nearing the end of his career. Bob Gross was a second-round pick who averaged in double figures only in his two seasons playing with Walton. Dave Twardzik was from the ABA, where he averaged fewer than ten points per game. Herm Gilliam was with his sixth team in seven seasons. Corky Calhoun was with his third team in five seasons. Lloyd Neal was a third-round pick. The best of them was Maurice Lucas, also from the ABA, a physical role player who played for six NBA teams in thirteen NBA seasons as well as two ABA teams.

"If you watched the 1977 Finals," said Inman, "and you never heard of Julius Erving and you never heard of Bob Gross, you only watched the series, and if you were asked who the best small forward was, who plays so well without the ball, gets himself open, is the better player, you'd have said Gross. Because if you were open, Walton found you. Most people never understood the impact he had because he was the constant provider for four other players. We had a good team, but everyone overrated the other players because Walton was so good."

It wasn't that same Bill Walton in 1986. The injuries had taken their drastic toll. But Walton was happier than he'd ever been because of the surprising new lease on his basketball life he'd been given. He'd been telling friends in 1982 that it was over, that he'd never play again. He missed two full seasons after being signed to a big free agent contract by the Clippers. He managed to play three seasons after that, but missed 91 of 246 games. It was a miserable, losing team on which Walton couldn't make an impact with his feet deteriorating further and his play limited to a game or two a week. He thought he might quit, though he still considered basketball his life and passion along with the Grateful Dead and his music (Walton is an accomplished classical pianist). He began attending Stanford Law School, searching for something else that might fulfill him. "Losing basketball was a miserable time for him," said Halberstam, who became a good friend. "It was like a form of death."

And then his feet started to feel better. He called the Lakers, but they weren't interested, so he tried the Celtics. Red Auerbach, wary of Walton and the angry departure from Portland, asked Bird what he thought. Bird said that if Walton could help, go ahead. And with that came the only season in his career Walton played at least eighty games. He was there just when the Celtics needed him.

He had some wonderful games that season coming off the bench, one in particular against the Lakers and Kareem Abdul-Jabbar, against whom Walton loved to compete. They no longer were basketball equals, as they had been in the Portland days. Then, Abdul-Jabbar would regularly out-statistic Walton, but Walton would come away with the win, like the 4–0 sweep in the 1977 Western Conference Finals. Walton punctuated the victory with a dunk over Abdul-Jabbar. "Bill had the ball at the free-throw line," recalled then–Blazers coach Jack Ramsay. "He turned and faced, which wasn't usual for Bill, dribbled straight at the basket and dunked over Kareem." It was one of those moments when Walton let the world—as well as his teammates and opponents—know that if he ever needed it, it was there.

But Bill Walton was about winning the game and helping his teammates. It never was about individual accolades. Walton never even kept his awards and mementos. His kids joke about the Bill Walton Museum in Alabama.

It seems a man named Rick Sherman once called Walton when he was with Portland. You could find NBA players in the phone book then. He said that he didn't know who Walton was, that he was a *Star Trek* aficionado, but his brother, Craig, was a huge Walton fan and could he do something for an upcoming birthday. "I thought,

Uh-oh, some nut," Walton recalled. So Walton sent the man's brother some signed souvenirs. A friendship developed, and to this day Walton sends Craig most of his major awards and trophies that record his individual accomplishments. It's not that he's not proud and grateful, but the thrill and enjoyment is in the playing and succeeding, not in being glorified for it. "What would I do with them?" he wondered.

Abdul-Jabbar was an early inspiration, although to this day Bill Russell remains his basketball idol, and Walton still considers meeting Russell one of the thrills of his life. It was Abdul-Jabbar, however, who helped persuade Walton to attend UCLA.

"Kareem was by far the best of them all," said Walton. "His skills were far superior to mine. That's the joke about this book, that I'm on the team and he isn't. I couldn't outjump him or outmuscle him, so I'd try to run him and minimize his strength. It's the way you play every player. You try to put them in position where they can't make the play they want to make. Like blocking a shot. I tried to make 'em miss by forcing them to take the shot they didn't want to take. When you try to block shots, you run the risk of foul trouble and being out of the game. I'd wait until they brought the ball to me. If a guy couldn't use his left hand, if he couldn't take a hook shot, whatever, it was about analyzing your opponent.

"With Kareem it was, 'He's not going to get that sky-hook.' You always can take something away," Walton said. "We accepted the fact we'd give up the baseline and make him turn away. On the right box, you make him turn middle. He wants to come right shoulder every time. I played my best basketball against him, and he'd still throw fifty in my face."

Walton always thrived on the best competition. He'd had bigger offers to go to the ABA after college, but rejected them. He wanted to play with and against the best. His standards were extraordinarily high. He was shocked when he came to the Trail Blazers and found that players couldn't dribble with their left hands, that their footwork was poor, that they couldn't dribble with their heads up. He told his teammates they wouldn't have gotten practice jerseys at UCLA. He talked about leaving the NBA to find a better league. No, Walton wasn't always the most popular teammate, especially in the conservative world of pro sports. He'd become a vegetarian and mocked teammates who were meat eaters. Things got so nasty around Portland at the end that some claimed Walton's change to eating vegetarian caused his foot problems.

With Boston in that 1985–86 season, Walton had big games off the bench (in one Celtics win over the Lakers he had eleven points, eight rebounds, and seven blocks). He rose to the big occasion like few others. But to this day, when he is asked about memorable games, the only ones he'll mention are the UCLA losses to Notre Dame and North Carolina State that cost a championship and broke the eighty-eight-game win streak. Walton takes blame for both losses.

And now the Celtics were staggering some, ahead two games to one in the 1986 Finals against the young, dynamic Houston Rockets of Akeem Olajuwon and Ralph Sampson. With a little over three minutes remaining in a tied game, Walton came in to replace Robert Parish. Walton rarely closed games by that point, but he did this time. Walton hit Bird on an inside-out feed, and Bird swished a three-pointer for a three-point lead. Rodney McCray hit a jumper, and then Dennis Johnson drove and the ball hit wildly off the rim. Olajuwon, Sampson, Bird, and McHale were battling for the rebound as Walton timed it right and went up among the four big men, grabbing the ball and going past Olajuwon for a backhanded layup and the final points in the game. Walton said he knew he couldn't grab the ball and pump-fake because of the leaping ability he was facing, so he made the move before Olajuwon could even react. That's precision to the nth degree.

Big moments had once been difficult for Bill Walton.

Any moment with the public had once been difficult because of a pronounced stutter. It helped lead Walton to basketball, because he could practice alone for hours. It's also why he gravitated to bicycle riding and playing the piano, activities he could pursue reclusively. His friends laugh and marvel at the transformation as Walton eventually became not only a national TV basketball analyst but a public speaker in great demand who travels at least two hundred days a year. "He's making up for lost time. You can't shut him up now," said Greg Lee, his UCLA teammate and still a close friend who lives near Walton in San Diego.

"At times it was painful to watch him," said Lee. "He couldn't start a sentence. Nothing would come out. Other than being a jockey, I can't imagine anything he'd have been less suited for than broadcasting."

Walton now says he's embarrassed over the many confrontations he had with the media in his college and early pro career, how difficult he could be. Some liken Walton's career to the career of George Foreman, a brooding, angry, condescending man when he was heavyweight boxing champion who became a beloved grandfatherly figure some two decades later. For Walton, it was the stuttering. Simple embarrassment. He was a perfectionist who believed he could handle anything he set his mind to. Yet he couldn't speak under stress, and stressful, pressure-packed moments were his greatest moments as a basketball player. He recalls being laughed out of a speech class in college at a time when he was the most famous amateur athlete in the world, the winner of the prestigious Sullivan Award.

With some of the establishment laughing at him, it was no wonder he rebelled against it. John Wooden remembered Walton telling him he wasn't going to cut his hair or shave, that Wooden didn't have the right to make him change his appearance.

"I told Bill, 'I have a right to say who plays and who doesn't, and, Bill, we're going to miss you.' Between practices he wanted to impeach the president," said Wooden, "take over the administration building." And it wasn't fashion that drove Walton in the '60s and '70s. He marched for social causes, for the migrant workers, mostly for the disadvantaged. It was never about him, but what he could do to help others.

Like in basketball. That was sacred. It was a religion, and as Halberstam liked to say, Walton was something of a basketball moralist. "He felt there was a right way to play and a wrong way. You didn't self-glorify. If the players all did the right thing on every play, it would work out. Everyone was there to play his role," said Halberstam.

Walton, in fact, did have a high sense of ethics and principles. Those principles seemed most obvious outside of basketball, but they developed the philosophy that governed his play.

Walton came from a liberal, athletic, Catholic house in San Diego. His brother Bruce went on to play in the NFL for the Dallas Cowboys. His father, Ted, was a social worker and nighttime adult educator. Ted, who'd attended Cal-Berkeley, wouldn't allow the conservative *San Diego Union* in the house, so they read the *Los Angeles Times,* which helped pave Bill's road to Westwood (along with the inspiration from one of the first TV games he saw, UCLA's win over Michigan for the 1965 championship).

"I'd never seen basketball on TV until 1965 [when he was thirteen years old]," said Walton. "We didn't have a TV. We couldn't afford one. I remember my mom [Gloria] at the dinner table once announcing they'd saved enough for a TV. But then my mom says she's done a lot of research and there's nothing on TV worth watching so we weren't getting one."

But eventually they did, and watching that UCLA game, Walton marveled at Michigan's size and strength. Cazzie Russell, Bill Buntin, and Oliver Darden were far more physical than UCLA's "scrawny guys," as he called them, and Walton believed UCLA had no chance.

"Until I saw the precision execution," said Walton. "It was incredible—the physical fitness, commitment to ball movement. I said right then, 'That's for me.' Basketball became my religion, the gym my church, and the game blessed sacrament."

Walton was playing by then and becoming proficient. A six-foot-one guard with incredible quickness, he was nicknamed "Spider" because he was so skinny with seemingly so many arms.

"The amazing thing," said then–Helix High School coach Gordon Nash, "was I saw him grow from six-one to six-ten-and-a-half, and he never lost a step of quickness."

The combination of size and speed was what separated him from the other big white kids, and he would begin developing into a phenomenon. Nash kept recruiters away from Walton, and Walton, because of his speech problems, would only do interviews with Nash by his side. Nash said that when there was a question that might provoke Walton's emotions, he'd tap Nash in a secret signal, and

Nash would answer the question for him. Walton was bright, an honors student, but he was inarticulate around everyone except friends and family.

"He didn't like anything that brought attention to him," said Nash. "He had absolutely no interest in being the high scorer. He did everything he could to shift the focus of attention. He always took delight in going into the low post, drop step, and then kicking the ball out to a guard or forward for a shot with everyone dropping on him. I'd take him a few seconds to the bench and explain this was not the game plan. He was more interested in giving someone else the opportunity to score, though he easily could have averaged fifty points. He loved rebounding, blocking shots, getting assists, and generating the fast break."

Early coaches, including grade school coach Rocky Graciano and later Wooden, believed one reason Walton developed his unselfish game was to avoid having to speak about it because of his speech impediment.

After Walton's freshman season in high school, he broke his foot fooling around in a football game. He likes to say that was the beginning of his athletic downfall, but it also laid another brick in the foundation of Walton's basketball philosophy. When he returned as a sophomore, he couldn't run as well, so he asked Nash if he could just play the defensive end of the floor, rebound, block shots, throw the outlet pass.

He'd grown another six inches from his freshman year and was now a force on the floor. Walton remembers one high school game where he'd blocked about a dozen shots and everyone was celebrating after the game. Nash came into the locker room and asked what the big deal was—most of the blocks had resulted in the ball going out of bounds and the opponent being able to run a set play. "It dawned on me, I had to control the ball to my teammates," said Walton.

So the pieces were coming together, the defense, the outlet, the block combined with Walton's incredible speed, quickness, and uneasiness. He never believed in standing still to get the ball. Larry Bird said he and Walton used to argue endlessly. Bird felt it was best to take a pass, let the defense react. If they double-teamed, then you made the pass. If they didn't, you made your move to the basket.

Walton insisted that it was constant movement that was vital, that that was how to wear down your opponent and react to his moves, almost like tai chi, the Asian martial art. Walton was like a tai chi master of basketball. He'd react to opponents coming to his one side or hand, then go for the other to get a pass or to shoot.

"Bill always wanted to be moving," recalled Lee, his UCLA point guard. "Watch the Memphis State game [forty-four points and an NCAA finals record-making twenty-one of twenty-two shots]. Left to right, high to low. It's why he was so great on defense. He never was waiting until something happened. They played a 3–2 zone, which was one of the stupidest things ever. I'd fake, and he'd be moving, and we'd get him a lob, and he'd drop it in or bank it, always based on where the defense played."

It was clear that this was a special, unique player, though someone who, as even he admits, could be a difficult teammate. Michael Jordan–like, really. It was that will to win, the absolute need to beat someone. As nice as they can seem in the interviews and the ads, they all had it: Magic, Bird, Jordan, Isiah, Jerry West, Oscar Robertson, Rick Barry, Kareem.

It wasn't just Walton's fiery red hair, but his personality, the flames of competition often singeing everyone around him.

"I was demanding and mean," Walton said. "I had to win. There's the story they tell you as a kid that it's not whether you win or lose. The guy was right. It's not whether you win or lose. It's whether *I* win or lose. I don't think my teammates enjoyed playing with me. I demanded the ball and asked too much of my teammates."

Though it was why his teams won.

Through high school, UCLA, and until he finally broke down in Portland.

"The word was 'passion,'" said Lee, his UCLA teammate. "He wanted to do the right thing every single time running down-court. And he wanted everyone else to do it too. Not just well . . . perfectly. His precision comes from his maniacal concept that we play right on every play. That's why we didn't have many of those strategic free throws or out-of-bounds plays. We got ahead by twenty points all the time after twelve minutes. If anyone didn't look for him when he was open, he'd say to the coach, 'I don't want to play with that guy. He doesn't give up the ball.' And it was his preparation.

"Before every game, we'd throw the ball back and forth between one another at incredible speeds, as hard as we could until our fingers were so red you wouldn't believe it," said Lee. "He was nuts. But then when the game started, it would be easy to catch the ball. You'd have a low pass, and it was no problem because there'd never be a harder pass than we threw at each other."

Yes, you need the talent. And Walton had it, the speed, quickness, innate ability, the size and attitude. But if there was a secret to his precision play, his ability to be at the right place at the right time and make the right decision, it was his obsession with repetition. Walton envisioned virtually every moment of the game before it started. It's what he does with most things in his life. Walton still lives by the maxims of John Wooden, his dear coach whom he calls almost every day no matter where he is.

Failing to prepare is preparing to fail.

Nate Walton, Bill's second-oldest son, a Princeton graduate, laughs when he hears the words. *Be quick but don't hurry. Do not mistake activity for achievement.* They are just a few of the life reflections that Wooden lived by and that so inspired Walton that he wrote them on the lunch bags of his sons every day for school. "The kids used to laugh and ask, 'What did your dad write today?'" recalled Nate. All the sayings are still on Bill's refrigerator at home, and he recites them regularly. And lives by them.

To the amazement and amusement of everyone who knows him, Walton is an accomplished and much-in-demand public speaker these days. Asked to talk for forty minutes, he'll often go on for two hours. Before every speech, he practices relentlessly in front of a mirror, much as he did as a player. He exercises the muscles in his jaw, he endlessly repeats what he'll say, and he anticipates almost any question so that there is little anyone can do to surprise him. He practices incessantly. He reads newspapers out loud at home. He talks constantly when he meets cabdrivers, waiters, doormen. He works on his verbal ability now as he once did on his basketball skills.

His teammates remember him deep in meditation before every

game, almost in a different state of being as he prepared and visualized every play, every move an opponent might make and what he would do.

On Martin Luther King Day in 2005, Walton was invited to participate in an NBA panel for a celebratory program in Memphis. At a luncheon there, about a dozen people—including Walton—were recognized for various awards. Each came up to the podium and politely thanked everyone after being introduced. Walton scribbled madly during each introduction. He was writing down the personal background of each recipient. When it was his time to speak, Walton was able to address each of the previous winners' accomplishments and biographies in detail before accepting his own award, a unique and special time in the presentation. When everyone walked away, they remembered Bill Walton.

"I like pressure and I like to work," said Walton. "I love to practice and get ready. I love the preparation. I loved the anticipation of the game. Coach Wooden taught us that being hot was not something to do with luck. It wasn't that hopefully you'd be in the zone. You create a routine by preparation, by how you lead your life, what time you go to bed, eating meals, everything leading up to the games. To this day I block out seven to eight hours for sleep, I regularly exercise, I'm up at five-thirty every day and visualize the event. I crave discipline. I love organization. I don't like it when there's not a schedule. I want to know when everything is. I want to know when everything is happening. I want to know the time so I can be ready. It's the way I played basketball. You prepare for everything that can happen. You see it in your mind a thousand times before it happens. What can this guy do? When does he want to do it? I memorized all their moves, all the moves of my teammates. Once your body has memorized every move, the outcome is the result of which button you push. Everyone thinks there are secret gimmicks. It's like music. You practice your chords, rhythms, beats, scales. The repetition and learning is incredibly enjoyable. I love the individual nature of it, which is why I like basketball, bicycle riding, playing the piano. And the speed, like a rock concert, everyone playing and dancing fast, six or seven musicians playing different songs at the same time that mean something. I hate sitting around. Music, bicycling, basketball, you can do it by yourself and practice all the time so that you are ready.

"I went down the Colorado River on a raft trip [in the summer of 2004]," recalled Walton. "I'm going down the river in my own boat. I'm the only guy, having the time of my life, doing everything perfect. Then they say I'll need some help for the next part, and this instructor tells me to listen to everything. That's the day I broke an oar, got thrown out of the boat. It's happening so fast you have to make the decisions, but they're telling me, 'Go this way, that way.' Like it was with Coach Wooden—once the game started, you didn't look at the sideline. He'd say there was nothing he could do for us anymore. It was time to go. I liked that."

Because of Walton's unselfish nature and injuries, the nation hadn't quite caught on to his special abilities when he was in high school. Tom McMillen was on the cover of *Sports Illustrated* and considered the nation's greatest prep hoopster.

Denny Crum, who went on to a great coaching career at the University of Louisville, was then an assistant and recruiter for UCLA. It was well known that Wooden didn't come to see high school prospects, but Crum said he had to make an exception.

"I told Coach Wooden I'd just seen the best high school player I'd ever seen play," said Crum. "He told me to close the office door and not to ever make a statement like that again. No one from San Diego had even been recruited to Division I programs. He said it wasn't logical. Coach Wooden isn't one to offer accolades, but he went down and watched him play and said, 'Well, he is pretty good, isn't he?'

"They were winning every game by like fifty points," recalled Crum. "They'd play a 1–2–2 zone with Bill at the point on defense. If the ball went to the wing, he'd drop back into a 2–3, and the other team could hardly get shots off. They'd have a 2–1–1 press, and he'd play back, get the block or rebound, and pass it to the other end. He dominated the game on both ends."

It was a style of play even the best were unaccustomed to. Rebounders, especially in the pros where they are paid on statistics, like to grab a rebound, cradle it, show they have it, and then walk it up to get into the offensive set. Walton just wanted to get rid of it as quickly as he could.

"I remember when I first started playing with him," recalled then–Portland guard Lionel Hollins. "He got the rebound, and as a guard since I was a kid, you'd come back to get the pass and dribble up-court. I started coming back, and he threw the ball over my head and said, 'You're going the wrong way.' As soon as he got the ball, he'd look up-court, and I learned to go. When a small guy was shooting free throws, I'd be standing at half-court, and Bill knew there would be a big guy guarding me, so he'd take the ball out of bounds and throw it to me knowing I'd have the edge against the big guy in the open court. He just understood everything.

"I remember this game against the Atlanta Hawks the year after we won, when we started 50–10," said Hollins. "We were both hot to open, something like 8–1. Today it would be the big game of the week. They had this attacking half-court press, so Bill just went to the high post and picked them off with passes to Lucas and Gross, and we won by forty-something. It was never about stats or showmanship with him, but that awareness of where everybody was and what to do."

It was Walton's way of breaking down the game into minute sections. Like players when they are in the so-called zone, who say that everything seemed to move in slow motion, Walton always was ready with the precise and correct movement because he saw things before they happened and thought about them constantly.

Walton was equally comfortable in the low post and high post, often beating his man with a straight-on move from the high post. But teammates remember most fondly his back-door passes, when it seemed as if he did have eyes in the back of his head.

"Bill would have his back to the basket with the ball," recalled guard Larry Steele, "and Lionel or Bobby Gross would be at the baseline. The weak side defender would see Bill and think the guy he was guarding was not in the play, and then he'd make a back-door cut, and the ball would be there, and it was such a difficult angle with a teammate coming from out of his eyesight that you wouldn't think he would even see that play. With Bill, you had to make a quick move. Sometimes you'd make your cut and wouldn't get the ball and think you were out of the play, but then you'd get the pass just at the right spot. So you learned to move quickly and never stop expecting the pass and you'd be rewarded."

Ramsay thinks that Portland team made more layups than any team in the history of basketball.

He vividly remembered Walton with Elvin Hayes on his back, then the ball quickly whisking by Hayes's head, millimeters from his ear, to a cutting Gross.

"That was typical," recalled Ramsay. "It would be just at the right time. He didn't need teaching. If you were open, Bill got you the ball. I remember in Game 5 in that Philly series, they're making a big run. Bill gets the ball in the high post with Lucas in the low post and Gross coming off a screen. Bill hits Gross for a short jumper that stopped their momentum and to me was the key play of the game. He had great technique for receiving the ball and always knew the right man to get it to."

Greg Lee likes to tell the story of when he, Jamaal (née Keith) Wilkes, and Walton were being recruited. They'd all gone to visit Stanford but were all leaning toward UCLA. Because they had never played against one another, they would go see the others play when possible. When Lee and Wilkes went to see Walton, it was a revelation.

"He had like fifty-two points and twenty-eight rebounds, his team was leading something like 72–6 at halftime," said Lee with a laugh. "At halftime he had like thirty-eight points and hadn't taken a shot yet. He'd just put in the misses."

Walton then went on to become college basketball's greatest winner. And he was a winner the first time he got healthy in the NBA. But the winning didn't last long enough. His career seemed over in 1982. The Clippers put together a team of a dozen world-renowned doctors, and their advice was to retire. They weren't even talking about basketball anymore—they were concerned about his ability to walk. In the end, Walton would have twenty-five operations on his feet and ankles, five on his knees, and two on his hands.

He would play again, first once or twice a week for the Clippers—angering teammates and management because he also simultaneously attended law school—and then again with the Celtics. The pain returned after the 1986 Finals, and in 1990 Walton's first ankle fusion surgery officially ended his hoop dreams.

"I was the most injured player ever," he said. "I remember I'm at the doctor's office one day, and they couldn't figure out what was wrong with my feet. They were operating on me every three months, and nothing was working. So this is the last guy, the ultimate doctor. The people who get to see this guy are either permanently on crutches or in a wheelchair. He sees the guys whose feet get crushed in industrial accidents, mountain climbing, motorcycle wrecks. I'm waiting, and out the door I see this young guy crutching up and down the hallway, burning off his anxiety, his frustration. Every time he goes past the door, he looks in.

"He does this six or seven times, and finally he comes into my room and closes the door behind him. I'm thinking, *I want to get out of here.* He looks me right in the eye and says he needs some help. I said, 'Sure, you need an autograph? I'll sign whatever you need.' He says it's nothing to do with that. He says, 'Look at me. I'm twenty-seven years old, and the doctor just cut off both my legs above the knees, and I'm having trouble staying positive in life. How do you do it?'

"I felt like the biggest schmuck in the world," remembered Walton. "There's a framed picture above my mantel at home. The Grateful Dead sent me what people say is a piece of memorabilia, a get well card. That doctor had told me if things didn't turn quick, I was looking at amputation. The Grateful Dead heard and sent me a big get well photograph with a card they'd all signed saying, 'Bill, we want to see you dancing.' It was an aerial photograph with everyone having the time of their life, smiling, jumping up and down. Mickey Hart wrote, 'Never look back.'

"Every day I stop by there and put my hand on that card and say, 'Here we go. I've got a chance. One more day.' I am, indeed, the luckiest guy in the world."

BILL WALTON'S PERFECT TEAM

Starters

Point Guard—Magic Johnson (unselfishness): Magic, along with Bill Russell, set the standard for team play and making their teammates the stars. Magic and Russell are really the same players—only with different names and faces. The only difference is that Magic always had the ball, while Russell was simply a conduit who moved it on.

Shooting Guard—Michael Jordan (competitive drive): Michael could and should be the winner in literally every category on this team. Everything said on this page and in this entire book can and should be said about Michael. He became Oscar Robertson after people forgot.

Forward—Larry Bird (leadership): The greatest player I ever played with—by far. . . . Larry remains the quickest player I ever saw. The opposition did everything imaginable to stop him—and they never had a chance.

Forward—Kevin McHale (confidence, instinct): He was the King. He carried himself as if the world belonged to him—and he was right. Kevin invented and forgot more things than anyone else could ever dream of. Trying to guard him was like being in the torture chamber. If you don't believe it—just ask him.

Center—Bill Russell (sacrifice): My hero. My favorite player of all time. The player I always dreamed of whenever I played. He dominated everything, yet wanted nothing in return save for the happiness and success of others.

Bench Players

Sixth Man—Kareem Abdul-Jabbar (dealing with pressure): The best player I ever played against. It's not even close. His skills were far superior to anyone's. I had to be, and was, at my best against him—and he still threw fifty in my face every time. His left leg belongs in the Smithsonian.

Guard—Oscar Robertson (versatility): There was nothing that Oscar could not do, and he did everything better than everyone else. As great and perfect as he was as a player, he was at least twice that good as a human being. Oscar was Michael Jordan long before even Michael knew it.

Guard—Jerry West (intensity): He never really lost at any-thing—sometimes they just stopped the game too early. Forget nu-clear energy—Jerry West radiated heat throughout the galaxies.

Forward—Rick Barry (precision): The personification of per-fection in all things after an early knee injury that would have ended anybody else's career, Rick fought back as an entirely different but ultimately better player. At the highest levels, success comes down to decision-making. Rick stands alone on the mountaintop where it matters most.

Forward—Maurice Lucas (courage): He was the greatest team-mate I ever had. Luke would do anything to help the team succeed, always demanding the toughest assignments, the ones that nobody else wanted any part of. Maurice was never interested in avoiding the difficult responsibilities. He always sought out the biggest and baddest guys: Artis Gilmore, Darryl Dawkins, you name 'em, line 'em up—and he always won. He would have gone looking for Wilt and Shaq.

Center—Wilt Chamberlain (will to dominate): He overcame all odds, because nothing he ever did was ever good enough. Never doubt for an instant that Wilt could, and did, do anything that he wanted to . . . *that's anything.* They had to permanently change the rules against Wilt to try to make it more fair. It didn't work. Noth-ing ever did. Wilt never had to promote himself or tell anyone else how great he was. Everyone already knew.

Center—Shaquille O'Neal (power): The purest definition of the indomitable force. Shaq is a remarkable teacher—the mere thought of him is the easiest way to convince the next generation and oppo-nent that your game better be based on skill, timing, and position. If it's not, you might as well pick another sport, because you'll have no chance when Shaq walks through the door.

Coach

KC Jones—Co-Head Coach with Jack Ramsay: K.C. was the most like John Wooden of any coach I ever played for. His sense of the human spirit is unmatched in my life. He knew exactly what to do at all times, in every situation—on and off the court. I never played for a finer coach or man.

BILL WALTON—CENTER/FORWARD

PERSONAL: Born November 5, 1952, in La Mesa, CA. . . . 6–11/235 (2.10 m/106.5 kg) . . . full name: William Theodore Walton III . . . Brother of Bruce Walton, offensive lineman with Dallas Cowboys (1973–75).

HIGH SCHOOL: Helix (La Mesa, CA).

COLLEGE: UCLA.

TRANSACTIONS/CAREER NOTES: Selected by Portland Trail Blazers in first round (first pick overall) of 1974 NBA draft. . . . Signed as veteran free agent by San Diego Clippers (May 13, 1979); Trail Blazers received center Kevin Kunnert, forward Kermit Washington, 1980 first-round draft choice, and cash as compensation (September 18, 1979). . . . Clippers franchise moved to Los Angeles for 1984–85 season. . . . Traded by Clippers to Boston Celtics for forward Cedric Maxwell, 1986 first-round draft choice, and cash (September 6, 1985). . . . Broadcaster, NBC Sports (1992–2002). . . . Analyst, ABC/ESPN (2002–present).

CAREER HONORS: Elected to Naismith Memorial Basketball Hall of Fame (1993). . . . One of the 50 Greatest Players in NBA History (1996).

MISCELLANEOUS: Member of NBA championship team (1977, 1986).

COLLEGIATE RECORD

NOTES: *The Sporting News* College Player of the Year (1972, 1973, 1974). . . . Naismith Award winner (1972, 1973, 1974). . . . *The Sporting News* All-America first team (1972, 1973, 1974). . . . NCAA Division I Tournament Most Outstanding Player (1972, 1973). . . . Member of NCAA Division I championship teams (1972, 1973). . . . Holds NCAA tournament career record for highest field goal percentage (minimum of 60 made)—68.6 percent, 109-of-159 (1972 through 1974). . . . Holds NCAA tournament single-season record for highest field goal percentage (minimum of 40 made)—76.3 percent, 45-of-59 (1973).

Season	Team	G	Min	FGM	FGA	Pct	FTM	FTA	Pct	Reb	Ast	Pts	RPG	APG	PPG
70–71	UCLA	20	—	155	266	.583	52	82	.634	321	74	362	16.1	3.7	17.1
71–72	UCLA	30	—	238	372	.640	157	223	.704	466	—	633	15.5	—	21.1
72–73	UCLA	30	—	277	426	.650	58	102	.569	506	168	612	16.9	5.6	20.4
73–74	UCLA	27	—	232	349	.665	58	100	.580	398	148	522	14.7	5.5	19.3
Total		87	—	747	1,147	.651	273	425	.642	1,370	—	1,767	15.7	—	20.3

NBA REGULAR-SEASON RECORD

HONORS: NBA Most Valuable Player (1978). . . . NBA Sixth Man Award (1986). . . . All-NBA first team (1978). . . . All-NBA second team (1977). . . . NBA All-Defensive first team (1977, 1978).

NOTES: Led NBA with 3.25 blocked shots per game (1977).

									Rebounds								Averages		
Season	Team	G	Min	FGM	FGA	Pct	FTM	FTA	Pct	Off	Def	Tot	Ast	St	Blk	TO	Pts	RPG	APG	PPG
74–75	Por	35	1,153	177	345	.513	94	137	.686	92	349	441	167	29	94	—	448	12.6	4.8	12.8
75–76	Por	51	1,687	345	732	.471	133	228	.583	132	549	681	220	49	82	—	823	13.4	4.3	16.1
76–77	Por	65	2,264	491	930	.528	228	327	.697	211	723	934	245	66	211	—	1,210	14.4	3.8	18.6
77–78	Por	58	1,929	460	882	.522	177	246	.720	118	648	766	291	60	146	—	1,097	13.2	5.0	18.9
78–79	Por								Did not play—injured											
79–80	SDC	14	337	81	161	.503	32	54	.593	28	98	126	34	8	38	37	194	9.0	2.4	13.9
80–81	SDC								Did not play—injured											
81–82	SDC								Did not play—injured											
82–83	SDC	33	1,099	200	379	.528	65	117	.556	75	248	323	120	34	119	105	465	9.8	3.6	14.1
83–84	SDC	55	1,476	288	518	.556	92	154	.597	132	345	477	183	45	88	177	668	8.7	3.3	12.1
84–85	LAC	67	1,647	269	516	.521	138	203	.680	168	432	600	156	50	140	174	676	9.0	2.3	10.1
85–86	Bos	80	1,546	231	411	.562	144	202	.713	136	408	544	165	38	106	151	606	6.8	2.1	7.6
86–87	Bos	10	112	10	26	.385	8	15	.533	11	20	31	9	1	10	15	28	3.1	0.9	2.8
87–88	Bos								Did not play—injured											
Total		468	13,250	2,552	4,900	.521	1,111	1,683	.660	1,103	3,820	4,923	1,590	380	1,034	865	6,215	10.5	3.4	13.3

THREE-POINT FIELD GOALS: 1983–84, 0-for-2; 1984–85, 0-for-2. Total: 0-for-4.

PERSONAL FOULS/DISQUALIFICATIONS: 1983–84, 153/1; 1984–85, 184/0. Total: 1298/17.

NBA PLAYOFF RECORD

NOTES: NBA Finals Most Valuable Player (1977). . . . Holds NBA Finals single-game record for most defensive rebounds—20 (June 3, 1977, vs. Philadelphia; and June 5, 1977, vs. Philadelphia). . . . Shares NBA Finals single-game record for most blocked shots—8 (June 5, 1977, vs. Philadelphia). . . . Shares single-game playoff record for most defensive rebounds—20 (June 3, 1977, vs. Philadelphia; and June 5, 1977, vs. Philadelphia).

									Rebounds								Averages		
Season	Team	G	Min	FGM	FGA	Pct	FTM	FTA	Pct	Off	Def	Tot	Ast	St	Blk	TO	Pts	RPG	APG	PPG
76–77	Por	19	755	153	302	.507	39	57	.684	56	232	288	104	20	64	—	345	15.2	5.5	18.2
77–78	Por	2	49	11	18	.611	5	7	.714	5	17	22	4	3	3	6	27	11.0	2.0	13.5
85–86	Bos	16	291	54	93	.581	19	23	.826	25	78	103	27	6	12	22	127	6.4	1.7	7.9
86–87	Bos	12	102	12	25	.480	5	14	.357	9	22	31	10	3	4	8	29	2.6	0.8	2.4
Total		49	1,197	230	438	.525	68	101	.673	95	349	444	145	32	83	36	528	9.1	3.0	10.8

THREE-POINT FIELD GOALS: 1985–86, 0-for-1. Total: 0-for-1.

PERSONAL FOULS/DISQUALIFICATIONS: 1985–86, 45/1. Total: 149/4.

NBA ALL-STAR GAME RECORD

Season	Team	Min	FGM	FGA	Pct	FTM	FTA	Pct	Rebounds Off	Def	Tot	Ast	PF	DQ	St	Blk	TO	Pts
1977	Por	Selected but did not play—injured																
1978	Por	31	6	14	.429	3	3	1.000	2	8	10	2	3	0	3	2	4	15
Total		31	6	14	.429	3	3	1.000	2	8	10	2	3	0	3	2	4	15

JERRY WEST—Guard

Dealing with Pressure

by Scott Ostler

O ver breakfast at a restaurant in Beverly Hills, a million miles from where Jerry West began his journey, he was asked to open for public inspection his personal hard drive, to reveal the physical and psychological characteristics that inspired his nickname—Mr. Clutch.

"Just give me the ball," West said, as if asking for the biscuit basket.

To Jerry West, basketball is a simple game, and his success playing the game can be explained simply. In pressure situations, he wanted the ball. He demanded it. He knew what to do with it. He was at home.

This could be the end of our search and our story, but inquiring minds wanted to know more. So West took us back to where it began, to a place so far back in the mountains of West Virginia that, as Hot Rod Hundley loves to say, "They had to pump the daylight in."

West painted a word-picture of a scene that the late Norman Rockwell would have loved, at first glance: the short, skinny, crew-cut country boy, maybe nine years old, is shooting by himself at a makeshift basket hanging over a dirt court, spinning hoop dreams.

Had Rockwell watched long enough, though, he would have noticed disturbing details that might not have played warm and fuzzy on the cover of the *Saturday Evening Post*. The kid is so scrawny that you can almost hear his stomach growl. He wears the intense look of a player under great pressure, hounded by invisible defenders. Every shot is desperation, and the stakes are huge.

It is growing dark and cold. Doesn't the boy have a home? Where are his playmates? He seems to be talking to himself. His pants are caked with dust and splattered with mud. His hands are bleeding, scraped raw by the ball and cracked from overexposure to the elements, yet he shoots and shoots.

"It's something I liked, okay?" West said. "I think the big thing was that I could see myself getting better, but never realizing or anticipating it would take me on a journey I'm not sure many kids could experience."

That scrawny kid never dreamed of someday actually playing in the NBA, or even at nearby East Bank High School. This wasn't about the future. He was in the moment, shooting crucial shots in an imaginary game, high as a kite on the here and now. Jerry West, Zen nerd.

That skinny kid would become rich and famous, feared and respected for being as cold-blooded and unstoppable as a shark. There is no statistical record of pressure shots taken and made, so Mr. Clutch's legend is built on anecdotal evidence, but even his worst enemies—the Boston Celtics—agree he was the ultimate go-to/can't-stop guy.

"He is the master," Celtic guard Larry Siegfried said in 1969.

"They can talk about the others, build them up, but he is the one. He is the only guard."

People still ask Mr. Clutch how he came to possess incredible composure under pressure. Practice, he explains. Before he took his first real shot on a real court in a real game against real people, he took a million crucial shots on that dirt court, into a blinding sun or driving snow, alone, with the game on the line.

Sure, most kids pretend. They put themselves in imaginary games and call their own play-by-play. Maybe what this little kid had was a bigger imagination, taking his fantasy so deep that it became reality, or at least blurred the distinction between the two.

"One of the things I used to do as a kid," West said, "I'd be by myself and I'd be the player, the coach, the announcer, the referee, and every shot was at the buzzer, and if I missed, I'd find a way to get another shot, or ten more. I wouldn't let myself fail. I'd always find a way, eventually, to make the last-second shot to win the game. I wanted to be the guy making that shot.

"People ask me what it felt like [to take shots under pressure], and I say it didn't really feel like anything, because it's something I'd done thousands of times, and it's something that stayed with me forever.

"I always—and I mean *always*—felt like I wanted to tackle [a teammate] if they were going to take a last-second shot."

Many NBA superstars forge their games in the inner city. Jerry West forged his game in the inner mind. He created an alter ego.

"I'm by nature a passive person," he said. "But basketball was like an out-of-body experience for me, because I wasn't the same person [on the court] at all. My body changed, my personality changed. I'm not by nature the most confident person in the world, I'm not, but there were times on the basketball court where you were *more* than confident you were going to do it. *More* than confident."

That elevator stop one level *above* confidence—that was West's world. Still is.

Mr. Clutch Moment: Before Game 7 of the 1969 NBA Finals against the Celtics, at the Forum in Inglewood, West has to be helped down the

*stairs to the locker room, where his right hamstring, badly injured in
Game 1, is shot up with Novocain.*

*Lakers center Wilt Chamberlain leaves Game 7 in the fourth quar-
ter with an injury, and Elgin Baylor is hobbled with bad knees, so it is
all on West. Dragging one leg into battle against a dynasty built
around nasty defense, West scores forty-two points and has thirteen rebounds and twelve assists. The Lakers lose by two points.*

Playing six games on one leg, West averaged 37.9 points for the
series.

After the game, several Celtics made a pilgrimage to the Lakers'
locker room. Bill Russell gave West a long, silent handshake. John
Havlicek told him, "Jerry, I love you."

West waited in the locker room until the arena was deserted so
that no one would see him hobbling painfully, one slow step at a
time, up that flight of stairs and out of the arena.

West's basketball legacy and legend are large. His L.A. Lakers career spanned thirty-nine seasons—fourteen as a player, two in retirement, three as a coach, three as a special assistant, and nineteen as
general manager/vice president. In the thirty-seven seasons West
was a Laker, they made the playoffs all but once, and won eight
NBA titles.

In West's fourteen playing seasons, the Lakers went to the NBA
Finals nine times, winning in 1971–72. As coach, West took a Lakers team that had missed the playoffs the season before and led them
to the league's best regular-season record; his three-year record as
coach was 145–101. Under West the executive, the Lakers made
eight trips to the Finals and won four NBA championships, and
they won another NBA title the year after West left, with the team
he had built.

West's achievements as player, coach, and executive inspired L.A.
sports columnist Lyle Spencer to dub West the all-time sports
MVP—Most Valuable Person.

The West legend not only lives but grows. He left the Lakers and
basketball in 2000, but two years later he accepted the challenge of
running the NBA doormat Memphis Grizzlies. A series of canny
moves was capped with a classic *West-did-whaaat?* moment—hiring
coach Hubie Brown. The basketball world wouldn't have been more

stunned had West hired Orville Redenbacher. By season two of the West Era, the Grizzlies were playoff contenders.

Zeke from Cabin Creek strikes again.

That's another West nickname, hung on him during his NBA rookie season by Lakers co-superstar Elgin Baylor. Two other Baylor nicknames for West: Louella, a reference to gossip columnist Louella Parsons, and Tweety Bird, in honor of West's high-pitched West Virginia twang.

Baylor was a better poet than cartographer. West's hometown is Cheylan (population back then: 500), but it's so small that Cheylanites picked up their mail in the more cosmopolitan Cabin Creek (population: 800).

West has a highway and a street named after him in West Virginia, but for all his fame he has been unable to put either of his hometowns on the map. Nearby pin-dots like Cyclone, Slab Fork, Big Chimney, Rumble, Nitro, Bald Nob, and Left Hand have made the Rand-McNally traveling squad, but not Cheylan or Cabin Creek.

It is coal country, once-lovely hills and valleys chewed up and spat out by mining machinery. West's father was an electrician in the mines. Strict, quiet, intelligent, and overworked, he had a wife and six children and no time for sports. The Wests lived in a simple two-story frame house and had no car.

Jerry, the fifth of the six children, was a loner. He admired his nearest brother, David, who was eight years older, but David was killed in the Korean War when Jerry was twelve.

When Jerry was about seven, he began hanging out at a neighbor's yard, where a hoop and backboard were nailed to the side of a storage shed. The older boys had no time for West, who sat courtside like a hungry dog watching a meat-juggling contest. When the big boys left, West would shoot by himself, mighty underhand heaves.

West recalled the moment when he finally summoned the strength and coordination to shoot the ball from his chest. "Oh, my God!" More Eureka moments followed. He discovered that if you hit a shot just right, the ball kisses off the inside of the back rim and bounces right back to you! If you use the exact same arm motion on every shot, the ball can't go anywhere but in the hole. *You* control *it!* Physics. Newton had the apple; West had the rock.

Jerry couldn't stay on the court forever, so he fashioned a hoop from a coat hanger, wedged it over his bedroom doorway, and shot a ball of socks, hour after hour.

West began listening to West Virginia basketball games on the radio from fourteen miles away in Morgantown, the announcer's voice and the cheers of the crowd fading in and out as the radio waves bounced along the valley. Now it was perfect. Now West had a context for his million practice shots, and no TV or video games to drain away his imagination. Alone on the dirt court or in his bedroom, he was the go-to Mountaineer.

The boy was always alone but never lonely. Near his home was a thin, elevated gas pipeline, a quarter-mile long and about five feet above the ground. West walked the pipeline, falling a hundred times until he became a master tightrope artist/daydreamer. He loved to fish and hunt by himself, but more and more the neighbor's dirt court drew him. As Hubie Brown would say in 1978, "Jerry was born to basketball."

"It was exhilarating," West said. "You go out there, the wind would be blowing, it's freezing cold, it would be hard to shoot the ball, and there's one second left on the clock, and you find a way, you find a way to shoot the ball five or six times in the last second, if you have to, to win the game. . . . It brought me pleasure, it really did. When I walked away and went home at night, I could feel good about myself."

West's parents worried. Lost in his dream world, Jerry missed meals. He became so gaunt that his mother took him to the doctor for vitamin shots. Whatever was driving him, it wasn't a tangible goal or a glimmer of athletic greatness. In junior high he was cut from the baseball, football, and track teams and rode the bench in basketball.

But the summer before his high school sophomore year West grew six inches, to six-three, and that season the future began to arrive. He played on the jayvee team but finally got a shot at the varsity.

Mr. Clutch Moment: West is put into a varsity game against a rival

high school and scores twelve or fourteen points in the last quarter.
East Bank wins the close game, a "huge thrill" for West.

"I didn't get to play any more that year because I broke a bone in my foot, but I really think that game was a breakthrough," West says. "I was really, really thin and gangly. You would probably look at me and say, 'Oh, my God, this kid could never be a basketball player,' and I was scared to death, and that [game] was a real confidence builder. Maybe once that happens for you, you're not afraid."

As a junior, West led East Bank to a 13–13 record, a shock to the town that had always looked upon basketball as a girls' sport. As a senior, West, the painfully shy loner, became a superstar, dazed by the sudden admiration and attention of his classmates and neighbors. He couldn't go to the barbershop without having his back slapped until it was as red as his cheeks.

Willie Akers, still one of West's best friends, recalled his first meeting with West, at a statewide leadership conference in Morgantown the summer before they were high school seniors.

"I was All-State as a junior, and I knew Jerry had been scoring some points, but our schools were about eighty miles apart," Akers said. "My buddies said he was a good player, so we went to an outdoor playground and had a pickup game. I was supposed to be the best high school player in the state, but there was no doubt who the best player in *this* game was. Jerry was skinny as he could be, but he could score every time. What impressed me most, though, was his defense. These were good players, and he was blocking shots like crazy."

West and Akers became pals. They visited one another's homes, and their two teams met in the semis of the state tournament.

Mr. Clutch Moment: "We were favored. His school wasn't known as much of a basketball school," Akers said. "I scored thirty-some points. We were knockin' Jerry around pretty good. We had a football player on our team, Rick Tolley, big tough kid—he tried to rough Jerry up, but it didn't work. He scored inside, outside, whatever, just jumping like crazy. He scored forty-three points."

Akers shook his head. "I coached high school basketball for twenty-four years, and I never saw anyone come *close* to doing what Jerry could do. He had just an unreal killer instinct. I've never seen anyone with more intensity."

West's team won the state championship, and he averaged 32.2 points and was named the state's Player of the Year. Then he enrolled at West Virginia University, as did Akers. West, having already scored a million points for the Mountaineers in his dreams, wasn't about to switch allegiance now.

He arrived in Morgantown with two pairs of pants and a sport coat. That first year he rarely left his dorm room. He didn't have a date until his sophomore year, and then with the girl who would become his first wife.

West's freshman team went 17–0. As a sophomore, he moved into the footsteps of graduated All-American guard Hot Rod Hundley, the '50s prototype of the hot dog superstar.

Hundley had been a perfect fit for coach Fred Schaus's program, which featured theatrics and wide-open ball. The players shaved their armpits and wore colorful unies. West hated the razzle-dazzle and only grudgingly led the Mountaineers onto the court before each home game by dribbling down a strip of carpet and slam-dunking a gaudy blue-and-gold basketball.

"There wasn't an inch, not one drop of showmanship in Jerry," laughed Hundley, now the play-by-play man for the Utah Jazz and still a close friend of West's. "He didn't even like to dunk in games—he felt like it was showing off." Whenever the Mountaineers won easily, West would score a quiet fifteen points and do a lot of passing and rebounding. But if the game was close, the ball found West, and vice versa, and he'd go for thirty or more.

"Nobody had to say anything," Akers said. "It was like, 'Here's the ball, Jerry.' I started every game in high school and college, and I can remember the few times I won a game with a basket. Very few. To Jerry, it was an everyday thing. We just knew he was gonna do it."

Akers could tick off the times West went off. "Our sophomore year, we were ranked number one in the country, and we played Villanova. They had a seventeen-point lead with four minutes left, and Jerry scored seventeen in a row and we won. In '59, Tennessee had [six-foot-nine bruiser] Gene Tormohlen. He beat us to death, and Jerry scored forty-four, his number, and we won."

Mr. Clutch Moment: "The Kentucky Invitational was a major hol-

iday tournament, and we won it twice," Akers said. "One year Jerry got his nose broken in the first half, stuffed cotton in his nostrils, could barely breathe, scored nineteen in the second half, and we beat Kentucky [79–70]. When [Kentucky] coach [Adolph] Rupp handed out the trophies, he told Jerry, 'Son, you're the gutsiest player I've ever seen play in this building.' "

West was building an oxymoronic reputation that fits him to this day: the reclusive life of the party.

Not that West lacked social graces. His senior season Villanova came to Morgantown with a center named George Raveling, the first black player ever in the WVU fieldhouse. The tension was thick during pregame warm-ups, but just before tip-off, West walked to midcourt, shook Raveling's hand, draped an arm around his shoulders, and welcomed him to town. The tension disappeared.

But off the court West was shy, and to this day he blushes slightly when someone recognizes him and asks for an autograph. It is one of many West character contradictions (the sum of which should deter any sane writer from attempting to psychoanalyze him in print): the man who thrived in the spotlight is allergic to the limelight.

He was nervous before games, yet come crunch time he demanded the ball. West didn't always make the shot, but he never choked, if choking is defined as diminished physical and mental ability caused by pressure.

West was the anti-choker. The hoop didn't get smaller for him in the closing seconds with two opponents guarding him—it yawned wider. The action didn't speed up into a confusing blur but rather slowed down and came into sharper focus. The game got easier and the pressure shifted to the opponent.

He led West Virginia to conference titles all three seasons and was All-American each year (second team as a sophomore), and as a six-three forward, he set a school career rebound record that still stands. In West's junior year WVU reached the NCAA championship game against Cal, and he scored 28 points. He got into foul trouble, though, and Cal won by 70–71. West averaged thirty-two points for five games and was voted the tournament's outstanding player, over Cincinnati's Oscar Robertson.

It was a great achievement, but West remembered it as the first

great failure of his career, one in a long line of huge disappoint-
ments that motivated him to play harder.

West and Robertson led the USA to an Olympic gold medal in '60,
then hit the NBA running. The Cincinnati Royals drafted Big O
with the number-one pick; the Lakers, who had just moved from
Minneapolis to Los Angeles, drafted West.

The fanfare was not loud. West wasn't aware that he had been
drafted until the Lakers phoned him two days later. They offered
him a one-year contract for $15,000 and a $1,500 bonus. Done.

The Lakers were pioneers, blazing an NBA trail to the West
Coast, bringing high-flying hoops to the hinterlands of Hollywood.
Off the court the Lakers were a traveling frat house, with all-night
card games, practical jokes, and brotherhood. Thanks to Baylor,
everyone had a nickname—Jim "Boomer" (as in flatulence) Krebs,
Rudy "Musty" (as in old socks) LaRusso, Tommy "Iron Jaw"
Hawkins, Frank "Pops" Selvy, Bobby "Slick" Leonard, Hot Rod
Hundley, Baby Ray Felix, and Zeke/Louella/Tweety. Baylor was
Motormouth.

The Lakers hired Fred Schaus as coach, and the players nicknamed him "Beef" because when he was angry his nose looked like
a raw pot roast. Beef, a former NBA star himself, let his thorough-
breds run, and he built team unity by rotating road roommates.
Decades ahead of his time in sports, Schaus kissed off the conventional wisdom that blacks are most comfortable rooming with
blacks, whites with whites. West and Tommy Hawkins, who was one
of two black players on that '60 team, became close friends, as did
their wives.

In '63, Hawkins had to deliver the bad news to West that his father had died, and they talked and cried together through the night.
Years later West encouraged Hawkins to become the Lakers' player
rep, and his role in helping negotiate a breakthrough labor agree-
ment led Hawkins to a successful career as a Dodgers executive.

West loved the NBA life immediately, but there was a catch:
Schaus didn't start his prize rookie until late in the season. To this

day Schaus is defensive about keeping West out of the starting lineup. And to this day West's jaw tightens when he talks about cooling his heels as a nonstarter. He made the All-Star team anyway and finished the season with a 17.6 scoring average.

Now the Lakers' stars—Baylor and West—were aligned for the next decade. It was the perfect Odd Couple. Baylor was the NBA's first playground-style superstar, making up the game as he went, an elegant and dominating force. West was the quietly unstoppable yin to Baylor's hang-'n'-bang yang. The Lakers, with a procession of journeymen at center, dominated the West for a decade and gave the mighty Celtics their greatest tests.

Mr. Clutch Moment: In West's second season the Lakers reach the Finals against the Celtics. They split the first two; Game 3 is in L.A. The Celtics lead by four near the end.

"I made two baskets to tie the game," West said, "and with three seconds left, Boston called time-out. They brought the ball in at mid-court, I stole the inbounds pass, and made a layup. Boston said, 'There's no way he can steal the ball and take it the length of the court in three seconds.' But I had a built-in time clock. I'm serious. I always knew exactly how much time was on the shot clock. Those are just things that you practiced."

What the Lakers got from West was spectacular consistency. This from a frail fellow full of quirks and nervous energy. West was, to borrow a phrase from James Taylor, a churnin' urn of burnin' funk. West controlled the burn of his churnin' urn by setting his daily routines in cement.

"I had a kind of ritual," West said, in great understatement. "I'd take a two-hour nap. If we were on the road, I'd carry a roll of tape, and I'd tape the curtains shut. The room had to be pitch-black, no noise. I was too nervous to eat, but I'd eat something at twelve-thirty, soup and a sandwich.

"If it was a home game and I was driving to the arena, there could be a 600-car pileup on the freeway and I was not going to change my route. I was always the first player to arrive, and the last one dressed, and I would always dress a certain way.

"I didn't want to talk to anyone. Writers didn't come into the locker room before games back then, but if they had, I would've gone somewhere and hidden out. I didn't want any interaction with anyone, and I hated loud noises in the locker room. I would try to get into a state of mind based on habits."

Hours before the game West's palms would begin to perspire. He told one of his sons that he knew it was time to retire when he noticed that he was going into games with dry hands.

"Even exhibition games were not meaningless," West said. "I can honestly say I never played a game when I wasn't nervous before the ball game. The thing you miss the most is what your body felt like. There was so much adrenaline running through your body, it felt like it was electric—it was the ultimate high. The intensity level, it's so hard to describe, it's like a controlled fury. You hear about rage killings and road rage. An athlete is like that, except it's controlled. You're thinking about the guy you're going to play against, how much you hate him. You didn't have to work at it, the feeling was just there.

"But sometimes you were so [emotionally] tired, it might take you half of the first quarter to kind of recharge yourself, particularly in the bigger games. You'd say, 'My God, how can I have so much energy and all of a sudden it's gone?' But it always came back. Early in my career I had to start quickly—Elgin and I really had to score for that team to be a success. As I moved along in my career I tried to build to the second half, particularly the last quarter."

Mr. Clutch Moment: Rod Thorn, who was a year behind West at West Virginia and later played in the NBA, said, "I was playing for St. Louis [Hawks]. We were one point up with eight seconds left, [and] the Lakers called time-out. We spent the whole time-out talking about double-teaming West, making him pass. He gets the ball, we've got three guys on him, he fakes, he makes a fifteen-footer."

Thorn remembered another Lakers-Hawks game. "We're leading, Jerry gets his fifth foul at the end of the third quarter, but they leave him in. We went at him the whole quarter, he scored fifteen in the quarter, and they win. No matter what, he would get a shot off, and it would be a good one. And if you foul him, he's going to make the free throws."

Tommy Hawkins referred to West's nervous system as "definitely high-twitch. His antennas were always twitching, though he was imperturbable. If ever there was a guy who could harness and focus his energy, it was Jerry. And if the other players didn't come out breathing fire, he couldn't understand."

Despite his inner fire, West kept cool. He rarely protested referees' calls and didn't get his first technical foul until his third season. He didn't bark at or criticize teammates. And owing to the West Reverse-Choke Syndrome, the greater the pressure, the calmer he became.

West couldn't avoid contact, but he stayed out of fights, even though it was a rough league. There's another West contradiction: this hard-nosed player got his nose broken nine times.

"People talk about how rough the league is now—it's not even close to what it was back then," West said. "It was dirty. You had some dirty players, in the sense that the fouls were going to be very hard. A lot of fights. You had one or two players on every team who didn't mind knocking you on your ass, or whatever it took. If they played now, they'd get fined every night. We called 'em enforcers.

"Tempers were short. Early on, I couldn't believe how physical the game was, nothing like college. In Detroit one night I was under the basket waiting for a rebound from a free throw. I saw an elbow, and I caught two of my front teeth in my hand."

The problem for opposing thugs was that West was more than willing to trade two front teeth for two free throws. He learned that there is gold in the lane if you can deal with the pain. He improved his free-throw percentage dramatically in his second season, from .666 to .769. In West's sixth season, he shot .860 from the line and set an NBA record for free throws made, 840.

West's stroke on free throws and jumpers was as grooved as any in the game, before or since.

"It's a lever," West once explained, stripping away the mysteries and complexities of the jump shot. "It's a simple lever."

West's lever had a devastating delivery system, the league's quickest stop-and-pop, thanks in part to one of the physics discoveries he made as a kid. If you pound your final dribble with extra force, the ball jumps off the dirt (or hardwood) harder and quickens your shot release. Perfecting that art came at a cost—bumps and scratches on Jerry's face and dings in his bedroom ceiling.

He recalled giving a shooting clinic at a basketball camp and making 186 consecutive jump shots. In one NBA game, he shot 16-

for-17 from the floor and 12-for-12 from the line (and also had ten rebounds, twelve assists, and ten steals, for a quadruple-double).

Mr. Clutch Moment: In his most famous shot, West sinks a sixty-two-footer at the final buzzer against the Knicks in Game 3 of the 1970 Finals in L.A.

West said it was lucky, then explained that maybe it wasn't.

"After practice, maybe a dozen times a year, I'd practice that shot," West said, "because those are the kind of shots you'll probably get an opportunity to shoot a few times in a season.

"What's the best way to get it up there? Is it two-handed? From that distance it's a little harder to shoot one-handed, but I felt the best way to keep the ball straight was to run into the thing and shoot one-handed."

Did he recall ever making another such shot?

"In one game I made two shots from half-court."

Defense was important to West. With his long arms, quickness, and feel for the passing lanes, he was Mr. Theft. But there's no hard evidence, since steals didn't become an official stat until his final season. Also, the league didn't select an All-Defensive team until five seasons before he retired, but West made the team all five times, four as a first-team pick.

West saw himself as a fairly mechanical player, and that's certainly true when he's compared to Baylor, who played basketball like John Coltrane played sax.

On the hot dog scale, West didn't register. He remained the polar opposite of his Lakers teammate Hot Rod Hundley. Hundley never matched his collegiate greatness in the NBA, but he never stopped working the crowd. He was the only NBA player of his day, post–Bob Cousy, to throw behind-the-back and wraparound passes. If a game was on ice, Hundley would shoot free throws with a hook shot.

West had no taste for hot-dogging or trash-talking, yet his game was never considered bland. And although he learned his hoops far from the inner city, his style was never categorized as "black" or "white."

West's skin color was never an issue, although then as now players made joking references to race. Just before the tip-off of an All-Star Game in which West was the lone white starter, Bill Russell cackled his famous cackle and said, "Surely you realize, Jerry, that you are the great white hope?"

When West played poorly, alarms and sirens went off inside his head. "I never saw Jerry have back-to-back bad games," Tommy Hawkins said. "Until he could replace a bad performance with a good one, his soul was not at rest."

In Game 1 of the '62 Finals, the first of the great Lakers-Celtics Finals, West scored only sixteen points.

"After the game," said Celtics guard K. C. Jones, a legendary defender, "I'm in the dressing room, surrounded by the media, and I got diarrhea of the mouth. I went off, explained how I'd held West to sixteen points. Next game he got forty-five."

Did Jones's boasting motivate West? West shook his head and said he never paid much attention to newspapers.

"*I* knew when I played a bad game or didn't do what I was supposed to," he said. "I was my own worst critic."

For West, it was less about answering critics and more about rising to the occasion. He dropped the forty-five on Jones not for revenge but out of necessity. And because he could.

In the NBA, just as in high school and college, West lived for the big moment, the crucial final minutes and seconds of a close game. He claimed that often near the end of a game, in the time-out huddle, he simply demanded the ball.

"I don't quite remember it that way," Fred Schaus said with a chuckle, "but giving him the ball *would* be a pretty smart coaching move."

The majority of players in the NBA occasionally experience mild choking symptoms, a loss of cool. West was a different cat. To him, the more there was at stake, the easier the game got.

"I think there are certain times in a player's career when physically you have an edge," said West, speaking as if his basketball psyche was standard-issue. "And it becomes a mental edge, and it allows you to read things quicker, but see them slower. The key to playing successfully at a high level has to do with seeing a game in slow motion.

"I never thought the game went real fast. At certain times quickness is an issue, but I never felt it was a real fast game, and the slower you see it, the fewer mistakes you're going to make. The game was never a blur, I never saw it that way.

"People ask me about it [the clutch reputation], and it's awkward to talk about it, people might think it's bragging or arrogant. It's not. It happened, okay? It happened. It was really, more than anything, probably a gift.

"I think it's an attitude, a faith in yourself that you can get the job done. Where did it come from? Mine certainly comes from my childhood, I don't think there's any question. None of us want to fail, but some people can just carry that burden a little bit better than others.

"I always felt I could get a good shot, that it might be easier to score [in crunch time] than at other times, because people don't want to foul you, because you're probably going to make your free throws. And if they double-team you, you probably have a greater advantage because one of them is more than likely going to foul you."

Mr. Clutch Moment: The Rick Barry–led Warriors are facing the Lakers in 1973 in the Western Conference Finals. "We had just beaten the Bucks, really a stunning upset, and the Lakers were worried about us," said Jim Barnett, a radio/TV analyst for the Golden State Warriors who played for that team. "They had just survived a tough seven-game series against the Bulls. If we win Game 1, I know we'll win the series.

"We lead the entire game, we know we've got it won, then we started throwing the ball away, and now it's 99-all, with thirty-two seconds left, and they've got the ball. I'm guarding West, and I make him go left, to the baseline, and I make him terminate his dribble, about twenty feet from the basket and slightly behind the plane of the backboard.

"I know he's going to pump-fake, and I don't bite on the fake. I do everything right! I'm all over him. He goes up and makes the shot, from behind the backboard."

Barnett had just been hustled by the Minnesota Fats of hoops.

"I had a shooting thing I'd do after practice, by myself," West said. "I'd practice really tough shots. I'd shoot from behind the backboard a lot, on the left side, because it makes you shoot very straight and a little bit higher than normal. It doesn't even look like you can make the shot. It really makes you concentrate. Even today when I go to a clinic, I show kids that particular shot."

Considering West's high expectations of himself, it was no surprise when he retired at age thirty-five, even though he was still able to pump in twenty-five a game and command a superstar salary.

Also not surprising is that West in retirement did not wear out a lot of hammocks. He is a fast talker, fast walker, fast eater. He thinks fast, drives fast, golfs fast.

"You go out with Jerry," Hundley said, "you hit eight places every five minutes. He comes in a place, takes a sip of beer, looks around, and says, 'Come on, let's go someplace else.' "

West the retiree took his nervous energy to the golf course. As his NBA playing career was winding down, so was his first marriage, to Jane, whom he had met at West Virginia and with whom he had three sons. West needed an activity to take his mind off real life.

Applying his engineering theory to the golf swing—"It's just a lever"—West became a scratch golfer. And a fast one. He read putts like Evelyn Wood reads books.

"He's very hyper on the course, always on the move," said Mitch Kupchak, who inherited West's GM job with the Lakers. "He walks up to the ball and hits. No practice swing, just steps up and whack."

Playing with Kupchak one day, West mashed a drive down the middle of the fairway, but the ball got plugged and West couldn't find it. He spent five minutes searching, clearly agitated. This surprised Kupchak, who expected West to simply drop another ball.

"I didn't realize until later that he was five-under-par at the time and he had a shot at the course record. Even with that two-stroke penalty, he shot 67."

"I rarely play anymore," West said. "I guess we all have addictions in life, and my addiction was basketball for a long time, and all of a sudden I wasn't playing, and my addiction turned to golf. It was a great addiction because it's a solitary game. I used to love to hit golf balls, to practice. It was a time in my life where I was kind of in tur-moil, and it was very much like basketball as a kid. Then I got to the point where I needed something to do with my life that was more meaningful than going to the golf course and playing cards every day."

He found it. Basketball recalled West to active duty. He had be-gun to miss the game desperately, and Lakers owner Jack Kent Cooke asked him to coach the team.

West loved his new job, and hated it. Winning was fine, but the losses were even harder to take than when he was a player, since now he could only sit and watch.

Under West, the Lakers, who had averaged thirty-five wins the previous two seasons, finished 53–29, the best record in the NBA. He took the team to the playoffs three seasons running, but suf-fered.

Assistant coach Stan Albeck described West's temperament after a loss: "Very quiet, morose . . . distraught. We'd go to his hotel room, and we didn't have any game video back then, but Jerry could recall the game in great detail, where everyone was on every play. . . . He was a great seether."

Hubie Brown, then coaching the Atlanta Hawks, said of West, "Sometimes he looks like he's gonna bust out of his skin."

Another West contradiction: he hates it when fans have unrealis-tic expectations for his teams, yet talking about his brief coaching career he once admitted, "It used to really piss me off when players couldn't do the things on the court I used to be able to do."

So West, his stomach knotted and his nerves frayed, retired from coaching. Cooke was selling the Lakers and begged West to stay and coach a team built around Kareem Abdul-Jabbar and an exciting rookie named Magic Johnson. West declined, but stepped into the front office as special adviser to the new owner, Jerry Buss.

Three seasons later Buss fired coach Paul Westhead and was hit with an inspiration: why not have co–head coaches—Pat Riley, the young and obviously talented assistant coach, *and* West? It would be the greatest duo since Batman and Robin.

Buss thought he had West's okay on the plan, but at the press conference to introduce the new coaching tandem, West leapt to the podium, took the microphone, and explained that while he would be helping from a distance, he would not be coaching in any way.

Not long afterward, general manager Bill Sharman stepped aside because of voice problems, and West moved into the GM chair. He inherited and nurtured the Showtime Lakers, keeping that Magic-Kareem machine humming with a constant supply of drafted stars and role players. Then West created the Kobe-Shaq Lakers, rebuilding the dynasty around two gifted players for whom a lot of basketball people had no use. Back then, few saw Bryant's potential or O'Neal's inner drive.

That was West's trademark as a GM: the courage to go against the grain, to create. In '89 he ignored the advice of his entire staff and drafted Vlade Divac, a questionable commodity because he hadn't played in America.

"Teams that drafted before us needed Vlade even more than we did," said Kupchak, West's assistant at the time. "One general manager told me, 'We just didn't have the balls to do it.' "

Divac helped the Lakers make the Finals in '91, and in '96 he was used as trade bait to land Bryant from Charlotte, which had drafted Bryant. O'Neal was courted and signed by West as a free agent. The pairing of O'Neal and Bryant seems like a no-brainer now, but Bryant was only a number-thirteen pick, and O'Neal was widely considered to be a great talent who was seriously flawed by a lack of fire and desire.

"I remember Jerry telling me he was going to try to draft Kobe Bryant," Hundley said with a laugh. "I'd never *heard* of Kobe. Jerry said, 'Let me tell you something, within five or six years he's going to be one of the top ten players in the history of basketball.' I said, *'Whaat?'* "

Easy call, said West. "I felt Kobe was the best player in the whole draft, though you knew you were going to have to wait a while. We traded a starting center for him, but we were trying to change the nature of our team."

West is considered by many to be the most astute judge of talent in the league, the best at discovering players. He took a virtually unknown A. C. Green with the Lakers' first-round pick in '85, and Green was a rock of the team for eight seasons. West is unafraid to trust his own judgment and draft a player well above the level assigned him by the "experts." This is risky, because a foolish draft can kill a team, and there is huge potential for embarrassment.

"Of all the general managers in basketball," said Rick Barry, "West is the least afraid to take a player where he's not slotted."

West said that criticism, or fear of criticism, doesn't faze him, because "I'm not here to be known as someone who's smarter than someone else. I would *rather* be criticized. I'll tell you why. Those same people who criticize you (anonymously) are the same ones whose teams don't do well. Soon the league will be thirty teams, and the best risk-takers ultimately are the ones who will have the best results."

When he was the Lakers' GM, the more successful the team was, the more stressful and the less satisfying West's work became. Player imperfections would drive him to deep bouts of exasperation. He clashed with Pat Riley, and then to a lesser extent with Phil Jackson.

More and more, West was Zeke the Bleak. In the playoffs he would pace the arena parking lot, ghostlike, during home games. He stopped traveling to away games.

"It just got to the point where winning wasn't fun anymore," West said. "I worked for an owner that was absolutely the best, but I was at the point where I couldn't even enjoy watching the two best players in the league playing together, when they were really playing well. I just couldn't watch. I expected everything to go wrong, and when you get to that point, you just know you've had enough. Physically and mentally, I was completely burned out."

That was it. West walked away from basketball for good . . . until the lowly Memphis Grizzlies challenged him in retirement to build them into a winner. West jumped.

"All of a sudden . . . I just got antsy," West said. "The [Memphis] owner here [Michael Heisley] was persuasive, and the thing I found out about myself is that I don't think any of us are worth a damn if we're not doing something that is challenging."

West moved to Memphis with his second wife, Karen, whom he married in 1978, and their two sons. He set out to do what he first did in 1960—turn around a losing NBA franchise.

West claimed that he is much more relaxed in Memphis, more Nice Jerry and less Zeke the Bleak. He claimed that he no longer cares what media critics say about him, which gives him a great feeling of freedom. Yet here came another West inconsistency: "Everything I've done since I've been here has been criticized. Everything. I have a number of [critical] articles I've kept here the last two years, and I read 'em every once in a while. It sort of motivates me, it really does."

Whatever inner demons he wrestles with, the public Jerry West is easygoing and personable, a gentleman, unfailingly polite to strangers, and a lively conversationalist. Quietly, he takes pride in a passage from Pat Conroy's recent memoir, *My Losing Season.* Conroy was a counselor at a basketball camp in Virginia in '64, when West, then a full-fledged NBA superstar, came to the camp for a day.

"He carried himself with a kingly, benign dignity and treated the boys around him with gentleness and good humor . . . ," Conroy writes. "Every boy who approached Jerry West was met with a gentlemanly kindness, a genuine engagement, and unfeigned courtesy.

"If you are one of those who think that great athletes shouldn't have to be role models for the young boys and girls, I offer you this: I have tried to treat everyone I meet as Jerry West treated those bedazzled boys who approached him, as he walked the grounds of Miller School. He taught me much about basketball, but he taught me much more about class and the responsibilities of fame."

West carries himself much the same way now and is accorded much the same respect-bordering-on-reverence by basketball fans and team staffers. The respect is for Jerry West the legend, but also for his Memphis miracle-in-progress.

When West hired Hubie Brown, the sixty-nine-year-old TV commentator who hadn't coached in fifteen years, jaws dropped around the league. No other team was remotely considering Brown as a coach.

A writer digs out notes from an informal interview with Brown on the subject of Jerry West, then the Lakers' general manager. Said Brown, prophetically, "I have the greatest admiration for his courage. He's not afraid to make moves that will pay dividends in the future."

West is a future guy and claimed he's not much for nostalgia. Years ago he threw out his trophies because he likes everything neat and they were a pain to keep dusted. When he scored his twenty-thousandth point, West took the ball home and gave it to his kids to play with in the driveway. His Olympic gold medal and his few scrapbooks were lost when his parents' home burned in '63.

Yet he hangs on to a few mementos, and when a writer brought up the subject of clutch performance, West dusted off an old mental snapshot. It was from the season he would finally help bring a championship to Los Angeles, even though he was struggling with a nagging injury that would soon end his career.

Mr. Clutch Moment: "This happened at the point in my career when I wasn't the same player I had been, I was not," West said. "I didn't have the same quickness, the jumping ability, the same ability to stop quickly and shoot the ball.

"It was the All-Star Game in Los Angeles in '72, the year we won the championship. We had a time-out [the score was tied], and Walt Frazier was guarding me, a very, very good defender, tremendous player. In the huddle I didn't ask for the ball, you don't ask for the ball when you've got a bunch of All-Stars on your team, but I knew it was going to end up with me, for some reason.

"I got the ball, and it's the top of the key, and Walt is all over me. It was hard for me then to get away from players who you felt you used to get away from pretty easily. I shot the ball and I said, 'That thing's in.' I can remember what you feel like, it's a tremendous feeling to do something like that. It was just kind of my last hurrah as a player. You remember those things."

The late Chick Hearn hung the Mr. Clutch label on West. At a charity event long ago, West was presented with an old automobile clutch mounted on a plaque. He was deeply embarrassed.

And yet decades later, West can still smell that clutch burning as, in his mind, he shifts into a higher gear with the game on the line.

"You can't wait to do it," West said quietly. "You can't wait to do it. You just can't wait."

JERRY WEST—GUARD

PERSONAL: Born May 28, 1938, in Cheylan, WV . . . 6–2/185 (1.88 m/84 kg) . . . full name: Jerry Alan West.

HIGH SCHOOL: East Bank (WV).

COLLEGE: West Virginia.

TRANSACTIONS/CAREER NOTES: Selected by Minneapolis Lakers in first round (second pick overall) of 1960 NBA draft. . . . Lakers franchise moved to Los Angeles for 1960–61 season. . . . Consultant, Los Angeles Lakers (1978–80 through 1981–82). . . . General manager, Lakers (1982–83 through 1993–94). . . . Executive vice president of basketball operations, Lakers (1994–95 to 1999–2000). . . . President of basketball operations, Memphis Grizzlies (2002–present).

CAREER HONORS: Elected to Naismith Memorial Basketball Hall of Fame (1979). . . . NBA 35th Anniversary All-Time Team (1980) and One of the 50 Greatest Players in NBA History (1996).

MISCELLANEOUS: Member of NBA championship team (1972). . . . Member of gold-medal-winning U.S. Olympic team (1960). . . . Los Angeles Lakers franchise all-time leading scorer with 25,192 points (1960–61 through 1973–74).

COLLEGIATE RECORD

NOTES: *The Sporting News* All-America first team (1959, 1960). . . . NCAA Tournament Most Outstanding Player (1959).

													Averages		
Season	Team	G	Min	FGM	FGA	Pct	FTM	FTA	Pct	Reb	Ast	Pts	RPG	APG	PPG
56–57	WVU	17	—	114	—	—	104	—	—	—	—	332	0.0	0.0	19.5
57–58	WVU	28	799	178	359	.496	142	194	.732	311	41	498	11.1	1.5	17.8
58–59	WVU	34	1,210	340	656	.518	223	320	.697	419	86	903	12.3	2.5	26.6
59–60	WVU	31	1,129	325	645	.504	258	337	.766	510	134	908	16.5	4.3	29.3
Total		93	3,138	843	1,660	.508	623	851	.732	1,240	261	2,309	13.3	2.8	24.8

NBA REGULAR-SEASON RECORD

RECORDS: Holds single-season record for most free throws made—840 (1966).

HONORS: All-NBA first team (1962, 1963, 1964, 1965, 1966, 1967, 1970, 1971, 1972, 1973). . . . All-NBA second team (1968, 1969). . . . NBA All-Defensive first team (1970, 1971, 1972, 1973). . . . NBA All-Defensive second team (1969).

														Averages		
Season	Team	G	Min	FGM	FGA	Pct	FTM	FTA	Pct	Reb	Ast	PF	DQ	Pts	RPG	APG	PPG
60–61	LAL	79	2,797	529	1,264	.419	331	497	.666	611	333	213	1	1,389	7.7	4.2	17.6
61–62	LAL	75	3,087	799	1,795	.445	712	926	.769	591	402	173	4	2,310	7.9	5.4	30.8
62–63	LAL	55	2,163	559	1,213	.461	371	477	.778	384	307	150	1	1,489	7.0	5.6	27.1
63–64	LAL	72	2,906	740	1,529	.484	584	702	.832	443	403	200	2	2,064	6.2	5.6	28.7
64–65	LAL	74	3,066	822	1,655	.497	648	789	.821	447	364	221	2	2,292	6.0	4.9	31.0
65–66	LAL	79	3,218	818	1,731	.473	840	977	.860	562	480	243	1	2,476	7.1	6.1	31.3
66–67	LAL	66	2,670	645	1,389	.464	602	686	.878	392	447	160	1	1,892	5.9	6.8	28.7
67–68	LAL	51	1,919	476	926	.514	391	482	.811	294	310	152	1	1,343	5.8	6.1	26.3
68–69	LAL	61	2,394	545	1,156	.471	490	597	.821	262	423	156	1	1,580	4.3	6.9	25.9
69–70	LAL	74	3,106	831	1,673	.497	647	785	.824	338	554	160	3	2,309	4.6	7.5	31.2
70–71	LAL	69	2,845	667	1,351	.494	525	631	.832	320	655	180	0	1,859	4.6	9.5	26.9
71–72	LAL	77	2,973	735	1,540	.477	515	633	.814	327	747	209	0	1,985	4.2	9.7	25.8
72–73	LAL	69	2,460	618	1,291	.479	339	421	.805	289	607	138	0	1,575	4.2	8.8	22.8

										Rebounds							Averages		
		G	Min	FGM	FGA	Pct	FTM	FTA	Pct	Off	Def	Tot	Ast	St	Blk	TO	Pts	RPG	APG	PPG
73–74	LAL	31	967	232	519	.447	165	198	.833	30	86	116	206	81	23	—	629	3.7	6.6	20.3
Total		932	36,571	9,016	19,032	.474	7,160	8,801	.814	—	—	5,376	6,238	81	23	—	25,192	5.8	6.7	27.0

PERSONAL FOULS/DISQUALIFICATIONS: 1973–74, 80/0.

NBA PLAYOFF RECORD

NOTES: NBA Finals Most Valuable Player (1969). . . . Holds single-series playoff record for highest points-per-game average—46.3 (1965).

														Averages		
Season	Team	G	Min	FGM	FGA	Pct	FTM	FTA	Pct	Reb	Ast	PF	DQ	Pts	RPG	APG	PPG
60–61	LAL	12	461	99	202	.490	77	106	.726	104	63	39	0	275	8.7	5.3	22.9
61–62	LAL	13	557	144	310	.465	121	150	.807	88	57	38	0	409	6.8	4.4	31.5
62–63	LAL	13	538	144	286	.503	74	100	.740	106	61	34	0	362	8.2	4.7	27.8
63–64	LAL	5	206	57	115	.496	42	53	.792	36	17	20	0	156	7.2	3.4	31.2
64–65	LAL	11	470	155	351	.442	137	154	.890	63	58	37	0	447	5.7	5.3	40.6
65–66	LAL	14	619	185	357	.518	109	125	.872	88	79	40	0	479	6.3	5.6	34.2
66–67	LAL	1	1	0	0	—	0	0	—	1	0	0	0	0	1.0	0.0	0.0
67–68	LAL	15	622	165	313	.527	132	169	.781	81	82	47	0	462	5.4	5.5	30.8
68–69	LAL	18	757	196	423	.463	164	204	.804	71	135	52	1	556	3.9	7.5	30.9
69–70	LAL	18	830	196	418	.469	170	212	.802	66	151	55	1	562	3.7	8.4	31.2
71–72	LAL	15	608	128	340	.376	88	106	.830	73	134	39	0	344	4.9	8.9	22.9
72–73	LAL	17	638	151	336	.449	99	127	.780	76	132	49	1	401	4.5	7.8	23.6

		G	Min	FGM	FGA	Pct	FTM	FTA	Pct	Off	Def	Tot	Ast	St	Blk	TO	Pts	RPG	APG	PPG
												Rebounds							Averages	
73–74	LAL	1	14	2	9	.222	0	0	—	0	2	2	1	0	0	—	4	2.0	1.0	4.0
Total		153	6,321	1,622	3,460	.469	1,213	1,506	.469	—	—	855	970	0	0	—	4,457	5.6	6.3	29.1

NBA ALL-STAR GAME RECORD

NOTES: NBA All-Star Game Most Valuable Player (1972).

Season	Team	Min	FGM	FGA	Pct	FTM	FTA	Pct	Reb	Ast	PF	Dq	Pts
1961	LAL	25	2	8	.250	5	6	.833	2	4	3	0	9
1962	LAL	31	7	14	.500	4	6	.667	3	1	2	0	18
1963	LAL	32	5	15	.333	3	4	.750	7	5	1	0	13
1964	LAL	42	8	20	.400	1	1	1.000	4	5	3	0	17
1965	LAL	40	8	16	.500	4	6	.667	5	6	2	0	20
1966	LAL	11	1	5	.200	2	2	1.000	1	0	2	0	4
1967	LAL	30	6	11	.545	4	4	1.000	3	6	3	0	16
1968	LAL	32	7	17	.412	3	4	.750	6	6	4	0	17
1969	LAL	Selected but did not play—injured											
1970	LAL	31	7	12	.583	8	12	.667	5	5	3	0	22
1971	LAL	20	2	4	.500	1	3	.333	1	9	1	0	5
1972	LAL	27	6	9	.667	1	2	.500	6	5	2	0	13
1973	LAL	20	3	6	.500	0	0	—	4	3	2	0	6
1974	LAL	Selected but did not play—injured											
Total		341	62	137	.453	36	50	.720	47	55	28	0	160

NBA COACHING RECORD

		Regular Season				Playoffs		
Season	Team	W	L	Pct	Finish	W	L	Pct
76–77	LAL	53	29	.646	1st/Pacific Division	4	7	.364
77–78	LAL	45	37	.549	4th/Pacific Division	1	2	.333
78–79	LAL	47	35	.573	3rd/Pacific Division	3	5	.375
Total (3 years)		145	101	.589	Total (3 years)	8	14	.364

NOTES: 1977—Defeated Golden State, 4–3, in Western Conference Semifinals; lost to Portland, 4–0, in Western Conference Finals. 1978—Lost to Seattle in Western Conference First Round. 1979—Defeated Denver, 2–1, in Western Conference First Round; lost to Seattle, 4–1, in Western Conference Semifinals.

Chapter Thirteen

PHIL JACKSON—Head Coach

Flexibility and the Power to Motivate

by Charley Rosen

> *The Zen wisdom is to always give your sheep a very*
> *large pasture. But unless the pasture has a fence, the*
> *sheep will get lost.*
>
> —Phil Jackson

If Phil Jackson is justly celebrated for his philosophical and psychological flexibility as well as his ability to motivate his players, it's no surprise that these defining characteristics are manifest in his offense of choice—the power triangle. Typically, Jackson explains the general principles of the triangle in cosmic terms: "It's a vehicle for integrating mind and body, sport and spirit, in a practical, down-to-earth form. It's five-man tai chi, awareness in action."

The basic idea of the triangle is to orchestrate the flow of movement in such a way as to lure the defense off balance and thereby create undefended spaces on the court. Once he carries the ball safely across the time-line, the ball-handler can initiate this movement by passing to any of his four teammates. The most effective of these possible passes would be directly into the center, stationed in the low post, because this creates the deepest ball penetration and forces the defense to make radical adjustments.

In certain situations, however, when the ball-handler is being pressured or the wing is overplayed, the center is required to move to the high post. "We call this the center-release," said Phil, "and what this option does for us is to leave the basket area undefended."

Since not all four possible trigger passes can be denied without making the defense vulnerable to reverses, back-door cuts, or alley-oops plays, the ball-handler always has a receiver available. Every possible entry pass keys a different series of movements. (A pass to the wing, for example, creates five distinct options for the passer—the corner fill, the basket cut, the diagonal cut, the outside cut, or the inside cut—depending on how the defense reacts.) Any subsequent passes create additional options.

"The fundamental principle," said Jackson, "is never to go head to head with the defense. In fact, the offensive players will always take the path of least resistance and move into open spaces. This kind of movement requires all the players to think and move in unison. Instead of moving along predetermined routes, the players must read the defense and be totally aware of what's happening on the floor. When executed properly, the triangle is virtually unstoppable because there are no set plays (only a series of possible options), so the defense can't predict what's going to happen next. If the defense tries to prevent one particular move or pass, there are always alternative moves and passes."

In the heyday of Chicago's dynasty, Jackson estimated that the Bulls operated with forty total options. "We didn't have any pop-up wing shooters," he explained, "so we didn't need any single-doubles or any motion actions, which would have added perhaps another ten options. By contrast, even with the single-double action installed to accommodate Glen Rice, the Lakers finished the 1999–2000 season with about twenty options. In my last season in L.A., we had about fifty. In theory, with sufficient time and sufficiently skilled players, the triangle's possibilities are almost infinite."

For the triangle to be most effective, the practitioners must be talented, mindful, and mature. Instead of trying to force the game to conform to the dictates of their own ego-power, the players must be capable of approaching defenses with an open mind. They must also trust that their teammates are likewise willing to subordinate their egos and go with the flow. Set the triangle spinning on any of its axes, and whoever winds up in an open space gets the ball and takes the shot. That's why Michael Jordan used to call the triangle "an equal opportunity offense."

Aside from the scoring opportunities the triangle creates, Jackson believed that any team with a coordinated, systematic offense has tremendous advantages over "playbook" offenses, i.e., a series of unrelated sets and plays. "First of all," said Jackson, "a system provides a clear purpose and direction with implicit goals. Secondly, players can learn exactly how they can contribute. Thirdly, it rewards unselfish behavior, which in turn renews the system. And lastly, it also relaxes the often tense relationship between a coach and his players because having a clearly defined set of circumstances to work with depersonalizes and reduces conflict. The players understand that the coach isn't attacking them personally when he corrects a mistake, but is simply trying to improve their understanding of the system."

According to Jackson, "a basketball team should work together like the five fingers on a hand. The thumb is more powerful than the pinkie, but the pinkie provides balance. And all the fingers move instinctively in conjunction to solve the problem."

So it is that understanding plus coordination equals flexibility.

While some players (most notably Scottie Pippen and Shaquille O'Neal) immediately accepted the principles of the offense, several did not (Michael Jordan and Kobe Bryant). Here's where Jackson's ability to motivate his players came into play.

"Bill Cartwright was the Bulls center when I first introduced the triangle in Chicago," said Jackson. "Because Bill wasn't a very good passer, and because he needed so much time and space for his post-up moves, that first version of the triangle generally focused on outside shooting and deemphasized one-on-one penetration. Michael began calling the triangle 'a white man's offense.' Michael's resistance was stubborn, so I had to out-stubborn him until he finally saw the light."

It was Jordan's competitive nature that finally brought him around. "He'd rather score thirty and win than score forty and lose," said Jackson, "which can't be said for all NBA players. What the triangle did for Michael was put him in so many possible spaces that the defense couldn't anticipate where he'd be when he received the ball and was unable to quickly double-team him."

Even with Jordan's grudging endorsement, the Bulls needed one and a half seasons to become fluent with the triangle. And it wasn't until Jordan returned to the Bulls from his fling with baseball in 1995 that he became a true believer.

Pippen and Shaq were "easy sells," but Kobe Bryant always resisted Jackson's system. "Kobe is so mesmerized by the ball," said Jackson, "that getting him to work hard without it has always been a problem." Bryant remained a stern and continuing test of Jackson's motivational skills. Jackson tried heart-to-heart talks over breakfast, where he used Jordan as an example, pointing out that M.J. was ringless in his first six NBA seasons until his awesome offense became triangulated. Jackson tried to convince Bryant that the whole is greater than the sum of its parts, that basketball is a team game, and that in the triangle (as in real life) the more you give the more you get. But Kid Kobe always resisted, arguing that the triangle was boring and stifled his creativity.

"I also tried tweaking Kobe during tape sessions," Jackson said. "I'd rerun portions of a game tape when he took on three or four defenders and lost the ball, or he forced up a shot before Shaq even crossed the ten-second line. There was Kobe, playing one-on-five. I'd just play the sequence over and over without saying a word. Sometimes it worked and sometimes it didn't."

Through it all, the youngster was increasingly resentful of what he perceived as Jackson's criticisms. Bryant wanted to score points and win championships *his* way. Anybody who attempted to force Kobe to do what he didn't want to do was dissing him. It's a mark of how highly evolved Jackson's motivational skills are that Kobe did take the bit often enough for the Lakers to win three championships.

Like any other personal skills and defining characteristics, Phil Jackson's intellectual flexibility and motivational tools were developed through hard work over long periods of time.

Both of Phil's parents (Charles and Elizabeth) were hellfire-and-brimstone Pentecostal ministers, so his childhood activities (in Deer Lodge, Miles City, and then Great Falls, Montana) were severely restrained. "Pentecostalism is a mystic, charismatic, proselytizing religion," he explained, "which teaches that the world is rapidly approaching its final destruction. With much fervor and desire, the message must quickly be spread to the four corners of the world to prepare for the imminent second coming of Christ."

Part of this preparation was to live a saintly life and shun the sinful "outside" world. "We didn't go to the movies," Phil noted. "We didn't dance or smoke or drink. We were taught a disdain for any other type of religion and [told] that we were practicing the truest and purest form of Christianity. The idea that people of our faith were excluded from the world was also handed down from my parents. We went into the world only to do things like go to school and shop for food, but then we would come right back into the tight circle of family and religion. The only secular reading material we had in the house was the local newspaper and the *Reader's Digest.*"

At the heart of the Pentecostal belief system was "a wishful faith." The Pentecostals took as their model the Old Testament tale of the Jews' forty years of wandering through the desert. "As long as we believed," Jackson said, "manna would fall from heaven."

At the same time, within what Jackson called "a weird and rigid structure," there was a certain degree of freedom. "The harsh winter weather in Montana made day-to-day life so difficult," he said, "that nobody could be overly dogmatic about anything. We also had prayer meetings on Wednesday nights where people would talk about following the spirit. The Lord told them to do this, or the Lord laid on their mind to do that. This kind of spiritual intuition was far more important than any apparent restrictions."

In later years, one reason the triangle so appealed to Jackson was the opportunity it offered of experiencing freedom within a system. Unlimited freedom led to chaos. And didn't Jesus promise rest, ease, and freedom to those who willingly assumed his "yoke" (Matthew 11:29)?

Jackson's first lesson in motivation was provided by his father. "Instead of delegating whatever work had to be done," Jackson recalled, "Dad always took on part of the load himself. I can remember my dad in overalls along with the rest of the work crew cleaning up the church grounds every spring. He worked right alongside the others and pulled his weight, even though he was the leader of the church. It was a very effective nonverbal way of motivating the congregation."

Playing sports was considered by the Pentecostals to be a physically healthy (if ultimately meaningless) activity for youngsters, and Jackson played baseball, football, and basketball throughout his high school years (but never on Sundays!). The basketball coach at Williston High School was Bob Pederson, who kept a tight rein on his players. "During my first varsity season," Jackson said, "Coach Pederson had us run a lot of patterns, and no freelancing was tolerated. I played the pivot with my back to the basket, and all I did was roll across the lane and shoot my left-handed hook shot. I very seldom was allowed to get more than ten feet away from the basket."

As Jackson became more adept, Pederson changed the offense, instituted an up-tempo game, and permitted him to explore the balance between freedom and discipline. Among other things, Pederson taught Jackson that a good coach should match his game plan to the particular talents of his players.

In 1964 Jackson accepted a basketball scholarship from Coach Bill Fitch at the University of North Dakota, and his attitudinal education took a quantum leap. "College was the first time I had ever lived away from home," Jackson said, "and like everybody else at that stage, I was very anxious to get away. Mom initialed all my clothing, my father patted me on the back, and suddenly I was gone."

There were eight thousand students at UND and only nine African Americans, all of them either basketball or football players. "Before then," said Jackson, "my various environments had been entirely homogenous. Except for a handful of Native Americans in high school (who were generally considered to be inferior beings), the only unique people I ever met were those who weren't named Johnson, Nelson, Peterson, or Hanson. The only Afro-Americans I had ever encountered was when I had a newspaper route and I had to go to the train station to pick up my copies of the *Minneapolis Tribune* from the Empire Builder during its ten-minute stopover in Williston. The 'Negro' conductors and railway workers let me walk through the Pullman cars, which was a big thrill for me."

Fitch knew that Jackson needed to expand his horizons, so he arranged for Jackson to have Afro-Americans first as suite-mates, and then as roommates. "One of the first real friends I made at UND," said Jackson, "was a black kid from Davenport, Iowa, named Jimmy Hester. He was a real quiet guy, but he had a fiery temper. One time we almost went at it when he mistakenly thought I had used the word 'nigger.' Jimmy was always a little tense because the only girls he felt comfortable with were a couple of black secretaries stationed at the Strategic Air Command base outside of town. Jimmy and I played lots of gin rummy."

Later, Jackson began rooming with another black hooper, Harold "Super" Bates. "Super had about seventy-five records," Jackson said, "and he introduced me to black music. 'By the time I'm finished with you,' he'd tell me, 'you're going to have some soul and you won't be square anymore.' Those spinning discs of Wilson Pickett and Otis Redding opened my heart to soul music, and Super opened my consciousness to include black culture."

Jackson's spiritual horizons were likewise expanding. "I became embarrassed about being a Pentecostal," he admitted, "when I took a sociology course and learned that Pentecostals were among the lower socioeconomic and intellectual groups in the entire country. In my other courses I read Plato, Nietzsche, the existentialists like Camus, Sartre, Heidegger, and Jaspers. *The Varieties of Religious Experience* by William James was my first intellectual contact with religious mysticism which made some of the Pentecostal practices, like glossolalia [commonly called 'speaking in tongues'] seem a bit more acceptable. Still, the Pentecostal idea that anybody outside their church was automatically a sinner turned me off, and I told my parents that I would no longer be attending church on Sundays. I even took a course called 'God Is Dead.' If I was no longer a true believer, I was more of an agnostic than an atheist. In any event, my mind became much more flexible and open to new directions."

For Jackson, motivation was (and still is) all about leadership and responsibility, and he learned a painful lesson early in his senior season. "Fitch had made me the team captain," said Phil, "and we had just lost a game to DePaul on the road. After the game, I had made plans to meet an ex-UND cheerleader in a bar in downtown Chicago. I was a big-shot senior by then, so I thought I knew my way around. But a snowstorm blew up, and I didn't get back to the hotel room until two o'clock. Fitch, of course, was waiting for me, and he cut me up pretty good. Fitch said that I had abdicated my responsibilities and that I was no longer the team captain."

The incident had two critical messages for Jackson: A leader must adhere to the same rules as the lowest scrub on the team. And off-court leadership is even more important than game-time leadership.

In the spring of 1967, Jackson was drafted by the New York Knicks in the second round (seventeenth overall). A crucial aspect of psychic flexibility is being able to experience the unexpected without falling apart, and Jackson was sorely tested on his first day in New York. "Red Holzman was the Knicks' assistant coach and scout," said Jackson, "and he picked me up at the airport when I arrived in New York to meet with the Knicks' front office. Red was a stocky, balding five-foot-nine individual who looked about as tough as I imagined anyone forty-seven years old could look. 'Go get your luggage,' he said in a gruff tone, 'and I'll drive you to your hotel.' I followed him to his 1967 Chevy, and we chatted politely as we drove into the city. We were riding down Queens Boulevard when we happened to approach an overhead pedestrian bridge. I looked up and saw a bunch of teenagers leaning over and laughing. As we passed underneath, one of them threw a rock at the car and it smashed the front windshield. I was stunned. Nothing like this had ever happened in Williston. Red was upset, but instead of freaking out, he told me this: 'Welcome to New York City. If you can take that, you'll do just fine here.' From then on, I expected anything and everything, and I was rarely disappointed."

Dick McGuire was the Knicks coach, but his lack of communication skills led him to be fired midway through the ensuing season. "Red took over," said Jackson, "and that's when my education really began."

According to Holzman, a coach motivates his players by earning their respect. He has to prove to his team that he understands the game, that his game plans are well researched and workable, and that he can adjust to any situation that comes up during a ball game. Since Holzman had had an outstanding nine-year professional career with the Rochester Royals, had been the savvy point guard of two championship teams (in 1946 and 1950), and had previously coached the Milwaukee Hawks and then the St. Louis Hawks (1953–57), his expertise could not be denied.

"Red was also a diplomat," said Phil, "and he always avoided public confrontations with his players. He could also accurately gauge the intelligence and temperament of everybody on the team. Some guys needed a pat on the back, some needed a kick in the pants, and Red was able to forge a personal connection with each of us."

Moreover, on every level of the game, players always know when their coach is lying to them, and vice versa. So Holzman was fair and impartial, and if sometimes he strategically failed to tell his players the whole truth, he never lied to them either.

Holzman knew that since the players were on the court and he was bench-bound, they had a better feel for how a ball game was unfolding. "During time-outs," said Jackson, "he'd ask us what was going on out there. And lots of times he'd ask the veterans what plays they thought would be effective. Because he respected us, it was easy for us to respect him."

This was a technique that Jackson later incorporated into his own coaching game plan. One difference between then and later, however, is that the modern-day player can't see the unfolding of a game nearly as acutely as his predecessors. "That's why when I asked for my players' input," said Jackson, "some guys would take the opportunity to complain that they needed more shots. We had a guy like that with the Knicks, and whenever he'd begin to gripe, [Dave] De-

Busschere would just tell him to shut up. Today's players are much more touchy about being scolded by anybody, so with the Bulls and the Lakers, I'd just ignore any blatantly self-serving suggestions."

Jackson likewise admired Holzman's flexibility: "Back then, NBA players were permitted to satisfy their military obligations by spending one weekend a month in either the National Guard or a Reserve unit back in their respective hometowns. Bill Bradley, Cazzie Russell, Howard Komives, and Dick Van Arsdale would leave the team after a Friday night game, serve a stint that usually began at six or seven o'clock the next morning, finish up about four that afternoon, then rendezvous with the team in whichever city we happened to be playing. If the Knicks were on the West Coast, they wouldn't miss any game time. But if we were somewhere near the Eastern Seaboard, they'd usually arrive midway through the first quarter. To save time, the guys would change into their uniforms on their way to the arena. It was all kind of helter-skelter, and Red was able to ride every wave."

Holzman's modus operandi was to give the players as much responsibility as they could handle. "With so many key players continuously coming and going," said Jackson, "Red didn't always put a lot of pressure on anybody to be here or there at a certain time. Shootarounds the morning of a ball game were strictly optional, and five or six interested players would pile into a cab if a court was available. Especially on the road, Red gave us enough room so that we were comfortable and agreeable whenever he did have to assert more control. At the same time, because of the mutual respect that the coach and the players had for each other, we were responsible enough not to take advantage of whatever freedoms he allowed us."

Holzman, like Fitch before him, always believed in the transcendent importance of team values—and Jackson's new teammates routinely promoted the same understanding. "In 1971," Jackson explained, "the NBA augmented its All-Star weekend with a one-on-one competition. But my teammates knew that this kind of emphasis would be detrimental to the way the Knicks had to play to win ball games. Individual play was the wrong kind of competition. So even though Dave DeBusschere, Willis Reed, Walt Frazier, and Earl Monroe were terrific one-on-one players, they refused to participate. Eddie Mast really wanted to do it, so we voted for him to represent us."

During his thirteen seasons in the NBA, Jackson continued to investigate the whys and wherefores of spirituality. He imbibed the wisdom of the I Ching, of Buddhism, and of Tao. He studied Christian thinkers like Joel Goldsmith and mystics like P. D. Ouspensky. Eventually, his consciousness was "reborn." By being able to see the truth in a variety of religious paths, "the scope of my existence was enlarged." He later came to define himself as a "Zen-Christian," the common ground between the two traditions being love and compassion.

By the time Jackson became a head coach in the Continental Basketball Association in 1983, he was on the verge of mastering the two skills—the ability to be open to the living moment and the ability to motivate a diverse collection of individuals—that would eventually win him a double-fistful of NBA titles. But there were still lessons to be learned, and a dramatic epiphany occurred in March 1984 when his Albany Patroons were battling the Wyoming Wildcatters for the CBA championship.

During his tenure with the Knicks, Jackson had been deeply impressed by Holzman's distribution of playing time. Barring unforeseen injuries, foul trouble, or ejections, each player in the Knicks' regular rotation knew when, and for how long, he'd be playing in every game. Jackson, for example, would be inserted into the lineup with four minutes left in the first quarter and remain on the court for about ten minutes. The same pattern would be repeated in the second half. Willis Reed would play the initial ten minutes of the first and third quarters, and the last eight minutes of the second and fourth quarters. Thus, the starters could maximize their downtime and the subs could prepare themselves for action. Jackson continued this tried-and-true pattern as coach of the Patroons.

Each round of the CBA playoffs was a best-of-five series, and the Patroons began their postseason efforts by recovering from a 2–0 deficit to defeat the Bay State Bombardiers. Next up, the Patroons closed out the Puerto Rico Coquis in four games, then squared off against Wyoming for the championship.

"The Wildcatters were coached by Jack Schalow," Jackson remembered, "and their best player was Del Beshore, a guard with some NBA experience. I was very rigid in maintaining the team's habitual rotation, but Beshore had a tricky behind-the-back move that our starting point guard, Lowes Moore, just couldn't handle. The series was knotted at two games each, and just before the deciding game, my assistant coach, Charley Rosen, insisted that Moore's backup, Mark Jones, could contain Beshore. I resisted as long as I could, but Beshore continued to overwhelm Moore, so I finally relented and sent Jones after him. This matchup turned the game around and enabled the Patroons to win the championship. And I was forced to realize that stubborn coaches operate under a self-imposed handicap."

The necessity of having an open-minded approach to the game was reinforced several times during Jackson's four and a half seasons in the CBA. Sudden roster changes were routine: players were constantly being called up to the NBA, while others opted to play overseas. Trades were commonplace, as were injuries and flunked drug tests. The average CBA team went through twenty-five to thirty players in a given season. Through it all, Jackson had to adjust, readjust, and be ready to coach whatever players were on hand.

After a two-year stint as a Bulls assistant, Jackson became Chicago's head coach in 1989 and readily embraced Tex Winters's triangle offense, mainly because it was flexible enough to accommodate a wide range of talents and personalities. "We didn't have many specialty plays, and I rarely called anybody's number," Jackson noted. "We just put the offense in motion, and sooner or later a defender's weakness would make itself known. Our success depended upon understanding, unselfishness, and execution."

Off the court, Jackson proved his respect for his players by ignoring conventional wisdom and granting them an unusual measure of personal freedom—no dress codes and no curfews on the road.

"The more rules you have," Jackson said, "the easier it is to break one of them. Besides, how can a single set of behavioral imperatives work for guys at opposite ends of the spectrum like Steve Kerr and Dennis Rodman?"

The motivational lessons Jackson had imbibed along the way likewise became part of his game plan: "Just as my father rolled up his sleeves and worked beside the members of his congregation, a basketball coach has to be willing to accept the burden of work that contributes to his team winning." That translates into studying game videos and formulating explicit and workable scouting reports. Also, Jackson's practice sessions were meticulously organized to always include fundamental skill drills and always avoid any kind of shortcuts.

"Unlike someone like Pat Riley," Jackson said, "I rarely gave motivational speeches. You can only ring the bell so many times over the course of a long season. My way was to create an environment that encouraged the players to motivate themselves." Jackson also trusted that this environment would be a self-correcting one.

So whereas the standard procedure is for a coach to call a time-out whenever the bad guys extend to a six-point lead over the good guys, Jackson's practice is to let his players play their way out of whatever difficulties they've gotten themselves into. He understands that peer pressure is always more effective than the imposition of discipline by a civilian authority. "The guys always know what they're doing wrong," he said. "They don't need me to nag them into playing the right way."

Above all else, Jackson intends that the team environment/community will be built on trust and respect and be entirely self-correcting.

Case in point: During the 1993–94 season the Bulls had the last possession of a tied game when Jackson instructed Scottie Pippen to inbound the ball to Toni Kukoc, who was designated to take the last shot. (Jordan was elsewhere trying to hit curveballs.) Pippen balked and took himself out of the game. Kukoc made the shot, and the Bulls won, but Jackson's subsequent handling of Pippen's mutiny was a perfect example of how his motivational environment functions: Jackson simply did nothing. In the postgame locker room, however, Pippen's teammates ferociously berated him for his selfishness, and Bill Cartwright had to be forcibly dissuaded from assaulting Pippen. Thusly chastised and corrected, Pippen went on to become the epitome of the selfless teammate.

But Jackson wasn't totally passive during games. He would chastise errant players during time-outs and bench them should they persist in their deviations from the acceptable protocol. During the half-time intermissions, he could be even more demonstrative.

In the privacy of the locker room, there were two extremes he could use to induce his players to play harder and/or smarter. The first was throwing a tantrum—overturning chairs and tables while screaming and cussing. "This is a tactic a coach can use only once or twice every season," Jackson noted. "More than that and the players will just tune you out."

The opposite motivational ploy is humor—which can range from the sublime to the ridiculous. The Bulls were involved in a fiercely contested game, and their efforts weren't helped by an uncharacter-istically inept performance by Scottie Pippen. Misdribblings, passes to nobody, and a score of flubbed shots. There were five minutes left on the game clock when Jackson signaled for a time-out. The play-ers were scrupulously attentive and were ready to hang on his every word. Jackson leaned into the huddle and said this: "Whatever you guys do, just don't throw the ball to Scottie." Pippen laughed along with his teammates and then proceeded to bag three crucial buckets to lead the team to victory.

On another occasion, the Bulls had been thumped by nineteen points in Portland and were subsequently in the throes of a four-game losing streak. Wearing a concerned expression, Jackson called the team to order in the postgame locker room. He then recited a litany of mistakes that had become habitual. Playing poorly to com-mence the third quarter. Somebody zigging when everybody else was zagging and thereby destroying the team's timing in critical sit-uations. During his impassioned recitation, Jackson noticed that many of the players were fidgety and inattentive—so he decided to change his approach.

"I've noticed that most of you come into the locker room at halftime and take a piss," he said with a straight face. "Now, how many of you take a piss before I talk? And how many take a piss after I talk?"

The players were bewildered. Was he serious? But they began comparing their own halftime urinalyses. After a while, they began to get the joke and began shaking their heads in bemusement at the unpredictable antics of their coach. Suddenly, their losing streak didn't seem so oppressive. Indeed, the Bulls subsequently embarked on a six-game winning streak.

When Jackson assumed command of the Los Angeles Lakers in 1999, he demonstrated just how infinitely flexible the triangle really was. In Chicago the perimeter aspects of the offense were emphasized to accommodate the special skills of Michael Jordan. With the Lakers, Shaquille O'Neal's dominating presence compelled Jackson to refocus the offense around the low post.

And with the Perfect Team, Jackson's offense would have enough flexibility to accommodate the specific talents of each player, alone and in every possible combination. Jackson would also be able to motivate and sustain the interests of every player. That's why Phil Jackson is the perfect coach for the perfect team.

PHIL JACKSON'S ASSESSMENT OF THE PERFECT TEAM

Magic Johnson (Leadership)

I think that Larry Bird and Michael Jordan were better team leaders because confidence and competitiveness are the real qualities of leadership. Besides, in the context of a workable team, only one true leader is needed. Otherwise, there's a battle for loyalty among the other players. And as for Magic specifically, just because he had the ball in his hands most of the time didn't mean that he was a leader.

Jerry West (Dealing with Pressure)

True, Jerry always wanted the ball whenever a game was up for grabs, but I'm not totally convinced that he was Mr. Clutch. Although the Lakers beat the Knicks in the 1972 championship series, Jerry played poorly throughout the playoffs that year. Fans don't remember all the times when celebrated clutch shooters like Jerry bombed out in the endgame.

I think that Jerry's best attribute as a player was his confidence. When he was the general manager of the Lakers, Jerry had to duck behind the stands whenever a close game came down to the wire because the pressure of watching was more than he could bear.

Michael Jordan (Competitive Drive)

Michael's will to win could certainly amp up his teammates. He'd say, "We're going to go out there and kick their ass," and I could see the fire building in everybody's eyes. Then he'd be diving for loose balls and hustling like a madman from the get-go. Hey, Michael worked harder in practice than most guys work during ball games. That's true leadership. But sometimes he'd go over the edge. I was an assistant when Doug Collins was the Bulls' coach, and Michael would freak out when Doug doctored the score of intra-squad scrimmages to keep them competitive. At the same time, Michael would think nothing of cheating during shooting games.

Larry Bird (Confidence)

Larry just couldn't accept losing, but he'd usually find a way to win that was within acceptable boundaries. And Larry was always astounded whenever he missed a shot. That kind of attitude is contagious and makes everybody on the team believe in themselves.

Bill Russell (Mental Toughness)

This is another quality that comes under the heading of leadership. Even more important than the way Magic played, Russ could provide leadership without having the ball in his possession.

Oscar Robertson (Versatility)

Of course, Oscar averaged a triple-double in the 1961–62 season. Later, he said that if he'd known that it was such a big deal, he would've averaged a triple-double for his entire career. And this wasn't just an idle boast. Oscar could do everything and do it well—pass, shoot, rebound, set picks, run, jump, and even play defense. In the modern game his only weakness would be an inaccuracy from the three-point line because his shot release was too high. Still, if Oscar played today, he'd probably average maybe fifteen points, five rebounds, and six assists—but that's only because he's sixty-seven years old.

Jason Kidd (Selflessness and Sacrifice)

Jason always makes the right pass and never misses finding the open man. Even with Jason directing the show, there's no way the Nets should've made back-to-back trips to the finals—but his incredible desire to win gets everybody's chops up. More than being selfless, I think Jason is a realist who understands the role he must play for his team to succeed. Jason's only downside is that he has to take a lot of shots to score.

Allen Iverson (Courage)

Allen plays with a great deal of arrogance. He'll beat the big men where they live even though he'll get knocked on his ass about ten times every game. Sure, it's courage all right. But in the end, if a little guy takes too many big hits, his body starts to fall apart. And that's why Allen is starting to lose it.

Bill Laimbeer (Intensity)

In the real world, the traits that Bill exhibited on the basketball court would land him in jail. His aggressiveness bordered on being mindless and was both negative and obsessive. I think it was Isiah Thomas's virulent competitive nature that egged Laimbeer on to do some of the things he did. The cheap shots and gratuitous violence were ruinous to the game.

Shaquille O'Neal (Will to Dominate)

This is a good definition of Shaq's attitude. He's the ultimate big man who likes to use his size to his advantage and who uses it well. But Shaq knows that the refs won't let him be a bully, so he must also use his skills to dominate opponents—and this is something that he's very proud of. Because of this, Shaq can dominate without humiliating anybody.

Bill Walton (Precision)

A very good call.

Red Auerbach (Basketball IQ)

More than anybody else, Red could recognize the kind of players whose talents could blend together to produce a winning team. He never judged a player strictly by size, strength, quickness, or the numbers the guy put in the scorebook. Red could see into a player's heart and mind. He always had an overview of what his team needed and of how certain guys could, or could not, fit in. And through all those years, Red made very few mistakes.

PHIL JACKSON—COACH

PERSONAL: Born September 17, 1945, in Deer Lodge, MT . . . 6–8/230 (2.03 m/104.3 kg) . . . full name: Philip D. Jackson.
HIGH SCHOOL: Williston (ND).
COLLEGE: North Dakota.
TRANSACTIONS/CAREER NOTES: Selected by New York Knicks in second round (seventeenth pick overall) of 1967 NBA draft. . . . Traded by Knicks with future draft choice to New Jersey Nets for future draft choices (June 8, 1978). . . . Waived by Nets (October 11, 1978). . . . Re-signed as free agent by Nets (November 10, 1978). . . . Waived by Nets (October 12, 1979). . . . Re-signed as free agent by Nets (February 15, 1980).
MISCELLANEOUS: Member of NBA championship team (1973).

COLLEGIATE RECORD

														Averages	
Season	Team	G	Min	FGM	FGA	Pct	FTM	FTA	Pct	Reb	Ast	Pts	RPG	APG	PPG
63–64	North Dakota														
64–65	North Dakota	31	—	129	307	.420	107	156	.686	361	—	365	11.6	—	11.8
65–66	North Dakota	29	—	238	439	.542	155	203	.764	374	—	631	12.9	—	21.8
66–67	North Dakota	26	—	252	468	.538	208	278	.748	374	—	712	14.4	—	27.4
Total		86	—	619	1,214	.510	470	637	.738	1,109	—	1,708	12.9	—	19.9

NBA REGULAR-SEASON RECORD

HONORS: NBA All-Rookie team (1968).

NOTES: Led NBA with 330 personal fouls (1975).

																Averages		
Season	Team	G	Min	FGM	FGA	Pct	FTM	FTA	Pct	Reb	Ast	PF	DQ	Pts		RPG	APG	PPG
67–68	NYK	75	1,093	182	455	.400	99	168	.589	338	55	212	3	463		4.5	0.7	6.2
68–69	NYK	47	924	126	294	.429	80	119	.672	168	43	168	6	332		5.2	0.9	7.1
69–70	NYK							Did not play—injured										
70–71	NYK	71	771	118	263	.449	95	133	.714	169	31	169	4	331		3.4	0.4	4.7
71–72	NYK	80	1,273	205	466	.440	167	228	.732	224	72	224	4	577		4.1	0.9	7.2
72–73	NYK	80	1,393	245	553	.443	154	195	.790	218	94	218	2	644		4.3	1.2	8.1

										Rebounds								Averages		
		G	Min	FGM	FGA	Pct	FTM	FTA	Pct	Off	Def	Tot	Ast	St	Blk	TO	Pts	RPG	APG	PPG
73–74	NYK	82	2,050	361	757	.477	191	246	.776	123	355	478	134	42	67	—	913	5.8	1.6	11.1
74–75	NYK	78	2,285	324	712	.455	193	253	.763	137	463	600	136	84	53	—	841	7.7	1.7	10.8
75–76	NYK	80	1,461	185	387	.478	110	150	.733	80	263	343	105	41	20	—	480	4.3	1.3	6.0
76–77	NYK	76	1,033	102	232	.440	51	71	.718	75	154	229	85	33	18	—	255	3.0	1.1	3.4
77–78	NYK	63	654	55	115	.478	43	56	.768	29	81	110	46	31	15	47	153	1.7	0.7	2.4
78–79	NJN	59	1,070	144	303	.475	86	105	.819	59	119	178	85	45	22	78	374	3.0	1.4	6.3
79–80	NJN	16	194	29	46	.630	7	10	.700	12	12	24	12	5	4	9	65	1.5	0.8	4.1
Total		807	14,201	2,076	4,583	.453	1,276	1,734	.764	—	—	3,454	898	281	199	134	5,428	4.3	1.1	6.7

THREE-POINT FIELD GOALS: Totals, 0-for-2.

PERSONAL FOULS/DISQUALIFICATIONS: 1973–74, 277/7; 1974–75, 330/10; 1975–76, 275/3; 1976–77, 184/4; 1977–78, 106/0; 1978–79, 168/7; 1979–80, 0-for-2; 1979–80, 35/1. Total: 1,375/32.

NBA PLAYOFF RECORD

																Averages		
Season	Team	G	Min	FGM	FGA	Pct	FTM	FTA	Pct	Reb	Ast	PF	DQ	Pts		RPG	APG	PPG
67–68	NYK	6	90	10	35	.286	4	5	.800	25	2	23	0	24		4.2	0.3	4.0
68–69	NYK							Did not play—injured										
70–71	NYK	5	30	4	14	.286	1	1	1.000	10	2	8	0	9		2.0	0.4	1.8
71–72	NYK	16	320	57	120	.475	42	57	.737	82	15	51	1	156		5.1	0.9	9.8
72–73	NYK	17	338	60	120	.500	28	38	.737	72	24	59	3	148		0.0	1.4	8.7

		G	Min	FGM	FGA	Pct	FTM	FTA	Pct	Off	Def	Tot	Ast	St	Blk	TO	Pts
										Rebounds							
73–74	NYK	12	297	54	116	.466	27	30	.900	15	42	57	15	10	5	—	135
74–75	NYK	3	78	10	21	.476	7	8	.875	5	20	25	2	4	3	—	27
77–78	NYK	6	50	4	8	.500	4	6	.667	4	6	10	3	3	0	4	12
78–79	NJN	2	20	1	3	.333	2	2	1.000	2	1	3	0	1	0	0	4
Total		67	1,223	200	437	.458	115	147	.782	—	—	284	63	18	8	4	515

PERSONAL FOULS/DISQUALIFICATIONS: 1973–74, 40/0; 1974–75, 15/0; 1977–78, 1978–79, 1/0. Total: 208/4.

HEAD COACHING RECORD

BACKGROUND: Player/assistant coach, New Jersey Nets (1978–79 and 1979–80). . . . Assistant coach, Nets (1980–81). . . . Broadcaster, Nets (1981–82). . . . Assistant coach, Chicago Bulls (1987–88 and 1988–89).

HONORS: NBA Coach of the Year (1996). . . . One of the Top 10 Coaches in NBA History (1996). . . . CBA Coach of the Year (1985).

RECORDS: Holds NBA regular-season record for highest winning percentage—.782. . . . Holds NBA playoff record for highest winning percentage (minimum 25 games)—.730. . . . Holds NBA career record for playoff wins—162.

CBA COACHING RECORD

		Regular Season				Playoffs		
Season	Team	W	L	Pct	Finish	W	L	Pct
82–83	Albany	8	11	.421	4th /Eastern Division	—	—	—
83–84	Albany	25	19	.568	2nd/Eastern Division	9	5	.643
84–85	Albany	34	14	.708	1st/Eastern Division	5	5	.500
85–86	Albany	24	24	.500	4th/Eastern Division	3	4	.429
86–87	Albany	26	22	.542	T2nd/Eastern Division	4	4	.500
Total (5 years)		117	90	.565	Total (4 years)	21	18	.538

NBA COACHING RECORD

		Regular Season					Playoffs		
Season	Team	W	L	Pct	Finish		W	L	Pct
89–90	Chi	55	27	.671	2nd/Central Division		10	6	.625
90–91	Chi	61	21	.744	1st/Central Division		15	2	.882
91–92	Chi	67	15	.817	1st/Central Division		15	7	.682
92–93	Chi	57	25	.694	1st/Central Division		15	4	.789
93–94	Chi	55	27	.671	2nd/Central Division		6	4	.600
94–95	Chi	47	35	.573	2nd/Central Division		5	5	.500
95–96	Chi	72	10	.878	1st/Central Division		15	3	.833
96–97	Chi	69	13	.841	1st/Central Division		15	4	.789
97–98	Chi	62	20	.756	1st/Central Division		15	6	.714
99–00	LAL	67	15	.817	1st/Pacific Division		15	8	.652
00–01	LAL	56	26	.683	1st/Pacific Division		15	1	.938
01–02	LAL	58	24	.707	1st/Pacific Division		15	4	.789
02–03	LAL	50	32	.610	T2nd/Pacific Division		6	6	.500
03–04	LAL	56	26	.683	1st/Pacific Division		13	9	.591
Total (14 years)		832	316	.725	Total (14 years)		175	69	.717

NOTES: 1983—Replaced Dean Meminger (8–15) and player/interim coach Sam Worthen (0–2) as Albany Patroons head coach (January 29) with record of 8–17. 1984—Defeated Bay State, 3–2, in Eastern Semifinals; defeated Puerto Rico, 3–1, in Eastern Finals; defeated Wyoming, 3–2, in CBA Championship Series. 1985—Defeated Toronto, 3–2, in Eastern Semifinals; lost to Tampa Bay, 3–2, in Eastern Finals. 1986—Lost to Tampa Bay in Eastern Semifinals. 1987—Defeated Mississippi, 4–0, in Eastern Semifinals; lost to Rapid City, 4–0, in Eastern Finals. 1990—Defeated Milwaukee, 3–1, in Eastern Conference first round; defeated Philadelphia, 4–1, in Eastern Conference Semifinals; lost to Detroit, 4–3, in Eastern Conference Finals. 1991—Defeated New York, 3–0, in Eastern Conference first round; defeated Philadelphia, 4–1, in Eastern Conference Semifinals; defeated Detroit, 4–0, in Eastern Conference Finals; defeated Los Angeles Lakers, 4–1, in NBA Finals. 1992—Defeated Miami, 3–0, in Eastern Conference first round; defeated New York, 4–3, in Eastern Conference Semifinals; defeated Cleveland, 4–2, in Eastern Conference Finals; defeated Portland, 4–2, in NBA Finals. 1993—Defeated Atlanta, 3–0, in Eastern Conference first round; defeated Cleveland, 4–0, in Eastern Conference Semifinals; defeated New York, 4–2, in Eastern Conference Finals; defeated Phoenix, 4–2, in NBA Finals. 1994—Defeated Cleveland, 3–0, in Eastern Conference first round; lost to New York, 4–3, in Eastern Conference Semifinals. 1995—Defeated Charlotte, 3–1, in Eastern Conference first round; lost to Orlando, 4–2, in Eastern Conference Semifinals. 1996—Defeated Miami, 3–0, in Eastern Conference first round; defeated New York, 4–1, in Eastern Conference Semifinals; defeated Orlando, 4–0, in Eastern Conference Finals; defeated Seattle, 4–2, in NBA Finals. 1997—Defeated Washington, 3–0, in Eastern Conference first round; defeated Atlanta, 4–1, in Eastern Conference Semifinals; defeated Miami, 4–1, in Eastern Conference Finals; defeated Utah, 4–2, in NBA Finals. 1998—Defeated New Jersey, 3–0, in Eastern Conference first round; defeated Charlotte, 4–1, in Eastern Conference Semifinals; defeated Indiana, 4–3, in Eastern

Conference Finals; defeated Utah, 4–2, in NBA Finals. 2000—Defeated Sacramento, 3–2, in Western Conference first round; defeated Phoenix, 4–1, in Western Conference Semifinals; defeated Portland, 4–3, in Western Conference Finals; defeated Indiana, 4–2, in NBA Finals. 2001—Defeated Portland, 3–0, in Western Conference first round; defeated San Antonio, 4–1, in Western Conference Semifinals; defeated San Antonio, 4–0, in Western Conference Finals; defeated Philadelphia, 4–1, in NBA Finals. 2002—Defeated Portland, 3–0, in Western Conference first round; defeated San Antonio, 4–1, in Western Conference Semifinals; defeated Sacramento, 4–3, in Western Conference Finals; defeated New Jersey, 4–0, in NBA Finals. 2003—Defeated Minnesota, 4–2, in Western Conference first round; lost to San Antonio, 4–2, in Western Conference Semifinals. 2004—Defeated Houston, 4–1, in Western Conference first round; defeated San Antonio, 4–2, in Western Conference Semifinals; defeated Minnesota, 4–2, in Western Conference Finals; lost to Detroit, 4–1, in NBA Finals.

Chapter Fourteen

RED AUERBACH—
General Manager
Basketball IQ
by Dan Shaughnessy

s it possible to be ahead of your time when you are almost ninety years old? It must be. Red Auerbach can still watch a basketball game (while smoking a cigar) and easily dissect the strengths and weaknesses of both teams on the hardwood. Put Red to work at any random tryout and he'd assemble the best team. He might not pick the five most talented players, but he'd put together the unit that would win the most games. He'd motivate his players, implement a simple system, work the officials, and get into the heads of his opponents. Red would win. Even now.

Simply put, Arnold "Red" Auerbach is the greatest mind basketball has ever known. He is also the only person in American professional sports who has been associated with his league for every day of its existence. Red Auerbach was a twenty-eight-year-old coach with the Washington Capitols when the Basketball Association of America was formed in 1946 (then changed to the National Basketball Association a year later), and he was in his fifty-fifth season as godfather of the Boston Celtics when the Green returned to the NBA playoffs in the spring of 2005.

No one was ever more adept at assembling a basketball team. Auerbach was a winner as a player, a coach, and a general manager. He was the best architect, the best motivator, and the best strategist. When other coaches were playing checkers, Auerbach was winning at chess. He was so good at picking pockets that other general managers stopped taking his calls. If Red wanted one of your guys, maybe you'd better reassess that player's value. You must not be seeing something.

Basketball IQ is not something that can be taught, and as with all geniuses, Red's gifts came to him naturally, with significant contributions from his family values and childhood environment. Like so many basketball giants, Auerbach was born in the fertile hoop borough of Brooklyn, New York. A child of the Depression born to parents who fled Russia when Eastern Europe was becoming increasingly unfriendly to Jews, young Arnold quickly developed the street smarts and cynicism that would serve him so well in his chosen profession. He grew up in a neighborhood that was populated by blacks, Russian Jews, Germans, Poles, Italians, and Irish. When Red was nine, he got into an argument with an Italian boy. The other kid swung first, and young Arnold was floored. It would be the last time Red ever let anyone else swing first. Another lesson came when Red met a man on the subway who was selling socks for five cents per pair. Red paid sixty cents for a dozen pair, then got home, unrolled his socks, and learned that none of them matched. He had been taken. In the year 2005, we are still waiting for another man who got the better of Red in any kind of deal.

Hoop IQ needs some inspiration, and for Red it came from Bill Reinhart, his college coach at George Washington. Reinhart was quarterback of Oregon's 1919 Rose Bowl loss to Harvard but made his name at GW as the man who invented the fast-break offense. It was pretty simple.

The idea was to defend the opposition, grab the missed shot, and fire an outlet pass to the wing while all your players broke for the other end of the floor. Players were instructed to fill their respective lanes and pass the ball back and forth without dribbling. Dribbling took too much time. Superior conditioning abetted the fast-break offense, and Reinhart and Auerbach always had players in top shape. Practices were short, but effective. No time was wasted standing around.

"Nobody ever sat down and taught me all this. I just picked up things along the way," said Red. "The main thing is common sense. The most important thing that I learned was the ability to communicate. It's not what you say, but how much they absorb. There are hundreds of coaches out there who know as much about Xs and Os as anybody, but I tried to make the game simple.

"My theory is that a win is just as good early in the season as it is late in the season. A lot of athletes, once they make the team, they don't come in shape anymore. They play themselves into shape. The seniors would come back, and everybody thinks they're going to be great, and they get the crap kicked out of them because they don't come back hungry and they gain weight and they're not in shape. In the NBA a guy like George Mikan would lose fifteen or twenty pounds during the season. I say you should maintain your weight year-round, and that way we were able to beat teams early in the year because we were in better shape. We ran with a purpose. Other teams would press and make a nice comeback—I figured, why can't you do it the whole game? When we did it against Philly, it would throw their pattern off. They weren't in good shape like we were."

Red played three seasons for Reinhart at GW. His antipathy for the Knicks and Madison Square Garden goes back to the year (1937–38) he felt his GW team was snubbed by the National Invitational Tournament (NIT) committee. After college, Red coached in high schools and in the armed forces before the formation of the NBA. In twenty seasons as an NBA head coach, he went 938–479, a winning percentage of .662. He made the playoffs in nineteen of the twenty seasons, winning nine NBA championships as head coach. He retired after winning eight consecutive NBA titles—an achievement that will never be matched.

  As a bench coach, Auerbach was known for his flamboyant style, his fiery temper, his vivid interaction with officials, and of course, the victory cigar. Red Auerbach's victory stogie was the original professional sports taunt. Long before NFL wide receivers started doing end-zone dances, and way before major league sluggers perfected bat flips and home run trots, there was Red, lighting up a Hoyo de Monterrey and sitting back on the bench—feet extended—enjoying the final minutes of a Celtic victory. Hall of Famer Bob Cousy says he hated the ritual because it provoked the opposition and forced the Celtics to play harder at the end of games that were already won. By any measure, it remains one of the top traditions of American sports, right up there with the Detroit Lions playing at home on Thanksgiving, "My Old Kentucky Home" at the Derby, and green blazers at the Masters. It would not happen today, since there are smoking bans inside just about every building in America, but it's also hard to fathom tolerance for such a repetitive, unsportsmanlike act.

  But a cigar is just a cigar, and there was more than smoke to Auerbach's coaching method. Auerbach has written seven books and been the prime subject of several other tomes, but his coaching philosophy was put forth best in his best-selling 1952 dime-store paperback entitled *Basketball for the Player, the Fan, and the Coach.* The book retailed for twenty-five cents, sold more than a million copies, and was translated into several languages. It was full of the commonsense tips that typified Red's philosophy. Red taught players to pass rather than dribble and to watch their man's hips when they were defending a player who had the basketball. He kept it simple. For decades the Celtics ran the same seven plays with a series of variations. Every opponent in the league knew what was going to happen when Boston's point guard called "zipper": a player from the high post would peel toward the basket and set a pick for a big man to run toward the foul line, catch the pass from the point, and hit a turnaround jumper or pass to a man cutting from the wing. When Celtic coach Bill Fitch closed practices in the 1980s, Kevin McHale cracked, "Yeah, we wouldn't want spies to come in here and steal these plays we've been running for the last thirty years."

"On every one of our plays, we had an alternative," said Red. "If you execute the play correctly, it doesn't matter if the defense knows what play it is. When I was in my late thirties, coaching the Celtics, I'd work on plays at the playgrounds in Washington during the summer. Right there on Connecticut Avenue. I'd go to the playground on Saturdays and Sundays and find the best players and try things out. I figured if the things worked there, they'd work in Boston. That's where I came up with the inbounding play from under your own basket, when you position your guys one in back of the other. I tried those things out with the young players, and if there was some semblance of success, I'd take it to Boston."

Some things you could not diagram. Red was a big-time advocate of gamesmanship. In his book he recommends, "When a player notices an official's indecision to an out-of-bounds ball, he should run over and pick it up with the full confidence that it is his." Other nuggets: "Faking injuries is used for many reasons such as stalling for time and giving the impression that a player will not be at his best." And "if the opposing team has a high scorer—keep reminding the other players of their uselessness because the scorer takes all the shots."

The book contains dozens of similar suggestions. Clearly there was more than strategy involved in the Auerbach system. Red was intent on getting into the psyche of the opposition, and he did it better than anyone in the history of sports. If Wilt Chamberlain were still alive, we could ask him to verify this claim. The Celtics consistently beat Wilt's teams in the playoffs, and it was always considered a win for team play over individual talent.

"I spent a whole summer writing that book," boasted Red. "And it's still applicable today. It's fundamentally sound. The Yugoslav coach told me that the only two books they used were my book and one of Adolph Rupp's books. Hank Iba once told me that he bought fifteen copies of my book to give to his son when his son started coaching."

Even the victory cigar was a mind game. It was Red's way of saying, "This game is over. I'm thinking about the next game." To this day Auerbach cringes when he sees a basketball coach stomping his feet and yelling at players in the final minutes of a game in which his team is comfortably ahead.

For Auerbach, basketball intelligence was never about the chalk-board Xs and Os. His basketball genius was rooted in anticipation, motivation, and getting the most out of his players. He didn't like the concept of "handling" players. Red treated his players like men.

He would not insult their intelligence. This got him the best results.

Hall of Famer Tom Heinsohn played nine seasons under Auerbach, then coached the Celtics for nine more years when Red was general manager. Heinsohn on Auerbach's coaching: "He put the style of play in, but Red's great ability was to get everybody's head involved and to use ideas that the players would come up with. In the last two minutes of a ball game, in the Celtic huddle, the first words out of his mouth would be, 'Anybody got anything?' What that meant was that he trusted everybody that was playing for him to act like a coach and spot little things. We had five coaches on the floor. So you'd come in and say, 'I can do this or that,' and he would listen to all that input and make a decision. And when you had stepped up and made a statement, that made it pride of authorship. You would try and make the goddamn thing work. He was great like that. He was not the dictator everybody thought he was."

"My players were all college graduates," Red recalled. "They were smart guys. They knew what the hell was going on, and I didn't treat them as babies. I treated them as men. A guy thirty-two years old—don't you think he might have something that could be of use? Heinsohn would say that his guy was overplaying him, and we'd think of a play we could use, and Cooz would call it and pull the string on the left side."

Auerbach could easily assess the basketball IQ of the opposition. "I liked guys who could perform in the clutch," said Red. "Dick McGuire, Jerry West, Oscar Robertson, Slater Martin. They were all smart players who would stay in control. You don't want to let your emotions take away from your skills. Don't make turnovers at the wrong time."

Another Auerbach innovation was the development of the Sixth Man. Auerbach was the first coach to keep one of his best players on the bench at the start of a game. He figured a rested talent could do some damage when the other starters were getting winded. Auerbach was the first to say, "It doesn't matter who starts, it's who's on the floor at the end of the game." Frank Ramsey, the original Sixth Man, John Havlicek, and McHale all made the Hall of Fame after starting their careers as Boston's first player off the bench.

"Here's the logic," explained Red. "I know, and my players know, that my five best players are the five that are on the floor at the end. But there's a lot of ego attached. All the players want to be recognized as starters. They want to be introduced to the crowd before the game. But as a coach, you've got to find a starting ballplayer who is willing to forgo that ego and fame and do things for the good of the ball club. That takes a certain type of kid."

Motivation was Auerbach's specialty. He was able to get the most out of his own players, put doubt in the mind of the opposition, and play the referees just enough to make everyone think he was gaining the edge. He paid Bill Russell one dollar more per season than Chamberlain. He told his center never to worry about statistics—it would not affect his salary. He knew that Russell hated to practice, but that was okay as long as he got forty-eight minutes of effort on game days. If he thought the other players were resentful, he'd make a deal with Russell and tell his center, "I'm going to yell at you in practice today, just to make it look good. But pay no attention to any of it. I just want the other players to see me yelling at you." He would get furious when newspaper reporters gave too many headlines to flashy players like Cousy.

Red also used ancient, drafty Boston Garden to his advantage. If he didn't like the way a game was officiated, he had the hot water turned off in the referees' dressing room. Rival teams complained about small, cold locker rooms, but Red always claimed he had no control over the building because it belonged to the Boston Bruins. Still, he knew it was an edge if the other guys merely thought he was trying to make them uncomfortable. A crafty big league pitcher knows that he really doesn't need a spitter as long as the other team thinks he's loading up the ball.

Though he was the most successful coach in league history (the NBA Coach of the Year award is a statue of Auerbach), Red will always have competition when folks get around to rating the best professional coach. Lenny Wilkens won more games, and Phil Jackson challenged Red's championship total. But only a fool would contend that there's ever been a man more ahead of his time when it came to making deals to assemble a winning basketball team. Between 1956 and 1986, Red won sixteen world championships and made his bones as the best dealmaker in the history of professional sports. He built teams that would win multiple championships three times.

Some of his attributes were rooted in his ethnicity and his early years in Brooklyn. As a Jew, he encountered prejudice and stereotyping at an early age. He had the advantage of growing up in the melting pot of Brooklyn, which exposed him to other races and cultures. He knew what it felt like to be a target of small thinkers. He also knew that it was okay to be different. And of course, like every city kid, he had street smarts. He knew how to make a deal and how not to be taken in a deal.

He also learned how to network. Keeping tabs on former teammates, coaches, ballplayers, and friends has served Auerbach for more than six decades of professional player procurement.

Red enlisted in the navy in 1943 and coached a lot of players at the Norfolk Naval Station before he was discharged in 1946. His tenure at George Washington and his stint with the navy gave him a working file of available ballplayers, and he tapped both sources when he took over the Capitols in the league's inaugural season of 1946–47. The network system never failed him, and to this day Red stays current with talent around the world by making calls to "his guys," a legion of ex-Celtics who are honored to be associated with the man they once called "coach."

After establishing himself as a fiery winner with the Capitols, Auerbach came to the Celtics in 1950. Oddly enough, his first great player acquisition was perfectly inadvertent and had absolutely nothing to do with Auerbach's basketball IQ. Red Auerbach got Bob Cousy when Cooz's name was pulled out of a hat. And in the moment, Auerbach cursed his bad luck.

The 1950 NBA draft—Red's first as the boss of the Celtics—forever established Auerbach as both lucky and good. No one can account for luck, but what made Red good was his ability to do what was best for his team regardless of conventional wisdom or ancient prejudices. With his first-round pick in 1950, Auerbach bypassed the popular Holy Cross guard Cousy and selected Bowling Green's six-eleven center Charlie Share. Red always liked big guys. He also

didn't want the burden of coaching what he termed "a local yokel."
He thought Cousy was too flashy and would be difficult to coach. In
addition, he was a tad jealous of Holy Cross's popularity in greater
Boston. The Crusaders routinely outdrew the Celtics in Boston
Garden. Cousy was originally drafted by the St. Louis Hawks, but
they couldn't sign him and traded his rights to the Chicago Stags.
When the Stags folded, the NBA called a meeting in New York to
divvy up the Chicago roster. The final three Chicago players to be
placed were Andy Phillip, Max Zaslofsky, and Cousy. The Knicks,
Warriors, and Celtics were the final three teams in the bidding.
Auerbach ranked both Phillip and Zaslofsky ahead of Cousy (remember, sometimes it is better to be lucky than good), but when the
names were pulled out of a hat, the Celtics got Cousy. Under Red
Auerbach, the Cooz would proceed to reinvent the professional
game with the Boston Celtics. Time to run. Time to fast-break.
Time to find the open man.

In the second round of the 1950 draft, Auerbach selected six-six
Duquesne forward Chuck Cooper. Cooper was an African American, and until that day—as unbelievable as this sounds now—no
one had ever drafted a black player to play professional basketball.
It says something about Auerbach that he would be the first. Auerbach was always about winning. He wanted the best players. And he
would let nothing stop him. Most of the NBA owners feared the
wrath of Abe Saperstein, who signed the best black players to play
for the Harlem Globetrotters, but Red wasn't afraid to anger Saperstein. In Red's mind, Cooper was the best available player when it
was the Celtics' turn to pick. When Cooper came on board, Auerbach saw to it that he roomed with Bones McKinney, the only
southerner on the Celtics.

"I would analyze players as much as I could, but let's cut the
crap," said Red. "I was doing this all by myself—the scouting, marketing, no assistant coaches. How much time did I really have to
break down the other players? I would talk to our guys a little bit
about the other players. I would talk a little bit about what I could
see were their skills, like saying that so-and-so is left-handed and
likes the right side of the court. Elgin Baylor was dangerous, not
just for his shot, but for the way he followed his shot. He was a tiger
going after it."

Auerbach's first six Celtic teams were winners and annual playoff entries, but they couldn't win the NBA championship because they lacked a big rebounder. Auerbach got the most out of what he had but could not win the big one without the big fella.

Enter Russell. The teaming of Auerbach and Russell produced the greatest dynasty in the history of professional sports and changed pro basketball. It established Russell as the greatest winner in American sports and demonstrated Auerbach's wisdom and vision. Red's critics correctly point out that he never won a championship before Russell—a charge that Auerbach gracefully acknowledges. But what the critics fail to grasp is that Red's genius was in knowing that he needed Russell and finding a way to procure this once-in-a-generation talent.

Young readers will have a difficult time comprehending pro basketball scouting as it existed in the 1950s. This was decades before ESPN and the nightly feast of college basketball games on television. There was no videotape. Coaches learned of potential prospects by talking to other coaches or making long road trips to see for themselves. There were no assistant coaches or scouts. Early NBA teams could not afford that luxury. These obstacles played in Auerbach's favor because he had more spies and contacts than any coach in the land. And he cultivated them. Red's "guys," his former players, were his eyes and ears across America. They told him where the players were, and he trusted them.

Historian David Halberstam, who has written two NBA books, noted, "Auerbach was so smart in an age when people weren't smart in professional sports in general, and in basketball in particular— when it was really embryonic, when everybody else was careless. Somebody who was a coach or general manager tended to be somebody who was a good player or a good guy. It was not yet a business, and it wasn't professional. He was smart and professional in thinking ahead and understanding an underdeveloped world of professional sport. The other thing is that he goes at life on a wartime footing. Everything is a struggle. It's probably from that immigrant background and being Jewish or whatever. Everything is a struggle, no one is going to give you anything, so you have to fight for everything."

He certainly fought for Russell. Auerbach first learned of the dominating young center when George Washington University (coached by his mentor, Reinhart) was crushed by the University of San Francisco in a tournament game at Oklahoma City in 1953. The S.F. Dons were led by Russell, a skinny, left-handed sophomore center who was not much of a shooter. Infinitely impressed, Reinhart told Auerbach that this kid could be the perfect centerpiece for Auerbach's running Celtics. Russell wouldn't put a lot of points on the board, and that discouraged coaches who were looking for "numbers." But the young man played great defense, helped the other players on defense, blocked shots while keeping the ball in play, rebounded everything, made the outlet pass, and ran the floor. Only the rebounds showed up in the box score, but Russell was the ultimate winner, and Reinhart told Red to keep an eye on the USF center.

In Russell's junior and senior seasons, the Dons won two NCAA championships and fifty-five straight games, but most NBA coaches rarely saw him play and were unimpressed with his skinny frame and his anemic offensive numbers. Auerbach saw Russell in the 1955 Holiday Festival and was convinced that Russell would perfectly complement his Celtic team. He knew Russell was the player who could take the Celts to the next level. So he went to work to acquire the San Francisco star.

Bob Cousy, then captain of the Celtics, remembered, "As captain, I would be privy to things occasionally if he thought he had a secret. Sometime in December I remember him telling me that he had a guy that he was going to draft that was going to change everything. That's why when it's said that this happened by accident, that's a bunch of crap. He knew that he wanted Russell, and he did whatever he could to get him."

In the spring of 1956, the Celtics were once again not good enough to win a championship, but too good to get one of the top picks in the 1956 NBA Draft. Auerbach knew he'd have to trade up to have any chance of getting Russell. He targeted St. Louis—which had the second pick in the draft. Red had a sometimes contentious relationship with Hawks owner Ben Kerner—he would later deck Kerner with a dandy right cross during a dispute before a playoff game in St. Louis—but Kerner was willing to listen to what Red had to offer. Auerbach knew that Kerner would often make deals without consulting his coach. He also knew that St. Louis might not be ready for a black star. He arranged to trade popular, high-scoring Celtic Ed Macauley plus forward Cliff Hagan in exchange for the second pick in the draft. He reminded Kerner that Russell had an Olympic commitment and would not be available to any team until December. Macauley and Hagan were talented, and they were white. The deal made sense to Kerner.

There was one more detail to be arranged, however. Rochester owned the top pick in the '56 draft, and Auerbach didn't want to make his deal with St. Louis only to have Rochester draft Russell. He had to make sure Russell would still be there when he picked second. Red had Celtic owner Walter Brown call Rochester owner Lester Harrison to work something out. These were the days when NBA owners were primarily arena owners who wanted to book plenty of winter dates for their big, drafty barns. Brown struck a deal. He offered Harrison the Ice Capades, a popular touring skating show. Brown owned the show and arranged for the troupe to play in Rochester if Harrison agreed not to select Russell with the first pick. The deal was made, and Rochester selected the immortal Sihugo Green, a Duquesne guard, with the first pick of the 1956 draft. The Celtics made the trade with the Hawks and used their second pick to select Russell. For good measure, Auerbach also drafted Holy Cross's Heinsohn and Russell's college teammate, guard K. C. Jones. Three Hall of Famers in one draft. Quite the hoop harvest.

The rest, of course, is hardwood history. With Auerbach on the bench, the Celtics won nine of the next ten NBA championships, including a record eight straight. Before the 1965–66 season, Auerbach announced that it would be his final season on the bench. He dared his opponents to beat him. And then he went out and won his eighth consecutive crown. The final cigar. During the 1966 Finals, there was one last bit of gamesmanship by the crafty old coach. Auerbach announced that his successor on the bench would be Bill Russell. This was significant in several areas. It gave the Celtics a lift in the middle of the Finals, and it also broke another race barrier. Russell would be the first black man to coach any major professional sport in America. (It should also be noted that under Auerbach the Celtics became the first NBA team to start five black players—Russell, Sam and K. C. Jones, Tom Sanders, and Willie Naulls.)

"Russell just had that competitive desire," said Auerbach. "He was human, like anyone else, with all the eccentricities. He liked the accolades, but he realized it was a tough place to get it. We were in Holy Cross territory, and Heinsohn and Cousy were from there, and him being black made it difficult. But he said nothing and played to win. That was the whole thing to him, and he was willing to sacrifice his own personal stats. He didn't have an agent. An agent would have said, 'Russ, stop giving up the ball so much. Make those plays yourself.' The agent would want him to average seventeen points a game instead of fourteen. Stop giving up the ball so much. If he was making $200,000, the agent would have said he could get him $400,000. So he didn't buy into any of that stuff. All he wanted to do was win. I remember once he had a bad game against Harry Gallatin. Russ was a rookie, and before we played them again I told him we could have Heinsohn take Gallatin. Russ said, 'Coach, I'd appreciate it if you let me take him,' and he shut him down."

When Wilt Chamberlain came into the league in 1959–60, there was considerable fear that the giant center would dominate the game for the next decade. Chamberlain was able to score fifty points a game over a whole season, but rarely was he able to beat the Celtics and Russell.

"I talked to Russ about this when we first had to face Chamberlain," recalled Red. "I told him there were two ways to handle it. He could play him by himself, or we could give him help. He said to me, 'He'll be difficult to handle, but I can do a reasonable job.'

"That's the answer I wanted to hear. Because I knew that no matter what Chamberlain did, we would do more. Once you start dropping off to help on him, the other guys are more free and have more time to shoot and do more things. Hey, even if Wilt gets forty, we'll score 106."

The Auerbach-Russell relationship stands as one of the most successful and significant pairings in the history of sport. Russell is a proud, intelligent man, and he immediately sized up Auerbach as someone who respected his ability and his intelligence. It's doubtful that Russell would have played as well, or as long, for any other coach. Auerbach gave Russell the rope he needed, treating his proud star with dignity and respect. He told the big guy not to worry about stats. Then he made him the first black coach in sports—knowing that the only other coach Russell would play for . . . was Russell. And all they did was win.

"Some writers claimed I had separate standards for Russell," said Red. "Nothing could be further from the truth. Russell never missed practice unless he asked permission. He would always travel with the team. I wouldn't let anybody do otherwise unless they asked. Still, you've got to be an idiot to say that you treat everybody the same. You don't. If Russ wanted to miss practice because he was tired, that was okay. Hell, the guy was playing forty-seven minutes a night in the games."

While coaching Russell and the world champion Celtics in the golden days of the 1950s and '60s, Auerbach continued to hone his skills as a king dealmaker. And he always used his network of former players to keep him current on new talent. After winning the first championship, on the advice of former player McKinney, Auerbach selected a no-name guard from a no-name college: Sam Jones. In 1962, with the last pick of the first round, he selected John Havlicek. On and on it went.

"A lot of it had to do with the age of the players I had," said Red. "I always looked around for a guy who was about to retire. I liked to bring a guy in for one more year with us if I thought he was a good guy. We did that with Arnie Risen. But there were always other facets of the team that we had to replace. Ramsey, for instance. When he retired, we had to replace him, so I drafted Havlicek.

"When it comes to spotting talent, I just don't know any secrets. You either have it or you don't. But you've got to realize that you're not infallible. You're going to make some mistakes. I won't make mistakes judging talent, but where you make mistakes is in personality. You just don't know if this guy is going to have the mentality or the disposition of a Bird or Ramsey or McHale. Or the brilliance of a Cousy. One year I drafted a six-nine guy from Colorado State, Bill Green. He was my number-one pick. You like to see a guy twice, but I saw him once and I knew. Then we got him and found out that he wouldn't get on an airplane. He refused to fly."

By the mid-1960s, the Green Machine was running itself, but Auerbach grew weary of doing so many jobs. A glance at the masthead of today's Boston Celtics organization would list at least two dozen people doing jobs that Auerbach did when he was coach of the world champions. He was coach, assistant coach, general manager, scouting director, traveling secretary, marketing guru, and team spokesman. He was happy to give up the coaching role after winning his eighth straight ring in 1966. He was ready to put his basketball IQ to work as a full-time general manager.

The year Red left the bench, a dominant Philadelphia 76er team, led by Chamberlain, snapped the Celtics' championship streak, but the Cs came back to win another pair of titles with Russell as player-coach. When Russell retired after the 1968–69 season, there wasn't much left, and the Celtics fell out of the playoffs. This was a new test for Red: he had to prove that he could rebuild a once-great franchise. No problem. Within five years, he had the Celtics back on top, winning championships in 1974 and '76. Havlicek was still around for those flags, but Red supplied new talent—JoJo White, Don Chaney, Paul Silas, and Dave Cowens. Cowens represented another draft coup. He played for Florida State, which had been placed on NCAA probation, and drew little attention. Auerbach saw something no one else saw: a competitive fire and typical Celtics selflessness. Cowens was only six-eight, but he was physical enough to guard Kareem Abdul-Jabbar. With Cowens in the middle, the Celtics won their first two championships without Bill Russell. The one and only constant was Red Auerbach.

When the Celtics bottomed out again in the late '70s, Auerbach did something that had never been done in professional sports: he rebuilt his team a second time. The 1977–78 Celtics went 32–50. In the springtime the Celtics had two first-round draft picks—one acquired from Los Angeles in exchange for Charlie Scott. With the sixth pick of the '78 draft, Auerbach selected Larry Joe Bird from Indiana State. Bird still had a year of college ball to play—he was draft-eligible because his original freshman class (Bird had transferred from Indiana) was graduating. Some teams thought Bird was too slow for the pro game. Others no doubt worried that fans would revolt if they had to wait a year to get a top pick. Red didn't worry. He drafted Bird, managed to sign him to the largest rookie contract in sports history, then bided his time while the Celtics went through another dreadful year.

"It was a gamble," he admitted later. "But I had to do it. I've always had the philosophy that you take the best kid that's available in the draft. Worry later. I felt the reputation of the Celtics was such that every kid would want to play here."

The Celtics made a dramatic turnaround in Bird's rookie season, improving from twenty-nine wins to sixty-one wins. After they were beaten by the Sixers in the playoffs, Auerbach again outfoxed his rivals, pulling off perhaps the best deal in NBA history. Before the 1980 draft, he sent the Warriors a pair of draft picks (one of them was the number-one pick in the draft) in exchange for Golden State's first-round pick (number three overall) and a young, underachieving center named Robert Parish. The top three players in that draft were Joe Barry Carroll, Darrell Griffith, and Kevin McHale. Auerbach wanted McHale. He thought he was the best player in the draft. He also knew the Warriors wanted Carroll. So he parted with the top pick, got the guy he wanted in the first place with the third pick (McHale), and got Parish as a "throw-in." Effectively, he got Parish and McHale, both Hall of Famers, for Joe Barry Carroll. And thus was born—with Larry Bird—the best frontcourt in basketball, which would yield three more NBA championships in the 1980s.

"Bird was exceptionally smart," said Red. "He got the most out of his natural ability. He was six-nine and wasn't quick, but just try to catch him. If he intercepted a pass, you couldn't catch him. And he had the determination that comes with hard work. I think it was a small-town thing with him. He figured there was no substitute for work, and he was willing to pay the price. When practice was over at ten-forty-five, he was still out there [at] eleven-thirty or twelve, just shooting around and working on all facets of his game. He and McHale did that almost every day. Other guys, practice is over and they are gone. Parish and Russell were like that. Cousy and Heinsohn too."

It was during the Bird era that Auerbach made his final series of brilliant moves. He drafted Danny Ainge even though Ainge had pledged allegiance to the Toronto Blue Jays. Then he talked Ainge into switching to basketball. When the Celtics were swept by the Milwaukee Bucks in the 1983 Eastern Conference Semifinals, Auerbach picked Phoenix's pocket, acquiring guard Dennis Johnson in exchange for Rick Robey. D.J. gave the Celts a defensive answer to Magic Johnson and brought strength and clutch play to the Celtic backcourt. He completed an already great team, and the Celtics won championships again in 1984 and '86. For good measure, Red brought in Bill Walton to fill the Sixth Man role in 1986. The 1985–86 Celtics went 40–1 at home, and a case can be made that they were the best basketball team ever assembled.

A year before the final flag in '86, Red made his last great deal. After a protracted contract negotiation (Red always hated agents) with guard Gerald Henderson, Red signed Henderson, then immediately dealt him to the Seattle Supersonics for Seattle's top pick in the '86 draft. As usual, Red didn't mind waiting for his reward, and he was gambling that the Sonics would tank and earn a lottery pick in '86. It all went exactly as planned, and after the '86 Finals the Celtics drafted Maryland's Len Bias with the second overall pick in the draft. It was too good to be true. The Celtics had the best team in basketball, then acquired the best player in the draft. (The first pick was Brad Daugherty, who turned out to be soft and disappointing, like Joe Barry Carroll.) With Bias in the fold, it looked like the string of flags would continue for several more seasons, but Bias died of cocaine intoxication the day after the draft, and the Celtics have not been the same since that day. Neither has Auerbach. Bias's death ushered the Green Team into a new era, and it's been difficult for an aging Red to keep pace with all the issues of today's NBA.

Like many people in the Celtics front office, Auerbach thought North Carolina Tar Heel Joseph Forte would be an excellent NBA player. The Celts drafted Forte in 2001, after his sophomore year at UNC.

"He was a great high school player and led the ACC in scoring for Chrissakes," said Red. "He had everything going for him. But he wanted to be a starter immediately, and as soon as he wasn't a star, he didn't know how to handle it and he fell apart. He became arrogant and started hanging around with the wrong people, and he never got out of it. He had the talent, but he didn't have the rest."

It's harder than it used to be, no doubt about it. Putting together an NBA roster and coaching twelve players is tougher than it was back when Red owned the league. The intricacies of the salary cap and the raft of talent from overseas and from American high schools have changed the landscape of professional basketball. But put all the players in one gym and let 'em show their stuff. When it comes time to choose up sides, Red Auerbach is still going to be the biggest winner every time.

RED AUERBACH'S PERFECT TEAM

Bill Russell: He made shot blocking an art. When he blocked a shot, most of the time, we got the ball back. He didn't just swat it out of bounds. Plus, there was his rebounding and his defensive efforts. His defensive presence altered the other team's game. He was intimidating.

Wilt Chamberlain: Wilt was probably the greatest offensive force in the history of the game. He was like Shaquille O'Neal, but I think he had more moves than Shaq. He was a little quicker and just as strong.

Bob Pettit: Relentless. He played two positions, center and power forward. He was a very fine shooter, but most of all he was relentless. He played the whole forty-eight minutes as if he was fresh the whole time.

Elgin Baylor: Elgin was a great offensive player. He had moves that nobody had done before, and there was no way to stop him. He was also very strong and quick.

Karl Malone: Here's another who was relentless, especially for a man his size. He could run up and down the court and shoot from outside. He could lead the fast break. A good rebounder. Great player.

Larry Bird: Brilliant. Whether you want to call him a power forward or a small forward, and I don't go for those terms, whichever he was, he was the greatest passer of his day. He was a great shooter and he played hurt. Very self-motivated.

Kevin McHale: Kevin was very innovative. He was one of the greatest pivotmen that ever played the game. He's the one who started all those double fakes in the pivot.

Jerry West: He fooled everybody. He was only six-three, but he had the arms of a guy six-six and he was a great shooter and a great defensive ballplayer.

Kobe Bryant: He's got it all. He plays hard at the defensive end, and he's highly motivated. He's got all the skills.

Michael Jordan: I think of him the same as Kobe, except that he did it for a longer period of time and he was a better shooter than Kobe. Michael also made everybody around him better. I'm not so sure Kobe has done that yet.

Bob Cousy: In my opinion, he was the ultimate when it came to leading the fast break. He was one of the greatest passers who ever lived. Cooz was also a good shooter, but above all, he was a leader.

Oscar Robertson: Oscar could do it all. All he needed was the ball. He could set up on the pick-and-roll. He was a great shooter. A good rebounder. He was big for a guard, at least it was big for a guard in those days.

Magic Johnson: I think Magic was the greatest point guard who ever played the game. He was big; he could run the break and see over you. That's what he had over Cooz. Magic could come down on the break, and other guards couldn't stop him because he just looked right over them. I came to admire him even more in his last few years because he went from being a fair shooter to being a great shooter.

John Havlicek: He was perpetual motion. He could run you around the floor and keep coming off screens, and he would just keep coming at you. A great defender.

Coach: I don't know. I would love to coach this team. We wouldn't lose many games, I'll tell you that.

RED AUERBACH—GENERAL MANAGER

PERSONAL: Born September 20, 1917, in Brooklyn, NY . . . 5–10/170 (1.78 m/77 kg) . . . full name: Arnold Jacob Auerbach . . . name pronounced "HOUR-back."

HIGH SCHOOL: Eastern District (Brooklyn, NY).

JUNIOR COLLEGE: Seth Low Junior College (NY).

COLLEGE: George Washington.

CAREER NOTES: Vice president, Boston Celtics (1950–51 through 1963–64). . . . Vice president and general manager, Celtics (1964–65). . . . Executive vice president and general manager, Celtics (1965–66 through 1969–70). . . . President and general manager, Celtics (1970–71 through 1983–84). . . . President, Celtics (1984–85 through 1996–97, 2001–present). . . . Vice chairman of the board, Celtics (1997–98 to present).

CAREER HONORS: Elected to Naismith Memorial Basketball Hall of Fame (1968). . . . One of the Top 10 Coaches in NBA History (1996).

COLLEGIATE RECORD

													Averages		
Season	Team	G	Min	FGM	FGA	Pct	FTM	FTA	Pct	Reb	Ast	Pts	RPG	APG	PPG
36–37	Seth Low					Statistics unavailable									
37–38	GW	17	—	22	—	—	8	12	.667	—	—	52	—	—	3.1
38–39	GW	20	—	54	—	—	12	19	.632	—	—	120	—	—	6.0
39–40	GW	19	—	69	—	—	24	39	.615	—	—	162	—	—	8.5
Total		56	—	145	—	—	44	70	.629	—	—	334	—	—	6.0

HEAD COACHING RECORD

BACKGROUND: Head coach, St. Albans Prep (Washington, DC). . . . Head coach, Roosevelt High School (Washington, DC). . . . Assistant coach, Duke University (1949–50).

HONORS: Coach of the Year (1965). . . . NBA 25th Anniversary All-Time Team coach (1970). . . . NBA Executive of the Year (1980). . . . Selected as the Greatest Coach in the History of the NBA by the Professional Basketball Writers Association of America (1980).

		Regular Season				Playoffs		
Season	Team	W	L	Pct	Finish	W	L	Pct
46–47	Wash (BAA)	49	11	.817	1st/Eastern Division	2	4	.333
47–48	Wash (BAA)	28	20	.583	T2nd/Eastern Division	0	1	.000
48–49	Wash (BAA)	38	22	.633	1st/Eastern Division	6	5	.545
49–50	Tri-Cities	28	29	.491	3rd/Western Division	1	2	.333
50–51	Boston	39	30	.565	2nd/Eastern Division	0	3	.000
51–52	Boston	39	27	.591	2nd/Eastern Division	1	2	.333
52–53	Boston	46	25	.648	3rd/Eastern Division	3	3	.500
53–54	Boston	42	30	.583	T2nd/Eastern Division	2	4	.333
54–55	Boston	36	36	.500	3rd/Eastern Division	3	4	.429
55–56	Boston	39	33	.542	2nd/Eastern Division	1	2	.333
56–57	Boston	44	28	.611	1st/Eastern Division	7	3	.700
57–58	Boston	49	23	.681	1st/Eastern Division	6	5	.545
58–59	Boston	52	20	.722	1st/Eastern Division	8	3	.727
59–60	Boston	59	16	.787	1st/Eastern Division	8	5	.615
60–61	Boston	57	22	.722	1st/Eastern Division	8	2	.800
61–62	Boston	60	20	.750	1st/Eastern Division	8	6	.571
62–63	Boston	58	22	.725	1st/Eastern Division	8	5	.615
63–64	Boston	59	21	.738	1st/Eastern Division	8	2	.800
64–65	Boston	62	18	.775	1st/Eastern Division	8	4	.667
65–66	Boston	54	26	.675	2nd/Eastern Division	11	6	.647
Total (20 years)		938	479	.662	Total (20 years)	99	70	.586

NOTES: 1947—Lost to Chicago in BAA Semifinals. 1948—Lost to Chicago, 74–70, in Western Division tiebreaker. 1949—Defeated Philadelphia, 2–0, in Eastern Division Semifinals; defeated New York, 2–1, in Eastern Division Finals; lost to Minneapolis, 4–2, in NBA Finals. Replaced Roger Potter as Tri-Cities head coach with record of 1–6. 1950—Lost to Anderson in Western Division Semifinals. 1951—Lost to New York in Eastern Division Semifinals. 1952—Lost to New York in Eastern Division Semifinals. 1953—Defeated Syracuse, 2–0, in Eastern Division Semifinals; lost to New York, 3–1, in Eastern Division Finals. 1954—Defeated New York, 93–71; lost to Syracuse, 96–95 (OT); defeated New York, 79–78; lost to Syracuse, 98–85, in Eastern Division round-robin; lost to Syracuse, 2–0, in Eastern Division Finals. 1955—Defeated New York, 2–1, in Eastern Division Finals; lost to Syracuse, 3–1, in Eastern Division Finals. 1956—Lost to Syracuse in Eastern Division Semifinals. 1957—Defeated Syracuse, 3–0, in Eastern Division Finals; defeated St. Louis, 4–3, in NBA Finals. 1958—Defeated Philadelphia, 4–1, in Eastern Division Finals; lost to St. Louis, 4–2, in NBA Finals. 1959—Defeated Syracuse, 4–3, in Eastern Division Finals; defeated Minneapolis, 4–0, in NBA Finals. 1960—Defeated Philadelphia, 4–2, in Eastern Division Finals; defeated St. Louis, 4–3, in NBA Finals. 1961—Defeated Syracuse, 4–1, in Eastern Division Finals; defeated St. Louis, 4–1, in NBA Finals. 1962—Defeated Philadelphia, 4–3, in Eastern Division Finals; defeated Los Angeles, 4–3, in NBA Finals. 1963—Defeated Cincinnati, 4–3, in Eastern Division Finals; defeated Los Angeles, 4–2, in NBA Finals. 1964—Defeated Cincinnati, 4–1, in Eastern Division Finals; defeated San Francisco, 4–1, in NBA Finals. 1965—Defeated Philadelphia, 4–3, in Eastern Division Finals; defeated Los Angeles, 4–1, in NBA Finals. 1966—Defeated Cincinnati, 3–2, in Eastern Division Semifinals; defeated Philadelphia, 4–1, in Eastern Division Finals; defeated Los Angeles, 4–3, in NBA Finals.